The Practice of Preventive Health Care

The Practice of Preventive Health Care

Edited by

Lawrence J. Schneiderman, M.D.
Associate Professor
Department of Community and Family Medicine
University of California, San Diego
La Jolla, California

ADDISON-WESLEY PUBLISHING COMPANY
Medical/Nursing Division • Menlo Park, California
Reading, Massachusetts • London • Amsterdam
Don Mills, Ontario • Sydney

To Rob, Claudia, Heidi and Tanya—and all our children

L'Chaim

Sponsoring Editor: Chester L. Dow
Production Coordinator: Helene Harrington
Copy Editor: Maggi Speer
Cover and Book Design: Michael Rogondino

Library of Congress Cataloging in Publication Data
Main entry under title:

Practice of preventive health care.

Includes index.
1. Medicine, Preventive. I. Schneiderman, L. J.
[DNLM: 1. Preventive medicine. 2. Primary health care.
WA 108 P943]
RA425.P69 613 80-39970

ISBN 0-201-07183-5

ABCDEFGHIJ-MA-8987654321

The authors and publishers have exerted every effort to ensure that drug selection and dosage set forth in this text are in accord with current recommendations and practice at the time of publication. However, in view of ongoing research, changes in government regulations and the constant flow of information relating to drug therapy and drug reactions, the reader is urged to check the package insert for each drug for any change in indications of dosage and for added warnings and precautions. This is particularly important where the recommended agent is a new and/or infrequently employed drug.

Addison-Wesley Publishing Company
Medical/Nursing Division
2725 Sand Hill Road
Menlo Park, California 94025

Contributors

Elizabeth Barrett-Connor, M.D.
Associate Professor
Departments of Community and Family Medicine, and Medicine
University of California, San Diego
School of Medicine

Phyllis Brown
University of California, San Diego
School of Medicine

Victor F. Froelicher, M.D.
Associate Professor
Department of Medicine
University of California, San Diego
School of Medicine

Igor Grant, M.D.
Chief, Consultation-Liaison Service and Mental Health Clinic
Veterans Administration Hospital
University of California, San Diego
School of Medicine

David S. Janowsky, M.D.
Professor
Department of Psychiatry
University of California, San Diego
School of Medicine

Barbaraterry Kurtz
Clinical Lecturer
Department of Family and Community and Preventive Medicine
Stanford University
School of Medicine

Barry S. Levy, M.D., M.P.H.
Assistant Professor
Occupational Environmental Health
Department of Family and Community Medicine
University of Massachusetts
Medical School

Leona M. McGann, M.S.W., M.P.H.
Assistant Professor
Department of Family and Community and Preventive Medicine
Stanford University
School of Medicine

Vicky Newman, M.S., R.D.
Nutritionist
Research Associate
University Hospital
University of California, San Diego
School of Medicine

William A. Norcross, M.D.
Assistant Professor
Department of Community and Family Medicine
University of California, San Diego
School of Medicine

William L. Nyhan, M.D.
Professor and Chairman
Department of Pediatrics
University of California, San Diego
School of Medicine

Charles M. Ross, M.D.
Director of Student
Health Services
University of San Diego
San Diego, California

Alan Ryan, M.D.
Editor-in-Chief
The Physician and Sports Medicine
Minneapolis, Minnesota
Secretary General
The International Federation of Sports Medicine

Lawrence J. Schneiderman, M.D.
Associate Professor
Department of Community and Family Medicine
University of California, San Diego
School of Medicine

Max H. Schoen, D.D.S., Dr.P.H.
Chairman of the Section of Preventive Dentistry and Public Health
University of California, Los Angeles
School of Dentistry

Martin T. Stein, M.D.
Assistant Professor
Department of Pediatrics
University of California, San Diego
School of Medicine

Joseph Stokes, III, M.D.
Professor
Department of Community and Family Medicine
University of California, San Diego
School of Medicine

David H. Wegman, M.D., M.S.
Director
Occupational Health Program
Harvard School of Public Health
Boston, Massachusetts

Preface

In this book we hope to give the primary medical practitioner—family physician, general internist, general pediatrician, physician's assistant, and nurse practitioner—both theoretical and practical information that will help in the provision of office-based preventive health care.

Classical preventive medicine divides its activities into three categories.

Classical preventive medicine divides its activities into three categories:

1. *Primary prevention.* This refers to measures taken to prevent the initiation of disease in someone who is healthy. An example would be dietary counseling of an adolescent to prevent obesity and its consequences.
2. *Secondary prevention.* This refers to measures that arrest the development of disease while it is still in its early, preclinical stage. An example would be treating asymptomatic hypertension to prevent stroke and heart disease.
3. *Tertiary prevention.* This encompasses the range of therapies designed to minimize the consequences of the disease after it has become clinically manifest. An example of this would be coronary bypass surgery for the patient with intractable angina.

As is evident from the few examples just cited, the process of prevention becomes increasingly difficult and expensive as one moves from primary through secondary toward tertiary prevention.

Spurred by soaring health care costs, policy makers have begun to cast a critical eye toward traditional medical practices. Ironically some of the most inexpensive procedures, such as screening, have undergone the most rigorous scrutiny. Several of these—mammography, cervical cytology, and testing for phenylketonuria and serum thyroxine—have been shown to be cost- and health-effective. Recommendations for the use and scheduling of screening procedures are emerging from various authoritative councils. However, because they come from different professional perspectives and are complicated by value judgments about quality of life and allocation of limited resources as well as by cost-benefit analysis, not surprisingly these recommendations have been embroiled in controversy.

Ironically some of the most inexpensive procedures, such as screening, have undergone the most rigorous scrutiny.

Those of us who advocate and practice preventive medicine can become infatuated at times with its remarkable possibilities. But not for long: inevitably we are brought up short by our limits. Trained to intervene actively in established disease we get used to the interventionist—indeed the controlling—role in health care. But how much can we do for patients who will not lose weight, take their medicine, drive with seat belts, or brush their teeth? How much can we do in a society that will pay vast sums of money to track down a miracle cure for lung cancer, while ignoring the simple, cheap, effective preventive measure that we already know about—avoidance of cigarette smoking?

This book is planned so that each chapter deals with a major aspect of preventive health care. Included are topics of current special interest such as nutrition, smoking, and athletic exercise. Also brought together are subjects usually not seen in one convenient text—genetic counseling, environmental hazards, psychiatric problems, and dental care.

The last two chapters of the book, with some unavoidable redundancy, review and summarize the material that has gone before and provide guidelines directed at the pediatric and adult age groups.

In presenting their recommendations the authors have attempted to convey the state of the art—what is known as well as what is not known. They may disagree in their advice on undecided issues. The reader must be the final judge. For example, in Chapter 9, "Prevention of Cardiovascular Disease," the authors have summarized the current status of evidence for the benefit of exercise. Some readers will be disappointed that more is not made of the effect of exercise on vigor, well-being, insight, self-esteem, and mood. We recognize the importance of these quality-of-life arguments; however, for the most part, they remain acts of faith. At the present time the only careful studies that have been done in substantial numbers are those attempting to answer the question: Does exercise prevent heart disease? Only these studies are reviewed in this book.

Finally, as previously alluded to, one of the most frustrating problems is how to get patients to reap the benefits of the little that we do know. Despite the simplicity of smoking avoidance, ideal weight maintenance, and compliance with antihypertensive regimens—all with solidly established benefits—physicians have been notoriously impotent in getting patients to modify their behavior. If ever there were an area of research that was unappreciated and underfunded, this is it.

Many people whose names are not listed among the authors provided help in writing this book. They reviewed, challenged, corrected errors, and offered opinions. They should not be blamed for the results, however, since their recommendations were not always taken. These people include Michelle Ginsberg, Michel Criqui, Henry Wheeler, Ruth Heifetz, Charles Khoury, Jan Soule, Robert Massad, John M. Peters, and Diane Mason. Most helpful of all was Helen Greenstein, who typed this manuscript many times over and attended to the myriad, maddening, necessary details; her contribution to this book can never be acknowledged sufficiently.

Lawrence J. Schneiderman

Contents

The Practice of Preventive Health Care

1 Screening, Case Finding, and Prevention

Lawrence J. Schneiderman

Dr. Schneiderman is a graduate of Harvard Medical School and served on the faculty of Stanford Medical School before moving to the University of California, San Diego, School of Medicine, where he began the Family Medicine program. He is board certified in Internal Medicine and Family Practice and has almost 20 years' experience in patient care, teaching, and research in the area of primary care.

Brief Contents

Overview

This chapter reviews the role of screening in prevention, presents important definitions and general concepts, and discusses the current status of the most commonly used screening tests. This material will enable primary medical practitioners to make informed judgments about the appropriateness of screening tests to their practices.

HISTORICAL BACKGROUND

> The Queen gives leave that. . .a Publick Brothel should be set up at Avignon. . .that on every Saturday the Women in the House should be singly examined by the Abbess and a Surgeon appointed by the Directors and if any of them have contracted any Illness by their Whoring that they be separated from the rest and not suffer to prostitute themselves for fear the Youth who have to do with them should catch their Distempers. —*Old Statutes of the Stews of Avignon (1347)*

As can be seen from the previous quotation, the idea of screening to prevent disease was not original to this century.* The practice commenced on a large scale in this country, however, during the 1930s and 1940s. Interestingly enough the venereal disease syphilis became the first target of modern health care professionals. This was followed by mass x-ray examinations for tuberculosis, blood sugar testing for diabetes, and cytologic screening for cervical cancer. The term *multiphasic screening* was first applied to a health survey in San Jose, California, in 1949 in which a large population was subjected to a battery of tests, including questionnaires, blood tests, urine tests, x-ray examinations, electrocardiography (ECG), anthropometry, spirometry, tonometry, psychometrics, and other tests.

Multiphasic screening of the general population has yielded only limited health benefits.

A few studies of multiphasic screening programs have been completed, and the results show limited benefits at best. One study of a large population, whose general health surveillance was carried out under the Kaiser-Permanente health plan, showed no reduction in overall mortality between a group urged to participate in periodic multiphasic health checkups and a control group. Significant reduction in the mortality rate was noted for colorectal cancer however, and a somewhat smaller difference was noted in mortality associated with hypertension. A limited cost-benefit study of periodic multiphasic examinations in this group suggests that the expense of screening might be justified for men in the 45-54 year age group. Similar cost benefits were not demonstrated outside this particular subpopulation.

---

*The reader will note that in the *Old Statutes of the Stews of Avignon,* the women were screened to prevent disease in men.

SCREENING AND CASE FINDING

Case finding, that is, screening of patients seeking medical attention is more likely to uncover illness than screening of the general population.

In assessing the value of screening programs one must draw a distinction between mass screening of the general (and generally healthy) population and case finding, that is, the use of screening technology in the evaluation of a patient seeking medical attention —the situation most likely to be encountered by the readers of this book. No studies comparable to the one noted previously have been carried out in the case-finding setting—the setting in which, of course, screening is more likely to uncover an illness.

In the clinical application of screening, precise distinctions are sometimes difficult.

Purists insist that the term *screening* be applied only to the asymptomatic person. In practice, however, the distinction is easily blurred (for example, the slightly nervous but otherwise healthy patient who on routine testing turns out to have an elevated T_4). In fact, the primary health care provider is most likely to be applying a combination of approaches for the patient who presents with some complaint. In the process of providing overall health care, the physician will most likely recommend a series of routine procedures to be undertaken then and in the future. Even further tailoring of individual tests to specific age and sex subgroups or to populations in which specific risks are known to be present (prescriptive screening) enriches the yield and hence health- and cost-effectiveness.

CRITERIA

Screening tests should be evaluated according to various practical criteria.

The following questions should be asked of each screening test or procedure:

Does the test detect a condition that will have a significant impact on health? Most biochemical screening panels confront the physician with a large mass of data. What should the physician do with an elevated serum uric acid? Does it represent an important disease? The physician must ask himself which is the greater risk to the patient's health—the elevated uric acid or the medications that lower it. What should the physician do with a borderline elevation in serum calcium? Are the risks and expenses of pursuing an occult parathyroid adenoma justified?

Will early detection make it possible to change the prognosis of the disease? Is the test health-effective? The failure to demonstrate any improvement in mortality through the use of screening x-ray examinations for lung cancer has led to the abandonment of this screening procedure. Other tests such as the measurement cholesterol and blood glucose, however, are in common use, even though there is still debate as to whether early recognition of hypercholesterolemia and hyperglycemia will lead to significant

A test that provides nothing more than early detection of a disease might give the spurious impression of improving the prognosis.

benefits to the patient. One should be aware that an artifact of observation may lead to a spurious justification for early disease detection. If one had not noticed a disease until it had reached its advanced, highly manifest state, one would obviously expect the prognosis of the disease at this point to be poorer than if one had detected the same disease early in its more subtle manifestation. This would be true even if one were unable to alter the course of the disease in any way. Disease detection through screening may thus appear to have a beneficial effect merely by uncovering the disease at an earlier stage.

Is the test and therapy acceptable to the physician and patient? Numerous studies have shown that physicians often ignore unexplained laboratory abnormalities obtained by a screening panel. Similarly, patients show poor compliance with simple programs whose benefits are unequivocal (for example, cessation of smoking). Periodic sigmoidoscopies are popular with neither physicians nor patients. The problem may lie with the nature of preventive medicine and its goals, which are long delayed and undramatic because of the absence of an event or consequence. Physicians as well as patients find it easier to respond to the dramatic, highly illuminated emergency rather than to take precautionary steps in what is comparatively a silent darkness.

Is the screening test cost-effective? For most tests, this question is unanswered. One of the few tests that has been demonstrated to be health- and cost-effective both in the neonatal and adult primary care setting is the screening T_4. Other tests such as the treadmill test with the ECG are more expensive and time-consuming, have little predictive value, and therefore are a waste of time and money in the general screening setting. Screening tests probably will be put under increasing scrutiny, particularly as the government becomes more concerned with controlling health care costs.

Are there any hazards associated with the screening test? Clearly the risk of a procedure should not outweigh the risk of the disease it is designed to uncover. Beside this obvious risk, however, there are more elusive ones that are not readily appreciated. In one study in which patients were screened for early detection of hypertension, the investigators reported that patients labeled with the condition, despite their successful treatment, altered their behavior in a way that resulted in diminished working days. Similarly the early sickle cell screening programs imparted information that made the recipients more anxious than enlightened about the meaning of positive test results. A so-called abnormal test result may label the person as abnormal; for example, a high blood glucose level may result in labeling a patient a diabetic. Or the opposite may occur: a normal test result may falsely reassure a

The hazards of screening are not always obvious, as in the cases cited.

person about his health in general. Or a nonspecific laboratory abnormality such as an elevated alkaline phosphatase might be judged by the physician to be clinically unimportant, only to be followed 5 years later by the discovery of metastatic malignancy. On medical grounds the connection between the abnormal test and the subsequent disease might be spurious; in the area of medical malpractice, however, the connection might be serious.

NORMAL VS ABNORMAL

The customary normal curve is a statistical concept, not a clinical one. On this curve there will always be normal persons who are abnormal.

It should be apparent on reflection that the customary curve that is drawn to establish normal values is based on a statistical concept rather than a clinical one. Abnormalities are laboratory values that lie outside some specified range (usually 2 standard deviations) from the mean. Thus in any general population that resembles the normal population from which the laboratory derived its normal range, one would expect 1 person in 20 to have an abnormality. The zealous pursuit of a false positive test results in unnecessary costs, risks, and anxiety on the part of the patient. Yet failure to pursue the true positive is also hazardous.

THE SUBSPECIALTY LOOP

The perils of the subspecialty loop are described.

Figure 1-1

In contrast to primary care physicians whose approach is to rule out disease in the patient, subspecialists tend to define their role as ruling out disease in their specialty. The hazards facing a patient in this system are not unlike those that faced the legendary Odysseus. As the patient is referred from one specialty to another in pursuit of the ubiquitous laboratory abnormality, he is haplessly swept into a maelstrom, which in modern terminology can be called the *subspecialty loop* (Figure 1-1).

Conceptually, prescriptive screening merely expands the general medical workup into promising areas where instruments are more effective in gaining information than the physician's own senses. In the ongoing debate over screening, it is interesting to note that laboratory testing has come under rigorous scrutiny. At the same time the more traditional and, in some cases, more expensive, time-consuming, and less productive components of the routine history and physical examination are taken for granted.

CONCEPTS AND DEFINITIONS

To interpret the usefulness of a screening test, one needs to understand a few basic concepts and definitions:

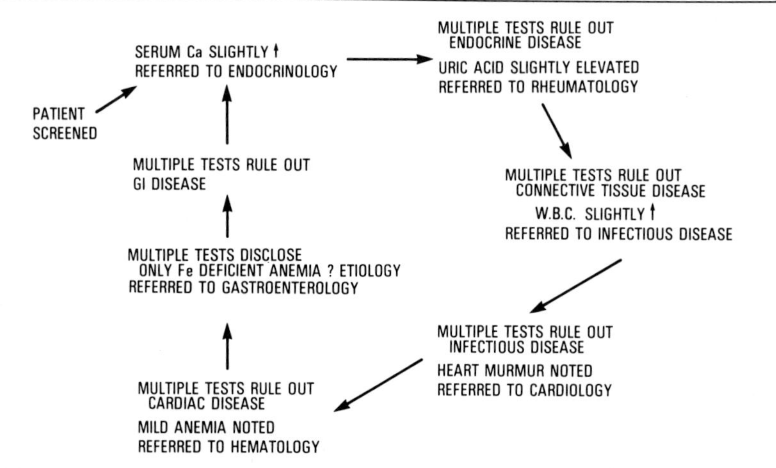

Figure 1-1 As patients are referred from one specialty to another in pursuit of the ubiquitous laboratory "abnormality," they may fall victim to an endless circle—the Subspecialty Loop.

Acceptability. The willingness of the physician and the patient to undertake the test or procedure (in spite of such factors as pain, cost, expenditure of time).

Accuracy. The ability of the test to provide a true measure of the quantity or quality in question.

Certain concepts are essential in evaluating screening tests.

Sensitivity. The ability of the test to recognize disease, that is, the fraction of positive test results in patients who have a particular disease.

Specificity. The capacity of the test to recognize nondisease, that is, the fraction of negative test results in patients free of the disease.

Predictive value. The ability of the test to predict the presence or absence of disease.

The predictive value of a test is determined by its sensitivity, specificity, and the prevalence of the disease in question. Often it is not appreciated that even the most accurate, sensitive, and specific laboratory test may mislead the physician. Simple calculations will illustrate this:

A sensitivity and specificity of 90% does not necessarily mean a good test.

For example, suppose we had a test whose sensitivity was such that the test was positive in 90% of diseased patients and whose specificity was such that it was negative in 90% of non-diseased patients. Intuitively we would tend to consider this a rather good test. Yet if we were to apply the test to a sample of 100 persons in whom the disease prevalence was 10% (that is, 10 were affected), because the test was 90% sensitive, it would correctly identify 9 out of the 10 affected persons. Because the test was 90% specific, it would be falsely positive in 9 out of the 90 unaffected persons. Thus in this situation the predictive value of a positive test would be 50%;* the test would be of no help at all. The rarer the disease the lower the predictive value of a positive test (Table 1-1); conversely, the rarer the disease the higher the predictive value of a negative test.

Table 1-1

Table 1-1 Predictive value of positive test as function of disease prevalence* (laboratory test with 95% sensitivity and 95% specificity)

Prevalence of Disease (%)	Predictive Value of Positive Test (%)
1	16.1
2	27.9
5	50.0
10	67.9
15	77.0
20	82.6
25	86.4
50	95.0

*From Galen, R. S. 1979. Selection of appropriate laboratory tests. In *Clinician and chemist.* Ed. D. S. Young Washington, D.C.: The American Association for Clinical Chemistry, p. 76.

PRACTICE GUIDELINES

A variety of protocols have been published as guides to the primary health care practitioner for using screening procedures in preventive health care (see Annotated References at end of this chapter). There is no unanimous agreement on screening protocols; indeed there is considerable controversy. For example, the Canadian Task Force on Periodic Health Examinations, American Cancer Society, and American College of Obstetricians and Gynecologists have taken substantially different positions on the screen-

Even committees of experts do not always agree on the best screening protocol.

*Predictive value of positive test = percentage of patients with positive test who have disease, or = true positives/(true positives + false positives) × 100.

ing Pap smear. The best of these guidelines take into account practical aspects of acceptability to both physician and patient, cost versus benefits, and the appropriateness of certain tests to specific age, sex, socioeconomic, and ethnic populations.

Since screening is undramatic and requires methodical record keeping and sustained motivation, it is a good place for teamwork and mutual reinforcement. Physician, nurse, nurse practitioner, physician's assistant and even nonmedical personnel can participate in the process and audit each other's activities.

Teamwork and mutual reinforcement can help sustain the methodical record keeping essential for good preventive care.

In this section the most commonly used screening tests will be reviewed and brief critical commentary as well as references for further follow-up reading will be provided. It would be ideal if each test could be evaluated along criteria presented in the preceding discussion. The reality is somewhat less than the ideal, however, for in most cases there simply are not adequate data. Also, although this chapter is limited to certain tests and procedures, the role of judicious history taking in prevention is by no means being ignored. This is covered in the chapters that follow.

Pediatric Age Group*

Phenylketonuria Routine measurement of blood phenylalanine is mandatory in most states. The initiation of a low phenylalanine diet early in infancy can prevent severe mental retardation. The high cost of institutionalization for phenylketonuria [PKU] (estimated average of about $200,000 per case) makes screening of neonatal blood samples using either the Guthrie or fluorometric test cost-effective (approximately $70,000 per confirmed case plus $1,000 a year for treatment). The reported incidence varies in different populations but approximates 1 per 15,000 births. (Families of Irish or Mediterranean descent have a higher incidence.) The sensitivity of the screening test is high, particularly if performed after 4 days of age. The specificity is low: only 5% of infants with elevated blood phenylalanine on screening are subsequently found to have classical PKU. Since infants may be discharged early, it is important for screening to be pursued after nursery discharge. Also rapid follow-up of positive tests is necessary to achieve effective prevention with dietary modification.

PKU screening is cost effective. It is most sensitive if done after 4 days of age.

Thyroxine Routine testing for congenital hypothyroidism is mandatory in some states. The incidence of this disorder—probably

---

* Hematocrit (Hct) and (Hgb) hemoglobin (Hgb) measurement and urinalysis are included under adult age group.

Screening for congenital hypothyroidism, probably the most common preventable cause of retardation, is cost effective.

the most common preventable cause of retardation—is 1 per 5000 births. Early treatment with thyroid replacement hormone prevents cretinism. Although the specificity of the screening thyroxine (T_4) is extremely low (about 10%), its low cost (approximately $10,000 per identified case) in contrast to the high cost of institutionalization (in the neighborhood of $200,000 per affected infant) makes this test cost-effective.

Vision Five percent of preschool children have visual defects including myopia, amblyopia, and strabismus or a combination of defects. The prevalence rises to approximately 25% during school age. Strabismus or a difference in refractive error between the two eyes can lead to amblyopia. Screening for vision defects begins with the newborn examination for anatomic defects. Well-child care should include regular checks for visual acuity and strabismus up to the school physical. Visual acuity can be checked again at about 13-14 years when myopia reaches its peak prevalence. Defects in color vision, transmitted as X-linked recessive traits, are prevalent in approximately 8% of males and 0.4% of females. Although such children may have difficulty recognizing colors at first, they usually adapt and have no learning impairment. Simple screening tests for color vision in the pediatric age group are not reliable.

Well-child care should include regular checks for visual acuity and strabismus.

Hearing Approximately one per thousand children has a severe hearing loss; 1%-3% have some degree of hearing impairment that may cause significant delays in speech comprehension, articulation, and social development. Although early recognition is desirable, reliable and practical neonatal screening technology is still in the investigational phase. Audiometric pure tone testing should be carried out routinely prior to school entry. Testing should also be done whenever there are suggestive findings, particularly any of the problems noted above or chronic middle ear effusion.

1%-3% of children have some degree of hearing impairment that may have significant consequences.

Adult Age Group

Weight Life insurance studies show that substantially overweight men and women experience an increased mortality rate, particularly from cardiovascular and renal disease, but also from diabetes, gastrointestinal disease, and even malignant neoplasms. In the broad range of ages from 15-69 years, the mortality rate among men who are 30% overweight is increased by a third. For women in the age range of 15-69 years who are 30% overweight mortality is increased about 25%. Weight reduction has been shown to have

The mortality rate among men who are 30% overweight is increased by a third.

a favorable influence on life span—an effect that persists as long as weight reduction is maintained.

Although obesity by itself may not predispose an individual to coronary heart disease, it is associated with other coronary risk factors, particularly hyperlipidemia and hypertension. Recent data suggest that being underweight also shortens one's life span.

A practical way to determine most patients' ideal weight is to ascertain what it was at the limit of skeletal growth (about age 18). Usually this period also coincides with the patient's greatest physical activity. Almost certainly any weight added after that time is excess fat. This ideal weight can be the approximate objective for any gradual weight reduction program.

Blood pressure Increasingly persuasive evidence is accumulating that maintenance of blood pressure below 140/90 is associated with significant reduction in mortality from stroke and heart disease. Prospective studies have been done on inpatient and outpatient populations, adult men and women, and blacks and whites. Some uncertainty continues to exist about the concept of labile hypertension. It is common experience to obtain a blood pressure recording on the first medical visit that is higher than subsequent recordings. Some investigators interpret the evidence gathered so far as indicating that any elevation above 140/90 should lead the physician to active treatment. Others maintain that treatment should be instituted only after persistent hypertension is demonstrated. One's therapeutic zeal must be tempered because of the problem of labeling a patient as hypertensive and the risks of therapy (minimal if one seeks first to lower blood pressure through procedures such as gradual weight reduction, salt reduction, and relaxation techniques).

One's judgment must be tempered because of the problem of labeling a patient as hypertensive.

Mammogram Evidence shows that for women over 50 years old an annual mammogram reduces the risk of death from breast cancer. Difficulty in interpreting mammograms in younger women has restricted the application of this technique. However, improved imaging developments have occurred, and future studies may show a reduction in mortality in all age groups through periodic mammography. Fear of excess deaths due to chronic radiation exposure probably can be assuaged now that a lower dose (0.3 rads) is being used. It is estimated that this dose will cause one excess cancer per year per million women after a 10-year interval. In contrast, 1000 cancer cases occur every year per million women at age 40 years and up to 2000 cancer cases every year per million women at age 70 years. Mammography should be considered an integral part of evaluation in any women with symptoms or signs suggestive of

By age 50 years a woman should have a mammographic examination with regular repeats every few years.

possible breast cancer. By age 50 years a woman should have a mammographic examination with regular repeats every few years, depending on findings thereafter. Women with fibrous cystic disease or a family history of cancer should be considered for early mammographic screening (see Chapter 12 for breast self-examination).

Studies show that an annual examination is unnecessary except for women in high-risk populations.

Cytologic screening for cervical cancer One of the oldest screening procedures is the annual Pap smear, a preventive measure that has played an important role in reducing the incidence of invasive cancer of the cervix. Attention has been directed lately toward maximizing the cost effectiveness of this procedure. Studies show that an annual examination is unnecessary except for women in high-risk populations, which includes young women of low socioeconomic status (who unfortunately tend to escape screening anyway) and women with herpesvirus infection. Invasive cancer is rare in women under 35 years of age. Since sexually active women are likely to seek medical care either for birth control or pregnancy, the primary health care provider has a good opportunity on these occasions to obtain the first Pap smear. The test should be repeated at least once to confirm negativity. Since observations on the natural history of cancer in situ reveal that it takes at least 10 years to develop into invasive cancer and that cervical dysplasia takes even longer, subsequent tests can be carried out on a 3-5 year interval until age 60 years. Women more than 60 years old who have had consistently negative Pap smears are unlikely to develop invasive cancer during their lifetime.

The PPD screening procedure is recommended for all persons who have been exposed to the disease.

Tuberculosis skin test Although no longer the scourge it once was, tuberculosis occurs in the United States at the rate of about 15 new cases per 100,000 population. This figure varies among different ethnic groups and is much higher in recent immigrants from Mexico and Southeast Asia. People who are in close contact with patients with tuberculosis have a 2.5% risk of developing the disease within the first year. They have a 5% risk if they themselves are purified protein derivative of tuberculin (PPD) positive. Overall there is approximately 0.6% risk per year for any patient with a positive skin test of developing active tuberculosis. Up to about age 35 years the risk-benefit ratio is in favor of prophylaxis with isonicotine hydrazine (INH). This screening procedure therefore is recommended for all persons who have been exposed to the disease—as relatives, patients, or health care personnel.

Blood glucose The value of maintaining strict control over patients with diabetes is controversial—even more so in the person with asymptomatic hyperglycemia without glycosuria. Most adult patients with elevated blood glucose levels will be obese, which is reason enough to have the physician recommend dietary modification; a screening for blood sugar would add nothing. Although the use of oral hypoglycemia agents to prevent the development of diabetes mellitus was once fashionable it is no longer so. Asymptomatic hyperglycemia provides no independent risk to atherosclerotic heart disease or mortality; hence the screening procedure is not warranted.

Screening for asymptomatic hyperglycemia is not warranted.

Serum cholesterol The association between elevated levels of serum cholesterol and coronary heart disease has long been recognized. Recent refinements have shown a direct relationship of morbidity and mortality due to coronary heart disease with levels of low-density lipoprotein cholesterol. A screening serum cholesterol test will have no particular merit, however, until there is conclusive demonstration that reduction of dietary cholesterol or fat (either of which will lower serum cholesterol) or a cholesterol-lowering agent reduces the risk of morbidity or mortality from coronary heart disease. (It is worth recalling that the treatment of renal disease once was directed at the proteinuria, that is, a low protein diet.) The comments regarding blood glucose also apply to serum cholesterol: the association between hypercholesterolemia and obesity is likely to lead primary care physicians to recommend weight reduction anyway—particulary in obese patients with a strong family history of heart disease and a sedentary existence.

Occult blood Death from carcinoma of the bowel occurs 90% of the time in the above-50-year-old age group, a fact that makes screening the stool for occult blood reasonable among the middle-aged and the older population. However, even the best test, Hemoccult slides, suffers from low sensitivity and specificity, particularly if the diet is not modified to be meat free and high in fiber. In one large-scale study of people more than 40 years old on meat-free diets, some 1%-2% had positive tests; of these only 10% subsequently were found to have cancer of the large bowel. Many more were found to have adenomas; however, the proportion of those that undergo malignant change is unknown. Since the regular physical examination usually includes a rectal examination (which can detect approximately 10% of large bowel cancer and also allows evaluation of the prostate gland), a stool sample can easily be tested as part of the general screening evaluation. The primary physician can also try guiding the patient toward early recognition of and response to symptoms of bowel

It may help to educate patients toward early recognition and response to symptoms of bowel neoplasm.

neoplasm—particularly blood in the stool, abdominal pain, changing bowel habits, and decreasing caliber of stool. Although the survival rate is much lower in symptomatic patients, the poor prognosis in symptomatic colorectal carcinoma in part may be related to patients' fear and delay in obtaining medical attention.

All things considered, sigmoidoscopy should probably be performed every 5 years on patients more than 50 years of age.

Sigmoidoscopy About 50% of large bowel carcinomas are visible by sigmoidoscopy. Screening of asymptomatic older patients with sigmoidoscopy has yielded 2-4 cases of cancer per 1000 examinations. Some 5%-10% of persons over the age of 40 years will be found to have polyps. Although considerable effort has gone into defining these lesions histologically, the proportion of polyps that undergo life-threatening malignant change is still unknown. In spite of medical exhortations to include periodic sigmoidoscopy in primary care screening of asymptomatic patients, the procedure has gained wide acceptance by neither physicians nor patients. The cost per curable case has been estimated to exceed $70,000. The major risk of sigmoidoscopy is perforation, which in some hands is equivalent to the cancer detection rate; in practiced hands, however, it is substantially less. All things considered, sigmoidoscopy should probably be performed every 5 years on patients more than 50 years of age and more frequently in patients with predisposing illness such as ulcerative colitis or with positive family history, particularly multiple polyposis.

Although a simple procedure, a screening Hct and Hgb test is probably of borderline justification.

Hematocrit and Hemoglobin The benefits of uncovering mild asymptomatic anemia have not been established; in fact harmful effects seem unlikely unless the hemoglobin is less than 10 gm/100 ml. (A prevalence of this magnitude is approximately 1% in females, less in males.) Thus, although a simple procedure, a screening Hct and Hgb test is probably of borderline justification except in those exposed to poor nutrition or environmental hazards (for example, the poor) or with a family history of anemia.

Urinalysis Routine urinalysis provides a variety of information in a simple noninvasive manner, including the presence of glucose, protein, and bacteria. All three findings deserve further evaluation and are of preventive value. Various surveys show that about 5% of females have significant bacteriuria, or greater than 100,000/ml of colonies; this prevalence rises with age. Kass first pointed out that the presence of visible bacteria on the side of an unspun sample coincides with pathogenic bacteriuria (colony counts in the 10^5 or more per milliliter range). Twenty percent of pregnant women will have significant bacteriuria; this group will be at greater risk of later developing symptomatic urinary tract infection.

That these women are more likely to develop hypertension, premature delivery, or perinatal death has been suggested but not clearly established. At this time there is no definitive evidence that treatment of bacteriuria in the adult woman prevents subsequent renal damage; prevention may be more promising in school-age girls. Many episodes of bacteriuria have been noted to resolve spontaneously.

Chemical panel Modern techniques of biochemical determination and multichannel recording have made it possible to run numerous tests on a single sample of blood. Whether this technological advance is useful as a preventive screening measure or is worth the cost is still under scrutiny. One puzzling paradox is that, although the biochemical screening panel has gained rapid acceptance in the medical community, most studies show that physicians ignore unexpected laboratory abnormalities almost half the time. One of the first to be evaluated is the T_4 component of a screening panel. It appears that the routine performance of this test in the general medical population is health and cost effective. Alkaline phosphatase determination, in contrast, is not.

Most studies show that physicians ignore unexpected laboratory abnormalities almost half the time.

ECG The routine baseline ECG has long been a fixture of periodic screening examinations. Only recently has its role been challenged. About one fourth of patients with myocardial infarction will have had previously normal ECGs. ECG abnormalities in the asymptomatic patient, whether obtained with or without exercise, have numerous false negatives and false positives (15%-20%). The predictive value of exercise testing is poor: in patients with high-risk and suggestive symptoms a negative test is usually falsely negative; in low-risk patients most positive tests are falsely positive. Therapeutic implications at this point are uncertain since most studies on bypass surgery have been done on the symptomatic patient, and symptoms certainly add an important prognostic variable to the clinical course of patients with heart disease. At this time a screening ECG has little to add to the information that physicians require in counseling patients on preventive measures regarding atherosclerotic heart disease.

At this time a screening ECG has little to add to the information that physicians require in counseling patients on preventive measures.

Chest x-ray examination Periodic chest x-ray examinations once were advocated as a screening procedure to reduce mortality from lung cancer. An evaluation of a large population undertaking x-ray examinations every 6 months showed no improvement in survival rate from lung cancer. At this time there is no rationale for employing chest x-ray examinations as a routine screening procedure.

Spirometry This procedure has been advocated as a means of uncovering lung disease in its early asymptomatic state; however, there is no evidence that presymptomatic recognition and treatment of chronic obstructive lung disease (COLD) yields any distinctive benefits. Indeed progression of COLD seems to be relentless and unaffected by treatment. At this time spirometry is useful only in following patients with recognized disease and not as a screening test.

Tonometry Routine tonometry has been advocated as a means for uncovering asymptomatic glaucoma. However the Schiotz tonometer has poor diagnostic accuracy and predictive value. Probably the best course of action is to refer a patient with a positive family history of glaucoma to an ophthalmologist, although the efficacy of preventive treatment has not been established clearly.

Special Populations

Sexually migratory

The value of screening for gonorrhea or syphilis is limited according to the likelihood of recurrent exposure.

Gonorrhea culture Gonorrhea is asymptomatic in about 75% of women. Contrary to earlier impressions recent evidence shows that the majority of infected males are asymptomatic also. In the sexually migratory patients the frequency of positive tests can be extremely high, but because of the likelihood of recurrent exposure it is almost impossible to put the screening culture to any significant preventive use. In the particularly vulnerable patient such as is seen in community health clinics, in association with counseling on the use of preventive measures of contraception (for example, condoms) and symptom recognition, culture of the cervix in women and first-voided urine in men (and the oropharynx and rectum in homosexuals) might have some justification.

Serological test for syphilis As with gonorrhea, syphilis is a recurrent risk in the sexually migratory person; 95% of cases occur in the 15-50 year age group. More than three quarters of patients with untreated primary syphilis will progress to tertiary complications. Thus, although there are cogent reasons for attempting to screen patients for syphilis, the populations in which this is usually done are not necessarily those at highest risk. Nearly every state now requires couples applying for marriage licenses to be screened for syphilis. The laws mandating this were enacted in the 1930s and 1940s as part of the social hygiene movement, which in its day was promoted with the same fervor as cost containment is today. A more promising application of syphilis screening would be in the community health clinic population, in urban homosexual males, and as part of a prenatal screening package.

Pregnant women

Screening pregnant women for elevated serum alpha-fetoprotein may well be reasonable.

Serum alpha-fetoprotein Neural tube defects such as anencephaly and meningomyelocele occur in 1-2 per 1000 live births. If an affected child is born, the probability that the parents will produce another is about 5 in 100 births. Alpha-fetoprotein, an alpha$_1$-globulin synthesized in the embryonic liver and gastrointestinal tract, has been found to be elevated in the amniotic fluid and serum of women bearing fetuses with open neural tube defects. Although measurement of alpha-fetoprotein by means of amniocentesis is indicated in women who have previously given birth to an affected offspring, such a procedure would not be cost and health effective in the general population in this country. A collaborative study in Great Britain raises hopes that a practical screening blood test can be developed. At 16-18 weeks of pregnancy, levels of serum alpha-fetoprotein above 2.5 times the normal median have a sensitivity of 80%-90% and a specificity of more than 95%. Women with these levels will have approximately one in ten chances of producing an infant with a neural tube defect. Screening pregnant women would be a useful first step in selecting those to undergo ultrasound and amniocentesis for confirmation of the diagnosis.

Rubella screening should be considered during premarital examination and contraceptive counseling, and for health care personnel exposed to pregnant women.

Rubella hemagglutination-inhibiting antibody (HAI) titer Screening for rubella antibody is now carried out in many prenatal workups as a routine procedure. The rationale is that if the woman at her first visit already has evidence of prior infection, any subsequent illness accompanied by a rash would not raise the diagnostic possibility of rubella or concern for the fetus. A better opportunity for rubella screening, however, is at an earlier time, perhaps at the premarital exam or during contraceptive counseling. Health care personnel who might be exposed to pregnant women should also be considered for screening. Surveys have shown a surprisingly low incidence of positive antibodies among health care workers —a situation that could lead to an outbreak of rubella and exposure of pregnant women patients. Women who have no detectable antibody can receive attenuated live virus vaccine. Ideally this should be administered before adolescence to avoid the risk to an unrecognized pregnancy.

Recommendations regarding use of RhoGAM have changed significantly.

Rh antibody This screening procedure is valuable since gammaglobulin directed against Rh antibody (RhoGAM) can be used to prevent the development of erythroblastosis fetalis. Rh negative unsensitized women should be detected as early as possible in pregnancy. Some patients are immunized by an Rh positive fetus during pregnancy; hence current recommendations are not to wait until delivery but to administer RhoGAM at approximately 28 weeks' gestation as well as following delivery.

Every primary care physician should be familiar with the indications for amniocentesis.

Amniocentesis This procedure involves removal of a small sample of amniotic fluid by needle aspiration, usually performed during the fifteenth week of pregnancy to allow time for cell culture and other studies to permit therapeutic abortion by the twentieth week of pregnancy. The indications for this procedure are: (a) increased maternal age (35-40 years or older); (b) previously affected offspring (chromosomal or metabolic disorder or neural tube defect); (c) a mother who is a presumed carrier of a serious X-linked recessive disorder); and (d) when both parents are known carriers of an autosomal recessive disorder. It is now possible to diagnose a large variety of fetal abnormalities, particularly chromosomal derangements (for example, Down syndrome), about 100 different metabolic disorders, and certain structural malformations (such as anencephaly, meningomyelocele), and even hemoglobinopathies. In experienced centers the risk of amniocentesis is small. It is important to note that a normal amniocentesis cannot guarantee a normal healthy child since the majority of birth defects still escape detection. On the other hand, in the general population the vast majority of births are normal: only some 3% of births are complicated by a major defect (see Chapter 3).

Ethnic groups with genetic disease

Sickle cell disease About 10% of blacks in the United States carry the hemoglobin S trait. Three out of every 1000 newborn blacks have sickle cell anemia. Sickle cell anemia is the homozygous manifestation; hence both parents must carry the trait in order for their offspring to be at risk. If both parents carry the trait—which except under exceptional circumstances of reduced oxygen tension is quite harmless—there is a one in four chance with each birth of producing an offspring with sickle cell anemia. Technical developments such as restriction endonuclease mapping (see Chapter 3) make it likely that sickle cell anemia will soon be detectible in the fetus by amniocentesis. Screening adolescent and adult Black individuals prior to their making reproductive decisions would seem to be of value; however, campaigns with this in mind have led to psychological and social problems through fear and poor understanding. Persons with the harmless trait have been adversely rated by insurance companies and have experienced difficulty in obtaining employment. Screening for this disorder therefore should be undertaken only with the most sensitive attention to and anticipation of these problems. If necessary, genetic counseling can be arranged through the nearest genetic counseling center (see Chapter 3).

Screening for sickle cell trait should take into account the psychosocial consequences.

Tay-Sachs Tay-Sachs disease is an autosomal recessive metabolic disease in which sphingolipid accumulates because of a block in its degradative pathway. Apparently normal newborns develop blindness at 4-6 months of age and begin a progressive neurological deterioration leading to death. Methods are available for detecting the heterozygote carrier. The disease is 100 times more frequent among Jews of Eastern origin (Ashkenazim) than among non-Jews. Approximately one in thirty of Ashkenazi Jews carries the gene for Tay-Sachs disease. Because the condition is highly concentrated in a defined population group, is of such devastating severity, and can be detected by an accurate and inexpensive blood test for carriers as well as by amniocentesis, Tay-Sachs disease lends itself to preventive screening. Many successful screening programs have already been carried out in conjunction with education and genetic counseling. The primary care health provider should be alert to the increased risk of the Tay-Sachs gene in Jewish patients (the majority of whom in this country are Ashkenazim) and advise them to contact the nearest genetic counseling center for screening (see Chapter 3). Since the condition is autosomal recessive, both parents must carry the gene in order for their offspring to be at risk. If both parents carry the trait there is a one in four chance with the birth of each child of producing an offspring affected with Tay-Sachs disease. Amniocentesis should be offered to such couples.

Primary care health providers should advise Jewish patients to contact the nearest genetic counseling center for Tay-Sachs screening.

SUGGESTED READINGS

Phenylketonuria

Holtzman, N. A.; Meek, A. G.; and Mellits, E. D. 1974. Neonatal screening for phenylketonuria. *J. A. M. A.* 229:7-70.

Holtzman, N. A.; Morales, D. R.; Cunningham, G., et al. 1975. Phenylketonuria. In *Pediatric screening tests*, ed. W. K. Frankenburg and B. W. Camp, pp. 92-118. Springfield, Ill.: Charles C. Thomas Publishers.

Thyroxine

Fisher, D. A. 1978. Neonatal thyroid screening. *Pediatr. Clin. North Am.* 25:423-429.

Vision

Bailey, E. N.; Kiel, P. S.; Akram, D. S., et al. 1974 Screening in pediatric practice. *Pediatr. Clin. North Am.* 21:123-165.

Ingram, R. M. 1980. The possibility of preventing amblyopia. *Lancet* 1:585-587.

Tibbenham, A. D.; Peckham, C. S.; and Gardiner, P. A. 1978. Vision screening in children tested at 7, 11, and 16 years. *Br. Med. J.* 1:1312-1314.

Hearing

Bailey, E. N.; Kiel, P. S.; Akram, D. S., et al. 1974. Screening in pediatric practice. *Pediatr. Clin. North Am.* 21:123-165.

Weight

Metropolitan Life Insurance Company. April 1960. Overweights benefit from weight reduction. *Stat. Bull. Metropol. Life Ins. Co.* 41:1-3.

Association of Life Insurance Medical Directors of America, Philadelphia and Society of Actuaries, Chicago 1980. *Report of the Ad Hoc Committee of the new build and blood pressure study.*

Pooling Project Research Group. 1978. Relationship of blood pressure, serum cholesterol, smoking habit, relative weight and ECG abnormalities to incidence of major coronary events: Final report of the Pooling Project. *J. Chronic Dis.* 31:201-306.

Mann, G. V. 1974. The influence of obesity on health. *N. Engl. J. Med.* 291:178-185, 226-232.

Blood pressure

Veterans Administration Cooperative Study Group on Antihypertensive Agents. 1970. Effects of treatment on morbidity in hypertension. *J. A. M. A.* 213:1143-1152.

Hypertension Detection and Follow-up Program Cooperative Group. Five-year findings of the hypertension detection and follow-up program. 1979a. *J. A. M. A.* 242:2562-2571.

Hypertension Detection and Follow-up Program Cooperative Group. Five-year findings of the hypertension detection and follow-up program. 1979b. *J. A. M. A.* 242:2572-2577.

Mammogram

Feig, S. A. 1979. Low-dose mammography. *J. A. M. A.* 242:2107-2109.

Cytologic screening for cervical cancer

Foltz, A. M., and Kelsey, J. L. 1978. The annual Pap test: A dubious policy success. Millbank Memorial Fund Quarterly. *Health and Society* 56:427-462.

Cervical cancer screening programs. 1976. *Can. Med. Assoc. J.* 114:1003-1033.

Tuberculosis skin test

Myers, J. A. 1965. The natural history of tuberculosis in the human body. *J. A. M. A.* 194:184-190.

Harris, A. A., and Karakusis, P. 1979. Diagnosis and management of tuberculosis. *Primary Care* 6:43-63.

Blood glucose

Cahill, G. F.; Etzwiler, D. D.; and Freinkel, N. 1976, "Control" and diabetes. *N. Engl. J. Med.* 294:1004.

Siperstein, M. D.; Foster, D. W.; Knowles, H. C., et al. 1977. Control of blood glucose and diabetic vascular disease. *N. Engl. J. Med.* 296:1060-1063.

Stamler, R., and Stamler, J., editors. 1979. Asymptomatic hyperglycemia and coronary heart disease. *J. Chronic Dis.* 32:683-837.

Serum cholesterol

Mann, G. V. 1977. Diet-heart: End of an era. *N. Engl. J. Med.* 297:644-650.

Stamler, J. 1973. Epidemiology of coronary heart disease *Med. Clin. North Am.* 57:5-46.

Stamler, J. 1979. Research related to risk factors. *Circulation* 60:1575-1587.

Occult blood

Kurnick, J. E.; Walley, L. B.; Jacob, H. H., et al. 1980. Colorectal cancer detection in a community hospital screening program, *J. A. M. A.* 243:2056-2057.

Winawer, S. J.; Miller, D. G.; Schottenfeld, D., et al. 1977. Feasibility of fecal occult-blood testing for detection of colorectal neoplasia. *Cancer* 40:2616-2619.

Sigmoidoscopy

Bolt, R. J. 1971. Sigmoidoscopy in detection and diagnosis in the asymptomatic individual. *Cancer* 28:121-122.

Winnan, G.; Berci, G.; Panish, J., et al. 1980. Superiority of the flexible to the rigid sigmoidoscope in routine proctosigmoidoscopy. *N. Engl. J. Med.* 302:1011-1012.

Dean, T. M. 1977. Carcinoma of the colon and rectum. *West J. Med.* 126:431-440

Dutton, J. J. 1978. Sigmoidoscopy as a periodic screening test. *J. Fam. Pract.* 7:1041-1046.

Morson, B. 1976. Polyps and cancer of the large bowel. *West. J. Med.* 125:93-99.

Hematocrit and Hemoglobin

Elwood, P. C. 1973. Evaluation of the clinical importance of anemia. *Am. J. Clin. Nutr.* 26:958-964.

Elwood, P. C. 1974. Anemia. *Lancet* 2:1364-1365.

Urinalysis

Asscher, A. W. 1974. Urinary-tract infection. *Lancet* 2:1365-1367.

Gillenwater, J. Y.; Harrison, R. B.; and Kunin, C. M. 1979. Natural history of bacteriuria in schoolgirls. *N. Engl. J. Med.* 301:396-399.

Lancet. Editorial. 1979. Bacteriuria: When does it matter? *Lancet* 2:1166-1167.

Chemical panel

Ahlvin, R. C. 1970. Biochemical screening: A critique. *N. Engl. J. Med.* 283:1084-1086.

Epstein, K. A.; Schneiderman, L. J.; Bush, J. W., et al. (In press). The "abnormal" screening serum thyroxine (T_4): Analysis of physician response, outcome, cost and health effectiveness. *J. Chronic Dis.*

Schneiderman, L. J.; DeSalvo, L.; Baylor, S., et al. 1972. The "abnormal" screening laboratory results: Its effect on physician and patient. *Arch. Intern. Med.* 129:88-90.

Young, D. S.; Uddin, D.; Nipper, H., et al., editors. 1979. *Clinician and chemist: The relationship of the laboratory to the physician.* Washington, D. C.: American Association for Clinical Chemistry.

ECG

Galen, R. S., and Gambino, S. R. 1975. *Beyond normality.* Chapter 14. New York: John Wiley & Sons, Inc.

Weiner, D. A.; Ryan, T. J.; McCabe, C. H., et al. 1979. Exercise stress testing. *N. Engl. J. Med.* 301:230-235.

Chest x-ray examination

Boucot, K. R., and Weiss, W. 1973. Is curable lung cancer detected by semiannual screening? *J. A. M. A.* 224:1361-1365.

Spirometry

Burrows, B., and Earle, R. H. 1969. Course and prognosis of chronic obstructive lung disease. *N. Engl. J. Med.* 280:397-404.

Tonometry

Graham, P. A. 1966. Screening for chronic glaucoma, *Proc. Royal Soc. Med.* 59:1215—1220.

Graham, P. A. 1972. Epidemiology of simple glaucoma and ocular hypertension. *Brit. J. Ophthalmol.* 56:223-229.

Gonorrhea culture

Cooper, D. L.; Bernstein, G. S.; Ivler, D., et al. 1976. Gonorrhea screening program in a women's hospital outpatient department. *J. Am. Vener. Dis. Assoc.* 3:71-75.

Handsfield, H. H.; Lipman, T. O.; Harnisch, J. P., et al. Asymptomatic gonorrhea in men. *N. Engl. J. Med.* 290:117-123.

Luciano, A. A., and Grubin, L. 1980. Gonorrhea screening. *J. A. M. A.* 243:680-681.

Serological test for syphilis

Felman, Y. M. 1978. Should premarital syphilis serologies continue to be mandated by law? *J. A. M. A.* 240:459-460.

Jaffe, H. W. 1975. The laboratory diagnosis of syphilis. *Ann. Intern. Med.* 83:846-850.

Serum alpha-fetoprotein

Brock, D. J. H. 1976. Prenatal diagnosis: Chemical methods. *Br. Med. Bull.* 32:16-20.

Hagard, S.; Carter, F.; and Milne, R. G. 1976. Screening for spina bifida cystica. *Br. J. Prev. Soc. Med.* 30:40-53.

United Kingdom Study. Report of UK Collaborative study on Alpha-Fetoprotein in Relation to Neural Tube Defects. 1977. Maternal serum alpha-fetoprotein measurement in antenatal screening for anencephaly and spina bifida in early pregnancy. *Lancet* 11:1323-1332.

Rubella hemagglutination-inhibiting antibody (HAI) titer

Farber, M. E., and Finkelstein, S. N. 1979. A cost-benefit analysis of a mandatory premarital rubella antibody screening program. *N. Engl. J. Med.* 300:856-859.

Lancet. Editorial. 1979. Rubella: Who needs a blood test? *Lancet* 2:1329-1331.

Rh antibody

Clarke, C. A., and McConnell, R. B. 1972. *Prevention of Rh-hemolytic disease.* Springfield, Ill.: Charles C. Thomas Publishers.

Amniocentesis

Omenn, G. S. 1978. Prenatal diagnosis of genetic disorders. *Science* 200:952-958.

Sickle cell disease

Petrakis, N. L. 1974. Sickle cell disease. *Lancet* 2:1368-1369.

Scott, R. B., and Castro, O. 1979. Screening for sickle cell hemoglobinopathies. *J. A. M. A.* 241:1145-1157.

Tay-Sachs

Kaback, M. M.; Rimoin, D. L.; and O'Brien, J. S., editors. 1977. *Tay-Sachs disease: Screening and prevention.* New York: Alan R. Liss.

ANNOTATED BIBLIOGRAPHY

Bailey, E. N.; Kiehl, P. S.; Akram, D. S., et al. 1974. Screening in pediatric practice. *Pediatr. Clin. North Am.* 21:123-165.
This is an excellent review of concepts and specifics related to pediatric screening. Provides many references.

Breslow, L., and Somers, A. R. 1977. The lifetime health monitoring program: A practical approach to preventive medicine. *N. Engl. J. Med.* 296:601-608.
This was one of the first screening protocols published which combined epidemiologic data and practical advice. Recommends prevention on an age-specific base.

Canadian Task Force on the Periodic Health Examination. 1979. The periodic health examination. *Can. Med. Assoc. J.* 121:1193-1254.
This is a solidly researched, authoritative report to the Canadian government evaluating a wide array of screening procedures. Provides good discussion and many references.

Dales, L. G.; Friedman, G. D.; and Collen, M. F. 1979. Evaluating periodic multiphasic health checkups: A controlled trial. *J. Chronic Dis.* 32:385-404.
One of the few excellent long-term studies of multiphasic screening by pioneers in this field.

Eggertsen, S. C.; Schneeweiss, R.; and Bergman, J. J. 1980. An updated protocol for pediatric health screening. *J. Fam. Pract.* 10:25-37.
A practical pediatric health maintenance protocol with many references.

Frame, P. S. 1979. Periodic health screening in a rural private practice. *J. Fam. Pract.* 9:57-64.
A brief update of selective screening procedures for the family physician with an emphasis on practical application in the rural practice.

Frame, P. S., and Carlson, S. J. 1975. A critical review of periodic health screening using specific screening criteria. *J. Fam. Pract.* 2:29-36; 123-129; 189-194; 183-288.

One of the first periodic health screening protocols proposed for the family physician based on a review of clinical evidence. Contains concise discussions and good bibliography.

Somers, A. R.; Bruck, T. L.; Frame, P. S., et al. 1979. A whole-life plan for well-patient care. *Patient Care* 83-153.
An excellent discussion of health monitoring presented in the highly readable style of the "throwaway" journal.

Young, D. S.; Uddin, D.; Nipper, H., et al., editors. 1979. *Clinician and chemist: The relationship of the laboratory to the physician.* Washington, D.C.: American Association for Clinical Chemistry.
A comprehensive review of many aspects of laboratory testing as it pertains to the physician. Provides discussion of concepts associated with the use and evaluation of laboratory data.

2 Health Hazard Appraisal

Charles M. Ross

Dr. Ross is a graduate of Washington University School of Medicine, St. Louis. He is on the clinical faculty of the University of California, San Diego, School of Medicine and Director, Student Health Service, University of San Diego. As a practicing physician he has been involved with health hazard appraisal for more than 10 years and developed the first operational computerized program. He is a past president of the Society of Prospective Medicine.

Brief Contents

Overview

Health hazard appraisal is a technique for estimating a patient's health risk factors from empiric mortality data. This approach forms the basis for motivating the patient to change certain hazardous behaviors and characteristics. It is too early to show the effectiveness of health hazard appraisal programs in reducing morbidity and mortality.

> Over 99% of us are born healthy and made sick as the result of personal misbehavior and environmental conditions.
> *John Knowles—"The Responsibility of the Individual"*

HISTORICAL BACKGROUND

Simple health habits regarding diet, alcohol, smoking, sleep, and exercise are associated with improved health and life span.

In the past decade there has been a surge of interest in the manner in which life-styles may influence health. Belloc and Breslow (1972), in a study of 7000 California residents, showed that health status and longevity varied in accordance with simple patterns of living. These workers found habits that were associated with good health included eating breakfast daily, eating regular meals without snacking, eating moderately so that normal weight was maintained, avoiding smoking, drinking no more than seven alcoholic beverages weekly and sleeping 7-8 hours a night. The more health habits persons followed, the greater their health and life span.

Sadusk and Robbins (1968) first proposed the technique of health hazard appraisal as a method of highlighting and computing a person's risk of death subject to these risk factors. An implied assumption behind the concept is that by encouraging patients to change their "personal misbehavior" they will improve their health and longevity.

STAGES OF DISEASE

In viewing prevention, one recognizes six basic time frames of a natural history of disease:

1. Essentially not at risk
2. At risk
3. Agent of disease present
4. Signs of disease present
5. Symptoms of disease present
6. Disability or death

For example, with atherosclerotic heart disease stage 1 would represent the very early childhood years in which essentially no

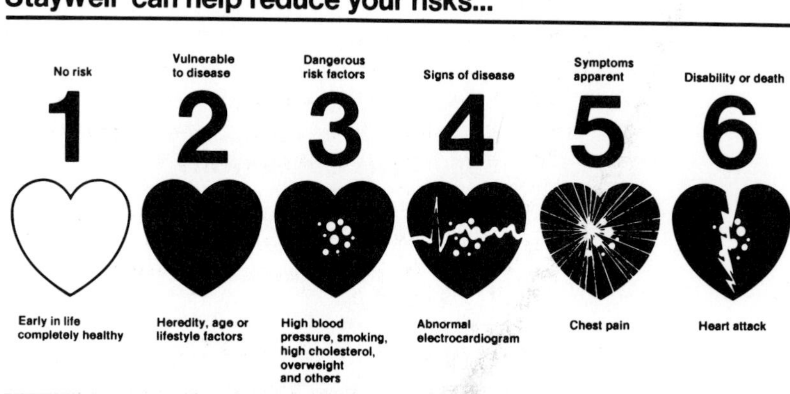

Figure 2-1 Progressive stage in the evolution of atherosclerotic heart disease.

Figure 2-1

risk is present (Figure 2-1). In stage 2 a person may become at risk through increasing age, overweight, a sedentary life-style, and so forth. A person would enter stage 3 when such conditions as hypertension were detected. In stage 4 the person might show abnormalities on the electrocardiogram though still be free of symptoms. By stage 5, symptoms such as anginal chest pain or dyspnea with exertion might become apparent. Stage 6 is when disability or death occurs as a result of myocardial infarction or congestive heart failure.

At present almost all medical care is provided as crisis intervention in stages 5 and 6. Periodic health testing would perhaps uncover signs in stage 4 but even if this were a successful time to intervene, the costs and the number of trained professionals required to perform millions of treadmill tests every year would be overwhelming. For this reason, medicine has to explore the possibility of successfully intervening in stage 1, 2, or 3. This concept forms the basis for action for proponents of what is called *prospective medicine.*

Health hazard appraisal estimates a patient's health-risk factors from the Geller-Gesner tables.

Health hazard appraisal is a way of estimating personal risk and providing the basis for offering practical advice to persons wishing to reduce that risk. The mechanism for estimating risk is not complex. For each age period from 5-75 years of age, tables have been developed identifying the leading causes of death in the ensuing 10-year periods. These data show that the top ten causes of death account for two thirds of all the deaths in each period. Since the remaining one third of deaths are scattered among 1000 or more causes, the incidence of each specific cause is extremely

Table 2-1 Leading Causes of Death in White Males Aged 40, 1974*

Rank	Cause of Death	Chance in 100,000 of dying from this
1.	Arteriosclerotic heart disease	1,629
2.	Cancer of the lung	348
3.	Cirrhosis	343
4.	Motor vehicle accidents	275
5.	Suicide	260
6.	Vascular lesions affecting the CNS (Stroke)	178
7.	Homicide	128
8.	Cancer of the large intesting and rectum	86
9.	Pneumonia	75
10.	Accidents due to machines nonmotor vehicle	63
	All other causes	1,750
	TOTAL CAUSES OF DEATH	5,135

*Adapted from the Geller-Gesner tables. Geller, H. 1963. *Vital statistics of the United States, 1960.* Vol. 2, *Mortality*, Part A. Washington, D.C.: U. S. Government Printing Office.

Table 2-1 Leading Causes of Death in White Females Aged 40, 1974*

Rank	Cause of Death	Chance in 100,000 of dying from this
1.	Cancer of the breast	342
2.	Arteriosclerotic heart disease	308
3.	Vascular lesions affecting the CNS (Stroke)	174
4.	Cirrhosis	170
5.	Cancer of the lungs	149
6.	Suicide	143
7.	Cancer of the ovary	101
8.	Motor vehicle accidents	93
9.	Cancer of the large intestine and rectum	87
10.	Cancer of the cervix	70
	All other causes	1,215
	TOTAL CAUSES OF DEATH	2,852

*Adapted from the Geller-Gesner tables. Geller, H. 1963. *Vital statistics of the United States, 1960.* Vol. 2, *Mortality*, Part A. Washington, D.C.: U. S. Government Printing Office.

Tables 2-1 and 2-2

low. These tables, known as the *Geller-Gesner tables*, are updated at regular intervals. (Tables 2-1 and 2-2 illustrates a Geller-Gesner table for white men and women aged 40 years.)

For each cause of death one can identify specific factors that are believed to be precursors, causing an elevated risk of death from the disease. For example, in atherosclerotic heart disease such factors include hypertension, hyperlipidemia, diabetes, family history of premature death from atherosclerotic heart disease, overweight, specific abnormalities of the electrocardiogram, smoking, age, use of birth control pills, and Type A behavior. For each factor the increased risk relative to that factor can be compared to the average. By convention the average risk is set at 1.0. An individual's risk can then be expressed as a factor greater than 1.0 for higher risk people or less than 1.0 for people with below average risk. The actual risk factor value is derived by comparing the mortality rate for an individual associated with a specific behavior or characteristic (for example, a cigarette smoker) with a mortality rate for an individual who does not have this behavior or characteristic (a nonsmoker of the same age, sex, and race). Figure 2-2 is a sample printout of a patient with an elevated mortality risk, based on several factors including sedentary activity and a one-pack smoking habit.

The method by which the actual risk factor value is derived is explained.

Figure 2-2

HEALTH HAZARD APPRAISAL

All the risks can be combined to give a composite risk, using either a mathematic formula or probability tables. Currently the mathematic formula method is used, with factors below 1.0 being multiplied together and factors greater than 1.0 being added to that result. When this composite risk factor is multiplied by the known average number of deaths from that specific cause and for individuals of that same age, sex, and race, the patient's risk can then be compared as being equal to, greater than, or less than an average person's risk.

Assuming certain interventions (and the success of those interventions), this composite risk can be recalculated.

A health hazard appraisal can be achieved by simple hand computation. Or computerized appraisals are available.

All of these calculations can be done by hand, as illustrated by Robbins and Hall (1979). Alternatively, physicians can enter brief medical history and physical examination data on a form that is used to obtain a computerized health hazard appraisal.*

*Such computerized appraisals can be obtained from many sources including Life Extension Institute, Control Data Corporation, Minneapolis, Minn.; University of Wisconsin, Stevens Point, Wisc.; Medical Datamation, Belleville, Ohio; St. Louis County Health Department, Duluth, Minn.; Division of Health Education, Center for Disease Control, Atlanta Ga.; and Project Well Aware, University of Arizona, Tucson, Ariz.

Case Example

Mary Jones is a 50-year-old Caucasian woman. Her blood pressure is 144/80; cholesterol, 200 mg/100 ml; triglycerides, 231 mg/100 ml. Her blood sugar is normal, but she is sedentary and smokes one pack of cigarettes a day. She is 30 pounds over her ideal weight; she has a normal resting electrocardiogram and no history of premature death in her immediate family from coronary artery disease. Her risk profile for atherosclerotic heart disease would therefore look like that depicted in Figure 2-2. This shows a 10-year risk of death from coronary artery disease as 2.3 times the average, or a chance of death of almost 2900 per 100,000 population in the next 10 years (compared to an average risk of death of 1260 in 100,000 for a woman of her age and race).

Figure 2-3

Now let us assume that Mary is one of those exceptional people who is totally motivated by her risk profile (and presumably her physician and perhaps her husband, children, and others) and changes all of her apparently detrimental life-styles. The weight drops to 134 pounds and with it her cholesterol and triglyceride levels, to 180 mg/100 ml and 150 mg/100 ml respectively. She begins a program of regular aerobic exercise under her physician's direction and gives up smoking. Figure 2-3 compares her current health risk profile with that which would be achieved with these changes. This shows that her individual risk factors would have fallen and her total risk of death from atherosclerotic heart disease in the ensuing 10 years dropped to 491 in 100,000 or only 40% of the average—a drop of almost six-fold. Unfortunately not everyone will be as responsive to health hazard appraisal as Mary Jones.

CURRENT STATUS

Health hazard appraisal is being used to motivate behavioral changes.

Any technique in preventive medicine is only as good as the results obtained by its use. Although health hazard appraisal has been around for about 15 years, it has only recently been combined with specific programs designed to encourage behavioral change. Only in the last few years have studies been initiated to evaluate the technique's effectiveness. At this time no definitive data are available. However, from a number of preliminary studies it is clear that changes in behavior do occur as a result of health hazard appraisal programs. Only the future will show whether such behavioral changes lead to a reduction in morbidity and mortality.

```
JONES, MARY                     HEALTH RISK PROFILE

STAYWELL PROGRAM                                       DATE   10-11-75  ID  000018251 F
- - - - - - - - - - - - - - - - - - - - - - - - - - - - - - - - - - - - - - - - - - - -
  CURR B.P.  144/080  PREV B.P. NOT GIVEN CURR CHOL. 200 MG %  PREV CHOL. NOT GIVEN
          HT. 65 IN. WI. 166 LBS. CURR TRIG. 231 MG %  PREV TRIG. NOT GIVEN
- - - - - - - - - - - - - - - - - - - - - - - - - - - - - - - - - - - - - - - - - - - -
 AVERAGE TEN YEAR RISK OF DEATH PER 100,000          6,489 YOUR PRESENT AGE       50
 YOUR CURRENT TEN YEAR RISK OF DEATH PER 100,000     8,893 YOUR CURRENT RISK AGE 54
 YOUR ACHIEVABLE TEN YEAR RISK OF DEATH PER 100,000  4,994 YOUR ACHIEVABLE AGE    47
- - - - - - - - - - - - - - - - - - - - - - - - - - - - - - - - - - - - - - - - - - - -
 AN AVG. WOMAN YOUR AGE HAS   6,439 CHANCES OF DYING PER 100,000 IN THE NEXT 10 YRS.
                   YOUR RISKS ARE   37% GREATER THAN THE AVERAGE.
                       YOU COULD REDUCE YOUR RISKS BY   43 %.
- - - - - - - - - - - - - - - - - - - - - - - - - - - - - - - - - - - - - - - - - - - -
      NOTE  SOME DATA SUGGESTS THE FOLLOWING DISEASES WHICH MAY SIGNIFICANTLY
           INCREASE RISK.
                      TUBERCULOSIS
      NOTE  THIS PROFILE DOES NOT INCLUDE ANY RISK FOR THE FOLLOWING DISEASE(S)
           DUE TO THE REMOVAL OF THE ORGAN FOR NON-CANCEROUS REASONS
                      CANCER OF CERVIX
                      CANCER OF UTERUS
- - - - - - - - - - - - - - - - - - - - - - - - - - - - - - - - - - - - - - - - - - - -
     FACTORS THAT MAY OFFER THE                        COMBINED ACHIEVABLE BENEFIT
     GREATEST REDUCTION IN RISK                        WITH CHANGE OF THESE FACTORS
          NOT SMOKING...................................... 2.7 YRS
          NOT DRINKING..................................... 1.1 YRS
          EXERCISE PROGRAM.................................  .9 YRS
          WEIGHT REDUCTION.................................  .4 YRS
          BLOOD PRESSURE REDUCTION.........................  .3 YRS
          CHOLESTEROL REDUCTION............................  .1 YRS
          OTHER............................................ 1.5 YRS
          TOTAL REDUCTION IN RISK.......................... 7.0 YRS
- - - - - - - - - - - - - - - - - - - - - - - - - - - - - - - - - - - - - - - - - - - -
                 YOUR RISKS IN DESCENDING IMPORTANCE. #1 IS HIGHEST.
     A RISK FACTOR OF 1.0 IS AVERAGE. A RISK FACTOR LESS THAN 1.0 CARRIES LESS THAN
     AVERAGE RISK. A RISK FACTOR ABOVE 1.0 CARRIES GREATER THAN AVERAGE RISK.
- - - - - - - - - - - - - - - - - - - - - - - - - - - - - - - - - - - - - - - - - - - -
 # 1 ARTERIOSCLEROTIC HEART DISEASE        (HEART ATTACK)
  AVERAGE RISK             1,260 **********
  YOUR CURRENT RISK        3,276 **************************               ( 2.6 X AVG)
  YOUR ACHIEVABLE RISK       743 ******                                   (  .6 X AVG)

 CONTRIBUTING FACTORS   RISK FACTOR    RISK REDUCING FACTORS      RISK FACTOR
 B.P. (CURR) ---144/080      .8        B.P. 120/80 OR LESS             .6
 CHOL (CURR) ---200MG%       .7        CHOLESTEROL 180 OR LESS         .6
 DIABETES-NO                1.0                                       1.0
 EXERCISE-SEDENTARY         1.4        SUPERVISED EXERCISE            1.0
 FH ASHD NO EARLY DEATHS     .9                                        .9
 SMOKER--1 PACK/DAY         1.9        NOT SMOKING                     .9
 WEIGHT-166 LBS.            1.2        WEIGHT-134 LBS. OR LESS        1.0
 NO HX. OF ABNORMAL ECG     1.0                                       1.0
 TRIG.--(CUR)--231MG%       1.6        TRIGLYCERIDES < 151 MG%        1.3
 EXCESSIVE STRESS MAY INCREASE RISK. EXACT RISK FACTOR NOT YET AVAILABLE.
- - - - - - - - - - - - - - - - - - - - - - - - - - - - - - - - - - - - - - - - - - - -
```

Figure 2-2 Health risk profile for "Mary Jones" prior to preventive measures. Prepared by Interhealth, Inc., San Diego, Calif.

```
# 1 ARTERIOSCLEROTIC HEART DISEASE       (HEART ATTACK)
 AVERAGE RISK          1,260 **********
 YOUR CURRENT RISK     2,898 ***********************                    ( 2.3 X AVG)
 YOUR ACHIEVABLE RISK    491 ****                                       (  .4 X AVG)

CONTRIBUTING FACTORS   RISK FACTOR    RISK REDUCING FACTORS      RISK FACTOR
B.P. (CURR) ---144/080      .8        B.P. 120/80 OR LESS               .6
CHOL (CURR) ---200MG%       .7        CHOLESTEROL 180 OR LESS           .6
DIABETES-NO                1.0                                         1.0
EXERCISE-SEDENTARY         1.4        SUPERVISED EXERCISE              1.0
FH ASHD NO EARLY DEATHS     .9                                          .9
SMOKER--1 PACK/DAY         1.9        NOT SMOKING                       .9
WEIGHT-166 LBS.            1.2        WEIGHT-134 LBS. OR LESS          1.0
NO HX. OF ABNORMAL ECG     1.0                                         1.0
TRIG.--(CUR)--231MG%       1.3        TRIGLYCERIDES < 151 MG%          1.1
EXCESSIVE STRESS MAY INCREASE RISK. EXACT RISK FACTOR NOT YET AVAILABLE.
- - - - - - - - - - - - - - - - - - - - - - - - - - - - - - - - - - - - - - - - -
# 2 LUNG CANCER
 AVERAGE RISK            386 **********
 YOUR CURRENT RISK       772 ********************                       ( 2.0 X AVG)
 YOUR ACHIEVABLE RISK    618 ****************                           ( 1.6 X AVG)

CONTRIBUTING FACTORS   RISK FACTOR    RISK REDUCING FACTORS      RISK FACTOR
SMOKER--1 PACK/DAY         2.0        NOT SMOKING                      1.6
                                      REMAIN STOPPED  5 YEARS           .6
- - - - - - - - - - - - - - - - - - - - - - - - - - - - - - - - - - - - - - - - -
# 3 CIRRHOSIS OF LIVER
 AVERAGE RISK            284 **********
 YOUR CURRENT RISK       710 *************************                  ( 2.5 X AVG)
 YOUR ACHIEVABLE RISK     57 **                                         (  .2 X AVG)

CONTRIBUTING FACTORS   RISK FACTOR    RISK REDUCING FACTORS      RISK FACTOR
ALCOHOL-25-40 DRINKS/WK    2.5        NOT DRINKING                      .2
LIVER FUNCTION             1.0                                         1.0
- - - - - - - - - - - - - - - - - - - - - - - - - - - - - - - - - - - - - - - - -
# 4 BREAST CANCER
 AVERAGE RISK            684 **********
 YOUR CURRENT RISK       479 *******                                    (  .7 X AVG)
 YOUR ACHIEVABLE RISK    342 *****                                      (  .5 X AVG)

CONTRIBUTING FACTORS   RISK FACTOR    RISK REDUCING FACTORS      RISK FACTOR
CURRENT FACTOR              .7        ACHIEVABLE FACTOR                 .5
FAMILY HISTORY-NO
MONTHLY SELF-EXAM-YES
YEARLY MD EXAM-YES
YEARLY MAMMOGRAPHY-NO                 YEARLY MAMMOGRAPHY
- - - - - - - - - - - - - - - - - - - - - - - - - - - - - - - - - - - - - - - - -
# 5 STROKE
 AVERAGE RISK            422 **********
 YOUR CURRENT RISK       405 **********                                 ( 1.0 X AVG)
 YOUR ACHIEVABLE RISK    177 ****                                       (  .4 X AVG)

CONTRIBUTING FACTORS   RISK FACTOR    RISK REDUCING FACTORS      RISK FACTOR
B.P. (CURR) ---144/080      .8        B.P. 120/80 OR LESS               .6
CHOL (CURR) ---200MG%       .7                                          .7
DIABETES-NO                1.0                                         1.0
SMOKER--1 PACK/DAY         1.4        NOT SMOKING                      1.0
NO HX. OF ABNORMAL ECG     1.0                                         1.0
- - - - - - - - - - - - - - - - - - - - - - - - - - - - - - - - - - - - - - - - -
# 6 CANCER OF INTESTINES AND RECTUM
 AVERAGE RISK            277 *********
 YOUR CURRENT RISK       277 *********                                  (  AVERAGE )
 YOUR ACHIEVABLE RISK     83 ***                                        (  .3 X AVG)

CONTRIBUTING FACTORS   RISK FACTOR    RISK REDUCING FACTORS      RISK FACTOR
INTESTINAL POLYP-NO        1.0                                         1.0
RECTAL BLEEDING-NO         1.0                                         1.0
ULC. COLITIS- NO           1.0                                         1.0
ANNUAL SIGMOID.-NO         1.0        ANNUAL IN FUTURE                  .3
- - - - - - - - - - - - - - - - - - - - - - - - - - - - - - - - - - - - - - - - -
```

Figure 2-3 Health risk profile for "Mary Jones" after carrying out preventive measures.

The model is flexible enough to allow for continuing revision of the Geller-Gessner tables as new mortality data are developed. Additionally, as new precursors are identified, they can be inserted, and any that fail to stand the test of further scientific scrutiny can be removed. Refinement of the risk factors themselves can also be accomplished as new information appears. Work in both of these areas is currently going on at the Center for Disease Control. Similarly, as benefits from changes in behavior or other interventions are confirmed, these data can also be incorporated in the calculations.

Health hazard appraisal should not be looked upon as an end in itself.

Health hazard appraisal should not be looked upon as an end in itself. It can be used in a primary care setting as part of the initial data base on each family member and kept up to date by periodic review. Nor should it be looked upon as more than one of many tools by which change can be carried out to a more "healthful behavior" by directing patients' attention to their quantitative personal risks. It should be coupled with appropriate intervention and follow-up procedures to help patients choose some alternative behavior.

To be effective physicians should probably offer some short-term gain to individuals.

To be effective physicians should probably offer some short-term gain to individuals in terms of improvement in the immediate or near-term quality of life after having drawn their attention to the dangers of long-term unhealthful life-styles.

Therapeutic medicine will always have an important role in health care. However, those in the medical professions should welcome measures directed toward changing an individual's life-style if those measures would be effective in delaying the onset of disability and death. Certainly it would seem a more economic way to achieve these goals than a commitment limited to creating more and better therapeutics.

ANNOTATED BIBLIOGRAPHY

Belloc, N., and Breslow, L. 1972. Relationship of physical health status and health practices. *Prev. Med.* 1:409-421.
Results of a study of the impact of specific health practices on health among California residents.

Knowles, J. 1977. *Doing better and feeling worse.* American Academy of Arts and Sciences.
Collected essays emphasizing the relatively small changes in measurements of life expectancy and other indicators, in spite of increasing expenditures for medical care in the last 30 years, and stressing the role of life-style change in maintaining good health.

LaDou, J.; Sherwood, J. N.; and Hughes, L. 1975. Health hazard appraisal in patient counseling. *West. J. Med.* 122:177-180.
The first article describing follow-up results in an industrial population making use of health hazard appraisal.

McQuade, W., and Aikman, A. 1979. *The longevity factor.* New York: Simon & Schuster, Inc. Publishers.
A detailed study of precursors in a group of individuals along with their health hazard appraisals before and after intervention attempts. It outlines some successes and failures and reasons behind them. It also provides information for calculating a personal health hazard appraisal. It is suitable for lay individuals.

Robbins, L. C., and Hall, J. H. 1979. *How to practice prospective medicine.* Indianapolis: Slaymaker Enterprises. Rev. ed. 1979. Indianapolis: Methodist Hospital Press.
A step-by-step manual discussing the theory of health hazard appraisal and describing the specific steps required to calculate individual appraisals. It contains sets of Geller-Gessner tables and other statistical information.

Sadusk, J. F., and Robbins, L. C. 1968. Proposal for health hazard appraisal in comprehensive health care. *J. A. M. A.* 203:1108-1112.
The original outline of a system of selecting certain precursors of death that increase risk when present and as applied against the most common causes of death in specific age, sex, and racial groups. It details the method of then applying specific risk factors to quantitate these risks for individuals.

Information on new developments in this field can be found in the *Annual Proceedings of the Society of Prospective Medicine*, published annually by the Society of Prospective Medicine, Suite 404, 4405 East West Highway, Bethesda, Md. 20014.

3 Genetic Counseling

William L. Nyhan

Dr. Nyhan received his M.D. degree from the College of Physicians and Surgeons, Columbia University, and served on the faculties of Johns Hopkins and the University of Miami medical schools before assuming his present position as Chairman of the Department of Pediatrics at the University of California, San Diego, School of Medicine. An active clinician and busy researcher, Dr. Nyhan has produced approximately 300 publications, mostly in the area of biochemical genetics, including the classic paper describing the Lesch-Nyhan syndrome.

Brief Contents

Overview

The role of genetic counseling in prevention has undergone dramatic changes with the recent development of techniques such as amniocentesis, prenatal diagnosis of metabolic and chromosomal disorders, and heterozygote detection. Genetic factors cause a significant burden of disease. The rapid pace of discovery is a challenge to the primary physician to remain current, yet offers unprecedented new approaches to health care.

DEFINITION

Genetic counseling is the providing of information by physicians or other specially trained health care professionals to those who consult them regarding the risks, diagnostic procedures, available treatments, and possible prevention of congenital or hereditary disorders.

HISTORICAL BACKGROUND

It has been difficult for the primary care physician to keep up with the explosive growth in genetic information over the past 20 years. In the latest edition of McKusick's (1978) catalogue of Mendelian disorders, there were 31,500 listings. By contrast, an earlier list assembled by Frazier (1954) included only 170 diseases, of which 110 were inherited in Mendelian fashion. Furthermore, the pace of discovery appears still to be accelerating; it is thus hard for those who provide health care to remain current.

The ways in which genetic disease is managed also have changed dramatically over the past 20 years. The advances in methodology that led researchers to decide with confidence the number of human chromosomes also led to the discovery of chromosomal diseases in 1959.

New techniques allow early intervention in the diagnosis and management of genetic diseases.

Before 1959, very little medical genetics was practiced. There were a few genetic counselors, most of them not physicians, and the process they employed was a relatively passive one by today's standards. Given the diagnosis of a disease known to be inherited in a Mendelian fashion, the task was to compute the probabilities for recurrence and to interpret this to the family so they could be guided in their planning for subsequent children. This is still an important part of medical genetics, but physicians are becoming increasingly involved with special techniques for diagnosis and treatment, which make possible earlier and earlier intervention. The discovery that the mental retardation of phenylketonuria could be successfully prevented provided the model for the management of genetic disease. This has led to preventive screening programs in most developed countries in the world. More recently methylmalonic acidemia, another inherited metabolic disease, has been successfully treated prenatally. Amniocentesis is now widely available, and a number of metabolic and cytogenetic disorders may be detected antenatally. For some conditions heterozygote detection is available. Where a gene is common in a population (for example, Tay-Sachs disease in Jews of Ashkenazi origin), a program for carrier screening is feasible and has proved to be of important preventive benefit.

GENETIC COUNSELING AND PREVENTION

It is important that primary care physicians incorporate genetics into their practice.

It is important that primary care physicians incorporate genetics into their practice. Books and articles are appearing in popular magazines, and patients are becoming increasingly sophisticated. As a result they are expanding their expectations regarding their health care, particularly with regard to preventive medicine.

The most common event leading to genetic counseling is the birth of a defective child to a normal couple.

Unfortunately the most common event that leads to genetic counseling is the birth of a defective child to a normal, unsuspecting couple. With the increasing awareness of preventive medicine, however, people are also seeking genetic counseling when (a) one or both partners contemplating marriage are concerned about a family history of genetic disease; (b) a married couple or a pregnant woman wishes medical advice about the risk of having a defective child; and (c) a member of a family afflicted with a genetic disorder is concerned about the probabilities of developing the condition.

Individual genetic diseases are rare, but the overall impact of genetic factors is great, as these figures demonstrate.

There is a tendency to think of genetic diseases as being rare. It is true that the diseases that follow simple Mendelian inheritance are individually rare. Nevertheless, in the aggregate they make up a sizable population. It is estimated, for example, that:

> Fifteen million Americans suffer the consequences of birth defects of varying severity.
>
> Approximately 80% of these defects—involving some 12 million Americans—are due wholly or partly to defective genes or chromosomes.
>
> Of all spontaneous abortions 36% are caused by major chromosomal defects.
>
> At least 40% of all infant mortality results from genetic factors.
>
> Genetic factors are contributory in about four fifths of mentally retarded persons.
>
> Genetic factors account for approximately one third of children admitted to hospitals.
>
> Genetic disorders rank second only to cancer as the cause of death in children under 5 years of age.

Each person is a heterozygous carrier of between five and eight serious gene defects.

Each individual is a heterozygous carrier of between five and eight serious gene defects that can be inherited by an offspring.

Certain genetic disorders such as sickle cell anemia (which affects mainly Blacks), Tay-Sachs disease (which affects mainly Ashkenazi Jews), and cystic fibrosis (a disease common in Caucasians) are single-gene defects that predominate in certain population groups. Other more common diseases such as atherosclerotic heart disease, rheumatoid arthritis, cancer, diabetes, and mental illness are apparently more complex multifactorial disorders resulting from the combined action of genetic and environmental factors.

Failure to warn a pregnant woman of genetic risks may have serious medicolegal consequence.

There are also medicolegal ramifications. The New York State Court of Appeals ruled in favor of two women who claimed their physicians did not warn them of the risks of giving birth to mentally retarded or physically deformed infants. One was a 37-year-old woman who was not warned about the increased risk of giving birth to a child with Down syndrome. The other woman, who had a previous child with polycystic kidney disease, was told that her chances of having a second child with the same defect were "practically nil." Both women gave birth to defective infants. The court ruled that physicians may be sued if they fail to warn a woman of the potential risk in such pregnancies.

MENDELIAN GENETICS

Normally human beings contain 23 pairs of chromosomes in their cells—1 pair of sex chromosomes and 22 pairs of autosomes. In the female the sex chromosome pair is made up of two so-called X chromosomes. In the male the pair is made up of an X chromosome and a much smaller Y chromosome. At meiosis all the chromosome pairs of the germinal cells divide in half to produce the sperm (in the male) and egg (in the female). The union of two germ cells at fertilization reestablishes a full complement of chromosomes to make a newly formed individual. Each person's chromosomal constitution is thus derived in equal parts from mother and father, each chromosome pair being made up of one maternally derived and one paternally derived chromosome. When it comes time for the offspring in turn to pass on genetic endowment, there is an equal chance of passing on, by the same process of meiosis, either the maternally derived or paternally derived chromosome of each chromosome pair. The same biologic mechanism apply to the sex chromosomes; however, the father must necessarily pass on his Y chromosome in order to produce a son, and his X chromosome to produce a daughter. Thus the father will never pass on any genes lying on his X chromosome to his sons and will always pass on such genes to his daughters.

Autosomal Dominant Disease

It is predicted that the chances are one in two that this disorder will appear in each offspring.

Table 3-1

A disorder is called *autosomal dominant* when it is manifested in either male or female and if it is a result of a single-gene defect. If either parent manifests an autosomal dominant disorder, it is known that the affected parent has an equal chance of passing on either a normal or the defective gene; thus it is predicted that the chances are one in two that this disorder will appear in each offspring. An affected child will have the same likelihood of passing on the disorder, while an unaffected sibling who does not have the condition thus has no chance of passing it on. Table 3-1 lists some of the important autosomal dominant diseases, exemplified by neurofibromatosis and Marfan syndrome. Although there tends to be extensive variation in the expression of autosomal dominant diseases and death may occur as early as childhood or young adulthood, they usually do not interfere with reproductive fitness.

Autosomal dominant diseases are characterized by variable expression; sometimes the signs of the gene are subtle.

Marfan syndrome is usually easy to recognize; neurofibromatosis is more difficult to identify, and an affected person may reach the childbearing age with no evidence of the disease except for a half dozen café au lait spots or some axillary freckles. Nevertheless, if a diagnosis can be made—even if the only manifestation is the presence of axillary freckles—the risk, as in all autosomal dominant diseases, is one in two for each offspring.

The problems of diagnosis and counseling posed by the patient with Huntington disease exemplifies those encountered in a large number of autosomal dominant neurologic degenerative diseases: by the time the patient develops the first symptoms of the disease, the childbearing years are usually over and the gene has already passed on to the next generation. The problem is compounded by the psychiatric manifestations of the disease, which leads not only to misdiagnosis and failure to recognize the gene but also to a tendency on the part of families to hide information from both their physicians and relatives.

The older the father, the greater is the risk of new mutations.

The sporadic appearance (that is, from normal parents) of patients with autosomal dominant disease is explained by mutation—a situation in which the risk of recurrence is exceedingly rare. (It is important to attempt to rule out alternative explanations such as unknown paternity and unrecognized disease in one of the parents.) The risk of mutation increases with the age of the father. Since male sperm is made continuously throughout repro-

Table 3-1 Selected Important Mendelian Disorders—By Frequency and Number of Affected Individuals

Genetic Disease	Frequency of Heterozygote	Number of Affected Individuals per Million Births
Autosomal recessive		
Adrenogenital syndrome		15
Albinism, tyrosinase negative		25
Albinism, tyrosinase positive		25
Alpha$_1$-antitrypsin deficiency, SZ Pi type		240 whites in
ZZ		600 Sweden
Cystic fibrosis	4% (American whites)	270 (whites)
Galactosemia		25
Hemoglobin		
S-S (sickle cell anemia)	8% (American blacks)	1600 (American blacks)
S-C	(3% of American blacks have hemoglobin A-C)	1200 (American blacks)
		600 (American blacks)
S-β thalassemia	1% (American blacks)	100 (American blacks)
β thalassemia	Up to 16% Italians	400 (American citizens of Mediterranean origin)
Metachromatic leukodystrophy		25
Hurler syndrome α-iduronidase deficiency		25
Sanfilippo syndrome		20
Phenylketonuria		70 (whites)
Tay-Sachs disease	3% (American Jews)	400 (American Ashkenazi Jews)
Autosomal dominant		
Achondroplasia		100
Acrocephalosyndactyly (Apert syndrome)		6
Aniridia		5-10
Dentinogenesis imperfecta		8000
Facioscapulohumeral muscular dystrophy		4
Huntington chorea		50
Hyperlipoproteinemia, type II (familial hypercholesterolemia)		10,000
Marfan syndrome		15
Neurofibromatosis		303
Polycystic kidneys (all types)		4000
Retinoblastoma		50
Thanatophoric dwarfism		15
Tuberous sclerosis		10
Waardenburg syndrome		250
X-linked recessive diseases	Frequency of female carriers	
Bruton agammaglobulinemia		10-15
Ocular albinism		10-15
Amelogenesis imperfecta		10
Fabry disease		2-5

Table 3-1 Continued

Genetic Disease	Frequency of Heterozygote	Number of Affected Individuals per Million Births
Color blindness (deutan)		2% of males
(protan)		6% of males
Diabetes insipidus, nephrogenic		0.1
Glucose-6-phosphate dehydrogenase deficiency (African type or A-minus variant)	24% of American black females	10-14% of black Americans
Chronic granulomatous disease		1-5
Duchenne muscular dystrophy		200-220
Factor VIII deficiency (hemophilia A)		100-120
Factor IX deficiency (hemophilia B; Christmas disease)		20-30
Hunter syndrome		20
Ichthyosis		200
Retinitis pigmentosa		1-5

Source Benirschke, K. et al. 1976. Genetic diseases. In *Prevention of embryonic, fetal, and perinatal diseases*, eds. R. L. Brent and M. I. Harris, pp. 219-261. Fogarty International Center Series on Preventive Medicine, Vol. 3. Washington D.C.: U. S. Government Printing Office.

ductive life, the chances of a copying error in the DNA going into the sperm increase with age. Thus the older the father is, the greater the chance he will sire an offspring with a spontaneously mutated genetic abnormality.

Autosomal Recessive Disease

In this situation there is a one in four chance at each birth of the parents' producing a heterozygous carrier like themselves.

A disorder is called *autosomal recessive* when it is manifested in either male or female and requires *both* genes at the same locus of a chromosome pair (alleles) to be abnormal in order for the condition to be evident. Thus two parents may appear perfectly normal though each is a carrier of the same gene defect. In this situation there is a one in four chance at each birth of the parents' producing a homozygous infant with the disease and two chances in four of producing a heterozygous carrier like themselves.

Consanguinity (genetic inbreeding)increases the chance of bearing an offspring with an autosomal recessive disorder.

The appearance of an infant with an autosomal recessive disorder is more likely when consanguinity (genetic inbreeding) has occurred. For example, the chances are one in two that a brother and sister share the same gene, and one in eight for first cousins; much higher odds than would be the case in nonconsanguineous matings, where the risks would be ten to a thousandfold less depending on the frequency of the gene in the population at large.

Some important autosomal recessive diseases and their frequencies are presented in Table 3-1. Most serious autosomal recessive diseases are rare, but some of those listed in Table 3-1 are relatively common in special populations.

X-Linked Recessive Disease

X-linked dominant inheritance implies expression in the female, as occurs in X-linked hypophosphatemic rickets.

A condition is called *X-linked recessive* when the gene responsible for the defect is carried on the X chromosome and occurs only in males. X-linked dominant inheritance implies expression in the female, as occurs in X-linked hypophosphatemic rickets. If the mother carries a gene defect on one of her X chromosomes, she will on the average convey this defect to half her sons and half her daughters. If her daughters receive a normal X from their father, they will all be unaffected. In contrast, because their Y chromosome lacks the paired alleles of the X chromosome, the sons will express the gene on their X chromosome; thus half the sons will be affected and half will be unaffected. In turn, an affected male will pass on his X chromosome bearing the gene defect to all his daughters but, since he conveys only the Y chromosome to male offspring, he will produce unaffected sons.

Some X-linked recessive disorders are shown in Table 3-1.

CHROMOSOMAL DISORDERS

Any child with a syndrome of multiple malformations that is not recognizable as Mendelian or nongenetic should be studied cytogenetically.

Cytogenetic analysis has defined a number of syndromes of congenital malformations—most of them associated with mental retardation. The development of the new banding techniques has permitted finely grained analysis of subtle variations from normality. Any child with a syndrome of multiple malformations that is not recognizable as Mendelian or nongenetic should be studied cytogenetically, using the banding techniques. This can be done using cultured fibroblasts but it is most conveniently done using short-term lymphocytes grown in 65-72 hours from a small sample of heparinized blood. The dividing cells are arrested in metaphase by the addition of colchincine, or a derivative; the chromosomes are dispersed by subjecting the cells to a hypotonic medium. The preparations are then simply squashed, air dried, and stained with one of a variety of techniques, most commonly Giemsa stain, to produce G bands (Figure 3-1). The preparations are viewed under the microscope and representative cells are photographed; then the individual chromosomes are arranged in pairs to form the karyotype. Most laboratories routinely analyze 10-40 cells. More may be required if mosaicism is suspected. The normal karyotype

Figure 3-1

Table 3-2 Selected Representative Cytogenetic Disorders—By Chromosomal Abnormality and Clinical Phenotype

Common Name	Chromosomal Abnormality	Clinical Phenytype
Down Syndrome	Trisomy 21 Translocation Mosaicism	Mental retardation, slanted palpebral fissure, epicanthal folds, small rounded facies, depressed nasal bridge, flat occiput, protruding tongue, iridal Brushfield spots, brachydactyly, clinodactyly, simian creases, wide gap between first and second toes, hypotonia, imperforate anus, intestinal atresia, congenital heart disease, leukemia, premature aging.
	Trisomy 13	Multiple congenital anomalies, including severe mental retardation; holoprosencephaly; major ocular anomalies such as anophthalmia, microphthalmia or colobomas; clefts of lip and palate; polydactyly; congenital heart disease; cutaneous defects of the scalp.
	Trisomy 18	Multiple anomalies including micrognathia, low-set, malformed ears; characteristically a failure of fisting in which the index fingers overlie the third fingers; hypoplasia of the nails, especially of the fifth fingers and toes; rocker-bottom feet. Also, low birth weight for gestational age and severe degree of retardation of growth and mental development, usually with early demise; congenital heart disease; narrow pelvis with limited abduction of the hip; low-arch dermal ridge pattern on the fingertips.
Turner Syndrome	XO	Shortness of stature, ovarian dysgenesis, sexual infantilism, webbed neck, shield chest, cubitus valgus, short fourth metacarpals, hypoplastic nails, multiple pigmented nevi, not associated with advanced maternal age; usually mosaic.
Klinefelter Syndrome	XXY	In the preadolescent patient, slim, eunuchoid body proportions with relatively longer legs, small testes, behavior problems, dull mentality; later, gynecomastia, underdeveloped secondary sexual characteristics, elevated gonadotropins, hyalinization and atrophy of seminiferous tubules; sex chromatin-positive buccal smear, 47 XXY karyotype.
Triple X Syndrome	XXX	Normal female phenotype; two sex chromatin bodies; 47, XXX karyotype, mild mental retardation is common.
Double Y Syndrome	YY	Tall stature, radioulnar synostosis, behavioral abnormalities; a phenotype that may be normal, extra fluorescent Y body, XYY chromosomal constitution.

contains 23 pairs or 46 chromosomes, 22 autosomes, and 2 sex chromosomes. Staining with quinacrine derivatives to produce fluorescent Q banding is particularly useful in studies of the Y chromosome, which has a particularly brilliant fluorescent band. In fact male whole cells can be recognized through such staining, without preparing chromosomes, by the presence of the fluorescent Q body.

A variety of abnormal karyotypes have been recognized. The most common is a deviation from the normal or euploid number,

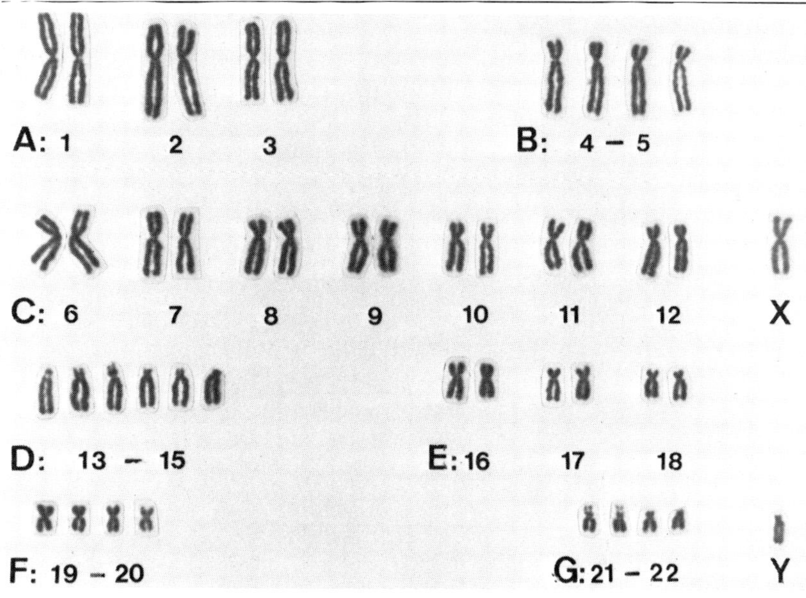

Figure 3-1 Normal human karyotype. The chromosomes were pretreated with trypsin and stained with Giemsa. (Reprinted with permission from J. Leisti. 1971. Structural variation in human mitotic chromosomes. *Ann. Acad. Sci., fenn. A, IV Biologica* 179:1-69.

The most common form of aneuploidy is trisomy in which there are three homologous chromosomes instead of the usual two.

referred to then as *aneuploid.* The most common form of aneuploidy is trisomy in which there are three homologous chromosomes instead of the usual two. Monosomy in which one of a pair is missing may also be seen. It appears that both trisomy and monosomy arise through nondisjunction. In this process the chromosomes divide during meiosis and, instead of separating normally to the opposite poles of the dividing cell, two chromosomes remain sticky and stay together, yielding one gamete that contains no chromosome and one that contains two. When the gamete that contains no chromosome is fertilized by a normal gamete the resulting organism is monosomic; when the gamete containing two chromosomes is fertilized by a normal gamete the resulting organism is trisomic. A different mechanism for trisomy or monosomy is that of nondisjunction during early embryonic mitosis, resulting in mosaicism, in which the individual that results has two cell populations.

The factor most commonly associated with nondisjunction and a trisomic fetus is advanced maternal age. The general order of magnitude of incidence of Down syndrome in relation to maternal

The older the mother is the greater is the risk of chromosomal anomalities.

age is approximately 1 in 2000 for women in their 20s, 1 in 300 for women in their 30s and 1 in 40 for women in their 40s. An incidence of 1%-2% is generally estimated for women over 40 years of age, but an incidence of 5% has been found among fetuses of women over 40 years of age studied by amniocentesis. Presumably some of these fetuses would ordinarily be aborted or stillborn rather than coming to term. Other forms of trisomy are also more common in women of advanced age. Now that the chromosomes derived from each parent can be identified by banding techniques, it has become apparent that advanced maternal and advanced paternal age both carry an increased risk of abnormal chromosomal segregation. Recent estimates are that abnormal segregation is paternal in origin in about one third of instances.

To a lesser extent, the risk of chromosomal anomalies also increases with paternal age.

Other chromosomal derangements occur through breaks, fusions, deletions, and derangements in meiosis.

Table 3-2

Down syndrome is the most common of the chromosomal syndromes (Table 3-2). It occurs in 1 in every 600-800 live births. It is due most commonly to trisomy of chromosome 21, but may also be caused in about 5% of cases by translocation of chromosome 21 to chromosome 14, or less commonly to chromosome 15 or 13, or to other chromosomes. In about 1% of cases there is mosaicism with two populations—1 normal and 1 trisomic for chromosome 21.

EMPIRIC RISK COUNSELING

The most common genetic disorders are probably multifactorial.

The most common disorders that have a genetic component in their causation do not follow a Mendelian pattern of inheritance and are considered to be multifactorial in their origin. Thus they might result from the interplay of a genetic susceptibility and environmental factors. Many common diseases such as diabetes, pyloric stenosis, and congenital dislocation of the hip fall into this category. Geneticists have assembled information that is of use in counseling from empiric information on recurrence and comparison with the random risk in the general population (Blyth and Carter, 1969).

Some interesting relationships have emerged. The prevalence of cleft lip and palate in the general Caucasian population is about 0.1%. The risk of recurrence in a second sibling is about 4%. Similarly, the risk of recurrence in the offspring of an involved parent is also about 4%. This relationship, in which the risk of recurrence is the same among siblings as it is from parents to offspring, is general among multifactorial conditions.

In general, the risk of recurrence is the same among siblings as from parents to offspring in multifactorial conditions.

The incidence of concurrence among monozygotic twins of cleft lip and palate is 31%, while the proportion of dizygotic twins that are affected is not different from that of siblings. These observations are also true generally of multifactorially inherited conditions and they tend to confirm their heritability. For isolated cleft palate the concordance among monozygotic twins is 40%; for psoriasis it is 63%.

Some disorders such as pyloric stenosis have a predominant incidence in one sex. Thus most infants with pyloric stenosis are males; congenital dislocation of the hip is much more common in females. When there is a sex predilection, an involved person of the sex in which the disorder is least common has a much greater risk of having affected offspring. It is as if it takes more factors or stronger factors to bring on the disease in the uncommonly affected sex, and these factors are felt in the next generation. Thus a woman who has pyloric stenosis as an infant has a 25% risk of having a child with pyloric stenosis, while an affected male has only a 4% chance of having a child with the disease.

In multifactorial conditions, unlike the situation in Mendelian inheritance, the risk of recurrence in subsequent pregnancies varies with the outcome of additional pregnancies.

It is also empirically true, unlike the situation in Mendelian inheritance, that the risk of recurrence in subsequent pregnancies varies with the outcome of additional pregnancies: thus the risk for cleft lip and palate of 4% applies to parents of an affected child; for parents of two affected children the risk of recurrence is 9%; similarly, with an affected parent the risk is 10% after the appearance of one affected child; it jumps to 18%-20% after two affected siblings.

AMNIOCENTESIS AND PRENATAL DIAGNOSIS

Amniocentesis and prenatal diagnosis have changed dramatically the practice of genetic counseling.

The development of amniocentesis and the prenatal diagnosis of genetic disease has revolutionized the practice of medical genetics (Benirschke, et al., 1976; Kaback, et al., 1979). It is this process more than any other that has changed genetic counseling from an essentially passive procedure to an active, interventive process. It has increased dramatically the number of patients coming to these practitioners.

The procedure sounds at first more like a negative than a positive intervention, involving as it does the termination of abnormal pregnancies through abortion. However, on reflection and with experience it is clear that these clients are not seeking prevention of disease: they are seeking a healthy child. Through the monitoring of pregnancies parents who before would not have risked a pregnancy are bringing unaffected babies to term.

Amniocentesis for prenatal diagnosis is performed by an obstetrician skilled in the procedure at 14-17 weeks of gestation. Ultrasound detection is usually employed first, in order to locate the placenta and to ascertain the presence or absence of twins.

Under sterile conditions up to 50 ml of fluid are removed, and ideally the fluid is hand carried to the laboratory. Some obstetricians have used the husband for this process; once the sample is safely in the laboratory the husband returns to take his wife home. We employ a nurse or genetic counselor who meets with the parents before the procedure, stays with the prospective mother through the procedure, and then takes the fluid to the laboratory. The sample is routinely split so that it is processed in two geographically separate laboratories. Thus if an incubator fails in one there is still another viable sample. When the sample arrives in the laboratory it is centrifuged. The supernatant fluid may be analyzed chemically for the diagnosis of certain inborn errors of metabolism. If this method is available, it provides the most rapidly specific approach to prenatal diagnosis. We have used gas chromatography-mass spectrometry and the presence of unique metabolites such as methylcitrate to make prenatal diagnoses of propionic acidemia and methylmalonic acidemia. Analysis for methylmalonic acid may serve the same purpose in the diagnosis of methylmalonic acidemia, and in this condition the diagnosis may be made antenatally by analysis of the maternal urine for methylmalonic acid.

The adrenogenital syndrome that results from a defect in adrenal 21-hydroxylase can be diagnosed prenatally by direct assay of amniotic fluid for 17 α-hydroxyprogesterone. This is best done at midgestation when levels are highest and the distinction between affected and normal is most clearly made. Diagnosis at this time also permits a decision as to interruption of the pregnancy. In late pregnancy, after 34 weeks, the concentration of 17 α-hydroxyprogesterone in maternal serum rises appreciably and the diagnosis may be made at this time by assay of the mother's blood. A diagnosis at this time permits the prompt initiation of treatment at birth, which may be lifesaving.

The cells recovered from the amniotic fluid are suspended in tissue culture fluid containing fetal calf serum and are grown in incubation rich in CO_2 until there are sufficient numbers of cells for analysis. This takes time. For cytogenetic analysis it is usually 2-3 weeks. For the analysis of enzymes in fetal cells in culture the interval is variable but always longer; 4 weeks is probably a minimum for the enzymatic analysis of an inborn error of metabolism.

The interval between amniocentesis and prenatal diagnosis is a difficult waiting time for parents.

This interval is a difficult time for parents. It is easy to become anxious while waiting. It helps to emphasize this inevitable time lag on the first interview, and if more time than usual is required it helps to call the parents to let them know. They might also be urged to call whenever they would like to progress report.

It is important to seek out a laboratory that has a record of success with the growing of cells from amniotic fluid.

Sometimes no cells grow. This is usually clear by 2 weeks and a second amniocentesis is performed. It should be emphasized that it takes a "green thumb" to obtain an analyzable culture from the cells that have washed off the fetal skin into the amniotic fluid; hence it is important to seek out a laboratory that has a record of success with the growing of cells from amniotic fluid.

Analysis of amniotic fluid cells for fetal chromosomal study is the basis for most prenatal diagnoses. The fetal karyotype is the simplest information obtainable from an amniotic fluid cell culture regardless of the indication for amniocentesis.

INBORN ERRORS OF METABOLISM

There is vigorous activity in the prenatal assessment of enzymes in cells in culture. This is the usual method of choice for the prenatal diagnosis of inborn errors of metabolism. Occasionally it is possible to make a diagnosis by assay of the fluid directly or of uncultured cells. The cells obtained at amniocentesis are generally large, with irregular borders and very small nuclei; they look like amnion cells or squamous epithelial cells. Occasional cells are round or oval and smooth bordered but they also have small nuclei. They are resistant to mechanical and physical methods of disruption. On cultivation the cells may be epitheloid or fibroblastic and are readily disrupted, by freezing and thawing or sonication, for preparation of cell-free extracts. Their fetal origin is supported by a considerable body of evidence such as the regular demonstration in the presence of male karyotypes.

In general any condition that can be diagnosed positively by studying enzymes in fibroblasts in cell culture can be diagnosed by assaying enzymes in cells cultured from amniotic fluid. So far this hypothesis has proved essentially correct. However, in the case of histidase the result depends on the type of cell studied. When amniotic fluid cells are cultured, epithelial cells and fibroblastic cells may be obtained. Epithelial cells are high in histidase, while histidase is lacking in fibroblastic cells. Thus only epithelial cells are useful for prenatal diagnosis of histidinemia.

A variety of genetic diseases have been diagnosed by the assay of enzymes in cell cultures derived from fluid cells.

A variety of genetic diseases have been diagnosed by the assay of enzymes in cell cultures derived from fluid cells. The X-linked disorders were the earliest to be approached by amniocentesis. It was recognized as early as 1956 that the sex of the fetus could be determined. In X-linked conditions such as hemophilia and Duchenne muscular dystrophy, recognition that the fetus of a known carrier is male has been considered grounds for interruption of the pregnancy. This is certainly a less than ideal criterion because such a male fetus has a 50% chance of being normal.

However, this approach to prenatal diagnosis remains all that is available in many X-linked disorders. Cultivation of cells and determination of enzyme content have put on a sound basis the prenatal detection of the X-linked disorders that can be diagnosed on a molecular level. Among these conditions, as in the case of the other inborn errors of metabolism, the assays for these enzymes that are suitable for prenatal diagnosis are available in only a few—sometimes only one—laboratories in the world. Arrangements should be made well in advance for the logistics of transport of the samples to where the diagnosis can be made.

Techniques coming from the forefront of molecular biology are already being applied to the problem of prenatal diagnosis. The most recent examples are of the use of restriction endonuclease mapping in the antenatal diagnosis of the thalassemic syndromes. In this work the DNA may be digested with restriction endonuclease and hybridized to specific ^{32}p-labeled cDNA probes and then subjected to autoradiography. Thalassemic syndromes due to gene deletions such as α-thalassemia and hemoglobin H disease can can be detected in this way. This approach requires cultivation of amniotic fluid cells in culture for 4-6 weeks to obtain enough DNA to permit analysis. Further refinement in technique in which restriction endonuclease maps are made require much less DNA. The occurrence of specific cleavage sites in DNA will doubless permit this technique also to be employed to detect the site of some single nucleotide substitutions in structural gene alterations. It is also possible to use these techniques by the analysis of a marker section of DNA that is linked to a specific gene. This approach is applicable to the prenatal diagnosis of a majority of cases of sickle cell anemia.

Thalassemic syndromes due to gene deletions such as α-thalassemia and hemoglobin H disease can be detected.

α-Fetoprotein (AFP) has been found to be a concomitant of neural tube defects and is useful for antenatal diagnosis. The concentration of AFP in the amniotic fluid surrounding fetuses with anencephaly or spina bifida is significantly higher than in normal amniotic fluid. This is the procedure of choice in a family at risk in which there has been a previous patient with one of these defects, and for AFP we routinely test fluid obtained for other purposes such as advanced maternal age. Fluid is obtained between the fourteenth and twentieth weeks. It is important that the length of gestation be recorded since the level changes with time. The procedure is highly accurate, but it does not identify all affected fetuses, and there is about a one in a thousand false-positive rate. Elevations of AFP may also be seen in other fetal abnormalities.

We routinely test fluid obtained for other purposes such as advanced maternal age.

Unfortunately more than 90% of these fetuses occur in families with no history of neural tube defect. Therefore interest has developed in the use of the level of AFP in maternal plasma to screen for these defects. This is particularly true in Great Britain where the incidence of 4.5 in 1000 births is at least twice that of the United States. Elevated levels are seen, and normative data have been obtained. In a British study the serum of women carrying anencephalic fetuses exceeded the normal median by 2.5 times in 90% of cases, and in the case of spina bifida in 80% of cases. Of normal pregnancies 3% were in this range. A positive test may be followed by determination of the amniotic fluid concentration and ultrasonography to rule out multiple pregnancy, which can elevate the level.

Ultrasound and x-ray examinations can be used to detect certain structural anomalies in utero.

Approaches to the visualization of the fetus may be useful in the delineation of congenital defects of morphogenesis. Of these, ultrasonography is the most readily available and the least invasive. Anencephaly can certainly be diagnosed in this way; so can spina bifida, although this is more difficult. The size of the head can be measured and autosomal recessive microcephaly may be diagnosed prenatally in this way. Hydrocephalus and encephalocele may also be detected. The short-limbed dwarfism of the Ellis-Van Creveld syndrome has been recognized prenatally, using ultrasound.

Radiographic examination is capable of detecting skeletal defects such as the radial aplasia of the thrombocytopenia-absent-radius syndrome. Amniography, in which radiopaque dye has been injected into the uterus, has been employed. This procedure may outline the limbs and assist in visualization; it is not reliable, however, in the detection of neural tube defects. Fetoscopy has been employed in a few centers for the direct visualization of the fetus; for instance, it was combined with ultrasound in the diagnosis of the Ellis-Van Creveld syndrome in which the polydactyly was actually seen. Fetoscopy may also be useful for obtaining a sample of fetal blood, though fetoscopy is still considered a research procedure.

The field of prenatal diagnosis offers a positive approach to genetic counseling and the management of genetic disease. Further research almost certainly will increase the number of disorders detectable prenatally. As techniques improve and become more widely applied, a variety of legal, ethical, and moral questions will be arising regarding therapeutic abortion; on the other hand, there are indications that society is prepared to deal realistically with these issues.

By monitoring pregnancies with amniocentesis and recommending selective abortion, one can guarantee selection of an unaffect-

Prenatal diagnosis and selective abortion allow families who would otherwise be afraid to risk pregnancy to try to produce a healthy offspring.

ed child. This permits families at risk to have healthy children, whereas they would otherwise be unwilling to risk bringing a diseased child into the world. Planned parenthood at its best is concerned not only with the quantity of human reproduction but also with its quality.

GENETIC COUNSELING

The key to accurate genetic counseling is accurate diagnosis.

Tracing surnames through ancestors may reveal the likelihood of consanguinity.

Genetic counseling centers can be consulted. They offer expertise in diagnosis and treatment and are helpful in dealing with the inevitable psychosocial problems.

As the foregoing discussion should have made clear, the key to accurate genetic counseling is accurate diagnosis. The primary care physician may wish to carry this out or cooperate with a genetic counseling center. Developing a family pedigree will enable the physician to decide whether a Mendelian pattern of inheritance, particularly autosomal dominant disease, seems likely. Obtaining medical records from other physicians and hospitals is essential for accuracy. If autosomal recessive disease is suspected the physician should have the couple trace surnames through ancestors on both sides of the family. The appearance of a common surname or any other suggestion of possible consanguinity (for example, the discovery that both sides of the family originated in an isolated geographical area) would support the likelihood that both parents share common genes. The counseling physician should advise prospective older parents of the increased risk of cytogenetic disorders. Increased maternal age raises the risk of chromosomal anomalies, and increased paternal age raises the risk of new mutations as well as of chromosomal anomalies. A careful physical examination should be carried out with attention paid to such subclinical manifestations of the disorders suspected as café au lait spots where neurofibromatosis is suspected, small extra nubs on the hands or feet where polydactyly is suspected, and dislocated lenses where Marfan syndrome is suspected. Since determinations of subclinical disease may sometimes require laboratory testing, it is wise to involve genetic counseling centers in the diagnostic workup. Furthermore, personnel at these centers have considerable experience with the psychologic and social impact of genetic disease and can often provide helpful assistance in conveying information and assisting parents in obtaining social support service (for example, funds for the treatment of hemophilia).

COUNSELING PREGNANT WOMAN

With each pregnancy every couple faces a 3% risk of bearing a defective offspring.

With each child every couple faces about a 3% risk that it will be born with a major defect of some kind. After concluding the workup of a defective offspring, the genetic counselor might predict that the couple faces a high recurrent risk (25%-50% in the case of Mendelian-inherited single-gene defects, to as high as 100% for certain chromosome anomalies) or relatively low recurrence risk (around 5% for most of the common multifactorial conditions).

Any pregnant woman over 35 should be advised about amniocentesis.

Any pregnant woman aged 35 years or older should be advised about the possibility of amniocentesis. There are a number of other situations in which the pregnant woman should be offered amniocentesis:

> If she has had a previous child with a chromosomal anomaly.
>
> If three or more of her past pregnancies have ended in miscarriage or if her husband's previous wife experienced several miscarriages.
>
> If she or her mate have a chromosomal abnormality.
>
> If there is a history of Down syndrome or some other chromosomal abnormality in her family or her spouse's family.
>
> If she has male relatives with serious X-linked disorders such as Duchenne muscular dystrophy or severe hemophilia.
>
> If her fetus is at usual or a higher risk for some hereditary error of metabolism detectable in utero or at increased risk for a neural tube defect.

All pregnant women should be advised to follow good prenatal care habits and, in particular, to avoid smoking and excess alcohol.

HETEROZYGOTE SCREENING

The persons consulting the physician may not be parents of an affected individual. A sister of a patient with galactosemia after getting married might come in with her husband and ask about their chances of having a baby that might develop cataracts, cirrhosis of the liver, death in infancy, or mental retardation as a result of galactosemia. Assuming that all the physician knew about her was what is known about most autosomal recessive conditions, he would proceed to calculate that her chances of being a carrier were two in three. In an autosomal recessive mating of the usual four genotypic possibilities—one affected, two heterozygotes and one normal—the first would be excluded since she is phenotypically normal; this leaves three possibilities, two of which are heterozytes. The heterozygote frequency of galactosemia in the United States is about 1 in 300—the chance they face that the husband is a carrier. Then assuming they both were heterozygous, the risk of an affected child would be one in four. Putting it all together, the risk of a galactosemic child from this union would be $2/3 \times 1/300 \times 1/4 = 1$ in 1800. This essentially would be no risk so the physician would tell the parents that it would be unrealistic to worry about it. However, in the case of galactosemia we can do much better than that today. It is possible to detect the presence of the gene in a heterozygote by assaying the blood for galactose-1-phosphate uridyl transferase, the enzyme that is defective in the patient. Generally the assay would be done on the patient's sister. If her enzyme activity were normal, then she could be reassured that she was not a carrier and that there would be no risk of galactosemia. If her activity were about half normal, it would be clear that she was a carrier, and her husband would be tested. Again, if he were normal there would be no risk. If by mere chance he too were to turn out to be heterozygous, then the pregnancy could be monitored by amniocentesis and assay of the enzyme in cultured cells. In the case of a positive prenatal diagnosis the parents might elect to terminate the pregnancy; or they might elect to go to term and treat the baby for life with a diet containing no milk products.

In some conditions tests can detect the asymptomatic heterozygote carrier of the abnormal gene.

The only effective method for reducing significantly the incidence of a disease in a population is to identify the presence of the gene in all carriers. Then amniocentesis could be performed on all carriers of an X-linked recessive trait or in all instances where both parents carry an autosomal recessive gene. Some persons who were carriers might not marry or might decide to adopt rather than have their own children.

If heterozygote detection were available for a common autosomal recessive disease such as cystic fibrosis, in which the gene is carried by 5% of Caucasians, a major campaign could be launched to eliminate the disease. Unfortunately, neither prenatal diagnosis nor heterozygote detection is available for cystic fibrosis, so the methodology for control is not in hand.

In the case of Tay-Sachs disease the gene is common, and programs have been established among the Jewish populations. The gene is carried by one in thirty of the descendants of the Ashkenazim, the Jews of Eastern Europe, who are ancestors of most of the Jewish population of the United States. It has been estimated that there are approximately 6 million carriers in this country. It should be possible to test all those of child-bearing age. A pilot screening program was established in the Baltimore-Washington area in 1971, and programs are now available in most major cities.

Screening programs are available in most major cities to screen for carriers of the Tay-Sachs gene.

The test is carried out on a small sample of blood, and the procedure is automated so that it can be done in a few centralized laboratories. Follow-up is done by people trained in genetic counseling so that the information obtained can be used intelligently by those receiving it. A couple is at risk only if both are found to carry the gene; for these couples monitored pregnancy is available using amniocentesis.

REFERRAL TO SPECIALIZED CENTERS

The primary care physician does not need to refer a family to a medical geneticist or to a specialized center for genetic counseling. Genetic disease is so common that it is important that genetic medicine be incorporated into primary care practice.

Once the diagnosis of a genetically determined disease is established, the principles of genetic counseling may be applied.

Once the diagnosis of a genetically determined disease is established, the principles of genetic counseling may be applied as laid out in this chapter. The first requirement in the counseling process is an accurate, definitive diagnosis. This is sometimes easy. On the other hand it may be for this reason that the patient is referred to a center specializing in genetic counseling. Many genetic disorders are rare, and few physicians have had experience with them. Particularly among the disorders of morphogenesis many conditions resemble one another; very similar phenotypic appearances may have entirely different modes of genetic transmission (Nyhan and Sakati, 1976; Smith, 1976).

Psychological support is an important part of genetic counseling.

In the process of counseling itself, the physician can perform a valuable service by filling the role of sympathetic physician, armed with precise information about genetic transmission. Couples may have had disheartening personal experiences. They may have a sizable amount of misinformation as to why they were singled out for misfortune. They may have guilt feelings that something they did caused the problem. It may be difficult for them to discuss their problems and their feelings. The role of the genetic counselor in the psychologic support of the family is an important part of the process. A skilled and knowledgeable counselor can help the emotional state of the family. To do this it is important to evaluate the concerns of the family. They may be the same kind of concerns that physicians have for the family, but on the other hand they may be very different. Genetic counseling is a process of communication. Communication of physician to patient is seldom as straightforward and easy as we think. It is often particularly difficult in genetic problems. Families may have trouble listening to what physicians are saying. Physicians must find ways of delivering their message so that it is understood.

A requirement for specialized testing provides an argument for referral. This is particularly true for prenatal diagnosis. At first the primary physicians may not know where to turn for such a specialized assay. Although even the facility for culturing amniotic cells may be available in only a relatively few centers often it is not necessary to send the patient herself. Even the highly specialized enzyme assays that can be done in only one place are generally available to those who know how to make the appropriate arrangement. It is important that the physician make the patient and the family an enlightened referral that gets them into the system.

Most medical centers have genetic counseling facilities.

In many states this information is available through the state health department or the closest university medical center. Most medical centers and university teaching hospitals have facilities for genetic diagnosis and counseling, or they can make an appropriate referral. Some of these institutions accept patients only if referred by a physician or other medical institution, but many now accept patients directly. In some areas the university medical center has set up satellite clinics in local communities.

Information is available through The National Foundation and the National Genetics Foundation.

The National Foundation-March of Dimes maintains information on the availability of genetic services in an "International Directory of Genetic Services." It is available free on request to physicians and other medical professionals from the Professional Education Department, National Foundation-March of Dimes.* The National Genetics Foundation coordinates a network of institutions in the United States and Canada that provide sophisticated genetic counseling and access to the specialized testing discussed throughout this chapter. Entry into the network may be obtained by writing the foundation.†

The National Institute of General Medical Sciences (NIGMS) has a Genetic Centers program. This program funds research in genetics in a small number of institutions throughout the United States. A critical concentration of investigators and other specialists in genetics has been assembled in each center. They all offer genetic services as well as pursue research. Information on these centers and their locations may be obtained by writing to NIGMS, National Institutes of Health, Bethesda, Md, 20014. Similarly, the National Institute of Child Health and Human Development (NICHD) supports mental retardation centers. In each there is a program for research into the causes of mental retardation. In most of the centers clinical services for the retarded and their families are available. Information about mental retardation centers and their locations and programs may be obtained by writing NICHD, National Institutes of Health, Bethesda, Md. 20014. The Health Services Administration (HSA) supports a

---

*P.O. Box 2000, White Plains, N. Y. 10602.

†250 West 57th St., New York, N. Y. 10019; or call (212)265-3166.

number of university-affiliated facilities devoted to a full range of services for the mentally retarded and their families.*

Some of the principal genetics centers in the United States follow:

University of California, San Diego, La Jolla, Calif.

University of California, San Francisco, San Francisco, Calif.

Columbia University, New York, N. Y.

Cornell University, New York, N. Y.

Albert Einstein College of Medicine of Yeshiva University, Bronx, N. Y.

Harbor General Hospital, Torrance, Calif.

Harvard Medical School, Boston, Mass.

Indiana University School of Medicine, Indianapolis, Ind.

The Johns Hopkins University Medical Institution, Baltimore, Md.

Los Angeles Children's Hospital, Los Angeles, Calif.

University of Michigan, Ann Arbor, Mich.

Mount Sinai School of Medicine, City University of New York, N. Y.

University of Oregon Medical School, Portland, Ore.

University of Pennsylvania School of Medicine, Philadelphia, Pa.

Stanford University, Palo Alto, Calif.

University of Texas Graduate School of Biomedical Sciences and M. D. Anderson Hospital, Houston, Texas

University of Washington School of Medicine, Seattle, Wash.

University of Wisconsin, Madison, Wisc.

Yale University School of Medicine, New Haven, Conn.

ANNOTATED BIBLIOGRAPHY

Benirschke, K.; Carpenter, G., Epstein, C., et al. 1976. Genetic disease. In *Prevention of embryonic, fetal, and perinatal disease,*

---

*Information about these facilities and their locations can be obtained by writing to HSA, Department of Health, Education, and Welfare. Public Information Branch, Room 14A-55 Parklawn Building; 5600 Fishers Lane, Rockville, Md. 20852.

eds. R. L. Brent and M. I. Harris, pp. 219-261. Fogarty International Center Series on Preventive Medicine, Vol. 3, Washington D.C.: U. S. Government Printing Office.
This monograph provides a comprehensive technical review of human genetics with a focus on preventive medicine.

Blyth, H., and Carter, C. 1969. *A guide to genetic prognosis in paediatrics.* London: Spastics International Medical Publications, William Neineman Medical Books.
This is the best source on assessment of risk in the many non-Mendelian genetic diseases.

Kaback, M. D.; Brent, R. L.; Crandall, B. F., et al., 1979. *Antenatal diagnosis.* NIH Publication No. 79-1973. Bethesda, MD: U. S. Department of Health, Education and Welfare.
This is the state of the art on prenatal diagnosis; coverage of ethical issues is extensive.

McKusick, B. 1978. *Mendelian inheritance in man.* 5th ed. Baltimore: The Johns Hopkins University Press.
The compendium of diseases determined by single Mendelian genes; frequently updated, this book is among the bibles of human genetics.

Nyhan, W. L., and Edelson, E. 1976. *The heredity factor: Genes, chromosomes, and you.* New York: Grosset & Dunlap, Inc.
This book is genetics for the patient and family. It is now available in Spanish.

Nyhan, W. L., and Sakati, N. O. 1976. *Genetic and malformation syndromes in clinical medicine.* Chicago: Year Book Medical Publishers, Inc.
This book addresses some rare genetic diseases and provides in capsule form the information needed for diagnosis and patient management. It is particularly strong on disorders of metabolism.

Smith, D. W. 1976. *Recognizable patterns of human malformation.* 2nd ed. Philadelphia: W. B. Saunders Company.
This book has a similar objective to that of Nyhan and Sakati. It covers more diseases in briefer fashion. It is particularly strong on abnormalities of morphogenesis.

4 Immunization

Elizabeth Barrett-Connor

Dr. Barrett-Connor is a graduate of Cornell University Medical College and was on the faculty of the University of Miami, School of Medicine, before joining the faculty of the University of California, San Diego, School of Medicine. In addition to her clinical practice in infectious diseases she has published extensively and has served on numerous national committees in the areas of epidemiology and infectious disease.

Brief Contents

Overview

The ability to induce disease-specific immunity by immunization is one of the triumphs of preventive medicine All presently identified infectious agents are immunogenic; in theory, vaccines can be produced against all of them. This chapter reviews briefly the general basis of immunization in disease prevention and provides specific clinical information and recommendations.

GENERAL PRINCIPLES

Smallpox vaccine has accomplished the first documented disease eradication in medical history.

The ability to induce disease-specific immunity by immunization (vaccination) is one of the triumphs of preventive medicine. The past 50 years have seen the introduction and application of over 25 vaccines. One of the oldest of these, smallpox vaccine, has actually accomplished the first documented disease eradication in medical history.

All presently identified infectious agents are immunogenic. In theory vaccines can be produced against them. Vaccines currently in use include bacterial toxoids and living or killed vaccines made from bacteria, viruses, mycoplasma, and Rickettsia. Different types of vaccine yield different durations of expected protection and different types of untoward sequelae. In general live virus vaccines produce the most sustained immunity; but this is by no means always true: tetanus toxoid, a nonviable reagent, produces immunity at least as sustained as that following vaccination with live vaccinia virus. Natural infection may boost artificially induced immunity, extending the duration of protection initiated by immunization. Untoward vaccine effects may be caused by the agent or by the vehicle in which it is grown or preserved. The frequency and type of side effects are also determined by host characteristics, many of which remain poorly delineated.

The paradox of immunization is that the risk of a successful vaccine may eventually exceed the risk of the disease it was intended to prevent.

An ideal immunizing agent is one that can produce long-term immunity through the administration of an agent sufficiently similar to the pathogen to induce protective antibody but sufficiently dissimilar to avoid any injury to the recipient. No such vaccine in fact exists. The paradox of immunization is that a successful immunization program may reduce disease incidence to a level where the risk of the vaccine exceeds that of the disease it was intended to prevent. Consequently immunization programs must be reevaluated periodically, as must the recommendations set forth in this text.

Simultaneous Immunizations

When vaccines commonly associated with side effects are given simultaneously, the side effects may be accentuated. Furthermore, the concurrent use of multiple vaccines limits the ability to ascertain the cause of any untoward reaction. Consequently, to offer the highest level of protection with the lowest frequency of untoward effects, the physician should individualize immunization regimens based on the characteristics of the patient and the indications for vaccination.

When there is limited patient access, impending foreign travel, or anticipated exposure to several infections patients may require several vaccines at the same time. Available evidence suggests that many active immunizations can be given safely at the same time without compromising the antibody response. For example, concurrent administration of pneumococcal polysaccharide vaccine and influenza vaccine at separate sites yields a satisfactory antibody response without increasing the incidence of side effects.

Concurrent administration of pneumococcal polysaccharide vaccine and influenza vaccine at separate sites yields a satisfactory antibody response without increasing the incidence of side effects.

Immunoglobulins should not be given until at least 2 weeks after a vaccine has been given, because passively acquired antibody can interfere with the response to the vaccination. (Passive antibody transmitted via placental circulation from mother to fetus is one reason for the high frequency of vaccine failure when immuization is attempted in infancy.) Passive and active immunizations are given concurrently only for the management of tetanus-prone wounds or for postexposure rabies prophylaxis.

Although several vaccines may be given simultaneously immunoglobulins should be postponed until at least 2 weeks after vaccine administration.

Hypersensitivity to Eggs

Vaccines produced from microorganisms grown on embryonated eggs may cause hypersensitivity reactions in sensitized individuals, including anaphylaxis. A relatively large amount of egg allergen is found in the duck embryo vaccine against rabies and in yellow fever vaccine. In contrast, influenza vaccine, although grown in

Persons who can eat eggs usually can be immunized safely with vaccines containing egg protein.

eggs, contains little egg allergen and is rarely associated with hypersensitivity reactions. Vaccines produced in embryonated eggs should not be given to persons with a history of egg allergy; persons who can eat eggs without adverse effects usually can be immunized safely with vaccines containing egg protein.

Altered Immunity and Pregnancy

Live attenuated vaccines should not be given to persons who have immune deficiency.

Avoid measles, mumps, and rubella immunization of any woman likely to be pregnant.

Live attenuated vaccines should not be given to persons who have immune deficiency diseases or who receive immunosuppressant drugs. Live virus vaccines are generally contraindicated in pregnant women on the grounds of potential risk to the developing fetus. Measles, mumps, and rubella vaccines should never be given to pregnant women or to those who are likely to become pregnant within 3 months of vaccination. Oral polio vaccine or yellow fever vaccine can be given during pregnancy when the risk of infection is believed to exceed the theoretical risk to the fetus.

Vaccination during Intercurrent Illness

Vaccination of persons with severe febrile illnesses should be deferred until recovery to avoid superimposition of adverse vaccine effects and/or incorrect attribution of sequelae to the vaccine. Minor illnesses such as an upper respiratory tract infection are not a contraindication to immunization.

Miscellaneous Vaccines

The following narrative relates to those vaccines available in the United States that the practicing physician is likely to use or be asked to use. Other vaccines available in this country for limited use are not discussed here. Details of the use of adenovirus vaccine, plague vaccine, and typhus vaccine, among others, can be obtained from the Center for Disease Control, Atlanta, Georgia.

There are currently under investigation several new immunizing agents that may become available in the near future. Two promising vaccines presently under preliminary clinical trial may provide active immunization against hepatitis and against gonorrhea.

Informed Consent

Immunization, like most forms of medical treatment, carries with it certain risks of side effects. Both for the sake of patient education and provider protection, the physician should make use of a

Table 4-1

simple information handout (Table 4-1) and record that the patient was advised on the risks and benefits of immunization.

VACCINES FOR GENERAL USE IN THE UNITED STATES

Diphtheria, Tetanus, and Pertussis

Immunization of infants and children against diphtheria, tetanus, and pertussis has been in general use in America for the past 30 years. The effectiveness of these immunizations is assumed on the basis of the decrease in the frequency of these diseases in North America.

At the present time there are usually less than 300 reported cases of *diphtheria* occurring each year in the entire nation. Most cases occur in unimmunized or inadequately immunized children. Although diphtheria is now relatively uncommon, many of the reported cases are severe, and 10% of patients with respiratory diphtheria die. Cutaneous diphtheria is a continuing problem, not only in children but also in adults with poor nutrition and hygiene.

Most tetanus victims are over age 50; presumably their immunization was allowed to lapse or they were never immunized.

Tetanus is relatively rare in the United States with an average of approximately 100 cases reported each year. All cases occur in unimmunized or partially immunized persons, or in those whose immunization was remote. More than half of patients are 50 years of age or older. Tetanus is potentially lethal and totally preventable.

Pertussis is a highly communicable infection. The highest attack rates and greatest severity of disease are seen in infants and young children. Approximately two thirds of reported pertussis deaths occur in infants less than one year of age. Pertussis morbidity and mortality have decreased dramatically since the vaccine was introduced in the 1940s. However, not all observers are convinced that this reduction in disease has been a consequence of widespread vaccination.

Vaccines Diphtheria and tetanus toxoids are prepared by formaldehyde treatment of the respective toxins. The toxoids are available in both fluid and adsorbed forms. Pertussis vaccine is a killed suspension of bacteria or a bacterial fraction. The toxoids and pertussis vaccine are available in several combinations and concentrations for specific purposes. The three preparations most widely used are (a) diphtheria-pertussis-tetanus (DPT) vaccine, which is designated for children through 6 years of age; (b) Td (tetanus and diphtheria toxoids) in which the diphtheria component is low (10%-25% of that in standard DPT) and which is

There are three common preparations that contain tetanus toxoids.

Table 4-1 Benefits and Reactions from Immunization of Children

Immunization can prevent crippling or fatal diseases. Outlined below are the dangers of these diseases and the benefits and side effects of immunization. Please review this information carefully; if you have questions, please ask them. The American Academy of Pediatrics recommends that all normal, healthy children in the United States be immunized against these diseases.

Disease	Vaccine
DIPHTHERIA • occurs primarily in children • attacks the throat and nasal passages • interferes with breathing • produces poison that damages heart, kidneys, and nerves • *10% of cases are fatal* TETANUS ("Lockjaw") • caused by contaminated dirt getting into wounds • causes painful muscular contractions • *50% of cases are fatal* PERTUSSIS ("Whooping Cough") • most severe in young infants • can cause ear infections, pneumonia, and convulsions; rare, but most serious is a brain disorder	TETANUS DIPHTHERIA TOXOID (Td) • almost all persons will be protected after completing a primary series plus a booster • common reactions include a sore arm or lump at the injection site and occasional fever for 12 to 24 hours after vaccination • more severe reactions are very rare and usually occur in adults DIPHTHERIA & PERTUSSIS & TETANUS TOXOIDS (DPT) • given to children under age 6 years • almost all children will be protected after completing a primary series and booster • common reactions include soreness, a lump at injection site, and fever for 12 to 24 hours after vaccination • very rarely causes brain disorder
POLIO • attacks the nervous system • causes paralysis usually of arms or legs but also the muscles you breath with • *10% of cases are fatal*	ORAL POLIO VACCINE (OPV, LIVE, SABIN) • 90% of persons receiving a primary series and booster will be protected • given by drops (no shots) • no common reactions • a paralytic reaction to the vaccine occurs in the person vaccinated or a close contact once in 3,000,000 doses INACTIVATED POLIO VACCINE (IPV, KILLED, SALK) • 90% of persons receiving a primary series and booster will be protected • no common reactions

Table 4-1 Continued

Disease	Vaccine
MEASLES • most serious common childhood disease • always causes high fever (103°-105°) and rash, usually lasts 10 days • may cause pneumonia or ear infection • causes deafness, blindness, convulsions, brain disorders in 1 of every 1,000 children who get the disease • of children who develop a brain disorder from measles, 1 in 10 dies	MEASLES VACCINE • 95% of persons receiving one dose of the vaccine will be protected • 10%-20% of children immunized may have mild fever and rash within 10 days • 1 person in 1,000,000 vaccinated may develop a brain disorder
RUBELLA • when contracted by pregnant women can cause miscarriage, stillbirth, or multiple birth defects including deafness and heart disease • usually a mild disease with mild fever, rash, and swollen glands • can cause joint pains, more frequently in teenagers	RUBELLA VACCINE • 90% of persons receiving one dose will be protected • about 1% of young children and 5%-10% of teenagers may develop temporary arm, leg or joint pains • very rarely vaccine may cause a rash • children of pregnant woman *can* be vaccinated
MUMPS • usually causes fever and swelling of salivary glands • may cause inflammation of testicles in adolescent and adult males • may cause inflammation of pancreas • may cause a temporary brain disorder • can result in permanent deafness	MUMPS VACCINE • 90% of persons receiving one dose will be protected • very rarely fever and swelling of salivary glands may occur after vaccination

Special Notes

Children under medical care for any acute or chronic medical condition should not be given vaccines in a school immunization program without their physician's approval.

Measles, mumps, and rubella vaccines can be given in combination (MMR) as one shot. Children who have had one of the diseases or vaccines can still be given the combination vaccine to complete their immunization.

Table 4-1 Continued

Pregnant females should not receive measles, mumps, rubella, or the combination (MMR) vaccine.

Keep the record for your child's immunization where you can find it: You will need it when you enroll your child in daycare or school.

Source: Marcuse, E. K. 1979. Benefits and reactions from immunization of children. *Pediatrics* 63:419-422.

designated for adults; and (c) T-tetanus toxoid, which contains antigenic material against tetanus only, in the same dose found in DPT or Td, and which is used to immunize adults specifically against tetanus.

Immunization with a diphtheria toxoid does not prevent pharyngeal carriage of the organism, but it does significantly reduce the occurrence and severity of clinical disease. Adequate immunization is followed by persistent antitoxin at protective levels for at least 10 years. Either a positive serologic test or the Schick skin test will reflect clinical immunity. The tetanus toxoid is an excellent immunizing agent and provides protection for at least 10 years after a complete immunization series.

Pertussis vaccine is seldom given to adults because they suffer more untoward effects of vaccination.

Although pertusis immunity after immunization does not persist into adult life, pertusis vaccine is generally given only to children because they suffer the most serious consequences of infection and because the vaccine produces more frequent untoward effects in older children and adults.

Vaccine use Primary immunization for children 6 weeks through 6 years of age consists of four intramuscular injections of the manufacturer's recommended dose of DPT. Three doses are given at 4-6-week intervals, and a fourth dose later. Ideally, immunizations should begin at the 6-week checkup, and certainly no later than at 2-3 months of age. It is recommended that children who have received this primary immunization receive a single booster injection of DPT at the time of entrance to kindergarten or elementary school (3-6 years of age), although the need for the revaccination against pertussis has not been established clearly.

Thereafter, and for all previously unimmunized persons, Td is the recommended vaccine. For previously unimmunized school children and adults a series of three doses of Td should be given intramuscularly with the second dose 4-8 weeks after the first, and the third dose 6 months to 1 year after the second. Td is the agent of choice for immunization of school-age children because per-

To avoid reactions to diphtheria toxoid give Td, not DPT, to an adult

tussis is no longer an important problem and because there is an increasing frequency of reactions to full doses of diphtheria toxoid with age. Booster doses of Td or tetanus toxoid should be given intramuscularly every 10 years. When a dose must be given sooner as part of wound management the next booster will not be needed for another 10 years. There is no benefit in more frequent doses, which indeed may be associated with an increased incidence or severity of side effects.

Give routine booster dose of Td or tetanus toxoid every 10 years. Give booster for severe wound and consider tetanus immune globulin.

Tetanus toxoid is indicated for any person with a wound, regardless of its severity or nature, if that person has received neither a complete series of four doses of DPT, Td, or tetanus toxoid nor a booster following a primary series in the last 10 years. When the wound is severe, neglected, or more than 24 hours old many experts recommend a booster injection if 1-5 years have elapsed since the last dose of tetanus toxoid. Passive immunization is not recommended because following a dose of tetanus toxoid antibodies develop rapidly in persons who have previously received at least two doses of toxoid. The main problem is assurance that a wounded patient has received adequate prior immunization. Good immunization records kept by the physician and by the patient would circumvent much anxiety and unnecessary immunization.

Guidelines are given for passive immunization with tetanus immune globulin.

Persons who have major, dirty, or old wounds and who have had less than two doses of tetanus toxoid, or who have not been immunized in the past 10 years, need passive immunization. Tetanus immune globulin (TIG) is the product of choice in that it provides longer protection than any toxin of animal origin and causes no undesirable reactions. Tetanus toxoid and TIG can be given concurrently, using separate syringes and separate sites. TIG, unlike equine antitoxin, must be given intramuscularly, not intravenously.

Asymptomatic unimmunized household contacts or other persons with intimate exposure to a patient with diphtheria should receive prompt prophylaxis.

Asymptomatic unimmunized household contacts or other persons with intimate exposure to a patient with diphtheria should receive prompt prophylaxis with penicillin or erythromycin, vaccination with diphtheria toxoid, and daily surveillance for 7 days for evidence of clinical diphtheria. Diphtheria antitoxin is recommended for asymptomatic household contacts only when close surveillance is not possible.

Untoward effects Serious untoward effects of diphtheria toxoid are extremely rare; transient local reactions and fever of 1-2 days' duration are common, particularly in previously immunized persons. The severity of reaction to diphtheria toxoid is directly proportional to the amount of toxoid administered.

Data on the frequency and severity of untoward reactions to pertussis vaccine are conflicting. Local reaction and low-grade fever occur in over half of immunized children. A high fever, a transient shocklike syndrome, excessive screaming, somnolence, or convulsions may occur in infants. Thrombocytopenia has been reported. The current controversy over the pertussis vaccine risks and benefits centers on the frequency of encephalopathy, permanent sequelae, or death. Some authorities in the United Kingdom believe that serious sequelae are more common than pertussis morbidity. However, in the United States the reported morbidity, mortality, and serious neurologic complications of immunization are significantly less than those of the disease. Fatal reactions are reported no more than once or twice for every 10 million doses. The cause of serious side effects to pertussis vaccine is unknown.

In children serious side effects to pertussis vaccine are uncommon.

Tetanus toxoid is remarkably safe: no deaths or permanent sequalae have been attributed to its use. Local and general reactions occur in 1% or 2%, minutes to several days after inoculation. Reactions can follow the first dose, but are most common in adults who have received more frequent inoculations than are necessary. Local reactions consist of pain and swelling around the site of injection, which may last 3-4 days. Urticaria with or without angioneurotic edema is the commonest general reaction. Inoculation into the gluteal region yields the fewest number of reactions.

Local and general reactions to tetanus toxoid occur in 1%-2% of cases.

Poliomyelitis

The number of reported cases of paralytic poliomyelitis has declined from more than 18,000 in 1954 to only 8 in 1976, since the introduction of specific immunization against poliomyelitis in the United States in 1955. This remarkable success story may not be sustained because immunization rates have fallen in recent years: Today one third of 1-4-year-old children in this country have not been vaccinated against poliomyelitis. In addition, inapparent infection with wild strains, previously a major source of immunity, has decreased in conjunction with the reduced circulation of wild viruses. Young parents who do not recall the terrors of the polio era must be counseled emphatically about the continuing importance of polio prevention.

Young parents who do not recall the terrors of the polio era must be counseled emphatically about polio immunization.

Inactivated poliovirus vaccine (IPV), licensed in 1955, was used extensively in the United States until the early 1960s when it was replaced by oral polio vaccine (OPV). Trivalent oral polio vaccine (TOPV) was licensed here in 1963.

Vaccines TOPV is a live attenuated vaccine that combines all three strains of polio virus. It has almost totally supplanted the individual monovalent antigens used in the early 1960s. Full

Full primary vaccination with TOPV produces immunity to all three poliovirus types in more than 90% of the recipients.

primary vaccination with TOPV produces immunity to all three poliovirus types in more than 90% of the recipients. The majority of recipients are protected after a single dose. The vaccine is given by mouth.

IPV, prepared from all three strains of killed polioviruses, had not been widely available in this country until the late 1970s: a Canadian product is now licensed for use in the United States. More than 90% of persons who receive 3-4 doses achieve good levels of antibody. This vaccine is given by injection.

Vaccine use Primary immunization with TOPV for infants, children, and adolescents through age 18 years consists of three doses: the first two doses should be given not less than 6 and preferably 8 weeks apart; the third dose should follow in 8-12 months. For infants the first dose is commonly given at the same time as the first dose of DPT. For older children and adolescents the third dose may be given as early as 6 weeks after the second if circumstances require.

On entering kindergarten or first grade, all children who completed the primary series of TOPV in early childhood should be given a single additional dose. This booster dose also serves to assure immunity to all three poliovirus types. All other children should complete the primary series. It is also recommended that anyone who has completed a primary TOPV series in the past and who is at significant additional risk should receive a single additional dose, although the need for this dose has not been established. The Institute of Medicine Committee for the Study of Poliovirus Vaccine has also recommended one dose of TOPV (or the full series if required) for all seventh graders. Primary immunization with TOPV for adults 18 years of age and older is recommended only when an epidemic exists or when travel to an endemic area is planned. Pregnancy is not a contraindication if protection is needed.

The Institute of Medicine Committee for the Study of Poliovirus Vaccine has also recommended one dose of TOPV (or the full series if required) for all seventh graders.

Untoward effects In rare instances OPV has been followed by paralytic disease. Vaccine-associated cases are defined as those occurring within 4-30 days of immunization or within 4-60 days of contact with an OPV recipient. (In such cases poliovirus isolated from the stool should be tested for temperature sensitivity or other markers suggestive of a vaccine strain.) From 1969 through 1976 there were approximately 190 million doses of TOPV distributed, and 10 cases of vaccine-associated paralysis occurred in otherwise healthy vaccine recipients. Paralysis, attributed to vaccine virus shed by other vaccinees, is somewhat more common; 39 such cases were reported during the same period.

When possible, persons with altered immunity should also avoid household contact with recipients of TOPV.

The only known contraindication to TOPV is immunodeficiency disease or an altered immune state. These persons experience a significantly increased risk and account for nearly 10% of all vaccine-associated disease. When possible, persons with altered immunity should also avoid household contact with recipients of TOPV for at least 3 weeks after vaccination. IPV (discussed in the next section) may be the preferable vaccine for immunizing all persons in a household containing an immunocompromised host.

IPV When IPV is the vaccine chosen, four doses are given as specified by the manufacturer. Three doses are given at approximately 1-2 month intervals; the fourth, 6-12 months after the third. This schedule can be integrated with DPT vaccination. A booster dose every 2-3 years has been recommended to sustain optimal levels of antibody, although a longer interval between boosters is probably adequate. The need for IPV boosters can be obviated by following the IPV with primary vaccination with TOPV.

Children or adults with immunodeficiency diseases or altered immune states should be vaccinated with IPV.

Children or adults with immunodeficiency diseases or altered immune states should be vaccinated with IPV. Their antibody responses cannot be assured, however.

IPV contains trace amounts of streptomycin and neomycin.

Untoward effects No serious reactions to IPV have occurred since the use of an improperly prepared batch of vaccine in 1955. Since IPV contains trace amounts of streptomycin and neomycin, there is a possibility of hypersensitivity reaction in individuals sensitive to these antibiotics.

Choice of IPV versus TOPV There can be no doubt that both parenteral and oral poliovirus vaccines are extremely effective immunizing agents. The reduction in paralytic poliomyelitis achieved in the United States with TOPV has been equaled in other countries that have used IPV primarily or exclusively. This country has elected to continue using TOPV as the primary polio vaccine—based on the ease of administration, the production of both humoral and intestinal immunity, the presumed enduring protection without the need for boosters, and the large proportion of recipients protected after only a single dose. It should be noted that similar levels of protection have been achieved with IPV in countries where more than 90% of the population is immunized and repeated booster doses are administered.

The relative risk of paralysis after TOPV and IPV is discussed.

The risk of paralysis after TOPV is 1 case in 11 million vaccinees and 1 case in 4 million household contacts. This small risk must be explained before immunization. Some may elect to use only IPV vaccine, or to precede a complete TOPV series with IPV immunization. In some situations IPV may be viewed as the vaccine of choice. As noted earlier, immunodeficient persons and their families should be immunized with IPV. Because TOPV-associated paralysis in immunocompetent recipients is most common after the age of 20 years, IPV is also recommended for primary immunization of adults. To reduce the possibility of paralytic disease in a household contact, some experts recommend two doses of IPV for unimmunized parents before the first child in their family is immunized with TOPV. This maneuver is not recommended if it unduly delays immunization of the child.

Parenteral polio vaccine (IPV) is recommended for primary immunization of adults.

Measles

Measles is a highly contagious and often severe disease caused by the rubeola virus. Death occurs in approximately one in every thousand cases. Overt encephalitis also occurs in one in every thousand cases, resulting in a 10%-30% mortality and in serious neurologic sequelae for up to 50% of the survivors. Electroencephalographic studies indicate that subclinical measles encephalitis with as yet undelineated sequelae is much more frequent. In addition, measles is often complicated by middle ear infection or bronchial pneumonia. Measles during pregnancy can induce premature labor or spontaneous abortion and is a possible cause of congenital malformations.

Killed measles virus vaccine and attenuated live measles virus vaccine (Edmonston B strain) were introduced in the United States in 1963. Killed vaccine was not licensed or produced after 1967. Live virus vaccine prepared from a further attenuated variant of the Edmonston B strain was licensed in 1968 and is widely used today.

Measles immunization has been associated with a 90% reduction in the reported incidence of measles in this country. Before the vaccine era most measles cases occurred in preschool and young school-age children: currently most disease occurs in persons 10 years of age or older. Immunization rates exceeding 90%—a nationwide goal—have not yet been achieved. In October 1978 the Secretary of the Department of Health, Education, and Welfare announced that the United States would seek to eliminate indigenous measles from the country by October 1, 1982. At present all states have laws or pending legislation that require measles immunization before entrance into public school.

At present all states have laws or pending legislation that require measles immunization before entrance into public school.

Vaccine The live measles virus vaccine available in the United States is prepared in chick fibroblast cell culture. The most widely used strain today has been attenuated beyond the level of the original Edmonston B strain and is therefore known as a further attenuated strain. Vaccine prepared from this strain is preferred because it causes fewer reactions than its predecessor. It is available in monovalent (measles only) form and in combinations with rubella and with rubella and mumps vaccines. All vaccines containing measles antigen are recommended for use at about 15 months of age. Earlier immunization may fail to induce adequate levels of antibody. When there is a high probability of exposure to natural measles, infants as young as 6 months can be vaccinated. However, to insure protection they should be revaccinated at about 15 months of age.

Measles vaccine produces a mild or inapparent noncommunicable infection. Antibodies develop in more than 95% of susceptible children vaccinated at 15 months of age or older. Antibody levels achieved after immunization persist for at least 15 years, although at lower titer than those following natural disease. Apparent vaccine failures may represent poor vaccine handling, in that the virus must be kept between 2-8 C and protected from light.

Apparent vaccine failures may represent poor vaccine handling.

Vaccine use Persons usually are considered immune to measles if they have documentation of either physician-diagnosed measles, laboratory evidence of measles immunity, or adequate immunization with live measles vaccine when 15 or more months of age. Most persons in the United States born before 1957 have been infected naturally and are not susceptible. All others are considered susceptible and should be immunized if not otherwise contraindicated. Because of the upward shift in age distribution of reported cases, the immune status of adolescents needs evaluation: measles eradication will require protection of all susceptibles. Therefore increased emphasis must be placed on vaccinating susceptible adolescents and young adults including persons who received inactivated vaccine or who received live measles vaccine before they were 12 months of age. There is some evidence to suggest that live measles vaccine, if given within 72 hours of measles exposure, may provide protection.

Increased emphasis must be placed on vaccinating susceptible adolescents and young adults.

A single dose of live measles vaccine is given subcutaneously as specified by the manufacturer. Immune serum globulin (ISG) is not indicated with further attenuated measles virus vaccine and is recommended only if Edmonston B vaccine is used. Live measles vaccine should not be given to pregnant women. Although this risk is primarily theoretical, concern about it constrains measles vaccination programs for adolescent girls. Persons with immune deficiency diseases or suppressed immune responses should not receive live measles virus vaccine. Their risk of exposure should be

Persons with immune deficiency diseases or suppressed immune responses should not receive live measles virus vaccine.

minimized by vaccinating their close susceptible contacts. If immediate protection against measles is required for such persons, passive immunization with ISG should be given as soon as possible after known exposure. Although ISG will usually prevent measles in normal children, it may not be effective in children with altered immunity.

Except for those born before 1957 (who were probably infected naturally), anyone immunized against measles before 1968 (with killed vaccine) should be reimmunized with live vaccine.

More than 1 million doses of killed vaccine were administered from 1963 to 1967. On exposure to natural measles many of these recipients are at risk of developing atypical measles characterized by high fever, atypical rash, pulmonary symptoms, and abnormal chest roentgenograms. Patients who have previously received only inactivated vaccine or who have received inactivated vaccine followed by a dose of live vaccine within 3 months should be revaccinated with live vaccine to avoid the severe atypical form of natural measles and to provide optimal protection.

About 1%-15% of vaccinees develop fever, sometimes exceeding 39 C, beginning about the sixth day after immunization.

Untoward effects About 1%-15% of vaccinees develop fever, sometimes exceeding 39 C, beginning about the sixth day after immunization and lasting up to 5 days. In children this fever is often surprisingly asymptomatic but adults may be confined to bed for several days. Other side reactions, also more common in adults, include transient rashes and eye pain. Encephalitis is rare. Cerebral complications are reported once in every million doses. Subacute sclerosing panencephalitis (SSPE), a slow virus infection of the central nervous system associated with a measleslike virus, appears to be reduced in frequency with the use of measles vaccine. However, there have been reports of SSPE in children who did not have a history of natural measles but had received measles vaccine. Nevertheless the recent decline in numbers of SSPE cases provides presumptive evidence of the protective effect of measles vaccine for the majority of recipients. There is no evidence of an increased risk of SSPE in persons receiving live measles vaccine who have been previously immunized or who have had measles.

Although live measles vaccine is produced in chick cell culture, it has not been reported to be associated with allergic reactions in persons allergic to eggs, chickens, or feathers. Some vaccines contain trace amounts of antibiotics to which persons may be allergic. Patients with an allergic history to antibiotics should be immunized with products that contain no antibiotics. No live measles vaccine contains penicillin.

No live measles vaccine contains penicillin.

Rubella

Rubella is a common childhood disease that often passes unnoticed and undiagnosed. Infection may be subclinical or may produce postauricular and suboccipital lymphadenopathy, arthalgia, and a transient erythematous rash. By far the most important consequence of rubella is the congenital rubella syndrome: the major objective of rubella immunization programs is to avert viremia in pregnant women and thereby prevent infection of the fetus.

Before rubella vaccine was available, most cases of rubella occurred in school-age children. Since licensure of rubella vaccine in 1969, the incidence of reported rubella in school-age children has decreased markedly, but there has been no significant change in the frequency of this infection in adolescents and young adults. Outbreaks of rubella continue to be reported in junior and senior high schools, colleges, the military, and places of employment. Although the number of reported cases of congenital rubella has decreased, current surveys show 15%-20% of young adult women in the United States have no rubella immunity.

15%-20% of young adult women lack rubella immunity.

A history of rubella is unreliable as a marker for immunity. The only good evidence of rubella immunity is specific antibody, determined preferably by the hemagglutination-inhibition antibody technique. When reliable laboratory services are available, routine premarital serology for rubella antibody is recommended.

A history of rubella is unreliable as a marker for immunity.

Vaccines Live rubella virus vaccines available in the United States are prepared either in duck fibroblast cell (HPV 77) culture or in human diploid cell culture (RA 27/3). Immunization with the human diploid strain produces a broader range of antibodies and higher and more sustained hemagglutination titers than the duck embryo preparation; however, no significant difference in protection or side effects induced by either vaccine has yet been demonstrated. Both vaccines are produced in monovalent form and in combination with measles and mumps virus vaccines.

A single dose of rubella vaccine at 12 months of age or older induces antibodies in approximately 95% of susceptible persons. Antibody levels are relatively low compared to those that follow naturally acquired rubella infection, but low levels of antibody persist for at least 9 years and long-term or lifelong protection is expected. Reinfection without illness can occur in persons with low levels of antibody. However, it causes neither detectable viremia nor sufficient pharyngeal excretion of virus to transmit infection to susceptible contacts; consequently, reinfection during pregnancy would be unlikely to cause congenital infection, and immunization of susceptible children whose mothers or other household contacts are pregnant is not contraindicated.

Low levels of antibody persist for at least 9 years and long-term or lifelong protection is expected.

Immunization of susceptible children whose mothers or other household contacts are pregnant is not contraindicated.

Vaccine use In the United States the rubella immunization program has been directed primarily toward children. Live rubella vaccine is recommended for all children 12 months of age or older. If given in combination with measles and mumps vaccine, immunization should be postponed to 15 months of age. Because a history of rubella is not reliable, all children for whom vaccine is not contraindicated should be vaccinated. A single dose of vaccine in the volume specified by the manufacturer is administered subcutaneously. There is no evidence that live rubella virus vaccine given after exposure will prevent illness or that vaccinating an individual incubating rubella is harmful. Live rubella virus vaccine is not recommended for patients who are immunosuppressed or who have immunodeficiency diseases.

When the policy of immunizing children was initiated, it was hoped that this method would provide sufficient herd immunity to protect pregnant women and thus reduce the risk of congenital rubella. Immunization of older children, particularly of females of childbearing age, was not recommended, although this was the target population for which protection was most desired. This was because of the theoretical risk to the fetus, should the immunized woman be pregnant or become pregnant within 3 months of vaccination. Presently the United States Public Health Service is placing an increasing emphasis on vaccinating unimmunized prepubertal girls and susceptible adolescent and adult females in childbearing age groups. The immunization of adolescent or adult males may be appropriate in selected populations such as colleges, hospitals, and military bases to reduce the risk of epidemic rubella.

Joint pain, usually of the small peripheral joints, may be noted in up to 40% of vaccinees.

Untoward effects Joint pain, usually of the small peripheral joints, may be noted in up to 40% of vaccinees, although frank arthritis occurs in less than 1%. Arthralgia and arthritis are more frequent and more severe in immunized women than children. Joint symptoms generally begin 2-10 weeks after immunization and resolve spontaneously in 1-3 days. An occasional vaccinee experiences persistent arthritic symptoms; it is not yet known whether this represents a complication of vaccination or coincidental disease. Rash, lymphadenopathy, or transient peripheral neuritis are less common sequelae.

Avoid rubella vaccine in pregnant women; advise women to avoid pregnancy for 3 months after immunization.

Rubella vaccine is not suitable for pregnant women. Rubella vaccine virus has been recovered from the placenta and fetus of women inadvertently immunized during pregnancy. Although approximately 70 susceptible women who continued their pregnancy after being immunized during early pregnancy have delivered infants without recognizable malformations attributable to rubella, there are theoretical risks to the fetus. When a pregnant woman is inadvertently vaccinated or becomes pregnant within 3 months of vaccination, she should be advised of the risks and counseled regarding the consideration of abortion.

Live rubella virus vaccine has not been reported to be associated with allergic reactions even in persons allergic to eggs, ducks, or feathers. Live rubella vaccine does not contain penicillin, but some rubella vaccines do contain trace amounts of other antibiotics. Persons administering vaccine should review the label information before deciding whether or not patients with known allergies to such antibiotics can be vaccinated safely.

Mumps

Mumps is primarily a disease of children, most cases occurring before the age of 12 years. Mumps is usually manifest as fever and unilateral or bilateral parotitis. Benign meningeal signs may be found in 15% of cases, but serious nervous system involvement is rare; nerve deafness is one of the most serious complications. Orchitis has been reported in up to 20% of postpubertal males with clinical mumps. Orchitis is usually unilateral, and sterility following orchitis is rare. Symptomatic involvement of other glands including the pancreas has been observed less frequently. Approximately one in three persons infected with mumps has no obvious illness and prior infection can be ascertained only by serologic testing.

Approximately one in three persons infected with mumps has no obvious illness.

Vaccine Live mumps virus vaccine is prepared in chick fibroblast cell culture. Although it was introduced in 1967, the vaccine has never achieved the level of use of other childhood immunizations, at least in part because the low morbidity of naturally acquired mumps makes this immunization of lesser priority than others. The vaccine produces a subclinical, noninfectious infection. More than 90% of susceptible recipients develop measurable antibody in lower titer than that following natural infection. Antibody persists for at least 10 years. The duration of protection is unknown, but it is anticipated that it may be lifelong.

Vaccine use Live mumps vaccine is recommended for all children over 12 months of age. A single dose of mumps vaccine is administered subcutaneously and no booster is required. Mumps vaccine is usually given in combination with measles and rubella antigens; if given in conjunction with measles antigen, it should be administered when the child is about 15 months of age (see measles vaccine).

As with other live virus vaccines, mumps vaccine is not recommended for pregnant women, for persons with severe febrile illness, or for persons with immunodeficiency states.

Untoward effects Side effects are uncommon. They include parotitis and allergic reactions, including pruritus and purpura. Febrile seizures, unilateral nerve deafness, and encephalitis occurring within 30 days of mumps vaccine are sufficiently uncommon that the relationship to the immunization is unclear. Almost all patients with complications have recovered completely.

IMMUNIZATIONS FOR SELECTED USE

Influenza

Influenza virus infections occur annually in the United States with consequences that range from asymptomatic seroconversion to death. Influenza viruses A, and to a lesser extent B, cause periodic widespread outbreaks of disease in both adults and children. During such epidemics an excess in the usual death rate is frequently observed. Influenza-related deaths occur primarily in persons over 65 years of age, and in persons of any age who are chronically ill.

Influenza A virus is classified into subtypes on the basis of hemagglutinin (H) and neuraminidase (N) antigens. There are four known types of hemagglutinin (Ho-H3) and two types of neuraminidase (N1-N2). Major shifts in these antigens occur periodically, so that the population is not immune to these "new" antigens, which result in epidemics of disease. There also may be sufficient antigenic variation within the same subtype over time (antigenic drift) so that previous infection or immunization fails to protect against a distantly related strain. Because influenza virus strains change almost annually, immunization with the prevalent strain(s) of the previous year often affords little or no protection to the current agent(s). Because influenza can spread with remarkable speed, it is not always possible to complete vaccine production and distribution in time to prevent an epidemic, even when the appropriate strains have been correctly predicted for the vaccine manufacturers.

Immunization with the prevalent strain(s) of the previous year often affords little or no protection.

Vaccines Killed influenza virus vaccine is prepared from virus grown in eggs. Evidence of influenza vaccine efficacy classically is based on antibody response rather than on actual protection. Age differences in antibody response are significant, presumably reflecting differences in prior experience with related antigens. Current preparations generally induce antibody in 70% of recipients. Whole virus preparations recommended for persons 21 years of age and older require only a single inoculation. Toxic reactions to the vaccine are more common in children; consequently a less immunogenic, split virus vaccine is recommended for them. Split virus vaccines require two doses to induce satisfactory antibody levels.

Vaccine use In the United States annual vaccination is recommended only for individuals at increased risk to serious sequelae of influenza. This includes persons with acquired or congenital heart disease, with any chronic pulmonary disorder, with chronic renal disease, with diabetes, or with altered immune states including certain malignancies and immunosuppressive therapy. Vaccination is also recommended for older persons, particularly those more than 65 years of age, who experience most of the excess mortality in influenza outbreaks. It should be noted, however, that many countries in the Western world do not use influenza vaccine routinely for older adults and limit its use, if at all, to persons with specific diseases.

The safety of influenza vaccine for use during pregnancy is unknown.

The safety of influenza vaccine for use during pregnancy is unknown. The decision to give a pregnant woman influenza vaccine probably should be based on the chronic illness criteria applied to nonpregnant persons and not on the existence of pregnancy per se, although in one or two pandemics, there appeared to be increased morbidity when influenza complicated pregnancy.

Local reactions are seen in approximately one third of influenza vaccinees.

Untoward effects Local reactions, consisting of redness and induration at the site of injection lasting for 24-48 hours, are seen in approximately one third of vaccinees. Systemic reactions include fever, malaise, and myalgia. These reactions occur most frequently in children and rarely last more than 48 hours. A less common systemic response is an immediate reaction that may include life-threatening respiratory hypersensitivity. These reactions are believed to derive from sensitivity to residual egg protein; therefore persons who are allergic to eggs should not be immunized with influenza vaccine. A third type of systemic reaction is the Guillain-Barré syndrome, a sequel apparently limited to the A/New Jersey (swine) influenza vaccine used in the massive influenza immunization campaign in 1976. The risk of Guillain-Barre syndrome is extremely low—just under 1 case per 100,000 vaccinations—and the consequent ascending paralysis is usually self-limited and reversible. But some patients suffer residual neurologic deficits, and up to 5% of cases may be fatal. Clearly the risk of this reaction must be weighed against the risk of influenza and its sequelae.

The risk of Guillain-Barre syndrome is just under one case per 100,000 vaccinations.

Meningococcal Disease

Meningococcal disease, primarily meningitis, is endemic in the United States. More than two thirds of all meningococcal disease occurs in single isolated cases, but secondary cases are more common in household contacts than in the general population. Periodic outbreaks among military recruits and the appearance of sulfonamide-resistant strains precluding chemoprophylaxis were incentives for the development of serogroup-specific vaccines.

There are three serogroups of meningococcus—A, B, and C. Serogroup B is currently the most common agent recovered in this country, and is the only serogroup for which no effective vaccine is now available. (However, serogroup B strains remain sulfa sensitive in many cases, unlike isolates of serogroups A and C.) Serogroup C vaccine has been given routinely to American military recruits since October 1971. Since then the incidence of meningococcal disease in the military has declined sharply.

Serogroup C vaccine has been given routinely to American military recruits since October 1971.

Vaccines Three meningococcal polysaccharide vaccines—monovalent A, monovalent C, and bivalent A-C—are licensed for use in the United States. These vaccines consist of purified bacterial capsular polysaccharides, each inducing specific serogroup immunity. The vaccine is administered as a single dose as specified by the manufacturer. The duration of protection is unknown. Neither serogroup A nor serogroup C vaccine appears to be effective in preventing meningococcal meningitis in the first year of life.

Vaccine use Routine immunization of civilians with meningococcal polysaccharide vaccines is not recommended because the risk of infection is very low in the general population. Serogroup-specific monovalent vaccines are recommended to control outbreaks of meningococcal disease caused by either serogroup A or serogroup C. Vaccination is also an adjunct to antibiotic chemoprophylaxis for household contacts, particularly when the disease is caused by sulfonamide-resistant strains. Approximately half of secondary cases occur more than 5 days after the primary case—long enough to allow vaccine-induced protection to occur.

Vaccination is also an adjunct to antibiotic chemoprophylaxis for household contacts.

Untoward effects Meningococcal vaccine rarely causes side effects. Infrequently mild localized erythema lasting from 1-2 days is noted. The safety of meningococcal vaccines for use during pregnancy is not established.

Pneumococcal Diseases

The pneumococcus causes several diseases including pneumococcal pneumonia, meningitis, otitis media, and bacteremia. Despite antibiotic therapy, pneumococcal pneumonia continues to have an overall case fatality rate of 5%-10%; and pneumococcal meningitis, a nearly 50% fatality rate. Pneumococcal pneumonia is most frequent and most lethal in the elderly, whereas over half of cases of pneumococcal meningitis occur in children between 1 month and 4 years of age. Pneumococcal meningitis causes permanent sequelae in approximately half of the survivors.

Most people with pneumococcal infection have no underlying disease. There is, however, an increased risk in persons with sickle cell anemia, anatomic, or functional asplenia, agammaglobulinemia, multiple myeloma, nephrotic syndrome, cirrhosis, and alcoholism. Pneumococcal meningitis may complicate basilar skull fracture with cerebral spinal fluid rhinorrhea.

Several types of pneumococcal vaccine were developed and tested as early as 1920. A combined polysaccharide vaccine, similar to the one currently licensed in the United States, was shown to prevent pneumonia in a young male military population with a high endemic rate of disease, and a trivalent vaccine appeared to be effective in one elderly population. A combined polysaccharide vaccine was licensed and produced in this country between 1945 and 1947. However, with the availability of effective antibiotics, this vaccine was used infrequently and the manufacturer discontinued production. The continued morbidity and mortality of pneumococcal disease despite the use of antibiotics led to the development of a new polyvalent pneumococcal vaccine in the 1970s. The appearance of some pneumococci resistant to penicillin and other antibiotics may ultimately extend the target population for pneumococcal vaccine use beyond the selected populations for whom it is currently recommended.

The emergence of antibiotic-resistant pneumococci may ultimately extend the indications for pneumococcal vaccine.

Vaccine The pneumococcal vaccine licensed for use in the United states contains 50 μg of each polysaccharide purified from the capsular material extracted from 14 of the 83 types of pneumococci. The types of pneumococci represented in the vaccine are 1, 2, 3, 4, 6, 8, 9, 12, 14, 19, 23, 25, 51, and 56, which together cause at least 80% of all bacteremic pneumococcal disease seen in the United States.

Pneumococcal vaccine has been shown in field tests to be effective in preventing pneumococcal disease in adults. Preliminary studies suggest that it may reduce the frequency of recurrent otitis media in children more than 2 years of age. Nasopharyngeal

Preliminary studies suggest that it may reduce the frequency of recurrent otitis media in children more than 2 years of age.

acquisition of the pneumococcal types included in the vaccine is reduced by immunization.

Most adults respond to vaccine with a severalfold rise in antibody against most pneumococcal types in the vaccine, but some apparently healthy persons show a deficient antibody response to some serotypes. Antibody persists for several years. Children less than 2 years of age and some asplenic or otherwise immunocompromised patients respond poorly to the vaccine.

Vaccine use Routine immunization of healthy persons is not currently recommended. Vaccine is recommended for individuals more than 2 years of age who have any of the specific diseases associated with increased risk to pneumococcal disease outlined in the beginning of this section. It should be noted, however, that vaccine efficacy is not yet clearly established for such persons. Pneumococcal vaccine may also be useful in persons more than 60 years of age, to reduce the morbidity and mortality of pneumococcal infection in this age group. At present the duration of protection is unknown and the need for booster doses is not established.

An occasional patient experiences high fever and extensive pain, redness, and swelling at the site of injection.

Untoward effects Serious side effects are rare. An occasional patient experiences high fever and extensive pain, redness, and swelling at the site of injection. The vaccine is not recommended for use during pregnancy, not because it has been shown to be harmful, but because there is no specific information about its safety during pregnancy.

Rabies

Fewer than five cases of human rabies are reported each year in the United States; however, the mortality from this encephalitic disease approaches 100%. Although infection in domestic animals has decreased the frequency of wild life infection is increasing. Each year more than 30,000 people in the nation receive rabies vaccine after possible rabies exposure.

Vaccines Semple-type rabies vaccine, made from mature nervous tissue, was effective but caused neuroparalytic sequelae in some recipients. It is no longer available in the United States. Duck embryo vaccine (DEV), a killed vaccine prepared in embryonated duck eggs, was introduced in the United States in 1956 in an attempt to avoid postvaccinial complications. DEV was safer than the older type of nervous tissue vaccines and probably was equally effective, but 15%-20% of persons receiving 16 or more doses of DEV failed to achieve an adequate antibody response (antibody titer ⩾ 1:16), and DEV caused unpleasant reactions in the majority of recipients. In 1980 a more antigenic and less allergenic, inactivated vaccine, prepared in human diploid cell cultures (HDCV) became available in the United States. All persons treated with 5 doses of HDCV have developed an adequate antibody titer, and the average peak titer is more than 10 times the average peak titer seen after 14 doses of DEV. HDCV should largely replace DEV.

In the 1950s it was established that the early addition of passive humoral antibody increases significantly the efficacy of postexposure vaccine. Two preparations of hyperimmune rabies serum are currently available—equine antirabies serum (ARS) and human rabies immune globulin (HRIG). Because ARS causes serum sickness in 15% of children and 40% of adults, HRIG is preferred when available.

Vaccine use Except for persons with excessive occupational or avocational exposure to rabies, rabies vaccine is used for postexposure prophylaxis in the United States.

The need for vaccine is determined on the basis of the probability of exposure to rabies. The species of biting animal is important: skunks, foxes, and bats are more likely than other animals to be infected with rabies. Bites of rodents have never resulted in human rabies in this country, and are not an indication for antirabies prophylaxis. Immunized domestic animals rarely contact and transmit rabies. Knowledge of the amount of rabies in the region is important in making a decision about antirabies treatment. An unprovoked attack is more significant than a provoked biting incident. Penetration of the skin by a bite is more apt to transmit rabies than are scratches or abrasions. When the individual has been bitten by a wild animal or in an unprovoked attack by an unvaccinated (or vaccine status unknown) cat or dog, HRIG and HDCV should be initiated. Immunization can be discontinued when a healthy domestic dog or cat shows no signs suggestive of rabies after observation for 10 days, or when the animal has been killed and the brain proved negative for rabies by fluorescent antibody examination.

Skunks, foxes, and bats are more likely than other animals to be infected with rabies.

Indications for stopping and starting rabies immunization are given.

The current postexposure regimen consists of local wound care, five 1 ml intramuscular doses of HDCV, and a single intramuscular dose of HRIG. Wound treatment includes thorough cleansing with soap, tetanus prophylaxis if needed, and measures to control bacterial infection. HRIG is administered only once; about half the dose of 20 IU per kg is infiltrated around the wound; the rest is administered intramuscularly in the buttocks. The first of five 1 ml doses of HDCV is given at the time that the HRIG is administered, as soon as possible after the exposure. This is followed by 1 ml doses on days 3, 7, 14, and 28 after the first dose. All persons who receive vaccine should have serum collected for rabies antibody testing on day 28 (at the time the last dose is given). If no antibody is detected this information should be reported to the state health department, another dose given, and another serum specimen collected 2-3 weeks later.

Local reactions to HDCV occur in about 25% of recipients.

Untoward effects Local reactions to HDCV (for example, pain, erythema, itching, and induration at the injection site) occur in about 25% of recipients. Headache, nausea, abdominal or muscle pain, and dizziness occur in about 20%. No serious anaphylactic or neuroparalytic reactions have been reported to date.

Smallpox

At the turn of the century, smallpox was a dreaded and often lethal disease of nearly worldwide distribution. The World Health Organization (WHO) launched a smallpox eradication effort in 1967, which appears to have eliminated this disease. No nonlaboratory-associated cases of smallpox have been reported since October 1977, and in December 1979 the WHO declared worldwide smallpox eradication. As a consequence of this remarkable achievement, the risk of smallpox is nil, and there is essentially no indication for smallpox immunization.

Though some countries still require it prior to entry, there is essentially no indication for smallpox immunization.

Nevertheless, at the time of this writing several African and Asian countries require proof of vaccination before entry. The physician is then presented with the choice of administering smallpox vaccine with its attendant risks (discussed later in this section) or of presenting the traveler with a letter indicating that there is a medical contraindication to vaccination. The letter need not specify a specific medical contraindication and the position can be taken that being in good health is a legitimate contraindication to smallpox vaccine.

Details of smallpox immunization are not given here since at the present time they are only of historical interest. Serious complications of smallpox vaccine were tabulated in the United States in 1968. Among approximately 5.6 million primary vaccinees and 8.6 million revaccinees and their contacts, there were 16 cases of encephalitis, 11 cases of vaccinia necrosum, and 126 cases of eczema vaccinatum. Nine persons died. Most deaths and complications occurred after primary vaccination. More than half of the complications occurred in persons with known contraindications—children less than 1 year of age; persons or household contacts of persons with skin disorders, most notably eczema; or altered immune states such as leukemia, lymphoma, disgammaglobulinema, and treatment with immunosuppressive drugs. Pregnancy is also a contraindication to smallpox vaccination.

There is no evidence that smallpox vaccination has any value in the treatment of recurrent herpes simplex infection.

It should be noted that there is no evidence that smallpox vaccination has any value in the treatment of recurrent herpes simplex infection. Such use is unjustifiable.

Yellow Fever

Yellow fever is a viral infection found only in Central Africa and South America. Illness is characterized by fever, jaundice, hemorrhage, and liver necrosis. In epidemics the mortality rate may be as high as 50%.

Vaccine The yellow fever vaccine available in the United States is a live attenuated virus preparation made from the 17D virus strain grown in chick embryo. Immunity persists more than 10 years.

Vaccine use Travelers to countries that require yellow fever vaccine should be immunized with a single subcutaneous injection of 0.5 ml of reconstituted vaccine. Until recently yellow fever vaccine was administered only at approved yellow fever vaccination centers. Now it is possible for physicians in most states to give yellow fever vaccine and to obtain the official stamp necessary to complete the international vaccination card. International health regulations do not require revaccination more often than every 10 years. To assure that effective immunization is given, the vaccine must be stored at less than 5 C until it is reconstituted. Unused vaccine should be discarded within 1 hour of reconsitution because the freeze-dried vaccine loses potency rapidly after reconstitution.

Yellow fever vaccine is not recommended or required for infants less than 6 months of age. Like all live virus vaccines it should be avoided during pregnancy, although no complications have been documented after use in pregnant women. Similarly, infection with yellow fever vaccine virus is not recommended for patients with drug-induced or disease-induced immunosuppression, although this risk remains theoretical. Because yellow fever vaccine is produced in chick embryos, it should not be given to persons clearly hypersensitive to eggs.

Untoward effects Five percent to ten percent of vaccinees have headache, myalgia, and low-grade fever 5-10 days after vaccination, but these symptoms are rarely severe. Serious sequelae are exceedingly rare. Although more than 34 million doses of vaccine have been distributed, only two cases of encephalitis have been reported in the United States. Trace amounts of antibiotics, indicated on the manufacturer's label, may cause allergic reactions in persons hypersensitive to these agents.

Cholera

Cholera is an acute illness characterized by massive loss of fluid and electrolytes from the gastrointestinal tract. Immunization with a cholera vaccine of whole killed organisms has been practiced for more than 75 years, but no adequately controlled studies defining its effectiveness were conducted until the 1960s. In these clinical field trials protection ranged from 30%-90% and persisted for 3-6 months.

Although the vaccine may prevent clinical cholera in approximately half of recipients for 3 months or longer, the risk of cholera in unimmunized American travelers is small. Furthermore the vaccine does not interrupt transmission or prevent acquisition of the carrier state. Therefore cholera vaccine is recommended primarily to protect travelers from the border immunization policies of those countries that still require evidence of vaccination.

Cholera vaccine is recommended primarily to protect travelers from the border immunization policies.

Vaccine Currently available cholera vaccine is a bivalent whole cell killed bacterial suspension of equal quantities of Ogawa and Inaba serotypes of *Vibrio cholerage.* The pandemic El tor biotype includes organisms that belong to either of these serotypes. For persons anticipating travel to countries that require cholera immunization, a single dose of vaccine is sufficient to satisfy international health regulations. When there is a threat or occurrence of epidemic cholera some countries may require evidence of a complete series of two doses, or a booster dose within 6 months before arrival. Complete primary immunization consists of two doses of vaccine given 1 week to 1 month or more apart. Dose volume differs by age group and by route of administration, as indicated in the manufacturer's directions. Booster doses may be given every 6 months if necessary. The primary series does not ever need to be repeated for booster doses.

Cholera immunization is not recommended or required for infants less than 6 months of age. There is no information about the safety of cholera vaccine during pregnancy and its use should be avoided.

Untoward effects Vaccination often results in 1-2 days of pain, erythema, and induration at the site of injection. This local reaction may be accompanied by fever, malaise, and headache. Although serious reactions to cholera vaccination are extremely rare, persons who have experienced a serious reaction in the past should not be revaccinated. Most governments will permit unvaccinated travelers to proceed if they carry a physician's statement of medical contraindication.

Typhoid Fever

Typhoid fever is an acute febrile illness caused by the ingestion and intestinal invasion of *Salmonella typhi.* Typhoid is common in parts of the world that lack sanitary water and sewage systems but is relatively rare in the United States.

Vaccines A variety of killed typhoid vaccines have been produced since the turn of the century; parenteral vaccine was introduced to the American army in World War I. Vaccine efficacy, however, was not evaluated prospectively until the 1960s. At least ten well-controlled field trials in five different countries have shown that acetone-dried or formalin-killed vaccines give 70%-90% protection. For example, in Guyana two doses of vaccine given 4 weeks apart to school children less than 15 years of age offered more than 80% protection for 7 years. Oral vaccines, currently under development, may prove superior.

Routine typhoid immunization is not recommended in this country. Nor is there any rationale for its emergency use when there is a major disaster in any country where the number of chronic carriers is small. On the other hand, the vaccine is recommended for persons traveling to developing countries where sanitation is poor.

Vaccine is recommended for persons traveling to developing countries where sanitation is poor.

The typhoid vaccines commercially available in the United States are prepared from killed whole typhoid bacilli; paratyphoid antigen is no longer included. The acetone-dried preparation is most effective. Heat-killed, alcohol-killed, phenol-preserved, or freeze-dried vaccine gives considerably less protection.

Vaccine use Primary immunization of adults and children 10 years of age or older is accomplished by 0.5 cc given subcutaneously on two occasions 4 or more weeks apart. Children less than 10 years of age receive half this dose on the same schedule. If there is insufficient time for two doses at the interval specified, it is common practice to immunize with three doses, each 1 week apart. A booster dose is recommended every 3 years. Only a single booster is recommended regardless of the interval of time since the primary immunization series was completed.

Untoward effects No serious side effects have been noted. From one fourth to one half of vaccine recipients experience local pain and some fever; fever rarely lasts more than 24 hours. Although less reaction follows vaccination by the intradermal route, the preferred acetone-dried vaccine should not be given by this route. Persons who experienced marked reactions to previous injections should be given reduced doses for booster injections.

Tuberculosis

Infection, disease, and death due to tuberculosis have declined steadily in the United States since the turn of the century. Nevertheless, some 30,000 new cases of tuberculosis and 3,000 deaths are reported annually. In the United States bacille Calmette Guérin (BCG) vaccine has had limited use; in many other parts of the world children are routinely immunized either in infancy or at school entry.

Vaccine BCG vaccine, derived from a strain of *Mycobacterium bovis* attenuated through serial passage, was first administered to humans in 1921. All BCG vaccines available in the world today are derived from the original strain. Nevertheless they may differ greatly with regard to efficacy and safety as the result of differences in the method of production or administration. Controlled trials of liquid vaccines prepared from different BCG strains have shown protection rates ranging from 0%-80%. Currently available vaccines differ from the products tested in field trials in this country prior to 1955, and their efficacy is therefore unknown. A recent field trial in India showed no benefit from two currently available vaccines; however, the incidence of tuberculosis in the unimmunized control group was surprisingly low.

Vaccines are freeze dried. They must be used within 8 hours of reconstitution and should be protected from exposure to light.

Vaccine use BCG vaccine is recommended only for uninfected persons who have repeated unavoidable exposure to infected cases and who are otherwise not likely to be followed closely or to accept alternate methods of prophylaxis. BCG vaccine should be considered for tuberculin-negative infants who have certain repeated household exposures to patients with ineffectively treated sputum-positive tuberculosis. BCG vaccine should also be considered for groups that have an excessive rate of new infections

BCG vaccine should be considered for tuberculin-negative infants who have certain repeated household exposures.

and no regular source of medical care, such as inner city and migrant worker populations. BCG has also been suggested for health workers in settings where the frequency of new infection, as measured by skin test conversion, exceeds 1% per year. It may also be recommended to travelers who will live and work in developing countries.

Although BCG can be given safely to persons who are tuberculin positive, it is recommended only for persons who are skin test-negative to 5 TU (intermediate strength) of purified protein derivative (PPD). Dosage is indicated on the package labelling. One half of the usual dose is given to infants less than 28 days of age. If the indications for immunization persist, these children should receive a full dose at 1 year of age. Vaccines are available in the United States for intradermal or percutaneous administration. Vaccination should be given by the route indicated on the package labelling. The intradermal vaccine apparently provides the most uniform and reliable dose and is preferred.

The PHS recommends a second dose of BCG vaccine if tuberculin positivity is not achieved by immunization.

Persons who receive BCG vaccine should have a tuberculin skin test 2 months later. Failure of tuberculin conversion does not necessarily imply lack of protection. Nevertheless the Public Health Service Advisory Committee on Immunization Practices recommends a second dose of vaccine if tuberculin positivity is not achieved by immunization. The tuberculin test reaction that results from BCG vaccine reaches its maximum size within 2 months of immunization. Consequently tuberculin skin testing can still be used for epidemiologic or diagnostic purposes when there is an accurate record of the diameter of skin test induration after immunization. Skin test reactions larger than the one induced by BCG vaccine strongly suggest infection with *Mycobacterium tuberculosis.*

Untoward effects The reported frequency of side effects varies greatly, and probably depends on the vaccine, the dosage, the age of the vaccinee, and the extent of surveillance. Ulceration and lymphadenitis occur in 1%-10%. Osteomyelitis occurs once per million doses and is most frequent in newborns. Lupoid reactions occur rarely. Disseminated BCG infection and death occur in less than one per million vaccines, primarily in children with altered immunity.

BCG should not be given to persons with impaired immune responses.

BCG should not be given to persons with impaired immune responses such as congenital immunodeficiency, leukemia, lymphoma, and metastatic cancer or who have been administered immunosuppressing drugs and radiation. BCG has no documented harmful effects on the developing fetus, but immunization during pregnancy is generally not recommended unless there is an immediate and unavoidable probability of exposure to infective tuberculosis.

Viral Hepatitis

At least three distinct viruses cause the disease known as viral hepatitis. Hepatitis A (formerly called infectious hepatitis) and hepatitis B (formerly called serum hepatitis) have been recognized as separate entities since the early 1940s. In the United States the incidence of hepatitis A has been declining since 1971, whereas the incidence of hepatitis B has continued to rise since the initiation of separate reporting in 1966. Hepatitis A is most common in children and adolescents; hepatitis B is rare in persons less than 15 years of age except in hospital settings. Non-A non-B viral hepatitis, usually a diagnosis of exclusion, probably accounts for most posttransfusion hepatitis in this country today.

Hepatitis A is caused by an RNA virus usually transmitted by the fecal-oral route. Common source outbreaks have been reported. Over half of the American adult population has serologic evidence of past infection. Viral excretion in the stool peaks in the late incubation or early prodromal phase of the illness, and falls off rapidly with the onset of jaundice. Viremia is transient; consequently hepatitis A virus is rarely a cause of posttransfusion hepatitis. Chronic carriers apparently do not occur. Most infections are subclinical or anicteric. Overt cases are characterized by fever, malaise, anorexia, nausea, and varying degrees of jaundice. The fatality rate for clinically identified cases is less than 1%.

Hepatitis B is caused by a DNA virus. The major source of hepatitis B is through inoculation by needle or through minute skin defects of infected blood or blood products. Saliva and semen can also infect, leading to sexual transmission. The frequency of transfusion-associated hepatitis has decreased dramatically with the screening of blood donors for the presence of hepatitis B surface antigen (HBsAg). Infection remains common in hospital settings, in drug abusers, and among homosexuals. Most patients have a subclinical or anicteric infection. Illness, usually of insidious onset, is manifest as anorexia, malaise, nausea, vomiting, and jaundice. There may also be arthralgia and arthritis. Morbidity and mortality appear to increase with the age of the patient. The case fatality rate approximates that of hepatitis A. Chronic carriers do occur, particularly but not exclusively, in immunocompromised patients. The carrier state may be asymptomatic or associated with active liver disease.

Immune globulins ISG is prepared by cold ethanol fractionation of blood or plasma from pools of at least 1000 donors. Federal regulations require that ISG contain defined titers of antibody against diphtheria, measles, and poliovirus. Standards for antibody against hepatitis A and B viruses have not been established. The level of antibody against hepatitis A virus vary between lots and manufacturers from 1:220 to 1:16,000. ISG prepared before 1972 often showed no detectable levels of antibody to hepatitis B; current preparations have a mean titer of 1:64.

The possibility that high titers of antibody to hepatitis B virus would yield greater protection led to the production of hepatitis B immune globulin (HBIG). Using donors with known high titers, HBIG with mean titers in excess of 1:100,000 are now available. HBIG is approximately 20 times as expensive as ISG and is in limited supply.

HBIG is approximately 20 times as expensive as ISG and is in limited supply.

Prophylaxis of hepatitis A Numerous field studies have demonstrated that ISG administered within 2 weeks after exposure to hepatitis A virus prevents illness in 80%-90%. Preexposure prophylaxis has also been shown to reduce the risk of hepatitis A in persons handling nonhuman primates and in travelers to developing countries. Depending upon the dose and timing, ISG may act by blocking both clinical disease and subclinical infection (passive immunization) or may result in subclinical infection with long-lasting immunity (passive-active immunization).

ISG administered within 2 weeks after exposure to hepatitis A virus prevents illness in 80%-90%.

Prophylaxis of hepatitis B Trials of ISG for the prevention of hepatitis B have yielded conflicting results, and there has been considerable controversy over its value for hepatitis B prophylaxis. Studies of preexposure ISG prophylaxis in naturally acquired infection in the military in Korea and in experimentally infected children in institutions demonstrated some protection against hepatitis B. More recent trials have been designed to compare HBIG with ISG prophylaxis, but they have not employed the necessary placebo groups to assess the efficacy of ISG. In two large multicenter trials—one involving preexposure prophylaxis of dialysis patients and staff, the other, postexposure prophylaxis of medical personnel after needle sticks—the incidence of hepatitits B at 2-8 months was lower in HBIG-treated individuals than in persons receiving ISG; however, it was not significantly different after a more extended 9-12 month follow-up. Reanalysis of the postneedle-stick prophylaxis showed that infection occurred equally in HBIG-treated and ISG-treated groups, but that the infection was more often subclinical in the HBIG recipients. This result suggests that HBIG permits the development of passive-active immunity to type B hepatitis, as discussed under hepatitis A.

HBIG has been shown to be of benefit for preexposure prophylaxis in hemodialysis units, in institutionalized children, and for postexposure prophylaxis of hospital personnel following needle sticks as well as in cases of spouse contacts of acute hepatitis B cases and of infants born to mothers with hepatitis B. Efficacy varies from 40%-90%. As noted, either passive or passive-active immunization may occur.

ISG is recommended for postexposure prophylaxis after household or institutional exposure to hepatitis A.

Preexposure prophylaxis is recommended for travelers who spend more than two weeks out of the usual tourist routes in a developing country.

ISG use ISG is recommended for postexposure prophylaxis after household or institutional exposure to hepatitis A; it is not generally recommended for school or employment contacts. Preexposure prophylaxis is recommended for persons handling nonhuman primates and for travelers who will spend more than 2 weeks outside the usual tourist routes in a developing country. While the currently recommended dose for postexposure prophylaxis is 0.02 ml/kg of body weight, 0.06 ml/kg of body weight may be more effective. For preexposure prophylaxis the dose is 0.05 ml/kg of body weight repeated every 4-6 months.

ISG is also recommended for postexposure prophylaxis of hepatitis B when HBIG is not available; the dose is 0.05 to 0.07 ml/kg of body weight, and is repeated 25-30 days later. Infants whose mothers are HBsAG positive at the time of delivery can also be given 0.05 ml/kg of body weight within 7 days of birth. Preexposure prophylaxis of hepatitis B is not generally recommended. If preexposure prophylaxis is undertaken, the suggested ISG dose is 0.05 to 0.07 ml/kg of body weight, repeated every 4 months.

HBIG is recommended only for postexposure prophylaxis or for an infant born to an HBsAG-positive mother.

HBIG use HBIG is recommended by the Advisory Committee on Immunization Practices only for postexposure prophylaxis following an accidental needle stick or mucosal exposure to blood known to contain HBsAG, or when an infant is born to an HBsAG-positive mother. The dose for adults is 0.05 to 0.07 ml/kg of body weight, repeated 25-30 days later. Infants receive 0.13 ml/kg of body weight as a single dose within 7 days of delivery.

Neither HBIG nor ISG is currently recommended to prevent posttransfusion hepatitis. Nevertheless, several studies suggest that ISG may modify non-A non-B hepatitis, and this position may be modified when tests for non-A non-B hepatitis become available.

Untoward effects Immunoglobulin preparations should be given intramuscularly; intravenous injection may cause a severe hypersensitivity reaction. Approximately 1% of recipients of intramuscular ISG have adverse reactions—usually pain of several hours' duration at the site of injection. Arthralgia, urticaria, rash, and unexplained fever have been reported. Children with gamma A immunoglobulin (IgA) deficiency who have repeated injections of ISG have allergic reactions more commonly. Antibodies may appear against gamma globulin, but their significance is unknown. Immunoglobulins as prepared in the United States have not been associated with hepatitis transmission, although this has been a problem elsewhere.

Pregnancy is not a contraindication to immunoglobulin preparations.

Pregnancy is not a contraindication to immunoglobulin preparations. Immunoglobulin should not be given concurrently with active immunization because of possible interference with antibody response. When gammaglobulin is used for preexposure prophlyaxis in persons who require other immunizations, it should be given 2 weeks after the last active immunization. Because of the theoretical risk of immune complex disease, HBIG should not be given to known hepatitis B carriers or persons with chronic active hepatitis.

HBIG should not be given to known hepatitis B carriers or persons with chronic active hepatitis.

SUGGESTED READINGS

Diphtheria, Tetanus, and Pertussis

Berg, J. M. 1958. Neurologic complications of pertussis immunization. *Br. Med. J.* 2:24-27.

Koplan, J. P.; Schoenbaum, S. C.; Weinstein, M. C., et al. 1979. Pertussis vaccine: An analysis of benefits, risk and costs. *N. Engl. J. Med.* 301:906—911.

Peebles, T. C.; Levine, L.; Eldred, M. C., et al. 1969. Tetanus-toxoid emergency boosters: A reappraisal. *N. Engl. J. Med.* 280: 575-581.

Scheibel, I.; Bentzon, M. W.; Christensen, P. E., et al. 1966. Duration of immunity to diphtheria and tetanus after active immunization. *Acta. Pathol. Microbiol. Scand.* 67:380-392.

Poliomyelitis

Nightingale, E. O. 1977. Recommendations for a national policy on poliomyelitis vaccination. *N. Engl. J. Med.* 297:249-253.

Measles

Krause, P. J.; Cherry, J. D.; Deseda-Tous, J., et al. 1979. Epidemic measles in young adults: Clinical, epidemiologic, and serologic studies. *Ann. Intern. Med.* 90:873-876.

Krugman, R. D.; Rosenberg, R.; McIntosh, K., et al. 1977. Further attenuated measles vaccines: The need for revised recommendations. *J. Pediatr.* 91:766-767.

Landrigan, P. H., and Witte, J. J. 1973. Neurologic disorders following live measles-virus vaccination. *J. A. M. A.* 223:1459-1462.

Martin, D. B.; Weiner, L. B.; Nieburg, P. I., et al. 1979. Atypical measles in adolescents and young adults. *Ann. Intern. Med.* 90: 877-881.

Weibel, R. E.; Buynak, E. B.; McLean, A. M., et al. 1975. Long-term followup for immunity after monovalent or combined live measles, mumps and rubella virus vaccines. *Pediatrics* 56:380.

Rubella

Modlin, J. F.; Herrman, K. L.; Brandling-Bennett, A. D., et al. 1976. Risk of congenital abnormality after inadvertent rubella vaccination of pregnant women. *N. Engl. J. Med.* 294:972.

Weibel, R. E.; Buynak, E. B.; McLean, A. M., et al. 1975. Long-term followup for immunity after monovalent or combined live measles, mumps and rubella virus vaccines. *Pediatrics* 56:380.

Mumps

Weibel, R. E.; Buynak, E. B.; McLean; A. M., et al. 1975. Long-term followup for immunity after monovalent or combined live measles, mumps and rubella virus vaccines. *Pediatrics* 56:380.

Influenza

Parkman, P. D.; Galasso, G. H.; Top, F. H., et al. 1976. Summary of clinical trials of influenza vaccines. *J. Infect. Dis.* 134:100-107.

Wright, P. F.; Dolin, R.; and LaMontagne, J. R. 1976. Summary of clinical trials of influenza vaccines. II. *J. Infect. Dis.* 134:633-638.

Meningococcal Disease

Peltola, H.; Makela, P. H.; Kayhty, H., et al. 1977. Clinical efficacy of meningococcus group A capsular polysaccharide vaccine in children three months to five years of age. *N. Engl. J. Med.* 297: 686-691.

Pneumococcal Diseases

Austrian, R. 1977. Pneumoccal infection and pneumococcal vaccine. *N. Engl. J. Med.* 297:938-939.

Rabies

Plotkin, S. A. 1980. Rabies vaccine prepared in human cell cultures: Progress and perspectives. *Rev. Inf. Dis.* 2:433-448.

Smallpox

Lane, J. M., and Miller, J. D. 1969. Routine childhood vaccination against smallpox reconsidered. *N. Engl. J. Med.* 281:1220-1224.

Yellow Fever

Rosenzweig, E. C.; Babione, R. W.; and Wisseman, C. L. 1963. Immunological studies with group B arthropod-borne viruses. IV. Persistence of yellow fever antibodies following vaccination with 17D strain yellow fever vaccine. *Am. J. Trop. Med. Hyg.* 12:230-235.

Cholera

Azurin, J. C.; Cruz, A.; Pesigan, T. P., et al. 1967. A controlled field trial of the effectiveness of cholera and cholera El tor vaccines in the Philippines. *WHO Bull.* 37:703-727.

Typhoid Fever

Ashcroft, M. T.; Singh, B.; Nicholson, C. C., et al. 1967. A seven-year field trial of two typhoid vaccines in Guyana. *Lancet* 2:1056-1059.

Warren, J. W., and Hornick, R. B. 1979. Immunization against typhoid fever. *Annu. Rev. Med.* 30:457-472.

Tuberculosis

Eickhoff, T. C. 1977. The current status of BCG immunization against tuberculosis. *Annu. Rev. Med.* 28:411-423.

World Health Organization. Trial of BCG vaccines in South India for tuberculosis prevention: First report. 1979. *WHO Bull.* 57:819-827.

Viral Hepatitis

Hoofnagle, J. H. Seeff, L. B.; Bales, Z. B., et al., and the Veterans Administration Cooperative study Group. 1979. Passive-active immunity from hepatitis B immune globulin. *Ann. Intern. Med.* 91:813-818.

Seeff, L. B., and Hoofnagle, J. H. 1979. Immunoprophylaxis of viral hepatitis. *Gastroenterology* 77:161-182.

5 Prevention of Sports Injuries

Allan J. Ryan

Dr. Ryan received his M.D. from Columbia College of Physicians and Surgeons and was formerly on the faculty of the University of Wisconsin-Madison. He has written extensively in the area of sports medicine, and is a consultant to the President's Council on Physical Fitness and Sports and editor-in-chief of *The Physician and Sportsmedicine.*

Brief Contents

Overview

The five main strategies for the prevention of sports and recreational injuries are (a) preparticipation evaluation of prospective participants, (b) preparation of the participants through careful training and conditioning, (c) provision of proper protective equipment, (d) development of correct participation techniques, and (e) control of the environment in which the sport will be practiced.

Recreational athletes can be classified roughly into two types: those who are dedicated to a particular sport and pursue it throughout the years, and weekenders who often try many different sports, and pick whatever is handy or seasonable. Those dedicated to one sport tend to keep themselves in some degree of conditioning suitable for their sport and seldom suffer an injury due to lack of preparation, unless they undertake a new aspect of the sport. Those who pursue available and seasonal sports typically prepare themselves for nothing, or if they have attempted any type of preparation, they have done either very little or the wrong thing.

Too often a coach is simply a former athlete who relies on traditional training methods that lack scientific validity.

Supervised school athletes should have an advantage with coaches possessing thorough knowledge of sports—a prerequisite essential to the proper preparation of the athlete. In spite of such knowledge, however, coaches may be lacking in information regarding basic exercise physiology, kinesiology, and biomechanics; if so, they would not be in a good position to provide effective preparation for the athletes under their charge. Too often coaches are simply former athletes who rely on traditional training methods that lack scientific validity.

Surprisingly, many recreational athletes take little pains to learn much about the sports they attempt, being satisfied with what they can pick up by observation and limited experience. As a consequence they don't know what to prepare for and, if they do know usually lack the specific knowledge to do it properly. It is possible, for example, to pick up enough basic technique in downhill skiing to negotiate a modest hill without realizing that if your quadriceps muscles are weak, several repeats in succession may result in a fall that can cause injury.

SPORTS INJURIES

Causes and Prevalence

Unsafe actions are characteristic of sports.

Unsafe actions are characteristic of sports. This is because the movements of the body are exaggerations both of those ordinarily performed and those not ordinarily performed, or those performed in such a way that they place an unusual stress on the parts involved. They may also call on performance qualities such as strength, speed, flexibility, coordination, agility, balance, and endurance, which, while they are essential to the skillful carrying out of the action, may be developed poorly or simply inadequate in the individual.

Physical preparation for any sport must be based on the particular demands and hazards of that sport. This is based on a thorough conceptual analysis of the usual and possible actions demanded by the sport, and supported by whatever experience and knowledge that is available about the occurrence of injuries in the sport. Anticipating such injuries identifies the particular qualities that must be developed and the body parts that need special attention. A sufficient period of time must be allowed to develop adequately the necessary qualities. Conditioning exercises must also be maintained, although at a reduced level, when active participation starts to prevent loss of the trained state. Following is a list of the most common and disabling injuries that occur in various sports:*

Archery Contusions of the forearm of the bow-hand side, tendinitis of the shoulder and elbow, and muscle strain of the latissimus dorsi are not unusual in archery, to say nothing of accidental wounds received from the arrow.

Badminton Badminton invites not only muscle strains of the trunk and extremities, bruises, ankle and knee sprains, and tendinitis of the elbow of the racquet arm but also eye injuries from the shuttlecock.

Baseball In spite of the protective helmet that is worn, the thrown or batted ball may produce a concussion or more serious brain injury, a contusion, a laceration, or a fracture. The throwing act may produce an acute injury such as a muscle or tendon rupture or a spiral fracture of the humerus or, more commonly, a chronic injury such as tendinitis or epiphysitis at the elbow or shoulder. The act of batting produces muscle strains as does running on bases or in the field. In general, fractures and dislocations of the fingers and sprains of the ankles and knees are the most common acute injuries.

Basketball Abrasions from contact with the wooden or composition playing surface and sprains or dislocations of the fingers

---

*Source: Ryan, A. J. 1980. Sports injuries. In *Clinical practices of adolescent medicine.* ed. J. T. Y. Shen. New York: Appleton-Century-Croft.

from catching the ball incorrectly are probably the most common serious injuries among basketball players. Muscle bruises of the thigh, lacerations of the head, stress fractures in the foot, and knee sprains are other reasonably common injuries.

Board surfing Nodules of connective tissue hyperplasia, often with ulceration of the overlying skin, occur on the knees and insteps from paddling in a kneeling position on the board. They gradually disappear, however, when the action is discontinued. Injuries to the head result from falling off the board and being struck by it. A concussion may result in drowning. Severe brain injury or a cervical fracture may be caused by being driven against the sea bottom by a wave. Exostosis of the external ear canal may result from repeated exposures to cold water.

Bowling Injuries to the fingers from the bowling balls in the return rack and to the toes from dropping the ball on them are relatively common. Formation of a neuroma of the digital nerve on the ulnar side of the thumb is peculiar to this sport. The most common muscle strain is in the adductor group of the thigh.

Boxing Most of the serious injuries occur in adult fighters; however, fractured and bloody noses, abrasions, hematomas and lacerations about the face, concussions, and fractures of the metacarpal bones are found frequently in adolescent boxers.

Cycling Chafing of the skin, abrasions, contusions and fractures in the upper extremities from falls, and concussions are the injuries seen most commonly in cyclists. Tendinitis around the knees and chondromalacia of the patella may occur in those who ride long distances in practice and competition.

Diving Injuries incurred from hitting the diving board include concussion, scalp lacerations, and wrist fractures. Shin splints and sprained ankles may result from actions on the board itself. Improper entry into the water may end by rupturing the eardrum. Strains of shoulder and back muscles and sprains of the neck and back also occur in the act of diving.

Fencing Bruises on the upper and lower extremities often follow saber fighting; while strains of the shoulder, back, and thigh muscles; sprains of the wrist, knee, and ankle; and wounds of the trunk from a broken epee blade can all occur during fencing.

Field hockey Contusions and hematomas from blows of the stick and sprains of the ankle and knee are no strangers to hockey players. Subluxation of the patella may be the consequnce of sudden turning and twisting of the weighted leg.

Football, American and Canadian The most common football injuries are abrasions and contusions. Deep muscle bruises, especially to the arm and thigh, are sustained more in football probably than in any other sport. In spite of the protective helmet that is worn, concussions occur with some serious, even fatal, brain injuries. Sprains and fractures of the cervical spine occur from driving the head into the opponent in blocking or tackling or from being driven down into the ground. Sprains, dislocations, and fractures of the fingers are very common. The occurrence of ankle sprains depends on whether or not the ankles are protected by taping or wrapping. Knee sprains are the most common serious and disabling injury. Shoulder sprains and dislocations are relatively prevalent and very disabling. The muscles most frequently strained are the groin, hamstring, and calf.

Golf Muscle strains of the neck, shoulders, and trunk; bursitis of the shoulder and the hip; and tendinitis of the shoulder, elbow, and wrist are the most common injuries in golf. Ankle sprains occur as the result of walking on uneven ground.

Gymnastics All kinds of injuries are common in this sport, especially from falls off the apparatus. Chronic tendinitis and bursitis result especially in the shoulder and upper extremities. Callosities of the hands frequently break down under the stress of hard practice.

Handball Hand bruises occur when players practice long hours and fail to wear proper gloves. The handball fits into the average orbital fissure and serious eye damage may occur, especially in doubles in the four-wall game.

Ice hockey Almost any part of the body may be injured in this game. Since facial lacerations have been the most common, helmets and mouth guards are now mandatory for all adolescents. The advent of face guards, now just coming in, will reduce facial injuries substantially. Contusions from the puck, sticks, and helmets cause deep muscle bruises. Knee injuries are less common than in football and ankle injuries are unusual because of the high skate boots. Shoulder injuries occur from being checked into the boards.

Judo The common injuries sustained in judo are hematoma of the pinna of the ear, chest wall contusion, rib fracture, fracture of the clavicle, sprain and dislocation of the shoulder, sprain and dislocation of the elbow, sprain of the knee, sprain and dislocation of the ankle, and contusions of the leg.

Karate In its classic form, physical contact in karate is only accidental; nevertheless, bruises, abrasions, lacerations, and sprains of the hands, head, ribs, and lower extremities are sustained.

Lacrosse Because of the protective equipment worn in lacrosse, abrasions and lacerations are infrequent except on the legs; contusions, sprains, and strains of the upper and lower extremities are common injuries.

Rugby Because little or no protective equipment is used in this rough contact sport, injuries are frequent. Contusions, abrasions, and lacerations are the most common; and although concussions, strains, and sprains are fairly common, serious intracranial injury is rare.

Skating Bruises from falls, sprains of the knee, and occasional head injuries and wrist injuries are among the relatively few injuries sustained in skating.

Skiing, Alpine There is a high injury rate in Alpine skiing and almost any kind of injury may occur, depending on many external as well as internal factors. The most common of the less serious injuries is abrasions and lacerations (from the ski itself). The more common serious injuries are sprains and fractures in the lower extremities.

Skiing, cross-country Serious injuries to cross-country skiers are uncommon but lacerations, sprains, and fractures occur. Extended runs may result in frostbite and snow blindness.

Soccer Every type of injury may occur in soccer. There is a higher occurrence of severe muscle strains than in other sports. Sprains of the knee and ankle are common serious injuries. Fractures are not prevalent, occurring mostly in the lower extremities.

Softball The hazards of softball are almost identical to those of baseball; the pattern of injuries, is therefore the same.

Swimming Although contusions and sometimes fractures occur from hitting the ends of the pool, swimming injuries are usually generated internally and tend to be chronic. They include bursitis and tendinitis of the shoulders and tendinitis around the knees.

Tennis Muscle strains, particularly in the calf, are relatively common among tennis players. Tendinitis occurs chiefly in the shoulder and the elbow of the racquet arm. Back strain is not unusual. Sprains of the ankle are common, but sprains of the knee are relatively uncommon.

Track and field Injuries sustained in running may occur from physical contact in races, including falls on the track. The great majority of running injuries, however, are a result of overuse and tend to be chronic. They include muscle strains and tendinitis in the lower extremities and stress fractures. In the weight events muscle strains and sprains in the lower extremities are the most common. In jumping events muscle strains and joint sprains are the common injuries.

Volleyball Minor injuries in volleyball are sprained and dislocated fingers and contusions and abrasions from diving on the floor to make saves. Sprains of ankles are the most common serious injuries. Back strains are not unusual.

Water skiing Burns from the water skier's tow rope are usually not serious, but fingers have been amputated when caught in a loop. Muscle strains and joint sprains may occur in taking off or in a fall. Injuries from the boat may be serious if a proper lookout is not kept.

Weight lifting Muscle strains from not warming up and using improper lifting techniques are the most common injuries. Stress fractures may occur in the lumbar spine from hyperextension. Knee cartilages may be damaged in doing squat lifts, and elbows may be dislocated in failing to make a lift of a heavy barbell.

Wrestling, free-style Injuries are common and often serious. Finger sprains and dislocations and lacerations around the head, although fairly common, are less serious. Sprains of shoulder, costochondral junctions, ankles, and knees are the more common serious injuries.

Strategies for Prevention

The five main strategies for the prevention of sports and recreational injuries are: (a) preparticipation evaluation of prospective participants; (b) their preparation by careful training and conditioning; (c) provision of proper protective equipment; (d) development of correct participation techniques; and (e) control of the environment in which the sport will be practiced. Each will have some effect independent of the others but if all can be brought to bear simultaneously the effects are synergistic.

PREPARTICIPATION EVALUATION

A medical examination prior to entering a new sport as a vigorous exercise program is an important preventive measure for the following reasons:

1. It establishes a baseline for observations of changes that later might be interpreted as being due to a fresh injury, whereas they might have been present before the supposed injury occurred. A good example is a chronic second-degree subluxation of the acromioclavicular joint.
2. Important physical conditions—some that might preclude participation in a sport—are sometimes found that were unknown to participants, their families, and even physicians who have supposedly examined them carefully beforehand. Examples are high blood pressure and heart block.

Some candidates for sports are physically not suited for the sports in which they desire to compete.

3. Some candidates for sports are physically not suited for the sports in which they desire to compete. Boys with long, thin necks are not suitable candidates for football, and girls with body fat percentage of 20%-25% are not suitable for gymnastics.
4. Athletes who have been injured in previous sports seasons may not have fully recovered from these injuries, or they may not be adequately rehabilitated. To admit them to sports without reexamination is to increase the possibility of reinjury or of exposing them to a new related injury.

Where competition is conducted in weight classes, it is desirable to have the physician make an assessment of reasonable goals for individuals.

5. In sports such as wrestling, boxing, weight lifting, and martial arts, where competition is conducted in weight classes, it is desirable to have the physician make an assessment of reasonable goals for individuals whose intention it is to reduce their weight.
6. The precompetition physical examination offers an opportunity for exchange between physician and athletes, at which time the athletes can ask questions regarding their condition as well as discuss their preparations for the season. Once the season is under way they may not have another opportunity to do so.

7. From the medicolegal standpoint, should athletes suffer illness, injury, or death as a result of being allowed to compete with some condition that might have been recognized during a physical examination, it could cause serious and damaging problems for the sponsoring agency.

Supervised School Athletes

Some type of evaluation by a physician is recommended, if not mandated, for interscholastic sports participation.

Some type of evaluation by a physician is recommended, if not mandated, for interscholastic sports participation. It is required for most collegiate participation but is not always repeated prior to each season after the athletes' initial examination. It is also required for most youth sports programs but is often done superficially simply because of the large numbers of youngsters involved and the limited hours of medical time available. Major professional team sports such as football, baseball, basketball, soccer, and ice hockey require all athletes to be evaluated prior to each season. Professional boxers are supposed to be examined when they are licensed and before each bout. Other professional and amateur athletes must arrange for their own evaluations if they wish to have them. An examination is required, however, to establish eligibility for some particular events, especially international sports competitions.

Examinations may be given immediately prior to the opening of practice for the sport season, or in the case of some high schools, just before the conclusion of the spring semester for those sports that will be starting the following fall. If athletes participate in a fall sport and do not become ill or injured during the summer, they are not usually reexamined before the winter and spring sports seasons. In some school systems complete examinations are now performed only every second or third year of participation.

Recently enacted legislation makes it difficult to exclude handicapped students from participation in high school sports unless it can be shown that the handicap would make it likely that the person would suffer further injury because of it. Parents usually make decisions about the participation of such students after receiving the recommendations of the examining physician and school authorities. The decision as to when athletes may return to play following an injury is the responsibility of the physician who examines or treats them.

Decisions as to when athletes may return to play following an injury is the responsibility of the physician.

The annual or periodic examinations of athletes should be recorded in detail and kept in a cumulative file during their period of participation. Should any of them move to another institution or team, a copy of their record should go with them, but this seldom happens. The record should include notes on all examinations and tests that might have been made during the interim between more complete evaluations.

Periodic examinations of the athlete should be recorded in a cumulative file; a copy should accompany the athletes who move.

A standard format for athletic examinations is available to all interested physicians.

The initial evaluation and periodic reevaluations should include a history of athletes' previous health and any serious injury, a physical examination, one or more laboratory tests, and probably the results of selected functional capacity and performance tests. There is no standard format for such evaluations, and the institutions or physicians tend to use their own. Some state scholastic associations have their own form, based generally on a model recommended by the National Federation of State High School Associations (P. O. Box 20626, 11724 Plaza Circle, Kansas City, Mo. 64195).

The content of an athletic history and physical examination is suggested.

The health history should include information about any serious illness or injury that has occurred since birth, the nature and results of any surgical procedure, a record of immunizations, and details of any past or present use of drugs, toxic substances, or medications. If there have been x-ray examinations for fractures, or electrocardiograms or other evaluations for suspected heart disease, the results of these examinations should be made available to the examiner. Any history of concussions or seizures is very important.

The physical examination should include the head, spine, lungs, heart, abdomen, male genitalia, and extremities. Vision should be recorded—with glasses or contact lenses as well, if they are worn. Missing or carious teeth should be noted. Hearing should be checked in each ear. The curvatures and mobility of the spine should be noted. Breath and heart sounds should be checked. The blood pressure should be recorded in both arms. The abdomen should be examined for scars, presence of enlarged organs, or any masses and possible hernia. The male genitalia should be examined to see if both testes are present and descended. Height and weight with minimal clothing should be recorded. If a Harpenden calipers is available, the sum of the subscapular, periumbilical, and anterior thigh skinfolds should be recorded.

Examination of the extremities should include range of motion, any scars or defects, muscle development, gross strength, and any unusual joint laxity. Any imbalance of strength between the same muscle groups in paired extremities, or in antagonistic groups in the same extremity, is a potential cause for injury.

Laboratory tests should include an examination of a freshly voided urine specimen and a hemoglobin or hematocrit.

Laboratory tests should include an examination of a fresh urine specimen and a hemoglobin or hematocrit. A blood smear should be examined in any athletes who show general lymphadenopathy or who have had a recent severe sore throat, since they may have infectious mononucleosis (and a spleen vulnerable to traumatic rupture). An electrocardiogram should be made if any significant abnormality is noted on examination of the heart, or if there is a history of heart trouble. The presence of abnormal breath sounds should require an x-ray examination of the lungs. With a history of convulsions or repeated concussions an electroencephalogram and possibly a brain scan should be obtained.

The urine should be examined for the presence of sugar and albumin, and under the microscope for cells or casts. If any abnormality is found another specimen voided on arising the following morning should be examined.

A sound medicolegal way to recommend participation in a sport is suggested.

The final recommendation based on whatever examinations and tests are performed should be to allow or disallow participation in a particular sport, given the understanding of the demands and possible hazards of that sport. For physicians' protection they should express it in such terms as "There is no apparent reason why X should not participate," rather than "It is safe for X to participate."

Unsupervised Older Athletes

Patients who request advice from a physician prior to beginning physical activity deserve a careful evaluation.

A frequent request today is for advice and examination regarding a regular program of unsupervised vigorous physical activity. Those who have continued to be very active physically from early life seldom make such a request since they have no doubts about their ability to tolerate exercise. As a consequence, those who do ask the physician's advice typically have been inactive since high school or college days but have come to the realization that they may have been missing something, or that they should undertake exercise as a means of forestalling the effects of the aging process.

Some of these "deconditioned" persons may feel perfectly well in the sense that they have no physical complaints but they may have so little tolerance for exercise that they are out of breath after climbing two flights of stairs or running a short distance to catch a bus. Others may have had some intimations of medical problems through symptoms such as occasional chest pain, shortness of breath, chronic cough, or rapid weight gain but have not consulted a physician. Whether people in either of these groups are young or old they deserve a careful evaluation by their physicans before embarking on a program of vigorous physical activity.

One of the best indices of generally good health is a history of regular employment with few absences from work over a period of years.

In taking a history from deconditioned patients, physicians should place major emphasis on any signs or symptoms that might indicate any past or recent disease affecting the heart and circulatory system, the lungs, the liver, or the kidneys. One of the best indices of generally good health is a history of regular employment with few absences from work over a period of years. The nature of the work performed may indicate the possibility of work-related illness, which may have produced only subclinical symptoms. A history of hospitalizations or of taking medicine on a regular basis should demand further investigation of the reasons for these actions.

The past record of physical activities including earlier participation in sports and games, outdoor recreational activities, or work requiring heavy labor may yield significant clues to the individual's ability to respond to exercise. Those who have once been well-conditioned are more easily reconditioned, even after a period of years, than those who have never been. The level of current physical activity either on the job or work related, is also important.

Evaluation of the person's general appearance will include weight, height, and body shape. Gross body weight can be deceptive if the approximate fat percentage is not determined. Heart rate and blood pressure should be determined in standing, sitting, and supine positions. The heart size and sounds are of particular importance. The breath sounds and ability to expand the chest are very significant. Physicians should look for any enlargement of the abdominal organs. The functional status of the extremities, especially the lower ones, may be critical, depending on the type of exercise to be recommended. Mechanical or circulatory deficiencies in the lower extremities may not only handicap exercise efforts, but they may be the cause later on of complications of physical activity.

It is probably not necessary to perform routine electrocardiogram on persons under 40 who are apparently healthy.

At age 40 years performance begins to decrease in the records of the British Association for Cycling Time Trials.

Although atherosclerosis and arteriosclerosis may begin in some individuals at a very early age (postmortem examinations of young adults dying accidental deaths may occasionally show partial or even complete occlusion of a coronary artery in a person who has never complained of chest pain or manifested any heart disorder) it is probably not necessary to perform routine electrocardiograms on persons under 40 years of age if they are apparently healthy, unless their history or physical examination suggests the possibility of heart disease. Even though 40 years of age is an arbitrary dividing line, abnormalities in the heart muscle or vessels—which might otherwise go undetected except by catheterization, arteriography, or echocardiography—begin to appear in rapidly increasing numbers at this time of life. It is of some interest that this is the precise age during which performance begins to decrease in the records of the British Association for Cycling Time Trials. All persons 40 years of age or more should have an electrocardiogram as a qualifying measure.

Candidates for exercise of all ages who have been physically inactive for some time and who have physically undemanding employment should have some type of test to determine their

The role of a test to determine maximum ability to perform sustained work is discussed.

maximum ability to perform work on a sustained basis. Physicians, depending on their interest, experience, availability of time, and equipment, may wish to perform this test in their office or they can refer their patient to a laboratory where it can be done. If a laboratory is chosen, those operating the laboratory and conducting the tests should be fully trained and competent not only to conduct the tests properly but also to observe the clinical reaction of the patient. They should be able to conduct resuscitative measures should these be necessary in the event of an unanticipated cardiovascular crisis.

Should these examinations uncover an unsuspected condition, it may be necessary to further evaluate the candidate before recommending unrestricted exercise. The following conditions would suggest such a need:

1. Any acute or chronic infectious disease
2. Diabetes that is not well controlled
3. Marked obesity
4. Psychosis or severe neurosis
5. Central nervous system disease
6. Musculoskeletal disease involving the spine and lower extremities
7. Active liver disease
8. Renal disease with nitrogen retention
9. Severe anemia
10. Significant hypertension
11. Angina pectoris or other signs or symptoms of coronary insufficiency
12. Significant cardiomegaly
13. Arrhythmias
    a. Second-degree A-V block
    b. Ventricular tachycardia
    c. Atrial fibrillation
14. Significant disease of the heart valves or larger blood vessels
15. Congenital heart disease without cyanosis
16. Phlebothrombosis, or thrombophlebitis
17. Current usage of drugs such as
    a. Reserpine

   b. Propanolol
   c. Guanethidine
   d. Quinidine, nitroglycerine, and other vascular dilators
   e. Procainamide
   f. Digitalis
   g. Catecholamines
   h. Ganglionic blocking agents
   i. Insulin
   j. Psychotropic drugs
18. An apprehensive or extremely negative view regarding exercise and its possible effects

The finding of certain conditions, although these would rarely be discovered in persons who present themselves as apparently well, is a contraindication to any exercise program of sustained and vigorous activity, and in most instances to any type of exercise program even if modified. The particular conditions contraindicating a vigorous exercise program are as follows:

1. Active or recent myocarditis
2. Recent pulmonary embolism
3. Congestive heart failure
4. Arrhythmias
   a. Third-degree A-V block
   b. Fixed-rate pacemakers
5. Aortic aneurysm
6. Ventricular aneurysm
7. Liver decompensation
8. Congenital heart disease with cyanosis

Persons with one or more of these conditions should be recommended promptly for appropriate treatment, which, if effective, might make them candidates at least for light exercise at some future date.

PHYSICAL TRAINING AND CONDITIONING

Supervised School Athletes

If any factors that may singly or in combination influence the occurrence of injury in sports are held constant, trained and well-

In general trained, well-conditioned athletes will suffer fewer and less serious injuries than untrained, poorly conditioned athletes.

conditioned athletes will suffer fewer and less serious injuries than untrained and poorly conditioned athletes. Individuals who lack strength would be unable to counteract the powerful forces that they might encounter in sports. If they lack speed of movement and a quick reaction time they would have great difficulty in avoiding forces or bodies directed toward them. If they lack balance and coordination their clumsiness could lead to an injury. If they lack endurance they would lose form from fatigue and become more easily injured.

The basic abilities or qualities that may be present naturally—and which may be improved by training—interact in a complex fashion. Strength is the chief independent variable, acting with cardio-respiratory function, speed of movement, and coordination to influence the dependent variables of endurance, whole body movement, power, reaction time, agility, flexibility, and balance.

Strength is the ability to exert tension in a muscle. No muscle that is normally innervated and is connected to a functioning control nervous system lacks strength, but if that muscle has not been exercised there is little strength there. This basic strength is due to a constant low level of excitation of the muscle generated through the muscle spindles, which act as stretch receptors. It is called muscle tone. Muscles adapt to the loads that are imposed on them; consequently most of us have muscles capable of sustaining only the effort of the activities of our daily lives. To improve muscle strength it is necessary to overload the muscles progressively. The resulting increased strength will serve to protect from injury the muscles and joints that they cross, and will enhance the other performance qualities insofar as they are dependent on strength.

Increasing strength protects from injury the muscles and joints that they cross.

Just as improvements in strength of the skeletal muscles are obtained by overloading, so the heart muscle can be strengthened by exercise that causes it to work at a rate beyond its accustomed pace. The chambers of the heart also dilate as a result of regular exercise so that a greater stroke volume is developed. The effects of training on the respiratory apparatus are similar in that it develops the muscles that control respiration. The most significant result is not in improving tidal volumes in the lungs, however, but in improving the ability of the muscle cells to take up and utilize oxygen through enlargment and increase in the mitochondria. The combined improvements in heart and respiratory function, together with the overall increases in muscular strength, develop the physical endurance of the individual. Since fatigue is a factor that may influence the occurrence of injury, this is a preventive measure.

One of the most common causes of muscle injury is lack of sufficient flexibility.

One of the most common causes of muscle injury is lack of sufficient flexibility. This may be due to the failure to develop muscle strength equally on both sides of a joint so that there is an effective loss of range of motion in the joint. Or it may be because of an injury to a muscle, which imbalances the joint, or because of failure to stretch muscles regularly to their full length. A muscle that has been injured previously requires special attention because at the site of injury there is fibrous scar tissue, which has a tendency to shorten. It therefore needs not only strength development but also a greater concentration on stretching than an uninjured muscle might need.

The concept that development of great strength makes athletes "muscle bound", or less flexible, is incorrect if strength development is carried out for both agonists and antagonists with equal intensity. It has been shown that athletes who have trained for great strength are more flexible than those who have not trained for strength.

Muscles should not be stretched by a rhythmic bounce but by a slow, steady pull, which is held for 6-8 seconds.

Muscles should not be stretched by a rhythmic bounce but by a slow, steady pull, which is held for 6-8 seconds. Light stretching to warm up and loosen up the muscle is done prior to practice or competition. If a muscle has been considerably shortened and requires heavy stretching to restore its normal resting length, this should be done following the workout. Overstretching a muscle before attempting to make a maximum contraction is a good way to set it up for a pull or tear. The most safe time is when it has been thoroughly warmed up and can rest after stretching.

Balance can be improved only by practicing balancing.

Balance can be improved only by practicing balancing. This can be done by walking or exercising on a narrow board or beam, by balancing on the hands, or by the use of a board balanced on a cylinder or a sphere. To be in balance is to be able to resist being upset, to control the contraction and relaxation of major muscle groups so that they will be less easily strained, and to be able to execute sports skills smoothly and effectively.

Coordination is the result of training neuromuscular reflexes. It is improved by repeated practice of the necessary basic and advanced sports skills. Lack of coordination causes uncontrolled movements, which in turn may cause injury by allowing too powerful a contraction of either the agonist or antagonist of paired muscles or muscle groups, so that one or the other is injured. Effective coordination depends on adequate strength, flexibility, and balance but also on two other qualities—agility and quick reaction times.

Power is an expression of how rapidly strength can be brought to bear in the performance of work. A muscle that is more powerful is one that can move the body or some object more rapidly and forcefully than another muscle. Speed is therefore critical in its production. Although speed of motion is to some extent an inherent quality with which some are more blessed than others, everyone can improve their speed. This is done by repeating skilled actions as rapidly as possible until they become almost automatic. Strength and endurance of muscles are necessary to enable this rapid repetition.

Reaction time can also be improved considerably by practice.

Reaction time can also be improved considerably by practice. As reaction time improves it becomes possible for individuals to apply their speed of motion more effectively. They shorten the period between the time they recognize the signal to react and the time their muscles respond, which is called the movement time.

Agility is that quality which combines speed of motion, reaction and movement time, and balance with coordination to enable individuals to move dexterously and efficiently through space in a connected series of skilled movements. Agility can also be improved by practice.

In their common application, training and conditioning programs for any sport do not develop these performance qualities in isolation from each other; they are exercised collectively, but sometimes with more emphasis on one than the other. The more that they can be exercised together and the longer this can be done in terms of weeks, months, or years, the more effective they will be in improving performance as well as in preventing injury.

Unsupervised Older Athletes

Exercise does not need to be "all out" to produce a training effect. In fact there are very good reasons for deconditioned persons and persons in the older age groups to avoid the "all out" efforts, which are more appropriate to the younger sports competitors. There obviously are exceptions: persons of middle and older age who have undergone intensive training over a period of time for the express purpose of reaching competitive levels consistent with their age; or the aging competitors who continue in a sport past the age when most of their former associates have retired because their skills can still compensate for what they may have lost in other physical qualities.

Good training effects can be achieved at 70%-80% of maximum effort.

Good training effects can be achieved at 70%-80% of maximum effort. This means reaching and maintaining a pulse rate of 140-150 for young to middle-aged adults and 120-130 or even less for older individuals. A simple method for estimating a person's optimal exercise level is to subtract the individual's age from 220. This gives an approximate maximum pulse rate for exercise. The resting pulse rate is then subtracted from the maximum pulse rate and 60% of the difference is calculated. When this is added to the resting pulse rate, it results in the rate that would be suitable for that individual to sustain through 20-60 minutes of continuous exercise. The self-control of exercise intensity by frequent estimations of the pulse rate can be learned easily by most individuals and does not require the use of automatic signaling devices, although these are available if the nuisance and expense are acceptable.

Exercise should allow participants to reach the desired pulse rate level but not compel them to exceed it.

The type of exercise selected is not critical, providing that it allows participants to reach the desired pulse rate level and does not compel them to exceed it. A sport such as bowling does not stimulate a circulatory response sufficient to produce a training effect or even a maintenance effect for youths but may for older people. Golf may produce a training effect in younger individuals who approach it vigorously, but will not for the golf cart set at any but advanced age. Many sports activities such as tennis may be modified by mutual agreement of the participants of older age to prevent reaching undesirably high pulse rates.

Exercise should be done regularly at least three to four times a week.

Whatever exercise is selected it should be taken regularly and with sufficient frequency. When training loads are calculated on a weekly basis it can be seen quite readily that if the number of days of participation is too few, perhaps the load on the days of exercise may be so high as to produce an undesirable fatigue and perhaps musculoskeletal problems. A frequency of three to four times weekly seems to be quite satisfactory, although six times is probably better from the standpoint of avoiding unpleasant side effects.

If the selected exercise is not enjoyable to the participants the chances of their continuing it are poor. Matters of convenience and availability must be considered as well. An activity that may have seemed quite attractive at the beginning may become boring through frequent repetition. A variety of exercises may thus become suitable for those who are lacking in dogged persistence. The camaraderie of group-exercise activities is a good motivating factor for many, especially the very outgoing and gregarious.

Precaution for beginning exercise All vigorous exercise should be preceded by some type of warm-up activity to set in motion the processes by which the pulmonary and cardiovascular systems will accommodate to exercise, to prepare the muscles by reducing their viscosity, to limber up the joints by gentle stretching, and to shorten reflex times by raising body temperature. Five to ten minutes should suffice for this.

Exercise should then start slowly and increase gradually during the sessions; the frequency of the sessions should also progress slowly. Beginners running, jogging, and then slow pacing should take about 20 minutes per mile, working up to 3 miles in 45 minutes, and so on.

In group exercises that are undertaken for conditioning purposes participants should set their own pace. Misguided attempts to keep up with others who have a greater exercise capacity can be dangerous. Challenges should be neither offered nor accepted.

Exercise should always be stopped if unfavorable symptoms, especially chest pain, appear.

Exercise should always be stopped if unfavorable symptoms, especially chest pain, appear. There is a tendency at times to push oneself against one's better judgment to avoid being thought of as a slacker or failing in self-esteem. It is stupid rather than heroic to ignore the body's signals that something is amiss.

Not feeling up to par may be a good reason to skip exercise on that day.

There are times when a person engaged in a regular exercise program has no specific complaint but feels vaguely uncomfortable and is just not "up to par." This may be a good reason to skip exercise on that day or at least to modify the program. Heart attacks are sometimes accompanied by these vague premonitory symptoms, and a number of myocardial infarctions and fatalities occurring during or shortly after exercise have been recorded under such circumstances.

Finally, in spite of all warnings and precautions, there are always those who want to do too much too soon. Aching and swollen muscles, tendons, and joints may be the result—in which case individuals lose rather than gain time in reaching their goals for conditioning. More fortunate and successful are those who heed the ancient motto, "Make haste slowly."

PROTECTIVE EQUIPMENT

Since athletes do not perform in the nude state (as they did during an extended period in early Greek games), except in swimming or diving where only a very brief garment is worn, the uniform in sports may be considered in some sense protective equipment. To the extent that it covers the skin it can cushion from blows and protect from abrasions or lacerations.

Shoes are worn in many sports, not primarily for protection but to provide support for the foot and ankle and to give purchase and traction. Sport shoes today are so specialized that there is a different type for almost every sport, even though the basic construction is often similar. The soles may be ridged or corrugated or fitted with cleats or spikes. Some are affixed to skates. Insofar as the upper portion of the shoe enfolds the ankle or lower leg it may provide protection not only from injury to the skin but to the joints and bones.

In some sports very little equipment is worn and in others a great deal is worn. Although rugby and American football are closely related sports, football is second only to ice hockey in the amount of protective equipment worn by the players, while in rugby the players use only a light shoulder pad sewn into the jersey and a crude ear protector for the forwards who make up the scrum. Serious injuries occur in rugby, just as they do in football, but tradition prevents the adoption of more protective equipment. Almost every item for protection that has been added in any sport has met with immediate opposition from the majority of players and coaches. Once the equipment has been accepted by all, or its use mandated, most players are unwilling to give it up.

Helmets are virtually the only piece of equipment that can prevent a fatality.

Gloves are worn as protective equipment in more different types of sports than any other item. Each is designed with the particular requirements of its sport in mind. Helmets are the second most common piece of protective equipment. They are critical devices since they are virtually the only piece of equipment that has the potential for preventing a fatality. As a consequence a great deal of research has gone into their development; we have standards for helmet performance that are recognized by the industry. In the case of football helmets these standards must be met for use in high school and university play.

Protective equipment varies in type from such temporary and disposable items as adhesive tape to soft pads, pads with hard plastic outer coverings, metal cages, mats, and flame retardant clothing. Some are worn on the athlete and some are placed on equipment and other objects with which he may be expected to make contact. Such equipment may function as a restraint or as a shock-absorbing device.

Special pieces of protective equipment should satisfy six requirements.

Special pieces of protective equipment worn by the athlete, such as shoulder pads or helmets, should satisfy six requirements: (a) they should afford maximum protection within reasonable limits for the body part that they are designed to protect; (b) they should not handicap the wearer in his actions; (c) they should be properly fitted and properly worn; (d) they should be durable; (e) they should be replaced when their protective qualities are seriously diminished or lost; and (f) they should not be hazardous to other athletes.

A soft wool hat will not provide the same protection as a hard-shell plastic helmet will against an impact to the head. At the same time the helmet must be prevented from "bottoming" on the head and the force should be distributed as evenly as possible Various suspension materials and devices are included inside the helmet to accomplish these objectives. On the other hand, no practical helmet system can completely prevent movement of the brain within the skull when the head is suddenly accelerated or decelerated. A good helmet simply does everything possible to protect the brain within these limitations.

A very large helmet that is filled with shock-absorbent material several times the size of the head might be very effective in neutralizing blows but could not be carried or worn by players and still allow them to participate effectively. A helmet that is reasonably comfortable for football players would not be practical for hockey players who need a more efficient system to eliminate the heat that they generate in what is now chiefly an indoor game. A helmet and face mask must also be designed in such a way that the wearer's field of vision is not severely restricted.

The best equipment may not be protective if it does not fit.

The most well-designed equipment made of the best available material may not be protective if it is improperly fitted to the person who is going to wear it. Equipment that is too small is less apt to be protective than equipment that is too large. If hip pads are built into pants and pants are worn too low on the hips the vital areas around the crests of the ilium will not be protected.

Equipment that sustains only one possible major force before it is replaced does not have to be durable. When it will be subjected to many shocks in the course of even one practice or game and may have to be used in many games during a long season it must be very durable. Proper care of the equipment during the season and during storage between seasons helps it to retain its protective qualities.

When these qualities are seriously impaired as the result of repeated impacts or other sources of wear and tear, the equipment must be either reconditioned to restore these qualities or discarded. Under no circumstances should it simply be passed on to other users at a lower level of play. Their need for good protection is just as great, possibly greater because of their inexperience.

Finally, the equipment covered with a hard-shell plastic may be hazardous to others who come into contact with it. Unfortunately there is equipment in both football and ice hockey that causes that risk today. The risk could be minimized by providing an outer covering of shock-absorbent material. In spite of requests from physicians the rules committees in both sports have failed to take action on this. As a result one study of high school football injuries showed the helmet to be the single most common source of injuries to players other than the wearer.

A player's equipment may cause injury to other players.

DEVELOPMENT OF CORRECT PARTICIPATION TECHNIQUES

Three elements are of importance in the development of correct techniques for safe participation in sports: (a) good coaching; (b) sufficient practice; and (c) knowledge and application of the rules of the sport.

The development of sport skills is something that comes very easily to some and very hard to others. Coaching plays a very important role for most athletes, some of whom can merely watch talented athletes perform and then imitate their actions. Unfortunately no such models are perfect so the other athletes imitate their mistakes as well as their talents. Others, once they become acquainted with the objectives of a sport, the equipment, and the general "rules of the game" can develop the appropriate skills almost instinctively, while improvising new skills and techniques of their own. Even these two types of athletes need some coaching—and most athletes need a great deal.

Experience in training allows athletes to develop a sense of pace, anticipation, and reflex reaction as they learn the movements characteristic of their sport and repeat them until they become instinctive. At that point they are in full control of their actions; they can thus devote their conscious attention to exercising judgment of their progress toward their objectives individually and vis-à-vis others with whom they are competing. The judgments that they make from moment to moment make up their strategy in participating in their sport. Based on previous experience their strategy may to some extent be preplanned, but successful athletes must be prepared to modify their judgment instantly as the situation requires. The mastery of this chain of thoughts and events makes a significant contribution to athletes' safety.

The coach's objectives are to teach athletes winning form and strategy, but these are inseparable from considerations of safe performance.

Good coaching enables athletes to develop this self-control, which in turn enables them to move gracefully and safely alone or in the midst of others, to anticipate and avoid sources of danger, and to react instinctively to unexpected threats to their body and extricate themselves unharmed from hazardous situations. The coach's objectives are to teach athletes winning form and strategy, but these are inseparable from considerations of safe performance. Athletes who are injured and disabled cannot ultimately be winners, except in unusual circumstances. A veteran coach will say that when experienced and inexperienced athletes are performing the same activities, the inexperienced athletes will be more frequently and seriously injured.

Because practice itself exposes athletes to the types of injuries that are characteristic of the sport, and because athletes usually devote many more hours to practice than to competition, more injuries arise in practice than in competition. Since activity in competition is more intense, the ratio of accidents to time of participation is greater. Athletes and coaches have the task, therefore, of balancing practice and competition in such a way that the advantages derived from practice in helping to prevent injury in competition are not outweighed by an inordinate number of injuries sustained through practice that is too intense or is unnecessarily prolonged.

In one study of high school football elimination of intersquad scrimmages reduced injuries without affecting the team's record.

In one study of high school football the elimination of intersquad scrimmages once the season had started reduced the number of player injuries overall without changing the ratio of games won to lost, in comparison with a control group of teams. Experienced distance runners learn that in practice sudden changes to greatly increased distances often result in crippling overuse injuries. A team that comes to competition in a fatigued state both physically and mentally will be more vulnerable to competitive injuries.

The primary purposes of rules in sports are to define the nature of play, to state how the winner will be determined, to set limits for play, and to provide for fair competition. A violation of the rules introduces an abnormal action that tends to disrupt the pattern, which is the reason why in sports where physical contact between the contestants is essential or even possible, rule violations tend to cause injuries. Once a sport is established, many of the changes in, and additions to, the rules have to do with the safety of the contestants. Penalties are provided for violation of the rules, but these cannot prevent the injuries that result from careless or deliberate transgressions, even though the rules and the presence of the officials tend to discourage such violations. It is therefore essential that athletes know all the rules of the games that they are playing and that their captains and coaches insist on their observing them.

The rules of American football have been revised repeatedly over the years to accommodate new developments in the game and changes in the average size and speed of the players. The rules presently in force have substantially reduced fatalities and total disability but still leave something to be desired as far as reducing less serious but disabling injuries, particularly to the knees. Coaches must be encouraged continually not to teach or allow their players to use techniques that are legal but only marginally safe.

Coaches must be encouraged continually not to teach or allow their players to use techniques that are legal but only marginally safe.

Officials are often in the best position to tell when an athlete is injured or in danger and should take action immediately to protect the player and to advise the team and coach. They should allow qualified persons to enter the playing area and give them reasonable time to attend or assist injured players. They should also act promptly to stop any game or call it off when the safety of the players is threatened. At all times they should be alert to the use of illegal equipment by any player.

CONTROL OF THE SPORTS ENVIRONMENT

There are three major factors in the control of the sports environment that can assist in the prevention of injuries: (a) elimination of physical hazards; (b) careful monitoring of the climatic conditions; and (c) control of the spectators. These controls involve input from coaches, officials, managers, and sports physicians.

Since sports are contested not only on playing fields but in indoor arenas, on and in the water, and even in the air, the possible environments and types of hazards, that may be encountered are almost endless.

Environmental factors can have considerable influence on athletic safety.

In indoor sports the environmental problems may arise from temperature, humidity, smoke, and lighting; from floor or ice surfaces; from obstacles in the playing areas; and from people and obstacles outside the playing areas.

In outdoor sports problems may arise from atmospheric conditions; field, court, track and water conditions; objects on or in the playing area; stands; spectators, officials, photographers and their equipment; and docks, trees, walls and other boundary markers.

Playing fields that are used for other purposes or to which the general public has unlimited access should be thoroughly inspected and cleaned up before a game to remove stones, glass, or other objects that might cause injuries to players; all holes and depressions should be filled, and any objects adjacent to the playing area should be removed to a safe distance. Spectators should be kept from encroaching in that area.

Should an area for a scheduled competition be judged unsafe an effort should be made to find a safer area to avoid postponement or cancellation of the event. Surfing competition, for example, might be moved to another beach if wave formations at the originally selected site are considered too dangerous for competitors.

Athletes performing in heat and high humidity can develop heat stress.

Athletes performing under environmental conditions of high temperature and relative humidity may develop symptoms of heat stress. These symptoms and the associated physical findings may be manifested in the development of heat cramps, heat exhaustion, and heat stroke.

Heat cramps occur in voluntary muscles when the sodium level in the blood falls below a critical level—a level that varies among different individuals. These cramps can be prevented by the prophylactic administration of sodium by mouth or by vein. Heat exhaustion is caused by dehydration and is accompanied by falling arterial pressure and rising venous pressure; if uncorrected it leads to collapse. Dehydration is prevented by maintaining a high water intake and is treated by rehydration orally or intravenously. Heat stroke represents a failure of the heat regulating mechanisms of the body to adapt to the increasing heat reception, decreasing heat loss and increasing heat production. If not treated promptly it may cause death.

The greatest danger is to football players who practice and play frequently under very hot and humid conditions in uniforms that cover their bodies almost completely and interfere with the cooling mechanism of sweating. The prevention of heat cramps, exhaustion, and stroke depend on taking seven measures: (a) gradual acclimation of the players to hot, humid conditions; (b) preseason physical conditioning programs; (c) exact observation of climatic conditions daily or more frequently, with appropriate scheduling of activities; (d) control of the wearing of uniforms by type and amount; (e) use of added salt prophylactically; (f) free intake of water before, during, and after practice and competition; and (g) thoughtful scheduling of practice and competition times.

The prevention of heat cramps, exhaustion, and stroke depend on taking seven measures.

In very cold environments the relative humidity is unimportant unless the clothing is soaked. The rate of air movement over the body is extremely important, particularly if the skin is exposed. Exposure to excessive cold may cause general hypothermia or frostbite. Hypothermia may result in death; and frostbite, in loss of tissue and amputation.

Clothing is protective against a cold environment insofar as it keeps the body dry, creates a dead space of air between the body and the outer surface of the clothing, absorbs radiant energy, resists penetration by wind, and does not increase work cost because of its bulk. Some acclimation to cold may occur as the result of chronic exposure, especially as far as the psychological reaction is concerned, but with acute, severe exposure everyone needs maximum protection.

When sportsmen go up to moderate or high altitudes, "mountain sickness" will occur in nonacclimated persons. Above 18,000 feet it may occur even in acclimated persons, and supplemental oxygen may be required. The most severe manifestation of this condition is pulmonary edema, which may result in death. Prevention depends on gradual acclimation to altitude, good physical conditioning, prevention of dehydration, and the use of oxygen. At high altitudes precautions must also be taken against cold stress since severe weather conditions may be encountered.

Above 18,000 feet "mountain sickness" may occur even in acclimated persons.

When sportsmen go down below the surface of the water they encounter problems caused by the increased atmospheric pressure. One additional atmosphere is experienced from every 33 feet of depth in sea water and 34 feet in fresh water. Since air is compressible and water is not, as a diver descends and continues to take in air, the air in his lungs is compressed and air passes from the blood vessels into the tissues. Pathological changes that can occur include sinus squeeze, rupture of ear drums, and nitrogen narcosis on descent; and decompression sickness, air embolism, and lung rupture on ascent. Prevention is accomplished by having proper scuba equipment in working order and using it correctly while both descending and ascending in the water. Accidents should be completely preventable if correct techniques are followed. Both dry and wet suits may be used to prevent excessive heat loss.

PREVENTION OF EXACERBATED INJURY AND CHRONIC DISABILITY

An important aspect of prevention includes keeping minor injuries from becoming major ones, and acute injuries from becoming chronic.

Although a majority of sports and recreational injuries could be prevented by following all the previous recommendations, realistically there are many gaps and failures in attempts to implement them. As a result, injuries that could have been prevented occur along with those that no amount of prevention would have stopped. An important aspect of prevention therefore becomes the efforts made by medical and other personnel to prevent minor injuries from becoming major ones and acute injuries from becoming chronic.

When there has been an injury, injury tends to recur if the original injury is not completely rehabilitated before the athlete returns to practice and competition.

Both the athlete and the coach must be convinced that injuries should be recognized and reported immediately.

This process must begin with the prompt recognition of injury and the early institution of definitive treatment. Since the coaches are the persons who spend the greatest amount of time in contact with athletes, they must be trained in the early recognition of injury and persuaded to report the injury immediately to the trainer or physician who is responsible for its care. The athletes themselves must be educated not to conceal or delay the reporting of an injury. The common reason for both coach and athlete to ignore or fail to report an injury in its early stages is a fear that the athlete will be held unnecessarily from practice or competition. While some injuries do subside without causing disability., neither the athlete nor the coach is ordinarily able to make this determination correctly.

Prompt treatment of an acute injury may require a brief period of disability from sport. If the injury is minor and is untreated or not treated adequately, it may become aggravated, changing its status to that of a major injury. Treatment will then almost certainly require a longer period of disability and there is less chance of effecting a complete cure. Also, if the acute injury becomes chronic as the result of neglect it will require an extended period of treatment and the chances of its recurring are greatly increased.

An example of a relatively minor injury becoming a major one might be a bruise to the quadriceps muscle of the thigh. Without prompt treatment by application of ice and pressure and relief from weight bearing, followed in 24-48 hours by active and later resistive exercises, damage to the thigh muscle and atrophy may be extensive and seriously disabling. The possibility of myositis ossificans is greatly increased, which would mean a prolonged and perhaps permanent partial disability.

An acute injury that could become chronic as the result of failure to treat it early and adequately is Achilles tendinitis. Early treatment may result in a disability of not more than 3 weeks. Failure to institute treatment while athletes are continuing to be active over a period of several weeks or a month may cause a disability that lasts a year or more and becomes very resistive to any treatment.

There are a number of reasons why the athlete may fail to complete his rehabilitation.

Anxious to return to practice and competition, athletes may fail to complete their rehabilitation because they fail to understand the serious potential for reinjury, because they are lazy, or because they become discouraged. Coaches, trainers, and physicians may have to share the responsibility because they have not informed them properly, have not restrained them from returning too early, have not motivated them adequately, or have not taken their complaints seriously.

Physicians may be responsible if their diagnosis of the injury is incorrect or incomplete or if their recommended treatment is inappropriate or insufficient. Or, if all their procedures are indeed correct they still may fail to communicate adequately with the athlete, coach, and trainer.

The athlete most apt to be injured is one who has already suffered an injury.

Experience shows that the athlete most apt to be injured is one who has already suffered an injury. Working with these athletes to prevent another injury or a reinjury can be one of the most productive areas of injury prevention because physicians are able to focus their attention on a group of athletes who are vulnerable but who should also be conscious of the necessity to cooperate in measures to prevent injury.

ANNOTATED BIBLIOGRAPHY

American Medical Association. Committee on Exercise and Physical Fitness. 1967. Is your patient fit? *J. A. M. A.* 201:117-18
Describes two simple methods for a rough evaluation of physical fitness. The first is a step test from which a recovery index is developed. The second is a continuous walk-run for 10 minutes with observation during and after.

Larson, L. A., editor. 1974. *Fitness, health, and work capacity: International standards for assessment.* New York: The Macmillan Company.
Offers methods for the complete evaluation of physical fitness including a description of basic exercise physiology, physical examination, estimation of body composition, standard assessment methods for all human performance factors, work capacity, and physical fitness measurements.

6 Environmental and Occupational Hazards

Barry S. Levy

Dr. Levy received his M.D. from Cornell University Medical College, and M.P.H. from the Harvard School of Public Health, and is on the faculty of the Department of Family and Community Medicine of the University of Massachusetts Medical School. He is an active teacher, consultant, and researcher in the area of occupational and environmental diseases.

David H. Wegman

Dr. Wegman is a graduate of Harvard Medical School, received an M.S. in Occupational Health at the Harvard School of Public Health, and served in the Massachusetts Division of Occupational Hygiene prior to his joining the Harvard School of Public Health faculty. He is currently director of the Occupational Health Program at Harvard, has served on numerous expert committees, and has published widely in the field of occupational and environmental health.

Brief Contents

Overview

Occupational diseases are—always in theory and usually in practice—preventable. This chapter will guide primary care physicians in the recognition of environmentally related disease; it will provide clues for obtaining an appropriate occupational history, and present recommendations for effective intervention.

ROLE OF PRIMARY CARE PHYSICIANS

The primary care physicians' role in relation to the recognition, management, and prevention of work-related diseases will be the major focus of this chapter. Further issues of concern—hazards in the general environment—will be covered more briefly.

Primary care physicians' responsibilities.

In general, primary care physicians' responsibilities are:

1. *Recognition, Diagnosis, and Management.* To detect cases of environmentally related disease, and for each case to take appropriate historical information to identify possibly related environmental factors, make the correct diagnosis, and treat the individual appropriately.
2. *Prevention.* To take appropriate measures to prevent recurrent episodes of environmentally related disease in a given patient; to derive information from individual patients and report it to appropriate government agencies or research groups; to institute measures of primary and secondary prevention among one's own patients; and to assist others in performing preventive activities.
3. *Education.* To inform individual patients and other health professionals as well as the general public about health hazards in the environment; and to serve as a resource for labor and management, community organizations, government, and other groups and individuals.
4. *Research.* To perform and cooperate with others in performing research to better understand the relationship between environmental hazards and human disease, and methods of preventing such disease.

5. *Advocacy.* To serve as a knowledgeable advocate for human health in the face of a variety of environmental hazards.

Physicians must be sensitive to environmentally related problems and willing to act in an ethical and responsible manner after identifying such problems. They must try to keep current about environmentally related diseases—their recognition, diagnosis, management, and prevention; about specific environmental (including occupational) hazards in the community; and about medical, legal, government, and other resources available to assist in dealing with these problems. It is crucial for primary care physicians to have a good understanding of the work and the workplace of patients, and of the environmental hazards in the local community.

OCCUPATIONAL HISTORY

Primary care physicians currently see in their practice more illness related to the work place than to the general environment.

The detection—and prevention—of occupational disease depends almost entirely on the occupational history.

Primary care physicians currently see in their practice more illness related to the workplace than to the general environment. They therefore need to know how to take a complete occupational history as well as when it is most important to take one. The detection—and eventual prevention—of occupational disease depends almost entirely on the occupational history. For those patients in whom the physician does not suspect an occupational disease, a brief statement concerning current job title, job tasks, and employer may be sufficient. But as the physician's suspicion increases that a problem may be work related, the degree of detail of the occupational history increases.

A complete occupational history includes five parts:

A complete occupational history is a crucial diagnostic tool for the primary care physician.

1. *Descriptions of all jobs* since completing education, including summer and part-time jobs. It is important to go beyond the job title of the individual: the physician should have a clear idea of exactly what the patient does at work. Sometimes it is useful to have the patient "walk through" a typical workday and detail certain work tasks. On a separate line the physician should record information for each job in which the patient has worked, including when the job began and ended, type of workplace, geographic location, and work tasks including unusual and overtime tasks that may be the most hazardous. It is important not to overlook "second" jobs and past service in the military.
2. *Exposures at work*, including biologic, chemical, and physical exposures and psychologic stress currently and in the past. These should include routine exposures as well as unusual

The worker may not know the name of a particular workplace substance, but this information can sometimes be obtained from the employer.

exposures such as leaks or spills of hazardous materials. Often a workplace substance is known to workers only by brand name, a slang term, or coded number. But physicians can sometimes obtain a list of its ingredients from the employer or the manufacturer of the substance. They should have patients quantitate the degree of exposure as accurately as possible. Physicians should also question patients concerning their use of personal protective equipment such as gloves, work clothes, masks, and respirators; their perception of the effectiveness of any protective engineering systems and devices in the work place (for example, ventilation systems); and their personal habits such as eating in work areas, which may increase bodily exposure to certain substances.

3. *Timing of symptoms* is often crucial in determining whether or not medical problems are work related. Physicians should ascertain when the symptoms begin and end and if they are related to certain routine work exposures or processes, to new exposures or processes, or to certain times of the workday or weekends or vacation periods. Physicians should determine whether or not the timing and "incubation period" of the individual's symptoms are compatible with what is known about the disease in question.
4. *Epidemiology of symptoms/illness among other workers* is useful information. Physicians should question patients about other employees at the same workplace or in similar jobs elsewhere who have the same symptoms/illness. Physicians should also ask workers to describe other things they have in common with these affected individuals.
5. *Nonwork exposure and other factors* should be considered, including smoking, alcohol or drug use, and hobbies or other nonwork activities. Questioning here should be similar to that in part 2 of the suggested history, and should include current and past exposures.

Two other types of questions are often useful: (a) Does the employer have information from preplacement and periodic examinations—such as pulmonary function and audiometry testing results or environmental measurements such as dust or noise levels—that may be helpful in making the diagnosis and determining whether or not it is work related? (b) Does the patient believe that the symptom or illness is work related?

WHEN TO TAKE A COMPLETE OCCUPATIONAL HISTORY

Since it is impossible for busy clinicians to take complete occupational histories on all patients, it is important to know when it is most useful to do so. In the following situations there should be a strong suspicion that occupational factors are having an influence, and a complete occupational history should be taken.

A complete occupational history should be taken for many respiratory disorders.

1. *Respiratory disease.* Almost any respiratory symptom can be work related. Cigarette smoking and respiratory viruses are much too often implicated as the only agents responsible for cases of respiratory disease. Adult-onset asthma is often work related, as is preexisting asthma with exacerbations as a result of exposure at the workplace. Pulmonary edema can be caused by chemicals at the workplace (for example, oxides of nitrogen from welding). This particular syndrome is difficult for patients to associate with work because onset is typically 12-18 hours after exposure, often awakening the worker from sleep.

About 90% of work-related skin disease consists of contact dermatitis.

2. *Skin disorders.* About 90% of work-related skin disease consists of contact dermatitis. Since its lesions are not pathognomonic in appearance, identification of the causative agent and determination of the work relatedness of the problem depend heavily on the occupational history.

Typically a hearing loss of around 4000 Hz occurs first in hearing impairment.

3. *Hearing impairment.* A hearing impairment is often overlooked since the patient will usually not complain of symptoms until the impairment is severe—and irreversible. Typically a hearing loss of around 4000 Hz (cycles per sec) occurs first in work-related hearing impairment.
4. *Back and joint symptoms.* Other than the work history, no tests or procedures differentiate occupational from nonoccupational problems. Many cases, of course, represent a combination of occupational and nonoccupational causes. Here physicians can evaluate the risks, which include lifting while twisting and regularly lifting more than 50 pounds.

A carcinogen has sometimes first been suspected after a clinician's report of an unusual number of rare tumors.

5. *Cancer.* The first suspicion that a substance may be carcinogenic has sometimes come from clinicians' reports based on their taking complete occupational histories and discovering unusual numbers of rare tumors or unusually young persons with common tumors.
6. *Exacerbation of coronary artery disease symptoms.* These may be due to stress, carbon monoxide, or other workplace factors. This needs a good clue from the history that the workplace is likely to cause of exacerbate the symptoms.

There are several well-documented hepatotoxins in the workplace.

7. *Liver disease.* Without a good occupational history it is all too easy to attribute hepatic disease to alcohol or hepatitis B virus. There are several well-documented hepatotoxins in the work-

place, including carbon tetrachloride, dinitrophenol, dinitrobenzene, and dioxan.

Over 100 chemicals, including virtually all solvents, can cause central nervous system depression.

8. *Neuropsychiatric problems.* Here too it is easy to ignore possible occupational factors when diabetes, alcohol abuse, and other causes may appear possible. Over 100 chemicals, including virtually all solvents, can cause central nervous system depression. Neurotoxins, including arsenic and lead compounds, mercury, n-hexane, and methyl butyl ketone (MBK), can cause peripheral neuropathy. Some neurotoxins such as mercury can produce behavioral abnormalities that can easily be misdiagnosed as psychoses or personality disorders.
9. *Any illness of unknown cause.*
10. *Ability to work.* A fairly complete occupational history is also useful in determining future work possibilities for patients recuperating from disorders such as acute myocardial infarction, and in assessing the potential impact of a patient's nonoccupational disease on the ability to work.

Every medical record routinely should contain the two occupations held longest.

Despite the vast array of modern technology available to the clinician today, the suspicion that a medical problem is work related and the determination that it is in fact work related depends almost entirely on the occupational history. For this reason it is advised that every medical record should contain routinely the two occupations held longest, when each was started and stopped, and especially the particular duties involved in each job.

PREVENTING OCCUPATIONAL DISEASE

Occupational diseases are, always in theory and usually in practice, preventable. There are several generic approaches to the prevention and control of occupational disease. Some approaches affect primarily the workplace: changing work practices; installation of engineering controls and devices; and substitution of a hazardous substance with a nonhazardous one. Others affect primarily the worker: education and advice concerning work hazards; use of personal protective equipment; and screening for early detection and management of disease.

Primary care physicians can play an active role in the set of prevention activities that involves the worker. They can inform workers about the health hazards of various exposures at the work place and ways of minimizing those exposures. Physicians can advise patients on the hazards of smoking in the work place or the feasibility of, and problems with using a respirator, or they can direct patients to a lawyer if legal issues such as workers' compensation are involved. Physicians can screen individual workers for certain diseases for which they may be at high risk, or they can advise the workers' employers to do so.

If the physician suspects a possible work-related illness there are several ways to work toward its prevention.

Much of the role of physicians in preventing occupational disease depends on what they do with the information on a possibly work-related case. There are several options for using this information to contribute to the prevention and control of a work-related disease. including:

1. *Inform the appropriate government regulatory agency.* The Federal Occupational Safety and Health Administration (OSHA) establishes and enforces standards for hazardous exposures in the work place; it inspects work places routinely and in response to complaints from workers, physicians, and others. In some states the program is implemented directly by OSHA, which is in the United States Department of Labor; in others the state department of labor or another state agency implements the program. If an occupational disease is serious or might be affecting other workers, it is prudent for the physician and/or the worker to enter a complaint with OSHA or the appropriate state agency. The law includes antidiscrimination measures that protect workers from jeopardizing their jobs when filing a complaint. It should also be noted that the Mine Safety and Health Administration (MSHA) is the regulatory agency for miners.

Contacting the patient's employer can be useful as an adjunctive measure to learn more about the patient's exposures.

2. *Contact the patient's employer.* Physicians may choose to report the problem to the patient's employer, without identifying the patient by name or in any other way. If the employer is sensitive to the workers' health and safety and if the employer has the staff to deal with the problem, this may be the more appropriate and more direct way of translating the diagnosis of a work-related case into preventive action. However, many employers in the United States do not meet these two criteria. Contacting the patient's employer nevertheless can be useful as an adjunctive measure to learn more about the patient's exposures and if other workers may be suffering from the same problem. In some cases the informing physician may be asked by the company to investigate the problem further and to advise the company about how to correct it.

NIOSH has two special sections that can address new problem areas.

3. *Contact an appropriate informational or research group.* Physicians may choose to inform the National Institute for Occupational Safety and Health (NIOSH), an appropriate state agency, a medical school or school of public health, or some other group with expertise, experience, and interest in researching a possibly work-related problem. NIOSH has two special sections that can address new problem areas: the first

is the Industry-wide Studies Branch, focusing on the most common and most hazardous types of employment; the second is the Hazard Evaluation and Technical Assistance Branch, designed to respond to worker complaints of possibly serious occupational health or safety hazards. Occasionally the reporting physician may choose to undertake or assist in a research project growing out of the recognition of a case of work-related disease.

Primary care practitioners can also play an active role in approaching disease prevention by focusing on the workplace. Many physicians are asked to advise, consult, or directly service an industry on a part-time basis to provide occupational health services. Traditionally this focuses on preplacement physical examinations, return to work evaluations, and workers' compensation reviews. Physicians, however, can and should do much more.

1. They should visit the plant to obtain sufficient information through direct observation and review its records to understand specific health and safety hazards.
2. They can establish an early detection and routine surveillance program to identify population trends in illness before individual illnesses occur.
3. They can give advice on the introduction of new materials or processes to anticipate and prevent, where possible, the development of new risks. They can inaugurate a total record review system so that past, present, and future medical screening and medical evaluation results will be used to their maximum for both individual and epidemiologic review of potential problems.
4. They can develop a cooperative working relationship with occupational nurses, safety specialists, industrial hygienists, and personnel managers to make certain that the best interests of workers' health are always paramount. If the other essential occupational health professionals are not employed by the company, physicians should identify such individuals in the community so they can be consulted when necessary.

CATEGORIES OF OCCUPATIONAL DISEASE

In this section are descriptions of the major occupational diseases and some examples of each. Given the limited amount of space in this chapter, some of these descriptions are superficial and do not include details concerning the spectrum of each of these diseases, which range from mild or even asymptomatic to severe and sometimes fatal cases (Table 6-1). Extensive lists or indexes describing the major hazardous exposures and work-related diseases for

Table 6-1

Table 6-1 Selected Common Toxins in the Workplace—by Use and Toxicology.

Toxin	Use	Toxicology: Specific Signs and Symptoms
A. METALS:		
Inorganic lead	Storage batteries, paint, ink, ceramics, ammunition, secondary lead smelters, lead foundries	GI disturbances (abdominal discomfort, constipation, weight loss), hypochromic/normocytic anemia, neuromuscular dysfunction (motor weakness, especially wrist and ankle extensors), encephalopathy, nephropathy, reproductive effects
Mercury	Electric apparatus, industrial control instruments, agricultural and industrial poisons, catalyst, antifouling paint	(Acute) severe respiratory irritation (cough, chest pain, dyspnea, bronchitis, pneumonitis); (chronic) tremor, psychic disturbances (insomnia, irritability), renal damage (with proteinuria), eye and skin irritation, stomatitis, muscle weakness
Cadmium (dust and fume)	Electroplating, solder for aluminum, constituent of easily fusible alloys, deoxidizer in nickel plating, process engraving, in cadmium-nickel batteries	Pulmonary irritation (cough, dyspnea, sense of constriction of chest, chest pain, occ. pulmonary edema), rhinitis, damage to olfactory nerve with anosmia, renal tubular damage (with proteinuria), and occasionally emphysema (with chronic exposure)
Beryllium	Hardening agent in alloys	Acute pneumonitis and chronic pulmonary granulomatosis. Also, conjunctivitis, nasopharyngitis, tracheobronchitis, hepatomegaly, contact dermatitis, skin ulcers, and granulomata in multiple organs.
B. CARBON COMPOUNDS:		
Benzene	Intermediate in organic chemical production; manufacture of detergents, pesticides, solvents, paint removers; research chemistry laboratories; additive in unleaded gasoline	(Acute) central nervous system depression (Chronic) depression of the hematopoietic system, aplastic anemia, and leukemia; also dry, scaly dermatitis
Toluene (industrial-grade toluene can be contaminated by benzene)	Manufacture of benzene and other chemicals, solvent for paints and coatings, component of gasoline	(Acute) central nervous system depression (Chronic) drying and fissuring of skin and dermatitis
Methyl bromide	Fumigant, methylating agent, fire extinguishing agent, in ionization chambers, degreasing wool, extracting oils	Neurotoxicity (including convulsions), pulmonary edema (with very high concentrations), peripheral neuropathy (with chronic exposure), eye irritation and conjunctivitis, and dry, scaly dermatitis
Trichloroethylene	Degreasing solvent, drycleaning, chemical intermediate	Central nervous system depression, mild respiratory tract irritation, injury to the cardiovascular system, gastrointestinal system, liver, and kidney

Table 6-1 Continued

Toxin	Uses	Toxicology: Specific Signs and Symptoms
Carbon disulfide	Solvent, insecticide, in preparation of viscose rayon fibers	Damage to central and peripheral nervous systems; may accelerate development of or worsen coronary heart disease; skin and eye irritation; possibly menstrual abnormalities; excessive rate of suicide in high exposures
Acrylonitrile	Manufacture of acrylic fibers, chemical intermediate, organic synthesis, pesticide fumigant	Metabolic asphyxiant; vapor causes severe eye irritation; possibly accounts for increased incidence of lung and colon cancer (recently shown to be an animal carcinogen)
C. ASPHYXIANTS:		
Carbon monoxide	Byproduct of incomplete combustion	Headache, dizziness, unconsciousness, and death. Also exacerbation of underlying coronary artery disease
Hydrogen sulfide	Byproduct of many industrial processes; around oil wells and in areas where petroleum products are processed, stored, or used; decay of organic matter	Low concentrations are irritating to the eyes and the respiratory tract; high concentrations can cause respiratory paralysis with consequent asphyxia
Hydrogen cyanide	Fumigant; and chemical intermediate for the manufacture of synthetic fibers, plastics, and nitrites. Also generates in electroplating.	Headache, vomiting, rapid weak breathing, tachycardia, hypotension, excitability, convulsions, and coma; pulmonary edema and lactic acidosis may occur

Source: Proctor, N. H., and Hughes, J. P. 1978. *Chemical hazards of the workplace.* Philadelphia: J. B. Lippincott Company.

specific types of work can be found in Key et al. (1977) and Stellman and Daum (1973). One of our objectives in presenting this chapter is to enable physicians to recognize occupational diseases at an early stage, at which time medical intervention is more likely to make a difference in the course of these diseases. Such intervention, of course, should include attention not only to occupational exposures but also to nonoccupational exposures (such as smoking) to prevent the individual from developing a disability associated with work.

Effects of Toxins

Toxic effects of substances in the workplace are among the most common occupational diseases, although the lack of occupational

Toxic effects of substances in the workplace are among the most common occupational diseases.

Table 6-2

histories often leads to their not being diagnosed. Toxic effects occur in many organ systems and tissues; some of these are summarized in Table 6-1 and 6-2. Useful sources of information include toxicology textbooks and poison information centers.

The hazard of a work-place substance is determined by many factors including (a) its toxicity, or inherent ability to cause injury to biologic tissue; (b) its absorption, distribution, metabolism, and excretion; (c) the speed with which it acts; (d) its warning properties; (e) its physical characteristics; and (f) how it will be encountered in the work place.

Inhalation is the most common route of entry for toxins.

Inhalation is the most common route of entry for toxins followed by skin absorption and, far less frequently, ingestion. Water solubility and particle size are two factors that determine how much of an inhaled toxin is absorbed through the lungs and degree of skin abrasion and inflammation determine how much of a toxin is absorbed through the skin.

Table 6-2 Selected Toxic Gases and Fumes in the Workplace and Their Effect

Toxic Gas or Fume	Effect
Carbon dioxide, nitrogen, methane	Asphyxia
Carbon monoxide, cyanide	Chemical asphyxiation
Acrylonitrile, hydrogen sulfide	Chemical asphyxiation, neurotoxicity
Ammonia	Acute laryngotracheitis, bronchitis
Chlorine	Inflammation entire respiratory tract, pulmonary edema
Nitrogen dioxide	Tracheobronchitis, obliterating bronchiolitis
Ozone, sulfur dioxide, hydrogen fluoride, osmium tetroxide	Acute bronchial irritation, probable chronic obstructive effects
Phosgene	Pulmonary edema, hypovolemia
Vanadium pentoxide	Acute bronchitis, pneumonitis
Mercury, chromates, zinc chloride	Tracheobronchitis and other effects
Manganese	Pneumonitis, neurotoxicity
Cadmium oxide	Acute tracheobronchitis, pulmonary edema, emphysema

Source: Morgan, W. K. C., and Seaton, A. 1975. *Occupational lung diseases.* Philadelphia; W. B. Saunders Company.

Dose-response relationships of toxins, usually determined from animal studies, help in gauging human response including determining the range between no-effect and lethal doses (margin of safety). Chronic toxicity usually cannot be predicted from acute manifestations. After suspecting a toxic effect from the history or physical examination, physicians can usually confirm the diagnosis through laboratory tests, which measure either the toxin or its metabolite in blood, urine, or another body fluid, or its effects, especially if they are specific.

There are two major standard-setting processes to help prevent toxic effects. OSHA and MSHA promulgate and enforce standards (permissible exposure limits) for some substances. The American Conference of Governmental Industrial Hygienists (ACGIH) recommends threshold limit values (TLVs) for many substances,* which are meant as practical guidelines, not fine lines between safe and dangerous levels.

Respiratory Diseases

The most important factors determining presence, location, and severity of work-related respiratory disease are discussed.

This segment will cover the major categories of occupational respiratory disease and give some brief examples. The most important factors determining the presence, location, and severity of work-related respiratory disease include (a) for dusts and aerosols the size of the inhaled particles, with those 5-15 μ being deposited in the trachea or bronchi, and those 1-5 μ in the alveoli; (b) the water solubility of toxic gases and fumes, with the very soluble ones such as ammonia being absorbed in and affecting the upper respiratory tract, and the relatively insoluble ones such as nitrogen oxides being absorbed in and affecting the entire respiratory tree; (c) antigenic quality of the particles inhaled; (d) immunologic status of the individual; and (e) underlying respiratory disease due to nonoccupational factors such as smoking.

Table 6-3

Pneumoconioses As shown in Table 6-3, there are several different agents that can cause these inorganic dust diseases, which have varying pathology and types of respiratory impairment. Asbestosis will be used as an example. Insulators, miners of asbestos, manufacturers of asbestos products, construction workers, and auto repair workers have a great deal of exposure. About 4.5 million American shipyard workers were exposed to asbestos during World War II. About 1 million auto repair workers are now exposed to asbestos in brake and clutch linings. The first symptom of asbes-

---

*Can be obtained from ACGIH, 6500 Glenway Avenue, Building D-5, Cincinnati, Ohio 45201.

Table 6-3 Selected Pneumoconioses—By Agent, Pathology, and Impairment.

Agent	Type of Pathology	Type of Respiratory Impairment
Silica:		
Simple	Nodular fibrosis	Restrictive, diffusion
Complicated	Conglomerate nodular fibrosis	Restrictive, obstructive, diffusion
Coal:		
Simple	Peribronchiolar macules, focal emphysema	Obstructive (small airways)
Complicated	Conglomerate nodular fibrosis	Obstructive, restrictive, diffusion
Asbestos	Interstitial fibrosis	Restrictive, diffusion
Beryllium	Interstitial fibrosis (granulomata)	Restrictive, diffusion

Source: Morgan, W. K. C., and Lapp, N. L. Diseases of the airways and lungs. 1977. In *Occupational diseases: A guide to their recognition,* ed. M. M. Key, A. F. Henschel, J. Butler, et al., p. 119. Washington, D.C.: National Institute for Occupational Safety and Health.

Although cessation of exposure is recommended for those with evidence of asbestosis, the disease progresses after asbestos exposure has ceased.

tosis generally is dyspnea on exertion, usually with a dry cough; and the earliest sign is bibasilar end inspiratory crackles (although this occurs in only 20% of cases). By the time these are present, however, significant pulmonary fibrosis has probably been present for several years. Although cessation of exposure is recommended for those with evidence of asbestosis, the disease progresses after asbestos exposure has ceased. Eventually weight loss and debilitation, cor pulmonale, and increased susceptibility to respiratory infections occur. X-ray features include opacities, which are more profuse in the lower lungs and initially consist of linear shadows 1-3 mm thick; these increase in number with progression of the disease, and gradually obscure the border of the heart, the diaphragm, and the vascular pattern (Figure 6-1). Eventually lung volume is reduced, and the heart and proximal pulmonary arteries enlarge. Pleural thickening and calcification, which indicate asbestos exposure and not necessarily disease, are often present (Figure 6-2). Pulmonary function tests include decreased vital capacity, total lung capacity, diffusing capacity, and eventually reduced pO_2. Primary prevention consists of substitution of nonhazardous material for asbestos wherever possible, control of asbestos dust in the workplace, and, only as a temporary measure, use of personal

Figure 6-1

Figure 6-2

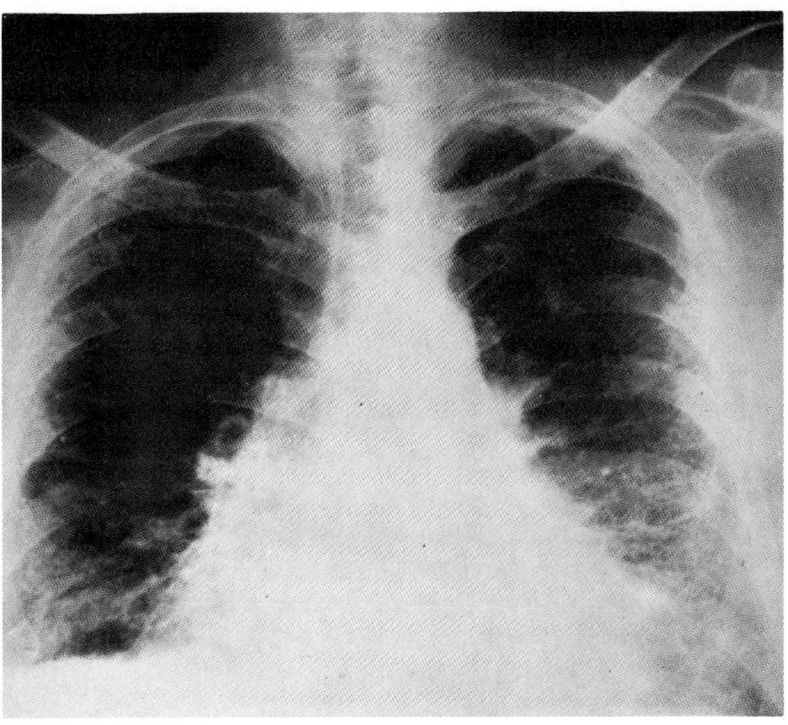

Figure 6-1 Final stages of asbestosis in a shipyard worker. Both lungs show diffuse fibrotic change, obscuring cardiac border. The heart is dilated; clinically this patient was in cardiac failure. (Source: Morgan, W. K. C. and Seaton, A. 1975. *Occupational lung diseases.* Philadelphia: W. B. Saunders Company).

protective equipment including NIOSH-approved masks and respirators. Secondary prevention, by regularly screening workers with pulmonary function tests and chest films and performing additional evaluation on those with abnormal results, is recommended, although these may fail to detect disease early. In addition to causing asbestosis, asbestos also contributes to the death of almost half of heavily exposed asbestos workers by causing lung and gastrointestinal cancer, pleural and peritoneal mesotheliomas, and other malignancies.

Asbestos also contributes to the death of almost half of heavily exposed asbestos workers.

Occupational Asthma In adults, new onset of asthma or exacerbation of previously quiescent asthmatic symptoms should raise suspicion of occupationally related asthma. Once again, work history is crucial in making this diagnosis. Symptoms are usually most severe at work and improve during nonwork hours

Asthma first appearing in an adult should make one suspect occupationally related disease.

including weekends and particularly vacation periods. Wheezing, dyspnea, and often rhinitis are present; cough and sputum production can also occur. A challenge test (done under controlled conditions in a hospital setting) by exposing the worker to the suspect allergen and measuring the timed vital capacity or peak flow rate may be necessary to confirm the responsible agent. Examples of high-risk workers are those exposed to grain dust, wood (especially Western red cedar) dust, enzymatic detergents, the flux often used in soldering aluminum, isocyanates including toluene diisocyanate (TDI), which is used in making polyurethane foam, and platinum salts. Management is identical to that of nonoccupational asthma with the important addition of reducing exposure to the etiologic agent in the work place.

Workers exposed to grain dust, wood dust, enzymatic detergents, and certain other chemicals are at high risk of developing occupational asthma.

Extrinsic allergic alveolitis In addition to asthma, inhalation of organic particles at work can lead to this condition, which affects

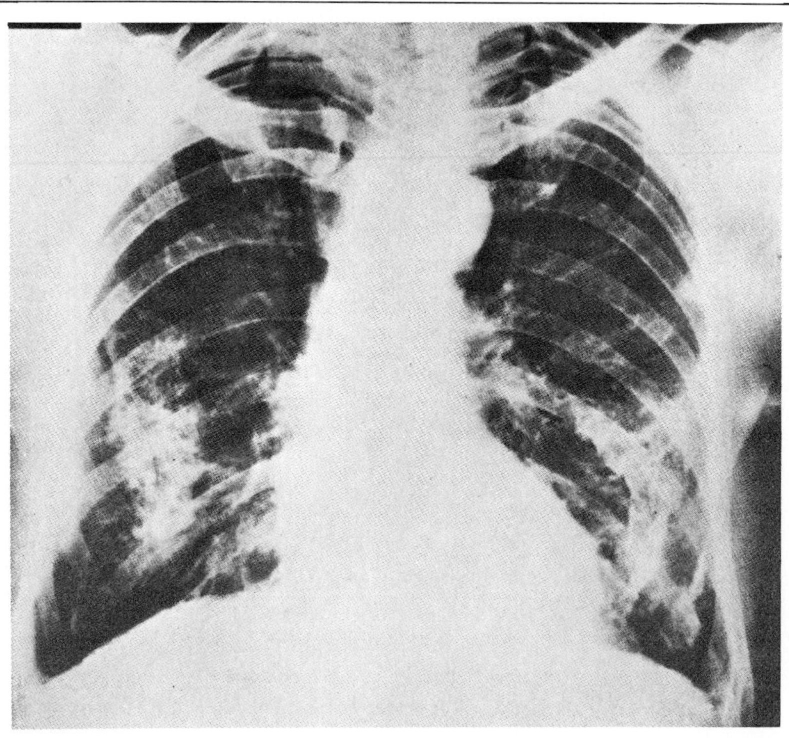

Figure 6-2 Bilateral pleural calcification as a result of asbestos exposure. (Source: Selikoff, I. J. and Lee, D. H. K. 1978. *Asbestos and disease.* New York: Academic Press Inc).

Table 6-4

the terminal air passages and lung parenchyma. Many inhaled allergens (Table 6-4), mostly fungal spores, can cause this syndrome. Fatigue, fever, chills, cough, and dyspnea occur usually within 4-8 hours after exposure to the allergen. Basilar inspiratory crackles are present on examination. The disease can be progressively severe and disabling.*

Byssinosis may be reversible in its very early stages.

Byssinosis Cotton, flax, and hemp workers develop this disease characterized initially by chest tightness on Monday (or day of return to work), and then by chest tightness, cough, and dyspnea persisting further into the work week. It is believed to be reversible in its very early stages if detected at that time by a history of typical early symptoms and evidence of decreased ventilatory capacity between the start and end of the first shift back to work. If it is allowed to progress, the end stage is believed to be severe obstructive disease and possibly emphysema.

Toxic gases and fumes As indicated in Table 6-2, there is a variety of gases and fumes (fine solid particulates) that can have irritant, asphyxiant, and other toxic effects. Those with high water solubility cause rapid onset of cough and tearing. They are generally so

Table 6-4 Selected Causes of Extrinsic Allergic Alveolitis—By Source and Precipitant Employed

Clinical Condition	Source of Offending Agent	Precipitant Employed
Farmer's lung	Moldy hay	*Micropolyspora faeni* *Thermoactinomyces vulgaris*
Bagassosis	Moldy bagasse	*Thermoactinomyces vulgaris*
Mushroom worker's lung	Mushroom compost	*Micropolyspora faeni* *Thermoactinomyces vulgaris*
Suberosis	Corkdust	Cork dust
Maple bark disease	Maple bark	*Cryptostroma corticale*
Sequoiosis	Redwood sawdust	Graphium *Aureobasidium pullulans*
Wood pulp worker's disease	Wood pulp	*Alternaria* species
Malt worker's lung	Moldy barley	*Aspergillus clavatus* *Aspergillus fumigatus*

Source: Morgan; W. K. C., and Seaton, A. 1975. *Occupational lung diseases.* Philadelphia: W. B. Saunders Company.

*This disease is also known as hypersensitivity pneumonitis.

irritating that workers will remove themselves unless trapped. For those with low solubility in water the effects may not occur until hours after exposure (as with phosgene, which causes pulmonary edema). Metal fume fever ("Monday morning fever") is due to inhalation of certain freshly generated metal fumes such as copper, brass, and zinc. Welders are at particular risk. Symptoms include thirst, a metallic taste, fever, and shaking chills. Polymer fume fever, a similar condition, occurs among workers (especially smokers) who are exposed to the polymer polytetrafluorethylene (Teflon).

Pulmonary malignancies These are briefly covered in the section on cancer later in this chapter.

Infectious diseases of the respiratory tract These are also briefly covered later in this chapter, in the section on infectious diseases.

Trauma, Back Injury, and Other Musculoskeletal Problems

It is estimated that there are approximately 20 million work-related injuries in the United States each year.

It is estimated that there are approximately 20 million work-related injuries in the United States each year. These range from minor abrasions, lacerations, and contusions to serious fractures, crush injuries, and amputations. Approximately 5000 work-related deaths, most due to injuries as opposed to diseases, are reported to the Bureau of Labor Statistics annually, and there are at least twice as many that are not reported. Injury rates are high in construction, manufacturing, mining, and agriculture; within manufacturing they are high in the lumber, metal, food, rubber, and plastic products industries. Many, if not most, of these injuries are preventable through better design of equipment and work tasks, development and use of safety equipment, education of workers and management, and particularly a reasonable pace of work. Important roles of primary care physicians include obtaining and recording accurately detailed information on the circumstances of the injury for medicolegal purposes, reviewing cases of occupational injuries to detect clusters or unusual trends, and reporting serious injuries and such clusters or trends to the appropriate government agencies.

Back problems are the leading work-related cause of time lost from work.

Work-related back problems are extremely common. They represent the leading category of workers' compensation payments, and the leading work-related cause of time lost from work. About half of all back injuries occur at work. Most affect the lower back. Work-related low back pain is usually intermittent. Most back injuries are nonserious strains that will heal within 1-2 weeks with conservative treatment (avoidance of physical stress, bed rest, physical therapy, low back exercises, and appropriate use of analgesics and muscle relaxants). Physicians should instruct the workers in lifting objects properly and, if necessary, advise them to change jobs. Back pain occurs most frequently among workers in their late 30s or 40s, and is most frequent among those who do hard physical work or sit for prolonged periods. There is much disagreement on the cause of back pain; muscle strain and intervertebral disc degeneration are two of the more accepted theories of causation.

It is usually difficult to determine whether or not a back problem is work related.

It is usually difficult to determine whether or not a back problem is work related; the determination of work relatedness often depends largely, if not entirely, on the patient's work history in conjunction with development of signs and symptoms. Complicating the problem is the great individual variability in tolerating physical stress.

Objects weighing more than 50 pounds, as a rule, should be lifted by machine.

Prevention of low back pain has been attempted through several approaches including physical fitness, job design, selection, and instruction. Regarding job design, objects weighing more than 50 pounds, as a rule, should be lifted by machine; regarding selection of employees, strength testing is being evaluated as a preventive approach. Lumbosacral spine x-ray films have been proven to be of no value as a screening technique to identify those at risk of developing back disease.

Primary care physicians' roles also include identifying workers at risk (predominantly through a symptom review regarding the back), advising on preventive measures, and determining the work relatedness of back problems.

Another common work-related musculoskeletal problem is tenosynovitis, most often resulting from unaccustomed strenuous use of forearm muscles in repetitive twisting or turning movements. It presents with pain, swelling, tenderness, and/or loss of function.

Cancer

It is estimated that 60%-90% of all cancer is caused or at least influenced, by environmental factors.

It is estimated that 60%-90% of all cases of cancer are caused, or at least influenced, by environmental (nongenetic) factors. This estimate is based on (a) temporal trends such as the tenfold increase in lung cancer mortality among American males in the past 50 years; (b) geographic comparisons such as the significantly higher bladder cancer mortality among American males in certain counties in the United States, mainly in the Northeast; and (c) migration studies such as the dramatic increases in colon and breast cancer and the decrease in stomach cancer among native Japanese who have migrated to the United States, as compared with those who remained in Japan.

Environmental carcinogens are present in air, water, and soil; in cigarettes, certain food products, and other consumer goods; and in the workplace. Our poor understanding of cancer etiology is reflected by the range of estimates that between 1% and 40% of cancer cases in this country are work related.

Basic facts concerning environmentally related cancer include (a) a long lag period between the time of the first exposure to the time of cancer diagnosis, often 20 years or longer; (b) the absence of evidence for a safe level (threshold) of exposure, at or below which environmentally related cancer will not occur; (c) a relationship between an individual's cumulative dose of a carcinogen and the probability of developing a related malignancy; (d) the more recent documentation of more than one substance influencing the development of a specific cancer, best exemplified by the synergism of cigarette smoke and asbestos in causing lung cancer (separately they increase risk by 5-10 times, together by more than 50 times); and (e) the inability to distinguish signs, symptoms, and the clinical course of environmentally related cancers from those that are not environmentally related (only the history of exposure differs).

Approximately 160 industrial chemicals could meet the proposed criteria for proven carcinogenicity.

Table 6-5

Of the more than 63,000 chemicals in American industry, approximately 160 could conceivably meet recently adopted OSHA criteria for "proven" carcinogens.* The best documented ones are shown in Table 6-5. Three approaches used to assess the carcinogenicity of substances, in order of increasing cost and time to perform, are (a) short-term in vitro assays such as the Ames test, which detects the mutagenicity of a substance in bacteria; (b) animal tests (long-term bioassays), usually performed on large numbers of rodents under tightly controlled conditions; and (c) case-control and cohort epidemiologic studies. Each approach has its strengths and limitations. Importantly, reports from clinicians have assisted in identifying more occupational carcinogens historically than any other method.

Since there are still only few effective screening (secondary prevention) approaches to control environmentally related cancer, primary prevention is essential. This focuses on identifying carcinogens and removing them from, or minimizing their levels in, the environment. The ideal approach is substituting carcinogens with substances not known to be carcinogenic (for example, substituting fibrous glass for asbestos insulation). Local exhaust ventilation with appropriate filter traps is another standard control operation. Much less effective is having workers use personal

---

*These criteria are cancer proven in humans *or* in two separate animal studies *or* in one animal study and positive results in two short-term in vitro studies.

Table 6-5 Selected Occupational Carcinogens—By Site of Cancer and Associated Occupations.*

Site of Cancer	Carcinogens	Occupations
Lung	Arsenic Asbestos Chromium Coal products Dusts Iron oxide Mustard gas Nickel Petroleum Ionizing radiation Bischloromethyl-ether (BCME)	Vintners, miners; asbestos and textile users, insulation workers, pipe coverers, shipbuilders, tanners, smelters, glass and pottery workers, coal tar and pitch workers, iron foundry workers, electrolysis workers, retort workers, radiologists, radium dial painters, chemical workers
Nasal cavity and sinuses	Chromium Isopropyl oil Nickel Wood and leather dusts	Glass, pottery, and linoleum workers; nickel smelters, mixers, and roasters; electrolysis workers; wood, leather, and shoe workers
Bladder	Coal products Aromatic amines	Asphalt, coal tar, and pitch workers; gas stokers; still cleaners; dyestuffs users; rubber workers; textile dyers; paint manufacturers; leather and shoe workers
Skin	Arsenic Sunlight	Insecticide makers and sprayers, oil refiners, vintners, smelters, farmers
Liver	Arsenic Vinyl chloride	Tanners, smelters, vineyard workers, plastic workers
Bone marrow (leukemia)	Benzene Ionizing radiation	Benzene, explosives, and rubber workers; distillers; dye users; painters; radiologists

Source: Cole, P., and Goldman, M. B. 1975. Occupation, In *Persons at high risk of cancer*, ed. J. F. Fraumemi, Jr., pp. 167-184. New York: Academic Press, Inc.

protective equipment when there is unavoidable intense exposure (for example, wearing masks, gloves, and/or special clothing at work) or getting them to change their personal habits (for example, motivating them to stop smoking cigarettes).

In addition to being sensitive to identifying and reporting unusual clusters of cancer cases that may be environmentally related, primary care physicians have an important role in advising patients to avoid, or at least minimize, exposure to proven or suspected carcinogens.

Hearing Impairment

More than 10 million Americans have permanent hearing loss as a result of occupational exposure.

Of those chronically exposed to 90 dBA of noise 15% will suffer significant hearing impairment.

More than 10 million Americans have permanent hearing loss as a result of occupational exposure. More than 4 million workers are exposed to noise that poses a threat to hearing. In general workers in the construction, lumber, mining, textiles, electronic music, and metal industries have more loud noise exposure at work than those in other occupations. At the current OSHA standard of 90 dBA for workplace noise exposure, it is estimated that 15% of those exposed will have significant hearing impairment.

Initially, as a result of loud noise, those exposed experience a reversible hearing loss because of a temporary threshold shift. With repeated exposure to loud noise, however, this hearing loss becomes irreversible because of permanent damage to nerve cells in the cochlea. It is estimated that the maximum temporary threshold shift experienced in the 16 hours after a full workday if experienced for 10 years is the amount of permanent loss that will be experienced by that individual.

The nonauditory effects of loud noise are not fully understood, but studies indicate that such exposure can at least transiently increase serum cholesterol, blood pressure, and heart rate; cause stress, fatigue, and impaired sleep patterns; reduce work performance; and, if workers are unable to communicate adequately, create safety hazards.

Figure 6-3

Secondary prevention of hearing impairment consists of screening workers at the time of employment and subsequently on an annual or semiannual basis.

By the time a worker notices hearing impairment, significant irreversible damage affecting the sound frequencies of human conversation has already occurred. Long before this, however, there are significant changes in the audiogram—first a dip at about 4000 Hz and then a broader and deeper abnormality (Figure 6-3). Secondary prevention of hearing impairment consists of screening workers at the time of employment and subsequently on an annual or semiannual basis if they are exposed to loud noise, and removing them from such exposure as soon as any significant abnormality develops. Primary prevention consists of (a) modifying the source of the sound or its path to the ear by such measures as building barrier walls, installing acoustical tiles or sound-absorbing hoods, venting loud compressed air exhausts to the outside, and maintaining equipment in good repair; and, less desirably, (b) providing the individual worker with hearing protection (ear muffs or well-fitted ear plugs) and encouraging its use. The role of primary care physicians in preventing work-related hearing loss should focus on (a) identifying workers at high risk and assuring that they are having audiograms regularly and using protective equipment; (b) where appropriate, advising employers to take primary prevention measures; (c) as necessary, advising employees with significant

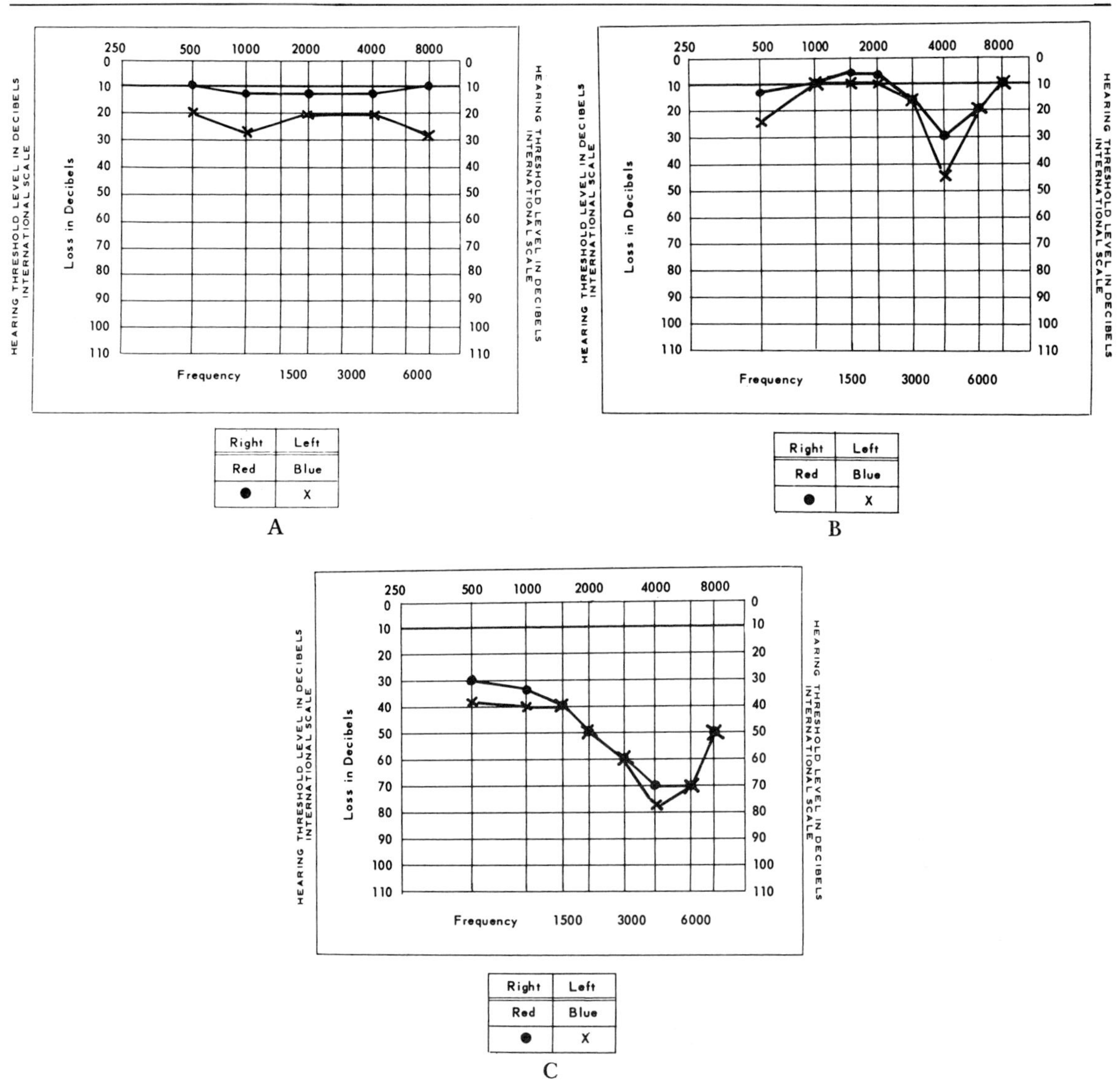

Figure 6-3 A, a typical audiogram showing hearing thresholds in the normal range. B, audiogram with notch at 4000 Hertz possibly could be early noise-induced deafness, probably asymptomatic to the worker at this stage. C, audiogram of worker after 25-30 years of exposure to extremely loud noise without hearing protection; impairment is beginning to be evident in the speech range. Reproduced with permission from Maas, R. B.: Occupational Noise Exposure and Hearing Conservation, in Zenz, C. (ed.) *Occupational Medicine: Principles & Practical Applications.* Copyright © 1975 by Year Book Medical Publishers, Inc., Chicago.

hearing loss to change their jobs if they are being exposed to loud noise at work; and (d) supporting appropriate workers' compensation claims for hearing loss.

Dermatologic Problems

The most frequently reported type of work-related disease is skin disorders.

The most frequently reported type of work-related disease is skin disorders. As examples of the many workplace chemicals that cause skin disease, automobile workers are exposed to dichromates, brake and cutting fluids, epoxy resins, gasoline, lubricants, oils, paints, plastics, polyester resins, solvents, and thinners; and clerks are exposed to adhesives, duplicating materials, inks and ink removers, solvents, type cleaners, and typewriter ribbons.

The seven main morphologic types of occupational skin disorders are:

1. Acute contact eczematous dermatitis
2. Chronic contact eczematous dermatitis
3. Folliculitis and acne
4. Pigment changes
5. Neoplasms
6. Ulcerations
7. Granulomas

The signs and symptoms of occupational skin disease are similar to those of nonoccupational skin disease, and the diagnosis rests largely on the patient's work history and the pattern of lesions in relation to exposure. Key history questions deal with the timing of symptoms in relation to exposure(s) and the presence of similar skin problems among other workers. Nonoccupational factors such as lack of personal cleanliness, preexisting nonoccupational skin disease, and excessively moist or excessively dry skin, may predispose the worker to work-related skin disease.

Figure 6-4

Contact dermatitis can be caused either by irritants or sensitizers in the workplace.

Most work-related skin disease is acute contact eczematous dermatitis, usually simply referred to as "contact dermatitis" (Figure 6-4). It is caused by (a) direct skin contact with irritants such as strong acids and alkalis, some metallic salts, simple metals, many organic compounds, and many oils; and (b) sensitizers such as nickel, mercury, and cobalt compounds, some bichromate salts, plastics, some chemicals used in rubber manufacturing, germicidal agents in soaps and cleansers, formalin, and poison ivy, oak, and sumac. Strong irritants act within a few minutes to a few hours by direct injury to the skin. Sensitizers cause an allergic reaction

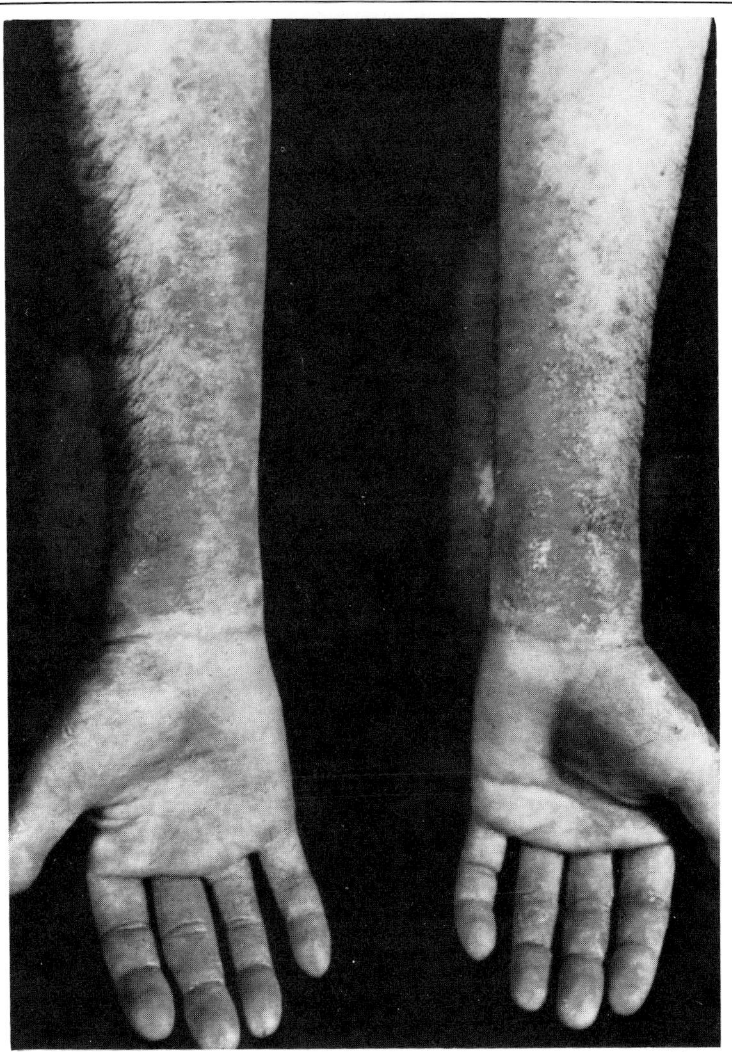

Figure 6-4 Occupational contact dermatitis. (Source: Key, M. M., Henschel, A. F.; Butler, J., et al., editors. 1977. *Occupational diseases: A guide to their recognition.* Washington, D.C.: National Institute for Occupational Safety and Health).

usually within a few days, although the first reaction may be as long as 20 days after exposure. Patch testing is sometimes used to determine which substance is responsible for allergic contact dermatitis.

Treatment consists of removing the worker from further

exposure to the suspect substance and a variety of nonspecific measures such as applying saline compresses, or in some severe, widespread cases, parenteral steroids. Most cases are preventable by enclosure of equipment and processes to prevent chemical exposures, ventilation, workplace and personal cleanliness, and gloves* and other personal protective equipment. Barrier creams are sometimes used when gloves cannot be worn. Still another preventive measure is removing those workers with certain skin diseases such as psoriasis and eczema from the jobs that involve contact with irritants or sensitizers.

Other Work-Related Medical Problems

There are many other categories of occupational disease; however, space permits only a few brief comments about some of them.

Reproductive system abnormalities Several exposures in the workplace, including metals, solvents, halogenated hydrocarbons and other pesticide ingredients, and radiation have been suspected of, or implicated in, causing such abnormalities. Specific examples include the pesticide dibromochloropropane (DBCP), which can cause irreversible sterility in males; lead, which causes abnormalities of sperm including hypospermia and congenital anomalies in experimental animals; and waste anesthetic gases in operating rooms, which may be associated with higher than expected rates of congenital anomalies among offspring of both men and women who are exposed.

Infectious diseases The most common work-related infectious disease in the United States today is viral hepatitis, type B. At high risk for this disease are clinical laboratory workers, renal dialysis unit technicians, nurses, dentists, and other medical workers—all of whom may come into direct contact with body fluids of patients likely to have acute hepatitis B or be chronic hepatitis B virus carriers. Other work-related infectious diseases include viral hepatitis, type A, anthrax, brucellosis, leptospirosis, tuberculosis and other mycobacterial infections, tularemia, and some fungal infections.

Renal disorders Examples of abnormalities include (a) decreased function (caused by such chemicals as mercury, carbon tetrachlo-

---

*Appropriate type of rubber or plastic varies considerably depending on the exposure.

ride, or glycols); (b) hematuria (caused by arsenic, cadmium, phenols, chlorobenzenes); and (c) albuminuria (caused by carbon disulfide, methyl bromide and chloride, mercury, and lead).

An occupational etiology should be considered in cases of acute or chronic liver disease.

Hepatic disorders It is tempting to diagnose almost all acute liver diseases as viral hepatitis and almost all chronic liver disease as alcoholic cirrhosis, forgetting to recognize occupational causes. Among the chemicals that may be responsible for hepatic damage are (a) metals and inorganic chemicals such as beryllium, manganese, cadmium, and antimony; and (b) organic chemicals including acrylonitrile, some alcohols, benzene, carbon tetrachloride, chloroform, phenol, toluene, trichloroethane, and trichloroethylene. In addition, exposure to vinyl chloride can cause chronic liver disease and rare malignant tumors known as hepatic angiosarcomas.

Hematologic disorders These include anemia, caused by lead, selenium, trichloroethylene, and other work exposures; leukopenia (and anemia), caused by arsenic, toluene, xylene, and glycol ethers; aplastic anemia, caused by benzene; and leukemia, caused by benzene, radiation, and perhaps certain pesticides.

ENVIRONMENTAL HEALTH— SOME AREAS OF MAJOR CONCERN

It is impossible in a chapter of this length to cover adequately the roles of primary physicians in the broad field of environmental health. Current areas of interest and concern include, among other problems, air pollution; disposal of toxic wastes; and pollution of water by toxins, carcinogens, sodium salts, and other substances. This section will focus on three hazards of great importance—lead, ionizing radiation, and pesticides. All three are present in the workplace as well as in the general environment.

Lead

One million tons of lead are produced in the United States each year. Many processes and products account for undue lead exposure in the general environment and in the workplace. Most lead in this country is used in batteries, antiknock additives for gasoline, cable covering, solder, pigments, and ammunition. Environmental exposure is primarily a problem for children who ingest chips of lead-based paint. Other environmental exposures include inhaling airborne auto emissions or house dust contaminated by lead workers' clothing; living near a lead smelter; and drinking liquids from improperly fired lead glazed containers, acidic water low in minerals from old lead pipes or illicitly distilled whiskey.

Possible industrial sources of lead exposure are discussed.

Occupational exposures include assembling new batteries and destroying and recycling the lead of old ones; demolishing ships, elevated railroads, and other metal structures; deleading homes; working at firing ranges or in motor vehicle tunnels or garages; structural steel painting and paint stripping; and plumbing.

Lead poisoning occurs by ingestion or inhalation of lead that has been heated (above 450 C), ground, or volatilized. Signs and symptoms include anorexia, metallic taste, constipation, pallor, nausea, malaise, weakness, headache, insomnia, irritability, muscle and joint pain, and tremors. An important sign is abdominal colic that can be so severe as to lead to exploratory surgery. Weakness of hand and foot extensors occurs, sometimes causing wrist or foot drop. Encephalopathy occurs with chronic exposure, usually in children.

Lead has no essential role in the human body. Its harmful effects include (a) interference with heme synthesis, leading to shortened life span of the red blood cells and anemia; (b) reproductive abnormalities including impotence and sterility in men, abnormal menstrual cycles and reduced fertility in women, and an increase in miscarriages and stillbirths in both exposed women and wives of exposed men (in animals it has been shown to be teratogenic); (c) reduced renal function; and (d) neuropsychiatric effects including encephalopathy and mental retardation. There is controversy over the effects on intelligence and behavior of children of mildly elevated lead levels: one recent well-designed study suggests that even mild elevations may lower IQs and cause nonadaptive behavior in children.

Early lead effects can be seen in tests of peripheral nerve function and tests for anemia.

Children are at increased risk because of greater exposure (pica and other hand-to-mouth activity) and more susceptibility (increased gastrointestinal (GI) absorption) to severe effects of lead. Of the 30 million American homes erected before World War II 95% have lead-based paint. One paint flake with 1% lead represents a dose of 10,000 μg of lead. The Centers for Disease Control, under the Lead-Based Paint Poisoning Prevention Act, operates a program to screen children at high risk of undue lead absorption and lead poisoning and to facilitate housing inspection and deleading.

One paint flake with 1% lead represents a dose of 10,000 μg of lead.

Lead-based house paint was banned for internal use in 1950 and external use in 1971. Such paint purchased since these dates contains only a small amount of lead (less than 0.06% by dry weight), making it very unlikely that a child would be poisoned by the lead unless an extremely large amount of it were ingested. There is one exception to be aware of: marine paint (used for boats) still contains a significant concentration of lead and is sometimes used (illegally) on the external surfaces of houses. Therefore, except for this, physicians can assure families in homes built after 1971 (unless they were painted with old paint) that the paint on and in these homes contain insignificant amounts of lead, which presents no danger to children.

Management of lead poisoning consists of stopping lead exposure for those with undue lead exposure and treating those with very high levels of lead or serious symptoms with chelating agents. Prevention consists of reducing lead in the work place and general environment, having workers with irreducibly high exposures use personal protective equipment, and screening those at high risk with (a) measurements of lead and zinc protoporphyrin in their blood, and (b) tests to assess the specific pathologic effects.

Ionizing Radiation

In recent years increased use of x-rays and radionuclides in medicine, research, and industry; nuclear power production; and nuclear weapons manufacture have increased exposures to ionizing radiation. The nuclear fuel cycle alone raises critical medical and sociopolitical issues concerning accidents at nuclear power plants, disposal of nuclear wastes, and proliferation of nuclear weapons. These, however, are beyond the scope of this chapter.

Deleterious health effects from ionizing radiation are determined by the type and energy of radiation, tissue penetration and distribution, and tissue half-life. Exposure to very high doses of ionizing radiation (more than 500 rads) in a short period can cause severe tissue destruction and rapid death. Exposure to approximately 100-500 rads can cause acute radiation syndrome with initial gastrointestinal symptoms and weakness, followed by fever, hemorrhagic lesions, hair loss, ulcers, bone marrow depression, susceptibility to infection, and death. But such exposures are rare. More common is exposure to lower levels of ionizing radiation, which can cause radiodermatitis, carcinoma and leukemia, cataracts, defects in the exposed fetus, gene mutations, sterility, and nonspecific life span shortening.

Occupational exposures to ionizing radiation are usually a result of inhaling radionuclide gases or particulates.

Occupational risks are usually due to inhalation of radionuclide gases or particulates. High-risk workers include those employed in nuclear power plants and in nuclear weapons production, users and makers of electron microscopes and high-voltage vacuum tubes, some military personnel, some physicians and nurses, x-ray technicians, and hard rock miners, in particular uranium miners.

Prevention is accomplished through minimizing exposure. To monitor radiation exposure there are a number of available methods: measuring external exposure by the use of film badges, screening with regular hemograms, and determining radioactive elements in the blood, urine, feces, and expired air of exposed people. The role of primary care physicians includes facilitating these preventive approaches, including avoiding unnecessary exposure to x-rays, and educating patients and the community about the dangers of these exposures.

Pesticides

Almost 2 billion pounds are produced in the United States each year. Most are chemicals used to kill weeds and insects; others are used to kill rats, molluscs, fungi, and worms. Their varied acute toxic effects and potential for carcinogenesis, mutagenesis, and teratogenesis pose substantial risks for exposed workers as well as the general public. Many pesticides accumulate in body fat and the liver, creating potential long-term health effects.

At highest risk of pesticide-related illness are the people who manufacture and apply the pesticides.

Most pesticides are readily absorbed through the skin, posing great risks for those in direct contact with them. At highest risk in this country are the almost 400,000 people employed in the manufacture and formulation of pesticides and the 100,000 commercial and 2 million noncommercial pesticide applicators. Other workers may be exposed unknowingly, for example, agricultural workers who enter a field too soon after it has been sprayed with pesticides. The general public is exposed in several ways including (a) eating fruit or vegetables that have been sprayed directly, or meat or fish that has a high pesticide residue as a result of the food chain, and (b) living near crop fields or forests that are being sprayed from the air.

Three of the major groups of pesticides are (a) the organophosphates (such as parathion, tetraethyl pyrophosphate [TEPP], and malathion), which act by inhibiting the enzyme cholinesterase and cause gastrointestinal, neurologic, and muscular symptoms, and in severe cases, paralysis and death; (b) the chlorinated hydrocarbons (such as chlordane, heptochlor, Kepone, and dichlorodiphenyltrichloroethane [DDT]), which cause central nervous system intoxication and may cause cancer in humans; and (c) carbamates (such as carbaryl), which also inhibit cholinesterase. Other groups include inorganic arsenicals, mercurials, cyanides, coumarins, and organic acids.

Under the Federal Insecticide, Fungicide, and Rodenticide Act (FIFRA) (Amended), the Environmental Protection Agency (EPA) has primary responsibility for pesticide regulation in the United States, including farmworker exposure to pesticides. All pesticides must be registered with the EPA. Each must be labelled with information on uses, dosages, and precautions. Restricted pesticides can be applied only by those who have received special training and have become certified to do so. The EPA, in conjunction with each state's cooperative extension service, operates an active program to train and certify pesticide applicators. Common-sense prevention measures include reading pesticide labels and carefully following instructions, handling pesticides in a safe manner, observing cleanliness, protecting farm workers and others in pesticide-contaminated workplaces, and observing precautions in the storage and disposal of pesticides.

ANNOTATED BIBLIOGRAPHY

Ashford, N. A. 1976. *Crisis in the workplace.* Cambridge, Mass. MIT Press.
An in-depth analysis of the technical, legal-political, and economic problems in occupational health and safety.

Birmingham, D. J. 1971. Cutaneous reactions to chemicals and occupational dermatoses. In *Disorders due to chemical agents*, in "*Dermatology in general medicine*," ed. T. B. Fitzpatrick et al., pp. 1044-1070. New York: McGraw-Hill Book Company.
A good review of the major work-related skin disorders.

Brodeur, P. 1974. *Expendable Americans.* New York: Viking Press.
A detailed account of the sociopolitical forces that have worked against dissemination of research information on occupational hazards and effective enforcement of occupational health and safety laws. Focus is on asbestos.

Center for Disease Control. 1975. *Increased lead absorption and lead poisoning in young children.* Atlanta, Ga.: Department of Health, Education, and Welfare.
An excellent review including screening, management of lead poisoning, hazard control, and educational approaches to prevention.

Dalrymple, G. V.; Gaulden, M.D.; Kollmorgen, G. M., et al. 1973. *Medical radiation biology*. Philadelphia: W. B. Saunders Co. Helps provide a good understanding of ionizing radiation.

Epstein, S. S. 1978. *The politics of cancer.* San Francisco: Sierra Club Books.
Documents the basis for the growing belief that most cancers are environmentally induced or related—and therefore preventable—and explores the questions that this raises. Demonstrates the failure to implement laws and put knowledge into practice regarding environmental carcinogenesis. Now in paperback with some added material.

Hricko, A., and Brunt, M. 1976. *Working for your life: A woman's guide to job health hazards.* Berkeley, Calif.: Labor Occupational Health Program and Public Citizen's Health Research Group.
A straightforward, comprehensive presentation of this project.

Kahn, K. L. 1980. *Health effects of nuclear power and nuclear weapons.* Watertown, Mass.: Physicians for Social Responsibility.
Includes useful information on ionizing radiation and its effects, and related sociopolitical aspects of ionizing radiation.

Key, M. M.; Henschel; A. F., Butler, J., et al., eds. 1977. *Occupational diseases: A guide to their recognition.* Washington, D.C.: National Institute for Occupational Safety and Health.
Occupational diseases are discussed in terms of occupational health hazards. Covers routes of entry and modes of action; chemical, physical, and biologic hazards; dermatoses; airway diseases; plant and wood hazards; chemical carcinogens; pesticides; sources of consultation; and references. Good lists and cross indexes of occupational hazards and potentially exposed groups of workers. A basic reference work.

Mackison, F. W.; Stricoff, R. S.; and Partridge, L. J. Jr., eds. 1978. *NIOSH/OSHA pocket guide to chemical hazards.* Washington, D.C.: National Institute for Occupational Safety and Health and Occupational Safety and Health Administration.
Key information and data in an abbreviated tabular format for 380 chemical hazards found in the work environment and for which there are specific federal regulations.

Morgan, D. P. 1977. *Recognition and management of pesticide poisonings.* Washington, D.C.: U. S. Environmental Protection Agency.
An excellent guide for the diagnosis and treatment of health effects of pesticides. This can be obtained from the Superintendent of Documents, U. S. Government Printing Office, Washington, D.C. 20402 (stock number 055-004-00013-7).

Parkes, R. 1974. *Occupational lung disorders.* London: Buttersworth.
An excellent reference reviewing in sufficient detail all occupational lung diseases.

Proctor, N. H., and Hughes, J. P. 1978. *Chemical hazards of the workplace.* Philadelphia: J. B. Lippincott Company.
Brief monographs on 386 chemical hazards, including basics about their chemical, physical, and toxicologic characteristics, diagnostic criteria, including special tests, and treatment and medical control measures.

Selikoff, I. J. 1980. Environmental health. In *Preventive medicine and public health*, ed. J. M. Last pp. 527-871. New York: Appleton-Century-Crofts.
An excellent review.

Shapiro, J. 1979. *Radiation protection: a guide for scientists and physicians.* Cambridge, Mass. Harvard University Press.
A manual for those who wish to become qualified in radiation protection as an adjunct to working with sources of ionizing radiation or using radionuclides in medicine. Provides the radiation user with information needed to protect himself and others and to understand and comply with government and institution regulations regarding the use of radionuclides and radiation machines.

Stellman, J. M. 1977. *Women's work, women's health.* New York: Pantheon Books, Inc.
A good presentation on occupational health and safety for women and related subjects. Helps to separate myths from realities.

Stellman, J. M., and Daum, S. M. 1973. *Work is dangerous to your health.* New York: Vintage Books.
A handbook designed to enable workers to recognize the health hazards in their workplace and to make concerted efforts to monitor and control them.

Waldron, H. A. 1979. *Lecture notes on occupational medicine.* Oxford: Blackwell Scientific Publications, Ltd.
A concise view of the subject, designed for medical students and for general practitioners. Stresses interaction between occupational medicine and other areas of environmental health.

Zenz, C. 1975. *Occupational medicine: principles and practical applications.* Chicago: Year Book Medical Publishers, Inc.
Broad and detailed review, designed primarily for physicians with responsibility for occupational medical departments in industry and elsewhere. Major sections focus on important administrative factors, clinical occupational medicine, the physical and chemical occupational environments, and behavioral or psychosocial considerations.

7 Anticipating Psychiatric Crises

Igor Grant

Dr. Grant received his M.D. degree from the University of British Columbia Medical School, and has been on the faculties of the University of Pennsylvania and of the University of California, San Diego, where he is now Chief of the Consultation-Liaison Service and Mental Health Clinic of the Veterans Administration Hospital. His publications are in the areas of relationship of life happenings to health status and behavioral measures of reversible and irreversible disturbances in brain function.

David S. Janowsky

Dr. Janowsky is a graduate of the University of California at San Francisco Medical School and had been on the faculties of the University of California, Los Angeles, and Vanderbilt before joining the University of California, San Diego, School of Medicine. He is principal investigator of the National Institute of Mental Health, Clinical Research Center at the University of California, San Diego, where he is involved in a wide range of clinical and research activities.

Brief Contents

Overview

Primary care physicians need hardly be reminded that emotional difficulties and behavioral disorders are commonplace among their patients. This chapter highlights the salient features of common psychiatric problems. Such information should help primary care physicians become more skilled observers of behavior, thereby enabling them to make early diagnosis and prompt preventive interventions. In particular this chapter will stress those conditions that primary care physicians might reasonably choose to manage themselves and indicate those that should probably be referred for specialized treatment.

THE PRIMARY CARE PHYSICIAN AS BEHAVIORAL SCIENTIST

Psychiatric crises do not occur in a vacuum. They are the product of biologic endowment, unique developmental history, and the social environment. Regarding the patient from a developmental perspective can be especially useful. The various stages in a patient's life (childhood, adolescence, early adulthood, middle adulthood, middle age and old age) represent repeated challenges (and opportunities) with which people must develop strategies for

Specific psychiatric syndromes have a propensity to occur at certain stages of development.

Table 7-1.

coping. Both successful and maladaptive (psychopathologic) coping change depend on age and past experience. Specific psychiatric syndromes, then, have a propensity to occur more at certain stages of development than at others, as illustrated in Table 7-1. Thus, when becoming separate and distinct from parents is an issue, maladaptive coping is more likely to take the form of antisocial behavior or drug abuse than during the retirement years, when the task is integration of personal achievements. Suicide occurs at all ages but incidence peaks are found during late adolescence and among the elderly. In the early years suicide might be seen as reflecting an inability to master the major life task of the early years—establishment of a clear identity with satisfactory self-esteem. In the later years suicide might represent despair over what the patient evaluates to be a dismal life performance or anguish concerning failing health or painful illness.

These examples illustrate how as behavioral scientists primary care physicians must have some awareness of life tasks, and some appreciation of the likely forms that maladaptive coping can take at different life stages.

Primary care physicians should use their knowledge to foster a relationship that will enable them to obtain information and influence the patient therapeutically.

The second task as behavioral scientists is for primary care physicians to use their knowledge of interpersonal dynamics to foster the kind of doctor/patient relationship that will enable them to obtain accurate and complete information from the patient, and to influence that patient in a therapeutic fashion. Requirements for a useful therapeutic relationship include empathy (insightful understanding of the thoughts and feelings of another), trust, and mutual respect. These conditions are facilitated by physicians who are mindful of patients' age, educational and social background, values, and beliefs and who also understand how their own appearance, behavior, beliefs, and authoritative role might affect patients. Finally, to be successful in managing psychopathology in their patients physicians must, to some degree at least, "know thyself." Such self-awareness will allow them to pinpoint their own potential overreactions (intolerance) or excessive identification (blind spots).

Know thyself.

DEPRESSION

Manifestations of Depression

Depression is probably the most common psychiatric condition that physicians will confront. Its manifestations are protean, and can include changes in biological functioning, mood, thinking, motivation, and interpersonal behavior.

Table 7-1 Psychiatric Disturbances from a Developmental Perspective

Age	Typical Psychosocial Tasks (Erickson, 1963; Piaget, 1962; Levinson, 1978)	Psychopathological States (listed under age periods where expected incidence is highest)	
		Milder	More Severe
1–5	Development of basic trust, autonomy (physical movement, bowel and bladder control, speech), initiative. Shift in cognitive functioning from sensorimotor to concrete operations.	Stranger anxiety, enuresis, delay in language.	Anaclitic depression, autism (childhood schizophrenia, hyperkinesis).
6–10	Industry—drive to master school, sports, games; cognitive—notions of conservatism, reversibility, decentering.	School phobia, stuttering, dyslexia—learning disability, obsessional signs.	Childhood schizophrenia. Hyperkinesis.
11–15	Cognitive—shift to abstract attitude, interest in values, concepts, principles. Development of adolescent identity. Initial efforts to cope with peer intimacy including sexual sharing, and to become distinct from parents.	Rebelliousness/fighting, shyness, experimentation with alcohol or drugs. Promiscuity/unwanted pregnancy.	Drug/alcohol abuse, antisocial behavior, suicide.
20	Early adult identity, choice of career or job. Detachment from parents. Marriage—development of adult psychosexual intimacy and	Excessive dependency, underachievement, failure to define career. Difficulties with meaning-	Schizophrenia (male)—bipolar affect disorder; schizophrenia (female)—severe neuroses (dissocia-

Table 7-1 continued

Age	Typical Psychosocial Tasks (Erickson, 1963; Piaget, 1962; Levinson, 1978)	Psychopathological States (listed under age periods where expected incidence is highest)	
		Milder	More Severe
25	sharing. Decisions regarding parenthood. Identity as parent (or childless adult, or single adult).	ful sexual relationships. Divorce	tive, obsessive, anxiety, passive, dependent).
30 35 40	Early midlife transition—recognizing that there are limits to what is achievable despite effort, excellence. Early coping with finiteness of life followed by settling into family/occupational role.	Phobic or anxious symptoms; situational depression, withdrawal from spouse (for example, into work, avocations, alcohol).	Alcoholism, paranoid states, and paranoid schizophrenia.
45	Midlife transition. Reevaluation of occupational, family commitments.	Intense time pressure, situational depression, infidelity/divorce.	Unipolar depression.
50	Recognizing frailty of body; sensing time is beginning to run out. Rededication to former family and career decisions versus new directions.	Preoccupation with fitness, diet, and so forth.	Presenile dementia, Wernicke-Korsakoff syndrome, involutional paranoid state.
55 60	Adjusting to life without children, planning for retirement.	Anxious depression, loneliness ("emptiness").	Unipolar depression, suicide, alcoholism.
65	Retirement. Coping with illness or reduced physical capacity, including sexual. Concerns with ability to maintain independent existence Development of identity as an elderly person. Sense of integration of life goals.	Hypochondriacal preoccupations. Anxiety, loneliness, disappointment, withdrawal.	Suicide, senile dementia

Depression can present as changes in or complaints about bodily functions. For example, depressed people frequently complain of sleep disturbances, with middle of the night or early morning insomnia. Other common bodily complaints include weight loss, loss of appetite, decreased sexual functioning, various aches and pains (especially back pain), a sense of unusual fatigue, constipation, and a preoccupation with physical problems (hypochondriasis).

Although depression is commonly thought to be a disorder primarily of mood, there are also thinking disturbances.

In terms of mood, the depressed person can feel sad, blue, helpless, hopeless, unhappy, irritable, or anxious. Although depression is commonly thought to be a disorder primarily of mood, there are also thinking disturbances. Indeed the depressed person's negative view of self, future, and environment has been termed the "cognitive triad" of depression (Beck, 1967). Depressed people often have altered motivations, that is, the things that "drive them" become different. For example, a normally active, self-reliant individual might become passive, dependent, and seemingly helpless. People who have a joie de vivre may begin questioning the value of their lives. In the interpersonal sphere, depressed people often become withdrawn, uninterested in their spouse and family, and may experience difficulties with their colleagues at work. These difficulties can be due partly to seclusiveness, or may be consequences of irritability or inefficiency. Depressed people often complain of difficulty in concentrating and in remembering. Careful psychologic testing usually fails to reveal significant memory deficits. The subjective "memory loss" probably reflects intense absorption in depressive thinking to the exclusion of normal cognitive functions.

Patients with depression often complain of memory loss that is not confirmed by psychological testing.

There have been many attempts to classify depression. Perhaps the most practical scheme is to partition the depressions into "major" and "minor" affective disorders. Minor affective disorders tend to be precipitated by life events and are limited in duration; severe grief reactions or depressions that occur after a loss are examples. Major affective disorders are characterized by episodes of greater duration (more than 2 weeks), often are more profound in degree, and have a tendency to occur repeatedly without there necessarily being an environmental precipitant.

A practical way to classify depression is to divide it into major and minor types.

Under major affective disorders, psychiatrists generally define two types of conditions: *primary affective disorders*—those that are independent of some preexisting disease; and *secondary affective disorders*—those that may follow the onset of some other important psychiatric (for example, schizophrenia or alcoholism) or medical (for example, dementia or metabolic disease) condition. The two subclassifications of primary affective disorders are *unipolar disorder* and *bipolar disorder*. Unipolar disorder describes repeated cycles of depression. This replaces the old categories of manic-depressive illness, depressed type, and involutional melancholia. Bipolar disorder describes episodes of depression that may be interspersed with episodes of mania (elation). (The equivalent older term is manic depressive illness, circular type.)

Primary affective disorders almost certainly have a substantial genetic component.

The primary affective disorders run in families, and there is almost certainly a substantial genetic component. In some series, persons with primary affective disorders have been found to have an unusually high prevalence of alcoholism in their blood relatives. The meaning of this apparent association of alcoholism and affective disorder continues to be a matter of debate.

Certain factors predispose a patient to depression.

There is uncertainty concerning the importance of environmental stresses as predispositions to depression. Age is a factor, since depression occurs more frequently in older people of both sexes. Certain severe losses also can trigger depression (for example, death of a loved one, severe financial reverses, or other disasters). The extent to which early childhood experiences predispose to depression is less clear. Some studies have suggested that early losses are important, but others have not confirmed this (Akiskal and McKinney, 1975). Medical illness predisposes to depression, and this is particularly true in people with severe illnesses such as cancer, or in people who have suddenly undergone a major alteration in their body image (for example, mutilative surgery, severe burns, amputations, or spinal cord injury). In addition, hypothyroidism, Cushing disease, and Addison disease as well as hyperparathyroidism and premenstrual tension can be associated with depression. Certain drugs induce depression. They include the central nervous system (CNS) depressants (hypnotics and minor tranquilizers) and drugs that tend to deplete centrally active catecholamines.

Management of Depression

Before physicians can develop a management plan for their depressed patients the following questions must be answered satisfactorily.

Before physicians can develop a management plan for their depressed patients the following questions must be answered satisfactorily:

1. *Is it possible that the depression is the result of a medical condition?* For example, is it possible that prescribed drugs, an infectious disorder (mononucleosis or hepatitis), or some metabolic disorder (for example, hyponatremia) is contributing to the present signs and symptoms? This is especially important in a patient who suddenly undergoes a profound change in mood in the absence of a personal or family history of affective disorder.

2. *Is the patient suicidal?* (For discussion of this issue, see the section on suicide later in this chapter.)
3. *What is the clinical picture?* The presence of "endogenous" signs—deep depression, psychomotor retardation, severe sleep disturbance, weight loss, anorexia, profound nihilism, severe withdrawal—all suggest that hospitalization and/or biologic treatment will be necessary. Deeply depressed persons with such endogenous signs do not tend to respond completely to psychotherapeutic intervention alone.
4. *What is the family and personal history?* People with personal histories of depression are more likely to require biologic treatment to prevent future relapses. The same may apply to people with family histories of mania or alcoholism.

Once an affective disorder has been diagnosed the next step is to decide whether the problem is of a serious enough nature that a psychiatric consultation should be obtained. If the decision is made that this is a problem of only mild or moderate severity, treating the patient with brief (1-10 sessions) psychotherapy might be considered. Such sessions need not be long (20-30 min may be adequate), but certain facts and principles should be considered. For example, most depressed people suffer from loss of self-esteem. Thus, any kind of counseling ought to be directed toward helping the person recognize this major difficulty and then find ways to self-correct. This chapter cannot outline the details of psychotherapy but rather only indicate a direction. In general patients should be encouraged to view themselves in a more positive light, to take affirmative action rather than to brood, and to make those changes in their lives that would improve their condition rather than remain passive. Some patients have difficulties extracting pleasure from their environment. Sometimes physicians can be helpful in suggesting ways in which patients can restructure their family or work situation so that it will be more satisfying.

Most depressed patients suffer from loss of self-esteem. Counseling should help them recognize this major difficulty.

Depressed patients, as a consequence of their illness, do not necessarily believe that all the above can be accomplished. Physicians should respond by acknowledging patients' feelings, while pointing out that in depression people often assess themselves and their situations more negatively than they might if they were "back to their old self."

If it is decided that the depression is of moderate or severe depth (that there are endogenous signs or previous history, as has been outlined) then a psychiatric consultation should be sought. There may be two outcomes from this: the consultant may recommend hospitalization of the patient, or an outpatient management plan may be developed.

In the outpatient setting it is usual to prescribe antidepressant drugs for the treatment of moderate to severe depression. There are currently three classes of drugs in use.

Of severe depressions 60%-80% will respond favorably to tricyclic antidepressants—usually after a latent period of 2-3 weeks.

Tricyclic antidepressants The tricylic antidepressants are all moderately effective in the treatment of endogenous and serious depression. Studies suggest that 60%-80% of severe depressives receiving these drugs will respond favorably (Morris and Beck, 1974). These drugs take time to act, however; there is usually a latent period of 2-3 weeks before a positive effect is seen. Also, they are only effective if used in adequate dosage. Physicians frequently make the mistake of prescribing homeopathic amounts (25-50 mg of amitriptyline a day). A healthy person in his midyears will generally require 200-300 mg of a tricyclic antidepressant to produce beneficial results.

Dosage of tricyclics should be adequate—generally 200-300 mg a day for the healthy person in his midyears.

Primary care practitioners may wish to discuss the use of tricyclic antidepressants with a psychiatrist. While effective, they produce many side effects and potential drug/drug interactions. Signs of autonomic effects (combination of adrenergic and anticholinergic) include dry mouth, dilated pupils, tachycardia, postural hypotension, constipation, urinary retention, delayed or uncomfortable ejaculation, and increased sweating. More serious effects are signs of cardiac irritability (for example, premature ventricular contractions) and exacerbation of narrow-angle glaucoma. Central anticholinergic syndrome, a delirious state akin to atropine poisoning, can occur following an excessive dose (the elderly or people with brain damage are especially sensitive). Overdose of these agents can be very difficult to treat, and death can result from profound hypotension, hyperthermia, or cardiac arrest. The arrhythmic effects of a tricyclic antidepressant overdose can persist for several days after other symptoms have cleared.

Patients who have started taking antidepressants generally need to continue doing so for a matter of months (usually 3-9 months). The decision to taper off or stop the drug should depend on the patient's having reached maximum improvement for a period of at least 6 weeks. The dose may be lowered by 25% every 2 weeks, with close attention being paid to signs of relapse. Minor recrudescences are common after drugs are discontinued and can be managed psychotherapeutically. More severe rebounds suggest that drugs need to be restarted.

A strategy is offered regarding when and how to discontinue antidepressants.

Psychological counseling should continue while antidepressants are being given. The general principles will be comparable to those described earlier. The long-term outcome is variable. Many patients require no further treatment. Others tend to keep relapsing with termination of their medications; such patients may require indefinite pharmacotherapy.

Tricyclics are toxic in overdose. In patients who may be suicidal prescribe no more than several days' supply or have someone close to the patient dispense the drug.

It is important to remember that tricyclic antidepressants are very toxic in an overdose, and that as little as a 2-week supply of drugs can be lethal. Thus in patients who may be suicidal no more than several days' supply of the drug should be prescribed. In some instances it is necessary that the drug be dispensed by someone other than the patient.

Monoamine oxidase inhibitors A second class of drugs used to treat depression are the monoamine oxidase inhibitors (MAOI). These drugs fell out of favor for a time but now are receiving some renewed interest since they are effective in the treatment of certain kinds of depression. It is recommended, however, that primary care physicians not assume the sole responsibility for the complex management of patients requiring MAOI; a psychiatrist knowledgeable in psychopharmacology should be consulted.

It is recommended, however, that primary care physicians not assume the sole responsibility for the complex management of patients requiring MAOI.

Lithium Lithium salts are the third class of antidepressant drugs. Lithium may have value in preventing or attenuating episodes of depression in persons with recurrent affective disorders. Generally speaking, lithium has not been advocated as the sole treatment for depression, however, because the primary indication for lithium is the treatment and prevention of mania. Further information on the use of this agent is presented in the next section on mania.

Hospitalization Only a few words will be said here about the patient who is hospitalized for depression. In general, the hospital is thought to benefit depressed people in several ways. First, it removes patients from a perhaps stressful environment and gives them some surcease. Secondly, good inpatient psychiatric units tend to support patient self-esteem, exhort passive patients into activity, and teach them new social skills. This can be accomplished with individual and group psychotherapy. Lastly, a hospital setting may be appropriate for attempting biologic treatments that are difficult to supervise in the outpatient setting. For example, elderly patients who might have adverse reactions to tricyclic drugs may be more safely begun on these agents in an inpatient setting.

Electroconvulsive therapy Another effective biological treatment is electroconvulsive therapy (ECT), which can be effective in 80%-90% of profoundly depressed patients. It is the treatment of

Electroconvulsive therapy is the treatment of choice for life-threatening depression.

choice for life-threatening depression. In general physicians should know that patients receive this treatment under brief anesthesia with skeletal muscle relaxation (for example, methyhexital and succinylcholine) so that risks of pain or vertebral fractures are minimized. An anesthesiologist is usually in attendance as well as the psychiatrist. There are no long-term adverse effects, though patients may be confused and have memory loss while undergoing a course of ECT. Thus the treatment is quite safe—indeed, it may be the treatment of choice in the severely depressed person who has cardiac disease.

It is important to consider what to do with the depressed patient once the depression has remitted.

It is important to consider what to do with the depressed patient once the depression has remitted. The depressed patient should be followed up at regular intervals (monthly or every other month) for signs of relapse, since depression is often cyclical. The depressed patient as well as the family should be made aware of the early signs of a specific patient's depression (feelings of futility, certain specific negative thoughts, lethargy, increased worrying, sleep disturbances, lowered mood, and so on), since these are often stereotyped from episode to episode. Physicians should ask to be informed immediately if the signs recur (for example, becoming more withdrawn, more pessimistic) so that they can intervene promptly. Patient education—and family education—sometimes do not succeed because lay people often write off a depressive prodrome as simple unhappiness in relation to some environmental circumstance. However, since previous depression is predictive it is important that this be emphasized to the family and that no time be lost if a depression begins to recur.

MANIA

Mania is much less common than depression. Manic persons are euphoric, and sometimes irritable. They speak and think more rapidly. Their behavior at the extreme tends to be frenetic and essentially uncontrollable. Biological signs include decreased sleep, increased energy, and increased sexual drive. However, it is in the social sphere that mania may be most dramatic. Expansive and grandiose manics may overspend (huge long-distance phone bills are typical) and overcommit themselves. Of equal importance is the fact that manic patients tend to enjoy their mania, especially in the early phases. They tend to deny that they have a problem, and while their decisions may seem plausible and rational at first, eventually their behavior may become more bizarre, and hospitalization is often needed.

Patients who have had a manic attack in the past usually have individual-specific signs and symptoms when another attack is

Manic patients usually present characteristic early-warning clues to attacks.

beginning. These are the orderly warning signals of mania. For example, a prodrome may be indicated for one patient when he begins to write his biography or for another by the making of long-distance phone calls and yet another by hypersexuality.

Very careful follow-up is necessary for the patient on lithium since its margin of safety is narrow.

Treatment often requires hospitalization, especially if the patient has frank psychosis (delusions, hallucinations, or thought disorder). Lithium is the agent of choice. As the margin of safety is narrow, plasma levels are monitored on regular occasions (1-2 times a week to start, then spaced out to once every few months if the level is stable). The therapeutic plasma concentration ranges from 1.2-1.4 mEq/1, although higher levels are sometimes required for severe mania. Levels exceeding 1.8 mEq/1 are usually accompanied by side effects (tremor, nausea, and diarrhea) and those above 2.0 mEq/1 can cause more severe toxicity (incoordination, delirium, somnolence, convulsions, coma, renal shutdown, and arrhythmias). Deaths have occurred at 2.5 mEq/1. Occasionally an antipsychotic drug is added to the lithium therapy during the early phase of treatment. How long to continue lithium is unclear. Long-term adverse effects (nontoxic goiter, hypothyroidism, perhaps interstitial fibrosis of the kidney) dictate caution and suggest that physicians seek to wean patients off of the drug. However, lithium is often effective in preventing manic and recurrent depressive episodes in serum concentrations of 0.8-1.0 mEq/1.

Once a patient has had mania, physicians may assist both the family and the patient in pointing out the early signs of mania, so that if the patient should begin to become manic again prompt treatment can be administered and hospitalization may thus be avoided.

SUICIDE

It has been estimated that there are about 10 completed suicides per 100,000 population per year in the United States. This figure has remained relatively constant since 1900. Nobody knows precisely how many suicide attempts there are each year, but it is estimated that they are ten times the number of completed suicides.

Suicidal ideas are very common. For example, in one college survey about 50% of queried students reported having had at least some ideas of killing themselves in the past several years (Lester and Lester, 1971).

In preventing suicide it is important to maintain a high index of suspicion and to be aware of people who are particularly vulnerable to suicide attempts or to complete suicides. More people complete suicide as they get older. The relationship is almost linear in men. In women completed suicides tend to increase into the 40s and 50s and then taper off. There may be some exceptions to this; for example, there is a peak in suicide rate in the late teens and early 20s. Young black males in urban settings may be especially vulnerable to suicide, as may other youthful members of minority groups. However, it is important to note that no age or ethnic group is immune. Indeed even small children have been known to commit suicide, as have younger adolescents.

Suicide occurs at all ages but tends to peak in late adolescence and in the elderly.

There are more completed suicides among men than women. This primarily seems to reflect the methods chosen. Men tend to commit suicide by use of firearms, hanging, or jumping off buildings or bridges; women more frequently use medications.

People who are seriously ill, and particularly those who have received a diagnosis of a fatal illness, are more vulnerable to committing suicide. In addition, people in severe pain or who have undergone a tremendous insult to their body image (for example, amputations of limbs, or operations on face or genitalia) may be more vulnerable. Thus physicians treating a seriously medically ill person, particularly one who has had an extremely severe accident or is in severe pain, should be alerted to the possibility that this patient may be suicidal.

In treating a person with a serious medical illness the physician should be alert to the possibility of suicide.

It has been estimated that as many as one fourth of all alcoholics end their life through suicide; thus they ought to be considered a very high risk group. These risks are probably the result, in part, of the fact that many alcoholics are depressed or at least go through episodes of profound depression, plus the fact that their judgment tends to be clouded when they are drunk. Additionally, alcoholics sometimes abuse sedative-hypnotic drugs (sleeping pills and minor tranquilizers). As a result a completed suicide can occur unintentionally through an overdose of alcohol and sedative-hypnotic drugs. Alcoholics who are suicidal may experience delay in being diagnosed: many physicians find it distasteful to treat them or may interpret what they are saying about suicide as manipulative.

Alcoholics have a high suicide rate.

Youthful drug abusers are also at increased risk to end their lives by their own hands. In some cases it is not clear whether they intended to kill themselves or simply misjudged the dose of drug. In general abusers of sedative-hypnotic and opiate drugs are at risk. It used to be said that lysergic acid diethylamide (LSD) predisposed to suicide, but there is little evidence for this. Phencyclidine abusers also may end their life inadvertently through serious errors in judgment (for example, in a dissociated state they may swim out farther than they had intended and drown, or they may provoke fatal violence).

A personal or family history of depression, combined with a suicide attempt, is a significant finding.

As stated earlier, serious depression tends to run in families. A history of depression in a family member, especially if associated with a suicide attempt, should make physicians alert to the possibility that this might occur in a patient. Even more important is a history of a previous attempt by the patient himself. If a patient has a past history of depression with suicide attempts, especially ones that are serious and might have been lethal except for luck, physicians should be particularly aware that the patient might commit suicide if depression sets in again. Indeed one study has indicated that as many as 15% of manic-depressive patients ultimately die by their own hand (Grant, 1979).

Forms of psychopathology beyond depression can predispose to suicide; for example, a schizophrenic patient may jump off a bridge because "God told him to do so" or "The voices told him to do so."

Any hints about suicide should be treated as a serious threat and explored thoroughly.

There are various hints that a suicidal patient might give.

Beyond being aware of patient characteristics that increase suicide potential, physicians should also be aware that suicidal patients often leave a number of clues regarding their intentions. For example, most suicidal patients will actually say to somebody that they are thinking of killing themselves, or that they feel like ending their life, or that their life is not worthwhile. Often these hints will be dropped to family members or people at work. Not uncommonly suicidal patients will make their intentions known to people in the health care delivery system, such as primary care physicians. The important issue here is that any hints about suicide should be treated as serious and explored thoroughly. The idea that if someone speaks of suicide they will not attempt it is a myth and should be discarded. Alert physicians can avert suicide by being attuned to more indirect clues. For example, a person who is either deeply depressed or seriously ill medically and who begins making moves to "tie up loose ends" (such as getting insurance policies together, transferring ownership on his house to a spouse, and opening joint bank accounts) should be considered a possible candidate for suicide. A person might in fact be preparing the way for his demise. Depressed people who indicate that they have recently purchased guns or other weapons should be considered high risk. Another risk factor that may be relevant is the fact that patients who are accident prone (for example, seem to have multiple accidents of various sorts, car accidents, or motorcycle accidents) may indeed be unconsciously acting out suicidal impulses, and such accident proneness may later develop into overt suicidal behavior. Lastly, if a depressed person suddenly seems much improved this may indicate that the patient has made up his mind to commit suicide and is relieved to have decided.

Talking With Suicidal People

Talking with suicidal people can be extremely challenging and difficult for physicians. Suicidal people are often extremely perturbed (that is, they express a sense of great anguish, anxiety, or depression, sometimes coupled with hostility) and at the same time are talking about things that tend to make physicians anxious. Furthermore, patients who are suicidal and in such severe distress often raise moral conflicts about "the right to die." Physicians may feel at some level that patients have the right to kill themselves and at the same time they may be trapped in a sense of great helplessness as to what to do.

There are a few principles that may be helpful guides in talking with suicidal patients (Lester and Lester, 1971; Schneidman, 1975; Grant, 1979). First, physicians should talk directly and honestly about the matter of suicide. Being indirect or using euphemistic terms are generally not helpful and may communicate to the patient that they really do not want to talk about these matters. It is better to ask, "Do you feel life is not worth living?" or "Are you thinking of ending your life?" Such direct questioning will not make a person more suicidal or make him more likely to kill himself. It might make the patient feel more comfortable to know that the physician is honestly willing to discuss these difficult matters.

Talk directly and honestly about the matter of suicide.

Another principle has to do with accepting the suicidal patient's feelings. Acceptance implies that the physician understands or has insightful feelings for the patient's dilemma. Acceptance should not be confused with agreement that the patient should actually commit suicide. Thus accepting physicians are those who indicate to the patient that they understand how the patient in this particular circumstance might feel hopeless, helpless, and worthless and that life is insufferable. At the same time there is no need to indicate an agreement that suicide is the only solution. It may be helpful for the patient to be told that the suicidal feelings, especially if they are related to depression, are caused by the disease of depression and that such thoughts are to be expected in depression. It can then be stressed that, although the feelings make it seem logical that suicide is indeed the best solution, that with proper treatment of the depression such thoughts will disappear.

Another principle has to do with accepting the suicidal patient's feelings.

A third principle of interaction with a suicidal patient is clarification of the patient's thoughts and feelings. Not uncommonly people who become suicidal are struggling with a sense of irresolvable conflict, either in their real life or in their fantasy life. If the patient can be convinced to articulate the dilemma, to put it into words, this is often useful for it suggests ways in

A third principle of interaction with a suicidal patient is clarification of the patient's thoughts and feelings.

which the patient can be helped to get out of that paradox. For example, a patient who is depressed and has suffered a series of difficult reverses might finally contemplate suicide because a major credit card account was cancelled. The physician can helpfully clarify that this seems to be a difficult problem only in the context of a whole series of difficult situations, that it is probably not unsolvable, and certainly is not one that requires the patient's death.

A final principle is the exploration of options beyond suicide.

A final principle is the exploration of options beyond suicide. Suicidal people have often reached the conclusion that there is no other way out. This is rarely the case in reality and usually reflects the distorted decision making of a person who is deeply depressed. As has already been said, without arguing with the patient, the physician can indicate that a person who is depressed is likely to make the kind of decisions that are not made except in a depressed state. The physician can also suggest that the patient not make any major life decisions while not thinking straight.

Management of Suicidal Patients

In deciding how to manage the suicidal patient, primary care physicians should evaluate several issues (Shneidman, 1975). The first of these is potential lethality. Does it seem likely that the patient will, if unprotected, attempt suicide? Here it is important to review again the potential risk factors discussed in the last section, particularly the presence of severe depression, previous suicide attempts, presence of complicating conditions such as alcoholism, drug abuse, or serious medical illness. The method chosen by the patient and the extent to which that patient has implemented a lethal plan should also be assessed. For example, if the patient is talking about using a gun, has that patient actually purchased a gun or ammunition?

In deciding whether or not to hospitalize a suicidal patient, several other issues should be considered.

In deciding whether or not to hospitalize a suicidal patient, several other issues should be considered. The first of these has to do with interpersonal resources. Does the patient have a family or other caring people with whom there is a meaningful relationship? Can these people be trusted to alert the physician to any change in the patient's condition? Another issue is the doctor-patient relationship. How well does the doctor know the patient? How strong is the relationship? Sometimes even very suicidal patients can be managed successfully as outpatients if there is a strong bond between the doctor and the patient. In general, a suicidal patient deserves a psychiatric consultation. An exception might be in the case of a physician who knows the patient very well and has the time and feels comfortable in doing some short-term psychotherapy with that patient. In any event, if the decision is made to hospitalize the patient, a psychiatrist should certainly be involved. Parenthetically, it is our impression that primary care physicians tend to underutilize psychiatrists in the evaluation of both depressed and suicidal patients. Generally it is best to err on the side of getting a psychiatric consultation on a patient in whom the question of suicide is raised. Beyond helping in the immediate circumstance, a psychiatric contact might make it easier for the patient to come for help earlier during a future episode. This is also our recommendation for patients manifesting severe depression, schizophrenia, drug abuse, and psychiatric concomitants of cerebral disease. Sometimes primary care physicians tend to use nonphysician psychologically-oriented individuals (for example, psychologists or social workers) in the treatment of psychiatrically ill patients. Such individuals have a definite place in the treatment of psychologically disturbed patients and can be most effective.

Generally it is best to get a psychiatric consultation on the possibly suicidal patient. The patient may get help earlier in the future.

With suicidal patients, and sometimes with psychotic or confused patients as well, the question of involuntary detention arises. Physicians tend to be uncomfortable with this circumstance, partly because they do not want to be seen as oppressors and partly because they are unfamiliar with the law. In most jurisdictions physicians have the authority to hospitalize patients against their will if it can be demonstrated that they pose an imminent danger to themselves or to others, or that they are gravely disabled (that is if the patients are pretty much incapable of looking after their health or personal affairs). It should be noted that although a psychiatrist ought to be consulted in these circumstances, this is generally not a legal requirement. Thus a physician who cannot immediately have access to a psychiatrist can in most jurisdictions act on his own to detain a dangerous or disabled patient on a temporary basis (for example, 72-hours). Failure to act promptly can have lethal consequences.

In most jurisdictions physicians have the authority to hospitalize patients against their will.

In the absence of a psychiatrist the primary physician can usually detain a dangerous or disabled patient on a temporary basis.

Assuming that the suicidal patient has been treated effectively for the acute episode and becomes nonsuicidal, several issues are important to consider. First, people who have felt seriously suicidal and/or have acted on this impulse are at increased risk to have a repeat performance. Statistics from the World Health Organization (WHO) suggest that 2% of people who have made a suicide attempt will die by their own hand within a year, and 10% will within 10 years (Grant; 1979). Therefore it is important to monitor the patient so that if the patient is beginning to fall into a suicidal mode of thinking, intervention can begin early. Continued psychotherapy by a professional and periodic monitoring by the primary care physician should help prevent a subsequent suicidal episode, or at least lead to its early recognition.

ANXIETY

Manifestations of Anxiety

Anxiety can contribute to symptoms in many patients seen by family practitioners. Subjectively anxiety is a highly unpleasant, sometimes unbearable sense of fearfulness and impending doom from dangers that are unknown. Since the source is unconscious, persons experiencing anxiety cannot tell the physician why they are feeling that way, even though they are feeling extremely uncomfortable and sometimes panicked.

Patients with anxiety can present with many physical complaints, which sometimes can be confused with other medical conditions. As a general rule the physiological concomitants of anxiety represent extreme arousal of the sympathetic nervous system, with diminution of parasympathetic activity. Thus a person may have dilated pupils and experience dry mouth, rapid breath, a sense of suffocation, tachycardia, mild hypertension, extrasystoles, gastrointestinal complaints (ranging from difficulty in swallowing or nausea to diarrhea or gas pains), increased muscular tension, aches and pains in various muscle groups (for example, headache, chest pain, or back pain), feelings of dizziness or unreality, weakness, and trembling. These various symptoms obviously do not occur in every case. Some patients who are mildly anxious or who have been anxious for long periods of time will have bodily complaints in only one or two organ systems.

The differential diagnosis of anxiety includes a long list of causes.

In terms of differential diagnosis the physician should consider the possibility of endocrinological disturbances (for example, hyperthyroidism, Addison disease, or hormone-secreting tumors such as pheochromocytoma or carcinoid syndrome), the effects of various drugs (for example, drugs with central stimulant properties such as amphetamines, methylphenidate, cocaine, phenmetrazine, pseudoephedrine, aminophylline, or excess caffeine or tea). Anxiety symptoms can also be produced by withdrawal from depressant drugs. Thus, alcoholics who have suddenly discontinued or reduced their drinking may feel irritable and have many of the symptoms of an anxiety attack. Similarly, persons who are dependent on sedative-hypnotic agents such as the minor tranquilizers (diazepam, chlordiazepoxide, oxazepam, meprobamate) or sleeping pills can experience anxiety symptoms and irritability when they discontinue or reduce taking these drugs. It should be noted that withdrawal symptoms can be produced by sudden discontinuation of rather modest daily intakes of diazepam (for example, 30 mg per day for several months) (Rifkin et al., 1976; Winokur et al., 1980). Another condition that can both mimic and cause anxiety is paroxysmal atrial tachycardia.

In attempting to forestall and treat anxiety, physicians should be aware of the general causes of this disorder. In simple terms, anxiety is usually regarded as an internal psychological sign that people feel a serious threat to themselves, or rather to their preferred view of themselves. The threat may be partially from the outside world (for example, news that they might be seriously ill, or that they might have to undergo a mutilating operation, or might lose a job or a loved one) or it might be essentially internal (intrapsychic). For example, persons going through certain life transitions (such as those entering their 40s) might be more vulnerable to anxiety on the basis of a challenge to their usual view of themselves as youthful, vital, sexually attractive, or invulnerable. Anxiety might result when these images are confronted by evident signs of becoming older and not so ominpotent. Other anxiety-inducing transitions may occur when women are entering menopause, when older people are retiring, and so on. For younger people graduation from high school and entering college or the job market may represent a similarly vulnerable time. For yet other people, developing their first meaningful relationships with members of the opposite sex, or getting married, or having a first child may be times of susceptibility to anxiety. This list of transitions is not meant to imply that each and every person will experience anxiety at each of these transitions, but rather to point out that some people with particular vulnerabilities might have more symptoms at these times, and that physicians who get to know those patients well over time may learn to anticipate these difficulties.

Persons going through life transitions are vulnerable to anxiety.

Anxiety can also occur when patients' self-regard or self-esteem is confronted by impulses that they consider alien. For example, patients brought up to believe that sexual desire is evil or base might feel anxious when experiencing such desires. Others might get anxious in anticipation of the mildest of confrontations because they have not disentangled destructive aggression from legitimate assertiveness. Often individuals are not aware of the cause of the anxiety since that cause is "repressed." The anxiety is a "signal" that the unconscious is being flooded by unpleasant, alien, or unwanted impulses. In such a circumstance individuals, when asked what is bothering them might reply, "I don't know" or "Nothing."

Management of Anxiety

It is hoped that primary care physicians will be able to avoid the following all too common scenario: An anxious patient presents with a number of somatic complaints, many of them vague or atypical. Doctors feel obligated to "do something," and focus on the physical complaint rather than on the emotional underpinning. They do an extensive work-up, ending usually with negative or equivocal findings, They then decide that the patient is anxious and prescribed meprobamate, diazepam, or chlordiazepoxide. They tell the patient that the problem is all psychologic; the patient become angry and leaves—to find another doctor, where the work-up is again repeated.

Clearly the best form of management is prevention. Unfortunately, prediction of vulnerability to anxiety attacks is difficult, and it will be only in retrospect that physicians will be able to piece together the causes and plan for secondary prevention.

The treatment of the acute anxiety attack depends on its severity.

The treatment of the acute anxiety attack depends on its severity. Mildly or moderately anxious people can best be managed through gentle exploration of potential sources of the anxiety, coupled with reassurance and some suggestions for physiologic management of their anxiety. For example, systematic relaxation, wherein a patient is taught to relax progressively various muscle groups several times a day, can be most effective in the management of mild anxiety. More complex techniques such as hypnosis, biofeedback, and meditation can also be useful. It is not recommended that sedative-hypnotic drugs or minor tranquilizers be administered to people with only mild or moderate anxiety. A psychologic approach is preferable.

The physician should adopt a full strategy in dealing with patients who have severe anxiety.

Severe anxiety (panic) attacks can be extremely dramatic and disconcerting to both family and physician. A patient may be hyperventilating at 40 breaths a minute, may be acting irrationally, panicked, irritable, and inconsolable. In such an emergency situation the following steps are recommended:

1. Panic is contagious. Remove from the scene persons who might be contributing to the anxiety by reacting in a panicky or angry fashion themselves.
2. Patients should be treated in a quiet and restful atmosphere by supportive people who are not easily rattled. Often all that is required is to remove patients from persons and circumstances that are aggravating their condition and to provide reassurance and explanation. For example, patients can be told that:
   a. They are experiencing what is called an "anxiety attack."
   b. Anxiety brings with it many unpleasant symptoms such as tingling of extremities, rapid breathing, dizziness, or whatever they might be feeling;
   c. These symptoms will soon go away even though they may feel dreadful at the moment.
   d. The physician will give them a medication that very quickly will make them feel better.

In such states of extreme anxiety and panic an antianxiety agent can be helpful as a short-term treatment. For example, physicians might wish to administer up to 40 mg of diazepam (Valium) by mouth and repeat with 10 mg every few hours as needed. It generally is not necessary and is excessively dramatic to give diazepam intravenously or intramuscularly. The key is to reduce arousal by pharmacologic means while following a psychologic management strategy emphasizing support, reassurance, kindness, and comfort. Occasionally patients who have hyperventilated so severely that they have become alkalotic may need to rebreathe through a mask or paper bag to restore their carbon dioxide level.

It should be emphasized that if physicians elect to use diazepam or similar agents in the acute treatment of a severe anxiety attack, they should not continue these agents for long periods of time. A few hours to a few days of treatment is generally adequate. These agents are not helpful in the long-term management of anxiety, because a tolerance develops to their beneficial effects. Chronic anxiety can be a serious and difficult management problem, which is probably beyond the scope and time available to the average family practitioner. Consultation with a psychiatrist is recommended for such patients.

PREMENSTRUAL TENSION SYNDROME

Some women experience irritability, mild depression, fatigue, a sense of bloating, anxiety, or affective lability in the few days preceding menstrual bleeding. Physical signs, such as cramps, may also be present. In a small proportion of women major psychiatric disturbances are linked to the menstrual cycle and include manic or depressive episodes, increased alcohol consumption, exacerbation of psychosis, or violent outbursts.

There is no consistent evidence that women with premenstrual tension are "neurotic." Rather such women may be experiencing exaggerated responses to hormone changes.

With the exception of the severe disturbances that tend to be part of an underlying psychiatric disorder, there is no consistent evidence to suggest that women suffering premenstrual tension are "neurotic." Rather it appears that, for reasons yet to be elucidated, such women experience exaggerated response to changes in ovarian hormones toward the end of their menstrual cycle. Premenstrual tension can occur after menopause, with cyclic mood swings occurring at the expected time when a menstrual period might have occurred.

The primary care physician can be of great help to the woman with premenstrual tension as well as to her family. The patient may be made aware of the problem and allow an intellectual defense against the problem to occur; that is, if the patient or her family determines that her upset state will be short lived and indeed is related to her menstrual cycle, she and/or her family can cope better during that phase of her cycle.

Drugs may have a role in the management of premenstrual tension.

Several alternative treatments can be considered for more severe cases of premenstrual tension. Probably most useful is the use of low progesterone content oral contraceptives, which will often alleviate premenstrual tension in many patients. Antiprostaglandins such as indomethacin can alleviate cramps and back pain. Antidepressants have also been suggested, but their efficacy is not established except for women who clearly have an affective disorder (see discussion under depression). Diuretics can ease the sense of bloating but do not affect the psychologic aspects of premenstrual tension. Antipsychotic compounds may be useful in the treatment of premenstrual tension if the individual becomes schizophrenic or psychotic during these episodes.

VIOLENCE

Manifestations of Violence

Violence is a serious social problem, yet its roots are poorly understood from a medical-psychiatric viewpoint. Perhaps this state of affairs partly reflects the fact that physicians are not commonly called on to manage violence: this task devolves on the criminal justice system. On the other hand, physicians frequently have to treat the sequelae of violent behavior.

A relatively small proportion of violent acts are committed by patients with clear-cut psychiatric diagnoses.

In the lay mind violence is often associated with mental illness. In point of fact, a relatively small proportion of violent acts are committed by patients with clear-cut psychiatric diagnoses (for example, schizophrenia, affective disorder, or cerebral disorder). Most violent people are classified as having various types of "character pathology"—which is tantamount to saying that these are people with warps in their personality whose etiology and amelioration are poorly understood. The commonest associations are between violence and antisocial personality, and violence and alcoholism.

The former is characterized by a long history of social maladjustment with symptoms evident in early school years: truancy; cruelty to siblings, other children, or animals; lying; stealing; and failure to learn from experience. In their teen years such children often dabble extensively with alcohol and drugs, tend to be active sexually at an early age, yet maintain a peculiar "affectlessness" for people; and become involved in criminal acts (for example, auto theft). Typically such teen-agers fail academically, drop out of school in grades 9-11, and become progressively more involved in actions that land them in juvenile hall and later on in jail. Most persons called antisocial are men, and most come from families in which one or both parents are themselves antisocial or alcoholic. Many have been abused as children. Antisocial people tend to regard violence as natural, as a legitimate means to gratify their needs or enforce their wishes. Their behavior tends to provoke violent counterresponses, which confirm antisocial persons' belief that violence is in the natural scheme of things, and that the main problem is how to avoid being caught and punished. Such mutually reinforcing transactions between criminals and society make meaningful interventions by physicians virtually impossible.

Physicians have more to offer in alcohol-related violence. Both men and women commit such acts, though men are more often responsible. The typical story is that of a man who is not ordinarily violent but who after a few beers or mixed drinks becomes progressively more irritable, finds frustration or fault with his wife and children, and then beats them. Contrary to the remorseless antisocial, this person tends (when sober) to regard his actions as wrong, to feel guilty, and to ask forgiveness. Such people often have family histories of alcoholism and child or spouse abuse.

Contrary to remorseless antisocials, violent alcoholics tend (when sober) to recognize their actions as wrong.

Physicians can help their patient by pointing out the linkage between violence and alcohol, that abstinence is the only safe solution. At the same time, they can teach the family strategies to avoid escalation of an incident into frank violence. Generally this involves the spouse's refusing to get into an argument with her drunk mate and, if necessary, physically leaving the scene until he is sober.

Violence to children appears to be a growing problem.

Violence to children appears to be a growing problem. Although much of it is alcohol related, one also sees parents with inadequate personalities and low self-esteem who are unable to tolerate even minor frustrations and reversals (which they tend to regard as personal assaults) without taking action. Sometimes frustrations from adult life are displaced toward children upon whom it is "safe" to vent hostility. Having diagnosed (or suspected) child abuse, physicians should report their findings to the local child protective agency. Although children and abusive parents are often separated, efforts are also made to teach alternatives to physical action in family or marital therapy.

Management of Violent Episodes

On occasion the clinician is confronted by a patient who threatens violence. The psychiatric disorders associated with assaultive acts include organic brain syndromes (delirium and dementia), schizophrenia, and alcohol or drug dependence (Tardiff and Sweillam, 1980). Neurotic conditions and affective disorders carry a much lower assult rate.

In managing potential violence the attitude of the physician is of great importance.

In managing potential violence the attitude of the physician is of great importance. Since many episodes of imminent violence, especially in psychiatric patients, are motivated by an underpinning of severe anxiety, a nonpunitive, reassuring, calming, yet firm attitude is needed. Beyond this the doctor should not attempt to combat a violent patient without adequate help. Indeed it is generally not possible physically to restrain a violent or panicked patient without the assistance of four to six people—one for each limb, one for the head and one to give medication. We are not here recommending that the doctor pounce immediately on a threatening patient with a hoard of attendants; rather the visible presence of such "reserves" can have a calming effect on a patient by underscoring that the physician is determined not to let a violent episode run out of control.

If a calm, reassuring, yet firm approach, coupled with the presence of visible assistants, fails to abort a violent outburst, measures must be taken to restrain the patient. The important principle here is to approach the matter in a coherent and unambivalent fashion: the attendants should all know what they are to do, and if medications are to be given, these should be available prior to beginning efforts to restrain the patient. For effective sedation adults in good health may require 50 mg of chlorpromazine, 5-10 mg of haloperidol, or 10-15 mg of perphenizine intramuscularly. Haloperidol and perphenizine, because they produce fewer hypotensive effects, are much to be preferred. On occasion patients who have not yet gone out of control but appear ready to do so will cooperate by taking liquid antipsychotic medications by mouth (for example, 100-150 mg of chlorpromazine liquid immediately, followed with additional doses of 50-100 mg as necessary while monitoring vital signs. The longer term management of the patient will depend on the nature of the underlying diagnosis and the physician's assessment of what triggered this particular episode.

SCHIZOPHRENIC RELAPSES

As with the development of manic and depressive episodes, symptoms of schizophrenia tend to repeat.

Acute relapses of schizophrenic illnesses or intensification of preexisting schizophrenic symptoms may qualify as a psychiatric crisis for the primary care physician. Schizophrenic symptoms may include delusions and hallucinations as well as other features of bizarre ideation, and such primary symptoms of schizophrenia as peculiar or inappropriate affect, intense ambivalence, autistic thinking, and illogical or loose associations. As with the development of manic and depressive symptoms, the symptoms of schizophrenia usually do not develop overnight, and specific ideas and symptoms tend to repeat with each new episode.

Though usually a relapsing disorder, schizophrenia occurs as a single episode in 20% of cases.

Although a small proportion (perhaps 20%) of schizophrenics will have only a single psychotic episode in a lifetime, schizophrenia tends to be a relapsing disorder. With a history of several psychotic episodes the chances are great of future episodes occurring.

It is important to be aware that early intervention at the beginning of schizophrenic relapse with antipsychotic drugs (for example, chlorpromazine, trifluroperazine, or haloperidol) may be extremely effective. Properly used, these agents at times abort a developing psychotic episode and thus avoid eventual hospitalization. Regrettably, inexperienced physicians sometimes use inadequate doses of antipsychotic medications and are thus ineffective in their treatments.

It is generally agreed that relapses are made less likely if a schizophrenic patient is maintained on antipsychotics over the long term. At the same time, evidence for irreversible toxicity is beginning to surface, as in the example of tardive dyskinesia (choreiform movements of the face, tongue, hands, and feet). Such toxicity poses the therapeutic dilemma as to how long a remitted schizophrenic should remain on antipsychotic drugs. At present we would recommend that an effort be made to lower gradually and discontinue antipsychotic durgs if a patient has remained stable for 4-6 months, but that this be done only with vigorous psychosocial monitoring and treatment.

We recommend that a schizophrenic patient who has been stable for 4-6 months be tapered off from his medications.

From a psychologic point of view physicians as therapists might usefully explore patients' misperceptions. While acknowledging that the perceptions may seem real to patients, physicians might indicate that that they do not necessarily seem real to them. Such acceptance, coupled with honest feedback, is better than trying to convince psychotics that their ideas are "crazy" or wrong.

The decision to hospitalize a psychotic patient may be a complex one.

With respect to hospitalization, it is usually best to hospitalize psychotic patients only when they are a danger either to themselves or to others, or are unable to provide for their needs. Another indication is when sufficient antipsychotic drugs given on an outpatient basis are inadequate. Obviously if schizophrenic patients have a strong network of friends or family who can help manage them, the likelihood is increased that outpatient management will succeed.

CEREBRAL INSUFFICIENCY

Physicians whose practice includes elderly patients must constantly be alert for the behavioral concomitants of cerebral insufficiency. By cerebral insufficiency we mean any physical or chemical insult that reduces the efficiency of brain function. When the disturbance is reversible the clinical syndrome is termed delirium; when it is irreversible it is termed dementia.

The cardinal symptoms of cerebral insufficiency are a decline in cognitive function in such abilities as attention orientation, perception, thinking, memory, and judgment. In cerebral insufficiency of gradual onset the earliest symptoms may be those of vague malaise, anxiety, mild depression, or general discomfort. It is as though patients sense that there is something wrong but cannot quite put their finger on what the matter is. Alternatively, the earliest clues to a dementing process may be observations by others (for example, spouses, family members, co-workers) that persons seem to be more forgetful, less reliable, and less efficient than they used to be. As the syndrome progresses, obvious deterioration of short-duration and intermediate-duration memory and disturbances in language such as aphasia, and in perception can become prominent. In the late stages, depending on the cause of dementia or delirium, there can be prominent neurologic signs such as seizures, disturbances in state of consciousness, sudden periods of weakness, and severe confusion.

The earliest clue of cerebral insufficiency may occur during an acute illness or drug treatment.

The earliest clue that a person has cerebral insufficiency may occur during an acute illness episode or during treatment with medications that have effects on brain function. For example, an elderly person might be functioning rather well and then develop pneumonia. During the febrile episode the patient may become frankly confused, disoriented, and psychotic. As the infection resolves the patient comes back to a normal or near normal level of functioning. If such a person had been investigated closely from a neuropsychologic standpoint, even before getting pneumonia, the physician might have observed definite decrements in cognitive function. It is important to note these early clues to a dementing process since some dementias are in fact reversible.

The usual causes of dementia in the elderly are "senile dementia" (also known as Alzheimer variant dementia) and dementia related to arteriosclerotic cerebrovascular disease. Some less common causes of dementia are normal pressure hydrocephalus, dementias related to nutritional deficiencies (for example, thiamine deficiency, vitamin B_{12} deficiency, and folic acid deficiency) and some of the dementias associated with endocrinopathies (for example, hypothyroidism and hyperparathyroidism).

Do not accept the fact that it is natural for an elderly person to become confused.

The basic principles to be followed by prevention-minded primary care physicians should be not to accept the fact that it is natural for elderly persons to become confused. Indeed there is good information that healthy elderly persons can retain excellent brain function even until they are in their 90s. Thus periods of confusion and disorientation should alert physicians to the possibility that there may be a specific disease affecting brain function, and this should lead them to look for reversible causes. Clearly, causes such as those related to infection, trauma, vitamin deficiency, exogenous intoxication by drugs (usually iatrogenic) and endocrinopathies are potentially reversible and should be considered in every case. Assuming that it has been established that the patient has a dementing process that is not reversible (for example, Alzheimer variant dementia or arteriosclerotic dementia), the next job will be to assure that the patient's level of function remains as high as possible despite the underlying illness: patients with dementia should be encouraged to do for themselves everything that it is possible for them to do. It is important not to infantalize patients or facilitate their regression into a childlike or helpless mode of being.

There is good information that healthy elderly persons can retain excellent brain function into their 90s.

As a general principle it is important to maintain a demented patient's sense of orientation and continuity with the past. Thus, to the extent possible, these patients should be managed in familiar settings and they should not be institutionalized unless and until absolutely necessary. Even when institutionalization becomes essential, it is important that patients be allowed to bring favorite and familiar articles of clothing and other belongings (things such as their teeth, hearing aides, glasses), and attempts at orientation be made (for example, night lights and decreasing sensory and personal isolation).

Demented patients can also do better if physicians and other helping people try to maximize the efficiency of those functions that are still preserved.

Demented patients can also do better if physicians and other helping people try to maximize the efficiency of those functions that are still preserved. For example, persons who have some aphasic difficulties might benefit if their room, instead of being labeled with their name, were labeled with some symbol with which they could identify. Similarly, a bathroom door might have a picture of a sink or a toilet on it rather than simply a word label. It goes without saying that every effort needs to be exerted to improve sensory function (for example, eyeglasses or hearing aids as appropriate). An informative and supportive attitude with families of demented patients might forestall premature institutionalization and recommend placement when it is clear that families have overextended themselves in a way that might be detrimental to the patient or family.

ALCOHOLISM

We prefer a definition based on problems related to alcohol.

The highest rates of alcoholism occur between 30-50 years of age.

Primary care physicians should obtain alcohol histories in all their patients.

Ethanol in the form of alcoholic beverages is the most commonly used of the recreational drugs in the United States. Because the majority of adults drink, physicians mistakenly do not always consider alcohol as a contributant to the health problems of their patients. There are many ways of defining alcoholism. We prefer a definition based on problems related to alcohol. In this diagnostic framework primary care physicians may consider that their patients are alcoholics if they answer positively to questions about marital separation or divorce, job loss or lay-off, multiple arrests, or physical disorders that are related to drinking. Using this sort of definition, it has been estimated that between 5% and 10% of the adult male population in the United States will demonstrate alcoholism sometime during their lives, and that 20%-35% of general medical or surgical patients are alcoholics. The highest rates of alcoholism are seen in people 30-50 years of age, and the usual age at which alcoholics first present for treatment for their disease is around 40 years of age.

Primary care physicians should obtain alcohol histories in all their patients. In particular, they should view with a high degree of suspicion patients who present with recurrent episodes of gastrointestinal disorders or evidence of recurrent accidents such as bruises and injuries and other nonspecific complaints that seem to have a cyclicity. Physicians should be aware that to get proper alcohol histories, they may have to ask repeatedly some very specific questions. People tend to deny their rate of drinking and also to deny the health and psychosocial consequences of drinking.

The early diagnosis of alcoholism is particularly important for a patient's future health. Doctors should be aware that alcoholics have increased rates of mortality from all causes over moderate drinkers and nondrinkers, and tend to manifest more diseases in a variety of organ systems—in particular, rates of gastrointestinal and urinary tract malignancies, ulcer disease, liver disease, neurological illness, arteriosclerosis, hypertension, and myopathy are higher among alcoholics. Thus alcohol along with tobacco are two important sources of morbidity and shortening of life span among patients. It is obvious that the early diagnosis, treatment, and prevention of alcoholism can serve to help prevent a whole host of illnesses and premature deaths.

Once it has been established that alcoholism is a definite or even probable diagnosis, physicians should urge their patients to seek specialized care for their condition. In general, physicians, psychiatrists, psychologists, and others in solitary practice are not very successful in the treatment of alcoholism. It is best to determine what facilities are available in the community and to refer patients for expert help. Such help might include inpatient alcoholism treatment units, Alcoholics Anonymous, special outpatient programs, and similar treatment resources.

Finally, bear in mind that even those people who have a clear diagnosis of alcoholism may, in fact, remit on their own. It has been estimated that perhaps as many as one third of all heavy drinkers and alcoholics manage to achieve stable abstinence without any professional help. Although it is beyond the scope of this chapter to discuss the many medical consequences of alcoholism, several useful guides exist (for example, Kissin and Begleiter, 1974).

Perhaps as many as one third of all heavy drinkers and alcoholics manage to achieve stable abstinence without any professional help.

DRUG ABUSE

The term "drug abuse" has become a wastebasket for all sorts of behaviors related to nonmedical drug use, ranging from occasional smoking of marijuana cigarettes to daily injections of heroin. Such lumping together of behaviors that are so clearly different has had the unfortunate effect of overly dramatizing trivial episodes of nonmedical drug use, while at the same time allowing some sections of society to deny the serious effects of other forms of drug misuse.

To clarify some of the confusion, it is worthwhile to remember that there are various patterns and stages of nonmedical drug use. Initial or experimental use suggests that a person has had, probably out of curiosity, only one or at the most a few experiences with a particular agent. Occasional use suggests that a person has had previous experiences but that such use tended to be unplanned, occurring fortuitously in social contexts where the drug was available. Regular use suggests a pattern where drug taking has become a matter of routine. Such regular use can be "recreational" (that is, occurring regularly at such events as rock concerts and parties) or it can be "functional" (for example the use of psychostimulants by truck drivers). The final category of drug use can be considered dependent drug use. This suggests that a person's psychologic or physical welfare is closely linked to the chosen chemical. Under psychologic dependence, we would describe circumstances in which persons come to believe that they need a chosen chemical to feel comfortable. Physical dependence (addiction) suggests that there will be physical withdrawal signs if the drug is abruptly discontinued.

By understanding these various patterns of drug abuse, family practitioners may be able to determine whether or not the drug use is "serious" (likely to have psychosocial or medical conse-

By understanding these various patterns of drug abuse, family practitioners may be able to determine whether or not the drug use is "serious."

quences). Another factor to consider, however, is the nature of the drug that is used. Some chemicals are inherently more dangerous to a person's psychologic or physical health. Thus in general drugs such as marijuana are regarded as being less likely to be harmful physically or psychologically than such CNS depressants as barbiturates. Lastly, in addition to the actual chemical used, doctors should be aware of individual differences in response to drugs. Some persons, particularly those with inadequate, antisocial, or dependent personalities, are more likely to enter a career of serious drug taking than are other people.

Recognizing drug use as a problem is similar to recognizing the alcoholic.

Recognizing drug use as a problem is similar to recognizing the alcoholic. Physicians should determine whether or not the use of drugs interferes materially with a person's marriage or family life, or work or school, gets the person in trouble with the law, or is causing physical harm. Early clues to drug abuse among children and adolescents are gradual and unexplained deterioration in scholastic performance, increasing difficulties with parents or peers, increased frequency of accidents, and unexplained absences from school. There are also some specific signs of specific chemical usage. For example, people abusing amphetamines tend to have periods of hyperactivity, grandiosity, and perhaps paranoia, cycling with periods of withdrawal, depression, and fatigue. On the other hand, persons taking CNS-depressant drugs might have periods of lethargy, confusion, nystagmus, and ataxia, alternating with periods of irritability and hostile outbursts, which correspond to early withdrawal.

Phencyclidine (PCP, angel dust) has become a popular drug of abuse in the last decade. Acute intoxication with this agent may produce intermittently a syndrome of confusion and combativeness, sometimes coupled with catatonia and convulsions. PCP overdoses can be life threatening, with hyperthermia, hypertension, convulsions, and respiratory arrest. Because of severe confusion and disorientation and the tendency for patients to wax and wane in their psychotic state, intoxicated PCP abusers can be particularly dangerous and should be isolated in a quiet place where they can do themselves and others no harm. Recovery from PCP can take several weeks to a month.

The general principles of treatment of drug use and abuse will depend in part on the pattern of drug use/abuse, underlying psychopathology (if any), the meaning of drugs to the individual and the specific drugs being used. It will frequently be important in the case of teen-age drug abuse to involve the family. For example, in some families we have noted that very trivial experimentation with marijuana can cause parents to label their children as drug addicts and, on the other hand, enormous denial can operate in other families so that a child who is using heroin might be excused as simply experimenting.

In the instance where primary care physicians determine that drug use is experimental or occasional, they might wish to undertake more of an educational-exploratory or supportive approach with patients. In many such instances it is sufficient to provide data about likely effects and side effects of drugs and advice about attitudes toward such drugs. On the other hand, if patients are dependent drug users, or entering into that arena, physicians should identify this problem to their patients and seek to refer them to specialized drug treatment agencies. As with alcoholism, established drug abuse can be an intractable problem and is not easily treated by the individual physician in the office setting.

IATROGENIC PSYCHIATRIC CRISES

Manifestations and Treatment of Iatrogenic Psychiatric Crises

A variety of psychiatric and medical drugs have side effects that can cause changes in mental function, mood, and behavior.

A variety of psychiatric and medical drugs have side effects that can cause changes in mental function, mood, and behavior. Depression can be induced by oral contraceptives and by those centrally acting antihypertensive drugs that deplete catecholamines. Reserpine (Serpasil) induced depression can present initially after a fairly long period of administration (4-6 months). Alpha-methyldopa (Aldomet) has been estimated to cause depression in 4%-6% of patients. Generally depression caused by antihypertensive drugs occurs in patients who have a propensity toward depression, either by family history or by previous depressive episodes.

Depression can also occur after cessation of psychostimulants such as amphetamine or sympathomimetic anorexigenics. In high doses such drugs can also cause an acute paranoid episode essentially indistinguishable from paranoid schizophrenia. This psychosis apparently is not related to preexisting psychopathology. The primary care physicians should thus be aware that any patient receiving a psychostimulant may develop such a psychosis. In addition, patients who have preexisting psychotic illness with symptoms, given a small dose of a psychostimulant, may have a dramatic activation of such symptoms.

The corticosteroids cause a variety of psychiatric symptoms including psychosis (delusions, hallucinations, and loss of touch with reality), elation, euphoria, and depression. Importantly, the corticosteroid-like drugs' ability to cause affect disorder is not really related to prior existing history of affect disorder. Treatment may involve withdrawal or decreasing the dose of corticosteroid and use of an appropriate antipsychotic or antidepressant drug.

Elderly psychiatric patients are at special risk for the central anticholinergic syndrome.

Many drugs can induce a delirious state, which has been termed the central anticholinergic syndrome. The agents include atropinics, antiparkinsonians, antipsychotics (especially thioridazine-Mellaril), tricyclic antidepressants, antihistaminics, and components of many over-the-counter cold and sleeping preparations. Elderly psychiatric patients are at special risk because they are sometimes prescribed combinations of antipsychotics, antidepressnats, and antiparkinsonians with cumulative atropinic effect. Patents may manifest aggression, agitation, anxiety, and most importantly, considerable cognitive impairment including hallucinations, confusion, loss of memory, and disorientation. The central anticholinergic syndrome in the elderly often can be mistaken for a senile state and thereby be missed. Furthermore, when the central anticholinergic syndrome occurs in psychotic patients, the picture is not dissimilar from that occurring in the original illness (for example, schizophrenic symptoms might be exacerbated in a schizophrenic). Thus a delirious patient may be misdiagnosed as having a relapse. The key to diagnosing the central anticholinergic syndrome is (a) recognizing that the patient's sudden or gradual mental deterioration is secondary to a delirium; (b) noting such typical physical signs as tachycardia, mild hypertension, dry skin and mouth, and dilated pupils; and (c) connecting these with agents being taken. Treatment involves discontinuation of the anticholinergic agent and/or injection of physostigmine (0.25-3.0 mg intramuscularly).

In the elderly the drug-induced central anticholinergic syndrome often can be mistaken for senility.

Treatment involves discontinuation of the anticholinergic agent and/or injection of physostigmine.

For prevention it is worthwhile to note that there are several medications that have peripheral anticholinergic properties but that do not have prominent central anticholinergic effects. In the elderly or in patients especially prone to having anticholinergic central toxicity, these preparations may be very useful (examples are glycopyrrolate and propantheline).

Digitalis preparations can also cause confusion, depression, lethargy, and hallucinations.

Beyond the anticholinergic agents, several other classes of drugs are capable of producing delirium. These include anticancer drugs such as cyclophosphamide and cis-platinum, which can cause confusional episodes, sometimes accompanied by psychotic thinking. Digitalis preparations can also cause confusion, depression, lethargy, and hallucinations. The antituberculosis drugs have been known to produce confusional, psychotic, and affective disorders. Disulfiram psychosis can occur in patients who have not ingested alcohol; the syndrome may range from a disoriented confusional state to symptoms mimicking a functional psychosis such as schizoprhenia or mania.

Another drug that can cause a variety of psychiatric symptoms is L-dopa. L-dopa therapy can induce confusion, depression, hypomania, paranoid states, and hypersexuality. These effects are often dose related. Lithium is also associated with tremor, ataxia, and delirium in high doses. Minor tranquilizers and sedative-hypnotics are sometimes associated with confusion, disorientation, and memory difficulties in the elderly.

Host and Environmental Factors Predisposing to Behavioral Toxicity

It is perhaps only common sense to note that drug toxicity does not occur in a vacuum. Different people respond variously to agents under different circumstances. For example, there are people who seem particularly sensitive to or even magnify the most subtle and early effects of various psychoactive drugs, noticing changes that most people would ignore. Such persons may have such reactions as excessive drowsiness, irritability, and dizziness to low doses of any drug that has psychotropic effects. Patients with such responses should probably not be prescribed psychoactive drugs unless they are clearly essential; if they are prescribed, the physician will have to pay special attention to reassurance, explanation, and empathetic listening to assure adherence to the regimen.

A person's current mental state may also determine drug effects. Thus a person who is chronically anxious might respond more unfavorably to stimulant preparations than a calm person would. A depressive individual might experience more profound depressant effects from a given tranquilizer than an ordinary person. Behavioral toxicity from levodopa has been linked to previous psychiatric history. Cerebral intactness might also determine behavioral drug effects: persons with early or moderate dementia, as with arteriosclerotic cerebrovascular disease or senile dementia, might respond unfavorably to even rather low doses of psychoactive medications. Such persons might experience extreme confusion, drowsiness, or psychotic behavior from low doses of chlordiazepoxide, antidepressants, or drugs with central anticholinergic effects.

Environmental conditions can contribute to drug toxicity.

Lastly, environmental conditions can contribute to drug toxicity. Every physician will be aware of the stressful effect of the intensive care unit (ICU), as an example. The ICU presumably exerts part of its effects through its sense of unreality, loss of track of time, loss of familiar persons and possessions, extreme fatigue, and monotonous stimulation. Similarly, elderly persons who might have some subclinical cerebral insufficiency are vulnerable to episodes of confusion, irritability, or psychosis when taken out of their familiar surroundings and removed from friends and familiar possessions.

Thus management of the psychiatric toxicity of medications requires the physician to understand not only which agents can cause what kinds of problems but also the individual characteristics and circumstances that tend to highlight the negative effects of such drugs. Finally, past history of toxic reactions is a very good indicator of future difficulties; thus an accurate history is important.

DEATH AND DYING

Considerable clinical research on patients' emotional reactions to life-threatening illness or death has occurred. With this information the primary care physician can be most helpful to patients who are weathering the storms of a serious or fatal illness. Many of the ideas that will be discussed have been developed by Kubler-Ross (1970).

The initial response to the news of having a serious illness such as a neoplastic disease tends to be shock, disbelief, and intense anxiety. Patients may become tearful or appear numbed. After these early initial reactions a period of denial may occur. Patients may ask to be seen by other specialists or to have their medical findings sent to experts in other centers to confirm the diagnosis. Although denial is a prominent aspect of the early stages of living with a life-threatening illness, it should be pointed out that it tends to wax and wane throughout the remainder of the person's life. At times when denial is less evident, patients may exhibit anger, depression, or a combination of these two. Anger could be expressed in terms such as "Why did this happen to me?" or it may be manifested by a patient's becoming hostile with physicians or family even to the point of suing the physician or hospital for alleged malpractice. Depression, on the other hand, can be manifested by many of the symptoms described in the section on depression, the most prominent signs being sadness, tearfulness, sleep disturbance, appetite disturbance, and lack of energy.

At times when denial is less evident, patients may exhibit anger, depression, or a combination of these two.

Kubler-Ross has also described a stage of bargaining. Here patients may in effect say, "If only I could do thus and so" (for example, live long enough for my child to graduate from college) "then I will do something else" (for example, agree to certain painful treatments). Many patients, particularly those who have a protracted illness, will reach a stage of some degree of acceptance of their condition. This may not mean that they are wholly comfortable with the thought of dying but rather that they feel somewhat detached and disengaged from their usual cares.

Kubler-Ross has also described a stage of bargaining.

Throughout these various stages there will be a waxing and waning of hope. It is important for primary care physicians to foster hope in seriously ill patients. This does not imply that they should lie or create expectations that will never be met. Rather they can tell patients that everything humanly possible will be done and that newer treatments are always being developed and will certainly be made available should they make sense.

Although these "stages" have been presented sequentially, this should not imply that a patient must go through or be "pushed" through them.

Although these "stages" have been presented sequentially, this should not imply that a patient must go through or be "pushed" through them to attain a "reasonable death." Many patients will experience primarily depression, anxiety, or anger. The role of physicians should be to give patients an opportunity to express their feelings, to provide comfort and emotional support, and to foster a sense of dignity. For this they must set aside some extra time to work with seriously ill or terminal patients. Perhaps more important than time is attitude. Physicians who spend 5 minutes in a hospital room standing in a posture that implies that they are ready to bolt out at any moment are providing less support to the patient than physicians who sit down face to face with patients for the same 5 minutes. Finally, physicians who are effective care givers with dying patients tend to be the ones who have considered their own death to some extent. Such physicians might not be comfortable with these thoughts but at least they recognize some of their own fears and anticipations.

ANNOTATED BIBLIOGRAPHY

Akiskal, H. S., and McKinney, W. T. 1975. Overview of recent research in depression: Integration of ten conceptual models into a comprehensive clinical frame. *Arch. Gen. Psychiatry.* 32:285-305.
A comprehensive review of recent thinking about the etiology of depression. Includes considerations of biologic, psychologic, and psychosocial models.

Beck, A. T. 1967. *Depression: Clinical, experimental and theoretical aspects.* New York: Hoeber Medical Division, Harper & Row Publishers.
An overview of the literature on depression, including classification, etiology, treatment, and treatment outcome. Since the book was written in the late 1960s, it is not quite up to date. However, the section on cognitive treatment of depression is excellent.

The section on cognitive treatment of depression is excellent.

Erickson, E. H. 1963. *Childhood and society.* New York: W. W. Norton & Company, Inc.

A classic work on man's "ages and stages" from a psychoanalytic-social frame of reference.

Grant, I. 1979. *Behavioral disorders: Understanding clinical psychopathology.* Holliswood, N. Y.: Spectrum Publications, Inc.
An introductory text on psychopathology addressing such issues as normality, interviewing, classification, and major syndromes from a biologic, psychologic, and social perspective.

Kissin, B., and Begleiter, H. 1974. *The biology of alcoholism.* Vol. 3. New York: Plenum Press, Inc.
Volume 3 of an excellent series, covering a wide range of topics in alcoholism, deals with topics such as the natural history of alcoholism, psychological factors in alcoholism acute and chronic effects of alcohol, and rehabilitation of the alcoholic.

Kubler-Ross, E. 1970. *On death and dying.* New York: The Macmillan Company.
A seminal work on psychological adaptation of persons to terminal illness, with suggestions as to the role of the physician.

Lester, G., and Lester, D. 1971. *Suicide: The gamble with death.* Englewood Cliffs, N. J.: Prentice-Hall, Inc.
A short but comprehensive review of the literature on suicide, including such topics as epidemiology, risk factors, and evaluation and management strategies.

Levinson, D. J. 1978. *The seasons of a man's life.* New York: Alfred A. Knopf, Inc.
One of the few books that deals with man's "mid-life." Some of the conclusions might be limited by virtue of the special sample of men that the author studied; nevertheless it represents an excellent start in a neglected field.

An excellent start in a neglected field.

Morris, J. B., and Beck, A. T. 1974. The efficacy of antidepressant drugs: A review of research (1958-1974). *Arch. Gen. Psychiatry* 30:667-674.
A good review of the literature on the efficacy of tricyclic antidepressants, monoamine oxidase (MAO) inhibitors, and lithium in the treatment of depression. The article was written in 1974; hence the review cannot be considered completely current.

Piaget, J. 1962. The stages of intellectual development of the child. *Bull Menninger Clin.* 26:120.
An exposition of Piaget's ideas about the cognitive development of children.

Rifkin, A.; Quitkin, F.; and Klein, D. F. 1976. Withdrawal reaction to diazepam (Letter to Editor). *J. A. M. A.* 236:2172-2173.
Describes a case report of a withdrawal reaction to diazepam (Valium).

Schneidman, E. S. 1975. Suicide. *Encyclopaedia Britannica.* 17:777-782.

An excellent review concerning suicide.

An excellent review concerning suicide including considerable emphasis on evaluation and management, written by one of the experts in the field.

Tardiff, K., and Sweillam, A. 1980. Assault, suicide, and mental illness. *Arch. Gen. Psychiatry.* 37:164-169.
Describes the relationship of violent behaviors to psychiatric diagnosis.

Winokur, A.; Rickels, K.; Greenblatt, D. J., et al. 1980. Withdrawal reaction from long-term, low dosage administration of diazepam. *Arch. Gen. Psychiatry.* 37:101-105.

Discusses the syndrome of withdrawal from long-term low-dosage administration of diazepam (Valium).

Discusses the syndrome of withdrawal from long-term low-dosage administration of diazepam (Valium).

8 Prevention in Dentistry

Max H. Schoen

Dr. Schoen is a graduate of the University of Southern California, School of Dentistry, and received his Dr.P.H. from the University of California, Los Angeles, School of Public Health. He has been on the faculty of the University of Connecticut, School of Dental Medicine, the University of Southern California, School of Dentistry, the School of Dental Medicine, State University of New York at Stonybrook, and is presently Chairman of the Section of Preventive Dentistry and Public Health at the University of California, Los Angeles, School of Dentistry. He has been a member of many expert committees and has published widely in the area of Public Health Dentistry.

Brief Contents

Overview

Many diseases have oral manifestations; two of them dominate the dental field and affect more than 90% of Americans at some time during their lives—dental caries (tooth decay) and peridontal disease (which attacks the supporting structures of the teeth). Dental caries can be prevented almost completely by a combination of systemic and topical fluorides supplemented by pit and fissure sealants and a diet low in refined carbohydrates. While no environmental preventive measure exists for periodontal disease, the combination of regular professional prophylaxis and good personal oral hygiene can prevent the disease or at least reduce its severity.

HISTORICAL BACKGROUND

Records of dental treatment date back to ancient civilizations, while some of the earliest efforts at prevention occurred in Arab medicine around the ninth century. A small wooden stick with a chewed brush-like end was used for oral hygiene. The importance of keeping teeth clean to prevent disease was emphasized by various authorities as early as the eleventh century. Subsequently dietary proscriptions on heavy concentrations of sugar were initiated in Europe in the fifteenth and sixteenth centuries. In the 1800s, dentistry became a recognized profession in the United States. A major step in the history of dental disease prevention was taken in 1973 with the establishment by Dr. Alfred Fones of the first school for dental hygienists in Bridgeport, Connecticut.

In the early 1930s fluoride in the water was identified as the cause of mottled enamel. Shortly thereafter, H. Trendley Dean and others established the relationship between optimum fluoride concentrations in drinking water and reduced dental caries. Controlled trials first started in the 1940s. By now this public health measure has been the subject of the most exhaustive investigations and trials. Its efficacy, safety, and low cost have been proved to a degree unsurpassed by any other disease-preventive agent.

CONSEQUENCES OF CARIES AND PERIODONTAL DISEASE

This discussion assumes that it is better to prevent dental caries than to treat and restore teeth, even if the restorations last many years. It also assumes that retention of teeth is almost invariably more desirable than teeth loss, usually from extraction.

No matter how good the restoration, the situation is never quite the same once a virgin healthy tooth requires treatment. In the first place, despite tremendous improvements in the restorative dental process, and resultant decreased discomfort, it still is not enjoyable to have an operation on a tooth. Surgery in any form— and operative dentistry is a form of surgery—should be avoided if possible. Second, restorations (fillings, onlays, and crowns) may be more sensitive to temperature and chemical change than the normal tooth. Third, the margins, or edges, of restorations are never perfect, can break down, and become areas that are more susceptible to plaque formation than untouched healthy areas. Plaque formation leads both to caries and to periodontal disease. Thus the more restorations present in a mouth, the greater the potential for disease. Finally, treatment is almost always more expensive than prevention.

Plaque formation leads to both caries and periodontal disease.

When periodontal disease is involved, treatment cannot replace destroyed structures as in the case of caries. Therefore the alternatives just discussed are not even available for consideration.

If possible, avoid tooth loss.

Regardless of which disease is responsible, tooth loss or extraction is considered the least desirable alternative. The loss of a single tooth rarely causes a noticable decrease in function in the short run. If loss occurs in the anterior region, it may result in a severe esthetic problem. Replacement of one missing tooth or even several teeth can be accomplished in both mechanically and esthetically satisfactory ways, but the same kinds of problems as those discussed previously occur in tooth restoration after removal of caries. However, if lost teeth are not replaced the adjacent and opposing teeth may tip or drift into the space. The changed architecture and loss of integrity of the oral structures make oral hygiene more difficult, clearly leading to greater plaque formation and consequently more disease.

As more teeth are lost, it becomes more difficult to chew unless replacements are made. But functional problems become even worse when all teeth are lost. Many persons adapt successfully to full dentures, but many do not. Since dentures rest on the mucous membrane and natural teeth are imbedded in bone, there is no comparison to the amount of chewing force that can be exerted. A denture is not permanent either, since tissues change and denture materials fracture. Comparing a denture to natural teeth is not much different from comparing a natural limb to an artificial limb. It is rare that a substitute is preferred over the original, even if the original has been repaired.

Most tooth loss is attributable to either caries or periodontal disease.

Since most tooth loss is attributable to either caries or periodontal disease, edentulism must be viewed as an indicator of the destructive effects of both.

Of the United States population from 65-74 years of age, 45% are edentulous.

Even in the 18-44 year age bracket, 4.1% of the population were edentulous in 1971-74 national health surveys. This prevalence rose to 23.8% of 45-64 year olds, 45.5% of 65-74 year olds (Kelly and Harvey, 1979), and 60% of those 75 years and older. Women have more edentulism than men, and whites more than blacks. The disparity by income and education is large. Those 45-65 year olds who have less than 9 years of education and earn less than $5,000 annually have an edentulism rate of 37%. Those with 12 years or more of education and incomes of $10,000 or more have a rate of only 12%. For persons 65 years and older, the comparative rates for the same socioeonomic levels are 60% and 30%, respectively (Burnham, 1974).

Although prevalence of dental disease is high regardless of variation in demographics, the outcome as measured by tooth loss is radically different. Despite a few small apparent or unexplained aberrations (for example, less edentulism in blacks than in whites and less in men than in women), there is a correlation with socioeconomic status.

DENTAL CARIES

Epidemiology

Evidence of the existence of dental caries in earlier times can be obtained from skulls with teeth that are generally well preserved. Although tooth decay existed several thousand years ago, it was far less prevalent (Caldwell and Stallard, 1977). It appears to have increased steadily as society evolved. The hypothesis that caries is a disease of modern civilization is supported by findings that even today primitive societies have a low caries rate, which increases rapidly on exposure to our culture, particularly the diet.

In the United States approximately 10% of children have decayed teeth by age 2 years.

Decay attacks the primary teeth shortly after they appear in the mouth. In the United States approximately 10% of children have decayed teeth by age 2 years (Caldwell and Stallard, 1977). The percentage of children with one or more decayed "baby" teeth and the number of teeth attacked per child increase with age. By 17 years of age 94% of youths have had at least one decayed permanent tooth. Most disturbing is the fact that more than

Up to the age of 35 years, it is generally agreed that most tooth loss is caused by caries.

one tooth per person has already been extracted by this age because of decay. Up to the age of 35 years, it is generally agreed that most tooth loss is caused by caries.

Although blacks have less decay than whites, a much smaller proportion of diseased teeth are restored. In general differences in treatment follow expected socioeconomic patterns regardless of race. Those with lower incomes and less education have more missing and decayed teeth and fewer filled teeth than their more affluent and better educated counterparts.

Although dental caries is most active in children and young adults, it continues to attack teeth throughout life. However, it is much more difficult to determine incidence after the age of 35 years, since the number of teeth at risk decreases with age and tooth loss may be the result of a variety of causes.

Pathogenesis

Destruction of tooth structures is irreversible.

Dental caries is a multifactorial disease that attacks the hard structures of the teeth. It is chronic in nature and largely irreversible; once destruction occurs, the body cannot repair the damage. It is so prevalent that more than 90% of the United States population are affected by it at some time during their lives.

Plaque bacteria destroy enamel and dentin.

Colonies of bacteria form on the tooth surface in a complex film called *dental plaque.* They ferment carbohydrates, primarily sugars, into acid, which demineralizes the tooth enamel. As this process continues, the bacteria invade the destroyed enamel and demineralization proceeds through the entire enamel layer. Next the dentin is attacked, with destruction spreading out laterally as well as to a greater depth. Since the dentin is not as hard as enamel, considerable undermining usually takes place. The tooth therefore may appear to be relatively intact even after considerable destruction has taken place. At some point the unsupported enamel collapses and a large cavity seems to appear suddenly.

The process continues until the central portion of the tooth, the pulp chamber, is affected. This chamber contains a rich nerve and blood supply and is often called the *nerve* of the tooth. As decay proceeds deeper into the tooth, considerable sensitivity can result from temperature change and from certain foods that cause a reaction in the pulp. Pain can become extreme.

After a further period of time the pulp tissue is destroyed, and the infection proceeds down the root canal and out of the apex of the tooth into the periodontal ligament and the bone. An acute phase may result in which considerable pus is formed. Until drainage is achieved, pain may be excruciating. After the acute phase, or often without it, the destructive process proceeds slowly, resulting in further cavitation of the bone around the apex of the tooth. This is the chronic abscess that is visible on dental radiographs. Over a period of years some of these get extremely large and can invade other structures. In the meantime tooth substance is continually being eaten away until the entire crown is destroyed and the roots are attacked.

Certain areas of the tooth are more susceptible than others. One particular area is that which consists of enamel pits and fissures. These junction areas where the enamel fuses during its developmental process often contain defects where plaque can form easily and where it can resist disruption from most cleaning processes. The area just below the point of contact of adjacent teeth is another such susceptible area since it too is a choice location for plaque formation.

Prevention

Caries can occur if four factors are present: (a) a susceptible tooth, (b) bacteria, (c) suitable substrate, and (d) time. If any of these factors are lacking, dental decay will not take place. Therefore preventive efforts can be directed toward each factor and achieve some success.

The most effective preventive measure is water fluoridation.

The single most effective measure to date has been water fluoridation. Classical epidemiologic studies, briefly described earlier, discovered that approximately one part fluoride for every million parts of water in the water supply reduced decay by about 60%. This level of fluoride is harmless, as verified by large number of studies. It is extremely cost effective: annual costs range from about $ .15 to $1.50 for each person, and no specific individual action is necessary for it to succeed (Burt, 1978). Water fluoridation appears to make the tooth enamel less susceptible to caries. Exposure, to be most effective should start at birth. Once all teeth are erupted, water fluoridation has little effect.

To be most effective fluoride exposure should start at birth.

At present about half of the population live in communities with either naturally or artificially fluoridated water. Unfortunately it has proved to be difficult to get authorities to institute this major public health measure in many communities. All manner of arguments have been raised, including concerns about the safety of fluoridated water, infringement of civil liberties, and accusations that it is a Communist plot. However, although all too slowly, fluoridation is gradually being extended to all communities with central water supplies.

In the event that there is no central water supply in a community, it is possible to get a significant drop in caries—up to

If there is no central water supply in a community it is possible to fluoridate the school water supply.

40%—by fluoridating the school water supply (Newbrun, 1978). Since consumption is limited to certain specific periods of time, a higher concentration is used—about 4½ parts of fluoride for every million parts water. Its decreased effectiveness is because preschool children are by definition not covered, and some permanent teeth are partially or fully mineralized by school age. Total costs of equipment, supplies, and labor amount to less than $1.50 for each child for one year.

Another systemic approach is the use of fluoride tablets or fluoride drops (Burt, 1978). Many pediatricians and dentists prescribe vitamins that contain fluoride. Parents can see that preschoolers get an adequate supply, and tablets can be given out daily to school children while in class.

The cost of tablets for school programs runs from $ .17 to $ .79 for each child for one year. Estimates of total costs including labor range from $ .50 to $5. for each child for one year. Caries reduction has ranged from 20%-35% for permanent teeth. The problem with nonschool programs is mainly one of compliance and secondarily one of increased cost. Except for those preschoolers in organized programs, individual prescription is the only approach possible in the absence of community water fluoridation. Thus a combination of parental administration for very young children and school administration when children commence formal education would appear to approximate the benefits of treating central water supplies, but at greater cost.

Several cautions are necessary at this point. Even if water fluoridation were to be authorized for a community or school, there is no guarantee that the chemical will be added in appropriate amounts. Regular monitoring is necessary to ensure that the correct amount is being added.

It also is essential that physicians and dentists are made aware of the fluoride content of local and school water supplies.

It also is essential that physicians and dentists are made aware of the fluoride content of local and school water supplies, whether natural or artificial, so that they can prescribe properly. Familiarity with the fluoride content of the community water supply (obtained from the local department of public health) will enable physicians to determine appropriate doses of drops or tablets for supplementation. Table 8-1 provides a supplemental fluoride dosage schedule.

Table 8-1

The major side effect of too much fluoride (unless intake is many times the optimum) is unsightly staining or mottling of the teeth. The anticaries effect continues but unacceptable esthetics occur.

Whether fluoride is present in water or not, topical applications provide added benefits.

Whether fluoride is present in water or not, topical applications provide added benefits (Burt, 1978). The first method discovered was the professional application of a 2% sodium

Table 8-1 Supplemental Fluoride Dosage Schedule—By Age

Age	Supplemental Fluoride Dosage (0-0.3)*	(0.3-0.7)*	(0.7)*
Birth to 2 years	0.25 mg	—	—
2-3 years	0.50 mg	0.25 mg	—
3-14 years	1.00 mg	0.50 mg	—

*Concentration of Fluoride in water (ppm).
Source: Newbrun, E. 1978. Dietary fluoride supplementation for the prevention of caries. *Pediatrics* 62:733.

fluoride solution to the teeth immediately following a prophylaxis performed by a dentist or hygienist. The solution is then applied three more times at weekly intervals. The entire process is repeated at ages 7 years, 10 years, and 13 years to cover the permanent teeth shortly after eruption. Benefits are about a 40% decrease in caries incidence. Similar disease reduction is achieved when different combinations of prophylaxis and different fluoride compounds are used at varying intervals. Costs tend to be relatively high and coverage of children in a community spotty unless performed on site in a school-based program. As with other forms of topical application, discussed later in this chapter, the benefit probably is not as lasting as with systemic fluoride since only limited penetration of the tooth surface occurs. In addition, unless the treatment procedure is followed carefully, benefits decrease markedly.

Costs vary considerably, depending on whether a dentist, hygienist, or assistant provides the therapy. It has been estimated that in a school-based program costs for treatments covering a 3-year period would range from $6.19 to $12.60 per child. Private practice costs would be much higher.

It has been discovered that weekly mouth rinsing with a 0.2% of sodium fluoride solution will provide about the same benefit.

More recently it has been discovered that weekly mouth rinsing with a 0.2% of sodium fluoride solution will provide about the same benefit. The advantages are that it could be supervised at school and it would be far less costly. Excluding salaries, since no new personnel would be required, the 3-year cost would be $1.50 per child.

Finally, fluoride in toothpaste also provides benefits. The only behavior required here is regular brushing with a toothpaste containing fluoride. Reductions of 15%-30% have been reported.

It is not yet clear what amount of additive effect would occur if, for example, water fluoridation were supplemented by supervised mouth rinsing and use of a fluoride toothpaste. The benefits are greater than when used singly but not to the degree reported earlier.

Pits and fissures can be protected by plastic sealants.

Fluoride is least effective in preventing caries in the pits and fissures of teeth. These areas, however, can be protected by sealants, which form a protective plastic film over the deep crevices and defects, thereby reducing tooth susceptibility (Burt, 1978). This coating must be applied carefully by dental personnel after prophylaxis and other chemical preparation of the teeth. The slight initial etching of the enamel enables the plastic to adhere to the teeth. The resin is cured either by ultraviolet light or chemical catalyst. When properly applied, the sealant appears to last at least 2 years and is almost 100% effective in preventing pit and fissure caries.

Its value is greatest where the incidence of decay has been decreased by fluoridation. In nonfluoride situations where smooth surface caries occurs interproximally, the resulting restorative treatment usually involves the fissure areas, whether decayed or not. Therefore much of the sealant benefit is lost. Sealants do not bond well to smooth surfaces; thus the two preventive measures supplement each other well.

One major problem with sealants is cost. If a dentist must apply the coating to the teeth, the process is about as expensive as the small restoration it would prevent. Since it must be reapplied at regular intervals and good restorations last much longer than 2 years, it is not at all cost effective. It could be argued that the avoidance of cutting into a tooth is worth the added expense, but these consequences are nowhere nearly as grave as other types of surgical intervention.

If, however, sealants were applied by paradental personnel in a school setting where almost all children would benefit, the cost effectiveness would be increased considerably. Dental assistants could be trained to perform this service and much simpler facilities than a typical dental office could be used.

It is not yet known exactly how much of this almost total prevention of caries in children and adolescents will continue into adult life. Certainly much of it will. Since the caries process seems to decrease after young adulthood, even a postponement will probably have a lasting benefit.

Sugar is the most important cause of caries.

Another effective approach to caries prevention is to reduce the amount of refined carbohydrates in the diet (Burt, 1978). Actually the critical concerns are dose and time. The sugars must be present in the mouth for minimum time periods and in sufficient quantity. Therefore, sticky substances such as certain types of candy and dried fruits are much more harmful than sugars in liquid form, which are swallowed quickly. Similarly, sugars with meals are less harmful than those consumed between meals since concentration is less and they are cleared from the mouth more rapidly. In addition, the more frequent the consumption is, the greater is the harm.

The main problem with this approach is that it has proved to be almost impossible to change the dietary habits of most of the population. Our culture is such that heavily sugared, sticky foods are considered to be a reward or a treat, and their removal is often considered to be a punishment. Television and radio commercials, vending machines, fund drives with candy as bait, and so on militate against change.

Concern for proper nutrition for children (and adults), however, has been increasing. Campaigns for removal of junk-food vending machines from school premises have been initiated. Bans on television commercials directed toward children are being considered. However, the substitution of heavily salted foods for those with high sugar content is changing the problem, not eliminating it. In this regard it is good to see the cooperation that is now taking place among the different public health disciplines.

Fluoride is the most effective preventive measure. Frequent prophylaxis and oral hygiene may also prevent caries.

Theoretically, if it were possible to removal all plaque from the surface of the teeth, decay would not occur. However, programs that have emphasized regular deplaquing have not been shown to have a significant effect on the incidence of dental caries. As will be discussed later, there is a definite correlation with periodontal disease. The exception to these findings has been a group of studies carried out by Axelsson and Lindhe (1977) in Sweden, where frequent prophylaxis combined with topical fluoride produced decreases in caries greater than those achieved by any other methods. Trained auxiliary personnel removed plaque from children's teeth every two weeks at the start of the experiment. Individual instruction in oral hygiene was given and repeated as necessary. The frequency was decreased to every 8 weeks over the course of several years. Although these frequencies are not nearly often enough to prevent plaque from forming in the intervals between treatment, it has been hypothesized that children brush better as a result of the increased attention and the good feeling of the polished teeth. These results have not yet been replicated elsewhere but are worth investigating further.

Similar results were achieved with adults when prophylaxes and home care instruction were given every 2 months and then every 3 months over a 3-year period (Axelsson and Lindhe, 1978). This too has not been replicated; although the periodontal findings are consistent with other studies.

PERIODONTAL DISEASE

Epidemiology

Childhood gingivitis is reversible; during late teens and adulthood gingivitis may lead to permanent destruction.

The complex of disease processes that affect the supporting structures of the teeth also begin their attack at an early age. In children through the age of 17 years, the usual form is gingivitis, or inflammation of the gum tissue surrounding the teeth. While most children have this inflammation at one time or another, it is reversible. However, during the late teens and early adulthood the periodontal ligament and supporting bone begin to be affected and an irreversible, destructive process sets in. In a recent survey, dentulous adults with periodontal disease increased from about 65% in the 18-24-year age group to over 90% of those 65 years and older (Kelly and VanKirk, 1965). The formation of pockets, or the deepening of the crevice between the gum cuff and the tooth surface, is a major indicator of bone loss. Persons with pockets increased from less than 10% in young adults to over 50% in those 65 years and older.

Unlike caries, both incidence and severity of periodontal disease are higher for blacks than for whites. Lower socioeconomic groups, regardless of race, have a higher prevalence and greater severity of the disease than the upper socioeconomic groups. Also unlike caries, periodontal disease is widespread in primitive and underdeveloped societies as well as in developed countries.

Pathogenesis

Periodontal disease becomes irreversible when the periodontal ligament is affected and when bone is destroyed.

Periodontal disease is primarily a chronic disease of almost universal prevalence; it attacks the supporting structures of the teeth. Younger people often have either acute or chronic gingivitis, which is reversible. However, once the periodontal ligament (which attaches the tooth to the bone) is affected and once the bone is destroyed the process is irreversible, although it can be halted. The exact mechanism of tissue destruction is not known but, as with caries, it involves bacterial plaque formation. The process proceeds apically around the tooth until sufficient support is lost so that the tooth becomes mobile and eventually nonfunctional (Figure 8-1). Usually before it exfoliates, the tooth becomes sufficiently painful to be extracted.

Figure 8-1

Certain sites seem more susceptible than others. Molar areas and the lower incisors are particularly affected. Least affected are the lower cuspids.

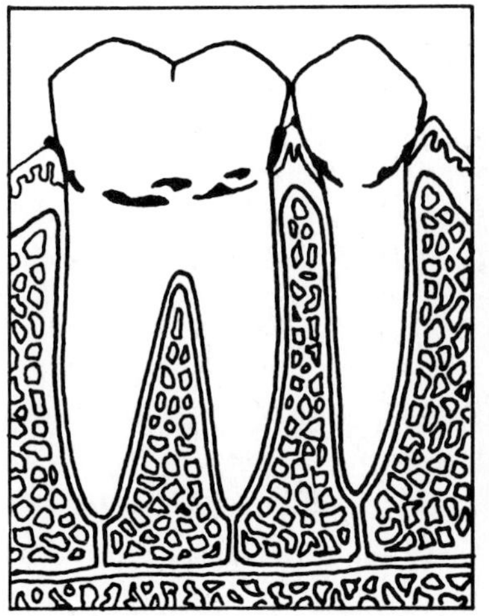

1

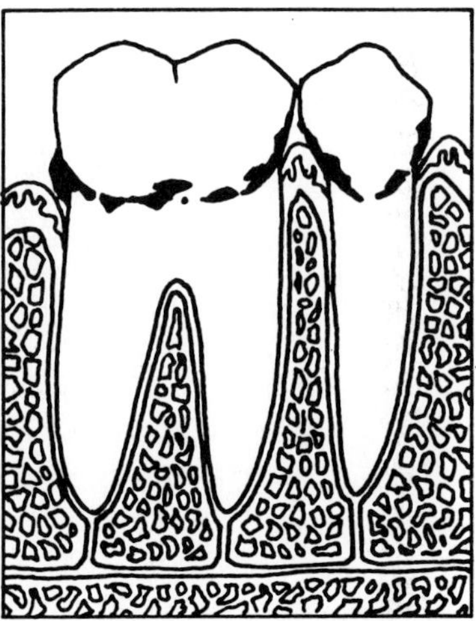

2

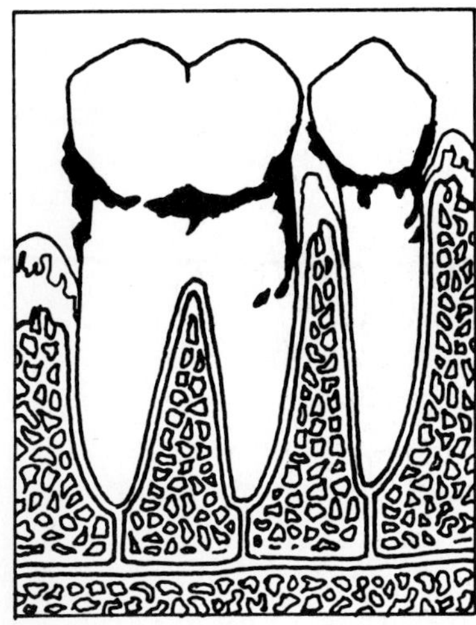

3

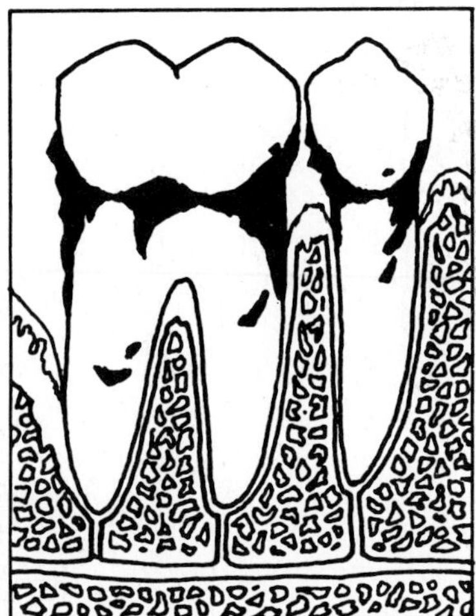

4

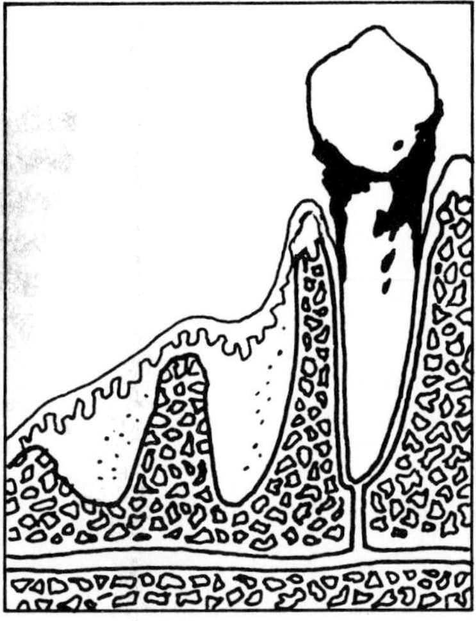

5

Figure 8-1 Progress of periodontal disease.

1. Gingivitis—plaque and hard deposit formation.
2. Initial bone destruction.
3. Increased bone destruction and pocket formation.
4. Severe bone loss, teeth becoming mobile.
5. Tooth loss.

Prevention

Oral hygiene and prophylaxis prevents gingivitis and periodontal disease.

No environmental measure similar to water fluoridation is available for the prevention and control of periodontal disease. However, there is a definite inverse correlation between prevalence and severity on the one hand and professional prophylaxis and oral hygiene on the other. The "cleaner" the mouth the less the disease. The correlation between increased plaque and increased disease has been verified by numerous studies conducted over many years in various parts of the world. This correlation applies to both gingivitis and the more destructive forms of periodontal disease.

Professional prophylaxis may greatly reduce rates of periodontal disease.

At least three controlled studies of the effects of professional prophylaxis (including deep scaling and curettage) on this disease in adults have been done. In two of the studies frequency of prophylaxis was every 3 months (Lovdal et al., 1961; Suomi et al., 1973), but in the third study it started on a bimonthly basis and then was reduced to the 3-month interval (Axelsson and Lindhe, 1978). In each study the various indices of disease were found to be reduced sharply when compared with matched controls. Gingival inflammation and pocket depth and height of bony support were far better in the experimental groups. In one study, even several years after the experiment was terminated, significant differences remained. Major improvement was noted even when home care was poor, although the combination of good personal oral hygiene with the prophylaxis produced the most dramatic results.

Far more needs to be done to determine appropriate intervals for prophylaxis. It is likely that this would vary with each individual. However, an organized program of thorough prophylaxis performed by hygienists at 3-month intervals, with exceptions for those who appeared to need it less frequently, would have the potential of resulting in a major decrease in periodontal disease in adults, in whom it is the most serious dental problem. While total cost might equal or exceed that resulting from neglect, this cost would be spread out evenly over a lifetime rather than occur as a large expense every few years. In addition, the possibility of reducing edentulousness to almost zero and tooth loss to a very low figure would be worth considering even if the total cost of dental care were not reduced.

No specific brushing technique has been found to be superior.

Many brushing methods and additional cleansing aids such as electric toothbrushes and water irrigating devices have been recommended. It appears that any approach that works for the individual is appropriate. Soft nylon brushes with rounded bristles minimize abrasion. Results of oral hygiene activities should be checked by hygienists or dentists for effectiveness in plaque removal and to ensure that damage from excessive diligence does not occur. The current recommendation is to brush thoroughly at least once a day. This frequency will prevent the plaque from organizing into a destructive matrix.

Brushing thoroughly at least once a day will prevent plaque from organizing into a destructive matrix.

Both professionals and the patient can determine whether or not the plaque has been removed, through the use of disclosing tablets or solutions. These consist of vegetable dyes, which after application and a rinse will leave a stain on areas covered with plaque. The cleansing technique being used can then be modified to ensure plaque removal from those areas that continue to show stain. Special brushes can be obtained that get at areas that are difficult to reach. Dental floss or tape can be used interproximally where brushes cannot reach. However, any method used could cause damage, and expert advice and observation are necessary to ensure efficacy of the process.

Dental floss or tape can be used for areas that brushes cannot reach.

The relationship of factors other than plaque to periodontal disease is by no means clear. Some diseases such as diabetes seem to increase the severity of the disease. Loss of teeth with consequent shifting of the remaining teeth may also contribute to increased disease. Effects of such factors as nutrition, smoking, and fluorides are minimal. The overriding factor is oral cleanliness and plaque removal. Although differences in individual susceptibility must exist, nothing definite as yet has been discovered.

The use of antiplaque mouthwashes such as alexidine has shown some promise, but it is not approved in the United States and is no substitute for mechanical removal.

MALOCCLUSION

Another condition that consumes a considerable amount of dental attention is malocclusion. This is not usually a disease per se but rather a condition in which the teeth do not interdigitate according to the norm. It can range from minor tooth irregularities, which interfere with neither function nor appearance, to major functional and disfiguring defects. In some cases the major underlying cause has been identified as a genetic defect and the malocclusion is only one manifestation of the problem. For example, a relatively common defect is that of cleft lip and/or cleft palate, which occurs about once in every 750 births.

Loss of teeth, thumb sucking, and other habits can give rise to malocclusion.

In some cases malocclusion can be traced to premature loss of either deciduous or permanent teeth; in other cases harmful habits such as finger sucking or pernicious swallowing patterns may be involved.

A 1966-1970 study of the prevalence and severity of malocclusion in 12-17 year olds found that 29% had severe enough deviations to warrant therapy.

A 1966-1970 study of the prevalence and severity of malocclusion in 12-17 year olds found that 29% had severe enough deviations to warrant therapy. Of these only 10.7% had had or were receiving therapy. As with the previously mentioned dental diseases, the percentage receiving care was much greater in the upper income brackets, reaching 29% for those children with family earnings of $15,000 or more.

Although malocclusion usually causes little functional difficulty it can have serious psychosocial consequences.

Except in extreme cases the significance of malocclusion is primarily one of esthetics. Neither function nor increased disease incidence appears to be a problem unless deviation from the norm is very great. However, in our society facial aberrations can have a serious effect on the quality of life—from the ability to get satisfactory employment to the ability to form friendships. Some people suffer severe psychologic damage as a result of disfiguring malocclusions.

Prevention

At the present state of the art the major malocclusions involving skeletal discrepancies and defects cannot be prevented. However, those caused by premature tooth loss, prolonged retention of deciduous teeth, or pernicious habits can be prevented or minimized. Early tooth loss is almost always due to caries. If this disease is prevented or treated, associated malocclusions will not occur. If tooth loss does occur, space maintainers can be constructed that will allow the permanent teeth to erupt into position.

ORAL CANCER

Although many disease entities occur in and around the oral cavity, only one will be discussed here—oral cancer.

In the United States malignancies of the buccal cavity and oral pharynx constitute 3%-5% of all cancers (Caldwell and Stallard, 1977). Treatment, even when successful, often leaves the patient severely disfigured. Function may be impaired markedly.

Oral cancer is more prevalent in males, smokers, and drinkers.

As with other malignancies the exact cause is obscure. However, oral cancer occurs much more frequently in men than in women and in heavy smokers and/or heavy drinkers. Lastly, risk is increased in mouths where dental disease is neglected and where oral hygiene is poor.

Prevention

Not much is known about the prevention of oral malignancies except that they are associated with increased use of tobacco and alcohol as well as with poor oral hygiene and untreated diseased teeth.

Most oral cancers are located in areas where they can be easily detected while still localized.

Most such cancers are located in areas where they can be detected easily while still localized. Physicians, nurses, and physician's assistants as well as dentists and hygienists can perform such inspections at regular intervals. They must be trained to recognize the early lesions in the mouth and not just look past the anterior pillars of the tonsils or solely at the teeth.

SPECIAL PATIENTS

There is a group of persons for whom prevention assumes a particularly important role. These are patients with severe systemic disease, the mentally retarded, persons on immunosuppressive therapy, those who have had radiation therapy to the head and neck areas, and so on.

Patients who are mentally retarded or who are on immunosuppressive therapy and others may benefit from special preventive dental care.

In many of these people dental disease, when it occurs, is difficult or even impossible to treat. A bacterial shower from extractions, scaling, or infection may result in death. The preventive measures enumerated in this chapter are effective, and many can be intensified for this special population. Topical fluorides can be applied daily at home, prophylaxes can be given more frequently, and special aids for oral hygiene can be designed and prescribed (for example, for those who can't use a toothbrush, sectional trays containing spongelike material with which patients can clean their teeth by using a chewing motion).

COOPERATION AMONG HEALTH DISCIPLINES

Dentists rarely look beyond the anterior pillars of the tonsils; other health professionals rarely look in front of them.

One problem in disease prevention or early detection is the separation of the health disciplines. Dentistry is infrequently practiced in close connection with the rest of health care. As a result dentists rarely look beyond the anterior pillars of the tonsils and other health professionals rarely look in front of them; serious and obvious problems must exist in either area for them to refer patients to the alternate provider.

Physicians should discourage excessively sticky sugars.

Good nutrition and diet apply to the entire body. Persons who consume excessively sticky sugars are everyone's concern. Whoever discovers the problem in a patient first should contact the other health professionals and coordinate their efforts. Since behavior is so difficult to change, such mutual support is essential.

Physicians should refer patients with plaque accumulation for prophylaxis

Physicians and nurses knowledgeable about plaque can discover persons with obvious major accumulations and refer them to the dentist. They can then support the concept of removal by professional prophylaxis followed up by good oral hygiene.

Support fluoridation.

Campaigns for fluoridation and school prevention programs require not only the support of the major professional organizations (which has been there for some time) but active participation of all health personnel to counteract the well-financed and well-coordinated attacks of the antifluoridationists.

In general, dental disease must be considered as being on the same level of concern as other health problems. There is the special factor, however: most caries and periodontal problems are preventable. At the present state of the art such prevention requires a combination of environmental measures, professional attention, and home care. None of these pieces is either very expensive or unusually time-consuming. The major problem is to apply current knowledge to the entire population, not just a small segment of it. A coordinated, cooperative approach by the various health disciplines can hasten the day when this might occur.

AGE-SPECIFIC RECOMMENDATIONS

The following schedule of recommendations for preventive oral health actions is appropriate for most cases. Obviously it should be modified according to special circumstances.

Age of Patient	Recommendations
Birth-2 years	Commence fluoride drops or tablets, 0.25 mg each day, in communities with no fluoride in the water supply.
2-3 years	Increase fluoride dose to 0.5 mg each day. Recommend first regular visit to the dentist; thereafter, frequency will depend on caries attack rate.
3 years	Increase dose of systemic fluoride to 1.0 mg each day; continue systemic administration until after second permanent molars are erupted (ages 12-14 years). Recommend annual topical application of fluoride by dentist or dental hygienist.
5 years	Recommend continued topical application of fluoride in dental setting unless a regular fluoride program is conducted at the school. Additional fluoride therapy is at dentist's option for high caries-risk individuals. Topicals should continue routinely to age 18 years—and beyond in special cases.
5-8 years	Recommend pit and fissure sealants for newly erupted first permanent (6-year)

	molars for children covered by optimum levels of systemic fluoride. Reapplications depend on retention, but appear to be useful at 2-year intervals.
6-13 years	Newly erupted permanent posterior teeth (for example, second molars and second bicuspids) should be treated with fluoride at about the age of 12 years. Recommend consultation for obviously malerupting permanent teeth. Include children with persistent pernicious habits such as thumb sucking and finger sucking and aberrant swallowing patterns. Most orthodontics is performed after all permanent teeth, except for third molars, are erupted (about age 11-13 years), but some conditions can be treated much earlier and thus malocclusion can be minimized at an earlier age.
19 years	Recommend regular dental visits. Professional prophylaxis assumes increasing importance, but the interval depends on the individual. It may vary from every 3 months to once a year, and rarely less frequently.
45 years	Incidence of neoplasms increases. Regular oral soft tissue examination at time of physical is indicated. Be sure to include the floor of the mouth and base of the tongue. High-risk persons include those with a history of smoking, alcohol consumption, and minimal dental care.

In general then, the following measures are important for primary care physicians in treating their patients:

1. Encourage fluoridation of water supplies, if levels are less than optimum.
2. Encourage good nutrition practices. Support efforts to decrease promotion and sale of "junk" foods, the worst ones from a dental standpoint being sticky sugar substances usually consumed as snacks.
3. Children too young to brush properly but who have teeth should be aided by parents. For infants a wash cloth may be used.

Infants may have their teeth cleaned with a wash cloth.

4. Recommend fluoride toothpastes
5. At present it is believed that a thorough daily deplaquing (toothbrush and dental floss) is sufficient.
6. Refer to the dentist persons with poor oral hygiene and/or gingivitis.

ANNOTATED BIBLIOGRAPHY

Axelsson, P., and Lindhe, J. 1977. The effect of a plaque control program on gingivitis and dental caries in school children. *J. Dent. Res.*, Special Issue C 56:C142-148.
This is a clinical study, using experimental and control populations, of a multiyear trial of the effects of frequent prophylaxis and oral hygiene instruction on the incidence of dental disease in school children. It demonstrated sharp reductions in both gingivitis and caries. It is the subject of much controversy in dental public health circles.

Axelsson, P., and Lindhe, J. 1978. Effect of controlled oral hygiene procedures on caries and periodontal disease in adults. *J. Clin. Periodontol.* 5:133-151.
This is a clinical study of a multiyear trial, using experimental and control populations, of the effects of frequent prophylaxis on dental disease in adults. Incidence of caries and the severity of periodontal disease were reduced drastically. Existing bone loss did not become worse.

Burnham, Clinton E. 1974. *Edentulous persons, United States-1971: Vital and health statistics.* National Health Survey, Series 10, Number 89. Washington, D.C.: U. S. Government Printing Office.
Results of an interview survey of adults conducted by the National Center for Health Statistics.

Burt, B. A., editor. 1978. *The relative efficiency of methods of caries prevention in dental public health.* Ann Arbor: University of Michigan.
A major compendium of knowledge of the current state of the art of caries prevention.

Caldwell, R. C., and Stallard, R. E., editors. 1977. *A textbook of preventive dentistry.* Philadelphia: W. B. Saunders Company.
An authoritative textbook on all aspects of preventive dentistry including descriptions of disease epidemiology causation where known. The effectiveness of various measures is discussed. Chapters are contributed by leaders in the field.

Carlos, J. P., editor. 1974. *Prevention and oral health.* Department of Health, Education, and Welfare Publication No. (NIH) 74-707, Washington, D.C.: U. S. Government Printing Office.

Designed for the nondentist reader.

A symposium on the current status of preventive activities in dentistry at the time of publication. Designed for the nondentist reader, the book concentrates on delivery and cost-effectiveness.

Dunning, J. M. 1979. *Principles of dental public health.* 3rd ed. Cambridge, Mass.: Harvard University Press.
One of the two major dental public health texts, it covers the entire field from epidemiology to dental care systems. It is very readable and contains an excellent bibliography.

Kelly, J. E., and Harvey, C. R. 1979. *Basic data on dental examination findings of persons 1-74 years—United States, 1971-1974: Vital and health statistics.* National Health Survey, Series 11, Number 214. Washington, D.C.: U. S. Government Printing Office.
This monograph is based on the examination of a scientifically selected sample of the United States population conducted every few years. It provides the best available data on dental disease incidence and prevalence.

Kelly, J. E., and Van Kirk, E. 1965. *Periodontal disease in adults—United States-1960-1962: Vital and health statistics.* National Health Survey, Series 11, Number 12. Washington, D.C.: U. S. Government Printing Office.
Results of the examination of a sample of United States population conducted by the National Center for Health Statistics.

Lovdal, A.; Arno, A.; Schei, O., et al. 1961. Combined effect of subgingival sealing and controlled oral hygiene on the incidence of gingivitis. *Acta. Odont. Scand.* 19:537-555.

National Institute of Dental Research, National Caries Program. 1977. *Preventing tooth decay: A guide for implementing self-applied fluoride in schools.* Department of Health, Education, and Welfare Publication No. (NIH) 77-1196. Washington, D.C.: U. S. Government Printing Office.
This booklet is exactly what the title implies—a practical manual for setting up a school fluoride program.

Suomi, J. D.; Leatherwood, E. C.; and Chang, J. J. 1973. A follow-up study of former participants in a controlled oral hygiene study. *J. Periodontol.* 44:662-666.
This clinical study involving both experimental and control groups lasted 3 years. It too demonstrated a positive correlation between frequent prophylaxis and oral hygiene instruction and reduced severity of periodontal disease. The effect lasted beyond the duration of the active treatment program.

9 Prevention of Cardiovascular Disease

Joseph Stokes III

Dr. Stokes is a graduate of Harvard Medical School and was on the faculty there and at Queens Hospital, Honolulu, before joining the University of California, San Diego, School of Medicine. He was associated with the well-known heart disease epidemiology study at Framingham, Massachusetts, and is a member of many expert committees on cardiovascular disease and preventive medicine.

Victor F. Froelicher, Jr.

Dr. Froelicher is a graduate of the University of Pittsburgh Medical School and is on the faculty of the University of California, San Diego, School of Medicine. His clinical activities and research are in the areas of exercise testing, cardiac rehabilitation, exercise physiology, and preventive medicine.

Phyllis Brown

Miss Brown is a student at the University of California, San Diego, School of Medicine.

Brief Contents

Overview

Cardiovascular diseases are the major cause of death for both sexes and all races in the United States. The pathogenesis of atherosclerosis is still obscure. Nevertheless several risk factors are associated with cardiovascular disease. In the presence of incomplete data, physicians are advised to recommend treatment of hypertension, weight reduction, cessation of smoking, regular exercise, moderation in alcohol, modification of salt and fat intake, stress reduction, and training in cardiopulmonary resuscitation. A special section on exercise and the prevention of heart disease is included to provide the current state of the art for this highly publicized issue.

EPIDEMIOLOGY

Coronary heart disease alone accounts for almost 40% of all deaths in the United States.

Coronary heart disease (CHD) and other cardiovascular diseases represent the "mega diseases" of all developed countries and dominate the causes of death for both sexes and for all races in the United States today. Nearly three persons now die of heart disease for every one dying of cancer. CHD alone accounts for almost 40% of all deaths in this country, and the addition of stroke and other types of cardiovascular disease increases this proportion to about two thirds.

Cardiovascular disease also ranks close to accidents and respiratory and gastrointestinal diseases as the most common reason for hospitalization. Except for musculoskeletal disease it causes more functional disability than any other health problem—three times that caused by mental disorders.

The 1973-1974 National Ambulatory Medical Care Survey found that asymptomatic hypertension accounted for 3.5% of all ambulatory health care services and that coronary heart disease accounted for another 2.4%.

The cost of these diseases is staggering and includes not only the direct cost of health care but also the indirect loss of income for the patient and loss of productivity for industry. Stroke alone cost the State of Massachusetts almost $380 million during 1975, 64% of which were direct costs; the remainder, indirect. This does not include the anguish of patients and of those to whom they are emotionally bonded.

Table 9-1

Table 9-1 summarizes the prevalence of hypertension and the three major etiologic types of heart disease that are encountered in family practice. Hypertension and CHD clearly dominate the list. These two categories are inextricably linked by virtue of the fact that elevated blood pressure is an important risk factor in the development of CHD and that both can cause congestive heart failure.

Based on the combined data of several prospective studies, one can estimate the 10-year outlook for an average cohort of 1000 men aged 40-49 years. Of these 1000 men:

1. Approximately 150 (15%) will develop symptomatic CHD by the end of 10 years.
   a. Forty (5%) will have angina as their only symptom.
   b. Seventy-five (7.5%) will have experienced acute myocardial infarction.
   c. Twenty-five (2.5%) will have died suddenly before it was possible to institute treatment.
   d. Twenty-five (2.5%) will have died of heart disease despite treatment.
2. Forty-five (4.5%) will have died from other causes.

Since 1968 cardiovascular disease mortality has declined.

One encouraging, although not clearly explained, observation is that since 1968 the crude death rate from cardiovascular disease has decreased from over 360 to less than 300 per 100,000 population. This improvement in mortality is paralleled by a

Table 9-1 Prevalence of Hypertension and the Three Other Principal Types of Heart Disease—By Men and Women Aged 18-79 Years

	Estimated Number Affected	Percentage of Population
Hypertension (>159/94 mm Hg)	17,000,000	15.2
Coronary heart disease	3,125,000	2.8
Rheumatic heart disease	1,250,000	1.1
Congenital heart disease	250,000	0.2

Source: Department of Health Education & Welfare. National Health Examination Survey, 1960-62. Washington, D.C.: U. S. Government Printing Office

decrease in morbidity as well. The incidence of stroke also appears to be decreasing. In Rochester, Minnesota, there was a 45% reduction in the incidence of stroke between the two 5-year periods of 1945-49 and 1970-74 (Garraway et al., 1979).

Despite these recent advances large gaps still remain in our knowledge, particularly regarding the pathogenesis of primary hypertension and the causes of most forms of congenital heart disease. Also, because cardiovascular disease is predominantly a disease of advanced age, there is a limit to the impact of prevention. Even if cardiovascular disease could be totally eliminated as a cause of death for all those infants born during the years 1969-1971, this miracle would increase their life expectancy by little more than 12 years (Tsai et al., 1978). A more achievable reduction of 30% for working-age men (those 15-65 years of age) would extend their life expectancy by only 7 months. In any event if risk factor modification is to be undertaken, it should be done as early in life as possible; some have suggested that adolescence may even be too late.

Risk factor modification has its most significant effect if undertaken early in life.

ATHEROSCLEROSIS AND CORONARY HEART DISEASE

Hyperlipidemia in the form of high-density lipoprotein cholesterol has an unexplained "protective effect."

Despite 25 years of concerted effort to unearth the cause of atherosclerosis, its pathogenesis remains controversial. Hyperlipidemia is generally recognized as a necessary cause, but the startling rediscovery of the "protective effect" of high-density lipoprotein cholesterol remains an empirical observation begging for an explanation. This also suggests that the word "malipidemia" should be substituted for hyperlipidemia since elevation of high-density lipoprotein cholesterol seems to be beneficial.

Hypertension appears to "drive" the fats and sterols into the arterial intima or to damage the endothelium so as to encourage such deposition, or both. Flow (rheologic) factors are also important since blood is a complex, non-Newtonian fluid, and atherosclerotic plaques usually first appear near bifurcations and the ostia of major arteries, which has led some investigators to suggest that turbulence either increases the "micromural" blood pressure (Bernoulli effect), or encourages mural thrombi, or both.

All agree that atherosclerosis eventually becomes thrombotic as the plaque begins to occlude the vessel; a few still adhere to Rokitansky's original suggestion, revived by Duguid, that the process is thrombotic from the outset and that the accumulation of lipids is secondary to the clotting process.

Nicotine can make platelets sticky, which, added to its effects on the electrical events in the heart, may explain most of the adverse cardiovascular effects of cigarette smoking. The fact that cigarette smokers recently have been shown to have lower levels of high-density lipoprotein cholesterol suggests another mechanism to explain their increased risk (Criqui et al., 1979).

Finally, the most important message to be gleaned from all the animal studies is that the disease is virtually impossible to produce in the absence of hyperlipidemia. Therefore, until more is known it would seem wise to focus efforts on lowering the low-density lipoprotein cholesterol and triglycerides and raising the concentration of cholesterol transported by lipoproteins of high density. The lowering of elevated blood pressure and the prohibition of cigarette smoking would also appear to be indicated.

Hypertension is the principal modifiable risk factor for stroke and congestive heart failure.

Hypertension represents the principal modifiable risk factor for both stroke and congestive heart failure and, except for "malipidemia," plays the same role for CHD. Marked elevation of blood pressure can also cause a gamut of renal manifestations ranging from proteinuria to frank kidney failure.

The concept of hypertension resists specific definition in that it has proved impossible to find a blood pressure level that clearly distinguishes between those who will become sick and die of the consequences of elevated blood pressure and those who will not. To put it another way, the relationship between the level of blood pressure and risk includes pressures (for example, 120/80 mm Hg) that are ordinarily thought to be normal. As far as mortality risks are concerned it seems that the lower the blood pressure the better. Obviously the curve must eventually become J-shaped when the point is reached where shock blood pressures make it impossible to perfuse vital organs, but such patients are never encountered in epidemiologic studies. (Incidentally, such studies have provided no support to the concept that the lethargy and fatigue so often encountered in young women is caused by hypotension.)

As far as mortality risks are concerned it seems that the lower the blood pressure the better.

Headache has long been associated with hypertension, but many clinicians have been trapped by post hoc, ergo procter hoc, reasoning. Some patients with marked elevation of blood pressure do complain of a characteristic occipital headache present upon first arising in the morning but which wears off during the day. Some of these headaches can be prevented either by using two to three pillows or otherwise sleeping with the head elevated. However, most patients with hypertension requiring treatment do not report such headaches and, if they wait for this or other symptoms to develop they have waited too long. The most important clinical lesson derived from the last 20 years of study of disease is that prognostically significant elevation of blood pressure can occur without any symptoms whatsoever.

Though hypertension appears to represent an ideal disease model for screening, such attempts often meet with difficulty.

Since most hypertension is both asymptomatic and remediable, it should represent an ideal disease model for screening. Unfortunately too many have interpreted this to mean either single-measurement, communitywide screening or as part of a multiphasic screening program, both of which depend on referral for treatment. Such programs have not proved effective not only because of incomplete public participation but also because of problems of both specificity and sensitivity. Some patients under good medical supervision have discontinued their antihypertensive medication when told that their blood pressure was normal in a communitywide blood pressure screen. These patients mistakenly assumed that they had been cured rather than merely controlled. Another unexpected consequence of hypertension detection was the discovery that labeling hypertensive workers (who were otherwise asymptomatic and well controlled) led to their increased absenteeism from work (Haynes et al., 1978).

An unexpected adverse consequence of hypertension detection was the increased absenteeism in otherwise asymptomatic patients.

As a result of these and other factors Weinstein and Stason (1976) conclude in their policy review of hypertension that a nationwide screening and treatment program for hypertension would not be cost effective.

Although the cause of primary hypertension is not known, a great deal has been learned about those risk factors associated with its occurrence. It is also known that modifying these factors will reduce the risk of developing sustained hypertension. Blood pressure increases with age and affects more men than it does women. Blacks are more likely to be affected, but this fact as well as the increased prevalence of high blood pressure in Japan may well reflect an environmental (for example, high salt intake) rather than a genetic effect.

Genetic factors presumably affect primary hypertension; studies of twins have shown greater blood pressure concordance in identical as compared with fraternal twins of the same sex. In addition, the mean blood pressure of first-degree relatives of hypertensive patients is significantly higher than that of controls matched by age, sex, race, or weight—controls who do not report hypertension in such relatives. Studies also suggest that blood pressure tendencies begin as early as infancy.

Obesity, salt intake, stress, and toxemia of pregnancy have been studied, particularly since they are modifiable and represent potential means of altering the natural history of the disease. All except obesity are still embroiled in controversy. The original Dahl salt hypothesis has been challenged by both epidemiologic and clinical data, and most investigators have been unable to find either increased salt excretion or intake in patients who have asymptomatic hypertension. Anxiety can elevate blood pressure during the acute flight/fright autonomic response: air traffic controllers have higher sustained blood pressure levels than those of matched controls. The best evidence suggests that pregnancy does not cause hypertension in normal women but merely represents physiologic (and perhaps psychologic) stress that reveals a latent hypertensive genotype in many of those who will later develop the disease.

Fortunately there are several well-defined causes of secondary hypertension and in most instances can effect radical cure such as that which follows reconstruction of a narrowed renal artery. Types of hypertension include the following:

I. Primary (essential) hypertension (90%-95%)

II. Secondary hypertension (5%-10%)
- A. Coarctation of the aorta
- B. Renal/endocrine disease
  - 1. Renal disease
    - a. Glomerulonephritis
    - b. Renal artery stenosis
      - (1) Fibromuscular
      - (2) Atherosclerotic
    - c. Other
  - 2. Adrenal
    - a. Medulla (pheochromocytoma)
    - b. Cortical
      - (1) Hyperaldosteronism
      - (2) Cushing syndrome
      - (3) Adrenogenital syndrome
- C. Central nervous system lesions

Unfortunately, the proportion of hypertension that is curable is less than was formerly thought. This change does not reflect any decrease in the prevalence of secondary cases but rather a growing appreciation for the magnitude of primary hypertension (that is, while the numerator has remained about the same the denominator now appears to be much larger than was previously realized). Most of this new insight has been gained through communitywide screening programs such as those that have been conducted under the auspices of The Hypertension Detection and Follow-up Program (1977, 1979). By extrapolating these data, we can now estimate that secondary hypertension represents only about 7% of the total cases and that "curable" high blood pressure includes only about 3% of that total. Conversely, about 90%-95% of adults with hypertension suffer from a disease the cause of which is still unknown. In children the proportion of

We can now estimate that secondary hypertension represents only about 7% of the total cases.

secondary cases is higher but curable forms still represent less than 10% of the total.

The physician's office seems to be the best place to screen for hypertension.

The physician's office seems to be the best place to screen for hypertension. The blood pressure should be measured by mercury manometer and recorded in a sitting position after at least 10 minutes at rest and prior to bloodletting and other stressful procedures. The arm and body position should always be noted when recording the blood pressure; many physicians do not realize that the systolic pressure may be as much as 25-30 mm Hg higher in the leg as compared with simultaneous measurement in the arm. This is not due to the fact that a thigh cuff may fail to transmit occlusive pressure to the femoral artery. Such may be true if the cuff is too small, but the paradoxical discrepancy remains even in thin patients. This is due to a water-hammer effect. In essence, the indirect method of blood pressure measurement yields an end rather than a lateral pressure, and the normal difference between the arm and the leg is an artifact of measurement.

Systolic, diastolic, and pulse pressures are affected by premature beats, atrial fibrillation, and other cardiac arrhythmias, all of which can alter stroke volume substantially from beat to beat.

Most experts now recommend recording the diastolic pressure at the point of disappearance of sound.

Some health professionals are taught to record diastolic pressure at the point of muffling rather than at the disappearance of the sound, assuming that this is a better measurement of the true diastolic pressure. Indeed there are data comparing direct with indirect measurements that would corroborate this fact. However, since disappearance is so much easier to measure and is reproducible, most experts now recommend using the point of disappearance.

Table 9-2

If both the systolic and diastolic pressures are normal by the criteria listed in Table 9-2, nothing further need be done other than recording the blood pressure again at the next clinic visit. However, if either pressure is elevated by these criteria, then the pressure should be measured again in the same arm after an additional 5 minutes of rest. If it is still elevated by these criteria, measurement should be made in the right arm and recorded; the patient should be evaluated as soon as is convenient according to the standard diagnostic protocol listed in the following outline.

I. Medical history
   A. Identifying information: age, sex, and race
   B. Past history of:
      1. Hypertension (dates and levels of blood pressure should be recorded)
      2. Headache (particularly occipital headache present upon awaking in the morning and then improving during the day)
      3. Body weight (weight at age 18 and at subsequent 5-year intervals)

Table 9-2 Blood Pressure Criteria—By Age (Systolic/Diastolic)

		Elevated	
Age	Normal	Borderline	Definite
0-6 months	< 105/50	105-114/50-64	> 114/64
3 years	< 110/75	110-119/75-79	> 119/79
5 years	< 115/80	115-124/80-84	> 124/84
10 years	< 120/85	120-129/85-89	> 129/89
15 years	< 130/90	130-144/90-94	> 144/94
25 years and over	< 140/90	140-159/90-94	> 159/94

Source: Committee on Arteriosclerosis and Hypertension in Childhood, of the Council on Cardiovascular Disease in the Young, American Heart Association. July 1975. *Pediatrics* 56:3-5. Copyright American Academy of Pediatrics 1975.

        4. Dietary salt intake
        5. Symptoms of hyperaldosteronism (muscle weakness, cramps, and polyuria)
        6. History of renal disease (for example, glomerulonephritis and proteinuria)
        7. Symptoms of pheochromocytoma (episodic headache, palpitations, and sweating)
    C. Family history of:
        1. Hypertension
        2. Stroke
        3. Congestive heart failure
        4. Renal disease
        5. CHD

II. Physical examination
    A. Height, weight, and adiposity
    B. Funduscopy (Keith-Wagener-Barker classification)
    C. Cervical examination (carotid pulse, bruit, and thyroid size)
    D. Heart, lungs, and abdomen
    E. Legs (palpation for femoral, popliteal, dorsalis pedis, and posterior tibial pulses)
    F. Screening neurologic examination

III. Laboratory
    A. Urinalysis and spot test for metanephrine
    B. Hematocrit and serum creatinine and K+ concentration
    C. Electrocardiogram
    D. Chest x-ray examination

The criteria for further screening and evaluation of patients suspected of having secondary hypertension are as follows:

I. Rapid excretion intravenous pyelogram
   A. History of renal disease
   B. Abnormal urinalysis (2+ or more proteinuria and/or microscopic hematuria)
   C. Elevated serum creatinine
   D. Palpable kidneys on physical examination
   E. Symptomatic hypertension
   F. Sustained, definite hypertension (160 mm Hg systolic/95 mm Hg diastolic)

II. Twenty-four hour urinary vanillylmandelic acid (VMA) and/or serum epinephrine or norepinephrine
   A. History of episodic headache, palpitation, and sweating
   B. Positive metanephrine spot test

III. Plasma urinary aldosterone determination
   A. Persistent hypokalemia
   B. Symptoms of muscle weakness and polyuria

IV. Plasma 17-OHCS after 7 mg of dexamethasone
   A. Physical or laboratory evidence of Cushing syndrome

V. Aortography
   A. Absence of pulses in the legs
   B. X-ray film evidence of rib notching or other evidence for coartation of the aorta
   C. Abdominal bruit or other evidence (for example, delay excretion of dye on intravenous pyelogram (IVP) for renal artery stenosis

One of the most important tasks when encountering hypertensive patients for the first time should be to screen out those few patients where the cause is clear and to refer to surgery those who are amenable. Even though those with curable high blood pressure represents no more than 3 patients out of 100, radical cure occasionally can be effected. Younger patients should be studied with special care since serious hypertension is far less prevalent under the age of 20 years than it is in adults and the cause can be determined in about one child out of four. The outline of causes on p. 219 does not attempt to estimate the relative frequency of the various types of secondary hypertension because even data pooled from a variety of clinical studies are not sufficient to establish these frequencies with any confidence. However, proper identification is important since curing patients may save them from a lifetime of tedious treatment with only partially effective therapy.

Serious disagreement still exists among the experts as to how to differentiate the curable.

Unfortunately, serious disagreement still exists among the experts as to how to differentiate the curable from other forms of hypertension. This disagreement reflects both lack of data and the fact that the consulting neurologist, nephrologist, vascular surgeon, endocrinologist, and family physician each views the problem from a different perspective. Nevertheless, most agree on the following points:

1. Curable patients tend to be younger, and fibromuscular renal artery stenosis is much more common in women than it is in men.
2. Secondary hypertension is more likely to be both symptomatic and of more recent onset.
3. Diffuse renal disease (such as chronic glomerulonephritis) is far more likely than "choppy" renal disease (such as polycystic disease) to elevate the blood pressure.

Several clinical trials have now been reported; they indicate that the treatment of asymptomatic moderate blood pressure elevation reduces the risk of suffering some of its serious consequences. The Veterans Administration (1967) first reported a striking reduction in serious morbidity in men in a treatment group as compared with a control group of men with diastolic blood pressures averaging between 115 and 129 mm Hg. Investigators in Sweden also found that treating middle-aged men with serious hypertension (systolic greater than 175 mm Hg and diastolic greater than 115 mm Hg) led to a significant reduction in coronary deaths and nonfatal myocardial infarctions. Later the Veterans Administration (1970) researchers reported a less striking but nevertheless convincing study showing that the treatment of men with less severe elevation of blood pressure (diastolic pressures averaging 90-114 mm Hg) also reduced morbid events over the subsequent 5 years 18%-55% below those that occurred among the untreated controls. These encouraging results prompted other studies, because it was recognized that the hospitalized veterans were all male and were not representative of patients seen in most primary care settings.

It is now well established that drug treatment of mild hypertension will significantly reduce mortality.

The Hypertension Detection and Follow-up Program (1977, 1979) reported one of the most careful, extensive, and encouraging clinical trials ever conducted in the field of cardiovascular disease. This study compared 5 years' mortality among a sample of 5000 men and women—both black and white, aged 30-69 years on entry who were assigned randomly to a systematic stepped-care drug treatment program—with a comparable group referred to community physicians for standard hypertensive care. This study demonstrated for the first time that aggressive drug treatment could lower the risk of patients with mild hypertension.

RISK FACTORS

Table 9-3.

Table 9-3 summarizes the modifiable risk factors for the development of cardiovascular disease and contrasts a high-risk profile and low-risk profile of two hypothetical men aged 45 years. Fixed factors such as age and sex are not included, although age is the most important risk factor, and four men are affected for every woman developing the disease under the age of 65 years.

Oral contraceptives increase the risk of thromboembolic disease, myocardial infarction, and stroke.

For women evidence has been accumulating that oral contraceptives increase the risk of thromboembolic disease, acute myocardial infarction, and stroke. These effects seem to reflect the fact that oral contraceptives alter serum lipids and elevate the blood pressure of some women.

There are also other genetic risk factors, which exert their effects through arterial blood pressure, lipid metabolism, and presence of diabetes mellitus. Presumably, all but the latter are modifiable, and there are still those who believe that controlling

Table 9-3 Estimated Coronary Risk of Two 45-Year-Old Men

Risk Factor (+ or −)	Level of Risk	
	High	Low
Blood pressure (mm Hg)	> 160/95	< 140/90
Serum		
DL cholesterol (mg/dl)	> 260	< 140
HDL cholesterol (mg/dl)	< 40	> 50
Fasting triglycerides (mg/dl)	> 150	< 125
Blood sugar (mg/dl)	> 140	< 100
Habits		
Cigarette smoking	> ++	0
Vigorous exercise	−	++
EtOH	0 or +++	+ or ++
Personality	Type A	Type B
Approximate risk of developing coronary heart disease over next 10 years	> 1:4	< 1:100

the blood level of glucose reduces the risk of developing atherosclerosis. Cigarette smoking and alcohol ingestion are also modifiable and it has even been suggested that the time-conscious personality characterized as Type A can be converted to the more relaxed pace of the Type B personality.

The hypothetical man represented in the left column of Table 9-3 who has elevated blood pressure, serum cholesterol (with low high-density lipoprotein cholesterol), fasting triglycerides, and random blood sugar; who smokes two or more packs of cigarettes each day, does not exercise regularly, and is either a teetotaler or drinks to excess (more than 10 ounces of absolute alcohol each week); and has a Type A personality, has almost a 50:50 chance of developing symptomatic CHD at some time during the subsequent 10 years. In contrast, his virtuous counterpart with the characteristics listed in the column on the right, runs a risk about 2% of that of his high-risk peer. Therefore, even though it may not be possible to prevent all CHD, it has certainly become one of the most predictable of all diseases.

Coronary heart disease may not be entirely preventable, but it is certainly one of the most predictable diseases.

Of course the rejoinder might be that such a virtuous life is not worth living. In addition, only scanty, early returns are in as to whether or not by modifying modifiable risk factors it actually changes the level of risk. In summary, the data on hypertension are very persuasive. With respect to diet, limited data from so-called "closed populations" (for example, residents of nursing homes) indicate that the risk of CHD can be reduced by dietary modification, limiting the amount of cholesterol and saturated fats and by reversing the usual ratio of saturated to unsaturated fatty acids (Dayton et al., 1969). With regard to smoking, the data are very persuasive that the risk of cardiovascular disease is reduced following cessation of smoking. The preventive benefit of vigorous exercise is widely proclaimed but has yet to be established conclusively. The current state of this controversy is reviewed in the section, "Exercise and the Prevention of Heart Disease." Studies of anticoagulant drugs have been carried out in this country and Canada. These studies show that aspirin reduced the risk of both stroke and death in men. Inexplicably, a similar reduction was not observed among women.

Daily aspirin reduces the risk of stroke and death in men—but not in women

The practice of clinical preventive medicine, as with all other aspects of the practice of medicine, requires that decisions be made even in the presence of incomplete data; therefore the following recommendations appear to be prudent at the present time:

The practice of clinical preventive medicine requires that decisions be made even without complete data.

1. Serum cholesterol and triglycerides should be measured at least once every 5 years. Those found to have marginal eleva-

tion of serum cholesterol should have their lipoproteins fractionated to determine which are carried in the high-density component as compared with other fractions.

2. Blood pressure should be measured annually and any significant elevation should be evaluated and treated if necessary despite lack of symptoms.
3. One should never start smoking cigarettes, and current cigarette smokers should be encouraged to stop or to switch to a less dangerous form of smoking. If this is not possible to accomplish they should be urged to switch to the brand of filter cigarette with the lowest nicotine content.
4. Jogging, swimming, and other forms of vigorous exercise should be engaged in for at least 15-30 minutes, at least three times each week.
5. Weight should be maintained either at, or somewhat below, the average for age and sex. Those more than 18 years of age can use their weight at 18 years of age as a realistic target figure unless they already were obese.
6. The diet should include no more calories than those necessary to maintain normal body weight, and should be reduced further if weight reduction is needed. A diet of 1200-1400 calories is far more realistic than those that are more restrictive (for example, less than 1000 calories). Complex carbohydrates such as the starch in rice and potatoes should be maintained at more than 45% of total calories and refined carbohydrates such as sucrose should be reduced to less than 15% of calories. Fat should be restricted to 30% of total calories and the ratio between saturated, monounsaturated, and polyunsaturated fatty acids should be 1:1:1. Cholesterol should be reduced to less than 300 mg a day (for example, that contained in the yolks of 1½ eggs).
7. Salt intake should be restricted to less than 3 grams a day. Such reduction can easily be effected by avoiding salty foods such as ham and heavily salted crakers and by not salting the water when cooking vegetables. Such care in the purchase and preparation of food should allow cautious use of shaker salt to improve the taste of food as it is eaten at the table.
8. One or two drinks each day, totaling 15-30 ml of absolute alcohol, is recommended unless there is a family history of alcoholism, in which case prohibition should be advised.
9. Those leading stressful lives should be encouraged to relax and to try to become less time conscious. However, such behavior change may be extremely difficult to achieve.

10. Oral contraceptives should be prescribed with caution to all women over 30 years of age, particularly if they are overweight. They are contraindicated for those women who have serious malipidemia, hypertension, withdrawal headaches, and a past history of thromboembolism.

11. Physicians should recommend that their patients learn cardiopulmonary resuscitation techniques. Those who live with patients suffering from CHD should be particularly encouraged to do so. Local affiliates of the American Heart Association and other agencies offer these courses.

Table 9-4
Table 9-5

Dietary intervention should be tried first for patients with lipid disorders.

Tables 9-4 and 9-5 summarize the various dietary and pharmacologic means of reducing very low-density lipoprotein, low-density lipoprotein cholesterol, and triglycerides as well as of elevating low high-density lipoprotein cholesterol. In each case, dietary intervention should be tried first and drug therapy used only if dietary means prove to be insufficient. To date cholestyramine has proved to be the most effective drug in the treatment of Type IIA hyperlipidemia, while clofibrate has proved the most effective agent in combined hyperlipidemia. The only recourse is diet for those with hypertriglyceridemia. The level of high-density lipoprotein cholesterol can be raised both by regular exercise and by moderate intake of ethanol. Unfortunately, a few

Table 9-4 Treatment of malipidemia

Type of Malipidemia	Diet	Drugs
Hypercholesterolemia (> 250 mg/dl) (Type IIa)	< 25% Fat S:U 1:2	Cholestyramine
Hypertriglyceridemia		
Mild (> 150-300 mg/dl) (Type IIb)	< 25% Fat < 5% Refined CHO	—
Severe (> 300 mg/dl) (Type I)	< 15% Fat 0 Refined CHO 0 EtOH	—
Combined types (Type IV)	< 30% Fat S:U 1:2 < 10% Refined CHO	Clofibrate (Niacin) (d-Thyroxin)
Hypo HDL Cholesterolemia (< 40 mg/dl)	↑ EtOH ++ ? 0 Cigarette smoking ↑ Exercise	

Table 9-5 Approved drugs for treatment of malipidemia

Drug	Mechanism of Action	Dose	Side Effects
Hypercholesterolemia (Type IIa):			
Cholestyramine resin (Questran)	Bind bile acids	16-32 g/day	Steatorrhea Vitamin A and D deficiency Constipation Drug interference
Colestipol HCL (Colestid)	Bind bile acids	15-20 g/day	? Folate deficiency
d-thyroxine (Choloxin)	↑ Catabolism	2-8 mg/day	Thyrotoxicosis Diabetes Digitalis and anticoagulant potentiation Coronary heart failure and arrythmias
Sitosterols suspension (Cytellin)	↓ Absorption	3-6 g t.i.d. a.c.	Diarrhea and bloating
Probucol (Lorelco)	?	500 mg b.d.	10% diarrhea and vomiting
Combined hyperlipidemia (Type IV):			
Clofibrate (Atromid-S)	↓ Lipoprotein synthesis	1 g b.d.	Nausea and gastrointestinal pain Weight gain Skin hypersensitivity Myositis Gallstones (2 × expected) Vitamin K antagonist
Niacin	?	250 mg t.i.d. to 1.0 g	Flushing

Source: Margolis, S. June 1978. Treatment of hyperlipidemia. *J. A. M. A.* 239:2696-2698. Copyright 1978, American Medical Association.

preliminary reports indicate that this may not be possible if the patient's hypercholesterolemia is due to inherited defect of the low-density lipoprotein cellular receptor.

CONGENITAL HEART DISEASE

Eight out of each thousand children born alive will manifest congenital heart disease of clinical significance. Despite the recent advances in both diagnosis and treatment, only about half of these children will survive to their first birthday. The other half will be reflected in infant mortality—deaths that have the greatest impact on life expectancy from birth. Therefore once again prevention, if it can be effected, is the best solution.

We cannot yet identify causes of more than 5% of all cases of congenital heart disease.

Unfortunately, we cannot yet identify causes of more than 5% of all cases of congenital heart disease and not all of these are preventable. Familial clustering suggests that more than chance is involved. Some are associated with rare genetic defects such as Marfan, Ellis-Van Creveld, and Hurler syndromes. Others are associated with chromosomal abnormalities such as trisomy 18 and 21 and Turner syndrome. More and more is being learned about the risk factors associated with these defects and all can now be identified by amniocentesis early enough in gestation to offer the mother therapeutic abortion as a means of preventing the defect if she is willing to make this difficult decision—a decision that is still beset by conflicting religious and ethical values.

A woman who acquires rubella during the first few weeks of gestation has about a one in three chance of bearing a child with a serious defect.

Even though we know little of the genetic determinants of congenital heart disease, we know even less about other causes. Rubella virus is the best identified environmental agent, and the risk is so high for any mother who acquires the natural disease during the first few weeks of gestation that she should be warned that her chances of spontaneous abortion are much increased, and that there is better than one chance in three that her child, if carried to term, will be born with a serious congenital defect, about one fourth of which will involve the heart. Fortunately immunization against rubella is not only effective and safe, but we can also measure circulating rubella antibody to determine the immune status of women during the childbearing years. However, in view of the fact that the vaccine is an attenuated live virus known to cross the placenta and to infect the fetus, it is not recommended that it be used during pregnancy even though no rubella antibodies are detected and despite the fact that the available data indicate that the vaccine (in contrast to the wild virus) is not teratogenic. Passive immunization can be used to protect those women known to be pregnant if they are inadvertently exposed to German measles. Unfortunately, most of those exposed during the first 3 weeks of gestation are not aware that they are pregnant. This illustrates a dilemma that frustrates the control of all birth defects; that is, the embryo is most vulnerable at a time when the mother is usually unaware that she is pregnant.

Passive immunization can be used to protect those women known to be pregnant if they are inadvertently exposed to German measles.

Only three chemical agents (thalidomide, lysergic acid diethylamide [LSD], and trimethadione or paramethadione) have been undisputably identified as causing congenital heart disease.

Only three chemical agents (thalidomide, lysergic acid diethylamide [LSD], and trimethadione or paramethadione) have been undisputably identified as causing congenital heart disease. Thalidomide and LSD are not approved drugs and trimethadione or paramethadione should be limited to the control of petit mal epilepsy; the patient insert of the drug packaging also advises that it should not be taken by pregnant women. Indeed, all drugs and chemicals should be considered suspect and used with caution during the first trimester of pregnancy. Some epidemiologic studies have implicated the coxsackie virus and perhaps influenza virus. These agents do cross the placenta, but at present the evidence is not so strong as to warrant recommending therapeutic abortion. The problem is further compounded by the fact that it takes sophisticated tests in order to identify positively the sporadic cases of either disease with any certainty. To help prevent congenital heart disease and other genetic defects, therefore, there are two important recommendations: (a) women should avoid all unnecessary medicine during pregnancy; and (b) physicians should administer attenuated live virus rubella vaccine to female patients prior to adolescence.

RHEUMATIC HEART DISEASE

Preventive cardiologists often point with pride to the decline in the prevalence of rheumatic heart disease as their crowning achievement. Although no one disputes that the disease is on the wane, legitimate debate persists as to whom (or to what) the credit should be given.

Skeptics continue to point out that the incidence of acute rheumatic fever began to decline well before the advent of sulfonamides and penicillin; they suggest that improvements in housing, nutrition, and other aspects of both the physical and social environment deserve at least as much credit as that claimed by medical research and by those who have translated such research into clinical practice.

Nevertheless copious evidence supports the fact that prompt identification and adequate treatment of pharyngitis and other infections due to Type A streptococci with either penicillin or alternative antibiotics virtually can eliminate the risk of developing rheumatic fever within the subsequent 3-6 weeks. We also know that acute rheumatic fever leads to chronic rheumatic heart disease in many of those affected, even though the initial attack may go unrecognized and manifestations such as the degree of stenosis of the mitral valve are more a function of time (the interval since the initial attack of rheumatic fever) than of either the number or severity of recurrences. We also know that some of those who are severely affected with acute rheumatic fever will develop congestive heart failure and that a few will die of acute myocarditis during the acute disease before scarring of the valves has had time to develop.

Either continuous penicillin or sulfadiazine prophylaxis can prevent most recurrences of rheumatic fever. To prevent rheumatic fever the following recommendation is made: treat all identified type A streptococcal pharyngitis with oral penicillin (or erythromycin) for full 10-day course, or with single dose of long-acting benzathine penicillin.

PRIMARY MYOCARDIAL DISEASE

A puzzling facet of the prevention of cardiovascular disease is provided by the primary myocardial disease associated with alcohol abuse and by the high-output congestive heart failure due to beriberi. Beriberi heart disease is rare in the United States even among alcoholics, although many drinkers get less than their recommended daily allowance (RDA) of thiamin (vitamin B_1). Alcoholics actually require more of this vitamin than normal due to the fact that ethanol impairs the intestinal absorption of the vitamin.

Low-output congestive heart failure due to alcoholic myocarditis need not be preceded either by beriberi or by other manifestations of thiamin deficiency such as Wernicke-Korsakoff psychosis. Indeed, in some cases it represents the only functional organ impairment due to alcohol abuse and is associated with consumption of ethanol subsumed under the euphemism "social drinking." The most likely explanation is that some other factor contributes to the effect. Thus to avoid primary myocardial disease, recommend moderation in all things including alcohol consumption.

BACTERIAL ENDOCARDITIS

The American Heart Association has recently revised its recommendations regarding the prevention of bacterial endocarditis. Dental procedures, incision and drainage of abscesses, and oral, genitourinary, and gastrointestinal surgery all can cause transient bacteremia.

There are no clear-cut criteria for antibiotic prophylaxis: presence of a prosthetic valve is a definite indication; mitral valve prolapse is still a question.

It is not easy to establish sharp criteria as to which patients with congenital, rheumatic, or other acquired valvular heart disease should be administered prophylaxis. However, it is clear that prosthetic heart valves represent a special risk requiring the use of both penicillin and streptomycin. At the other end of the spectrum, most atrial septal defects do not require prophylaxis. Although endocarditis has been described in patients with mitral valve prolapse, this appears to be a relatively rare complication and the need for prophylaxis has not as yet been firmly established.

EXERCISE AND PREVENTION OF HEART DISEASE

That exercise can be effective in the prevention of CHD is a popular conception. If exercise is to be evaluated for either its relation to, or its role in, the prevention of CHD it is necessary to delineate the natural history of the disease, the extent of the disease process, and the effects of intervention. This section will deal with more recent investigations of the role of exercise at primary, secondary, and tertiary levels of prevention (see Introduction).

Role of Exercise in Primary Prevention of Coronary Heart Disease

Epidemiological studies The association between physical inactivity and the underlying atherosclerotic process is weak compared to other factors such as serum cholesterol, cigarette smoking, and hypertension. There is no evidence of an inversely proportional association between the level of activity and degree of atherosclerosis; nor does physical inactivity necessarily precede the atherosclerotic process. The capacity of physical inactivity to predict coronary events has not been reproducible when applied to different populations; nor has the exercise hypothesis been supported by animal studies (Froelicher, 1972). Following is a list (Froelicher, 1977, 1978) of the major epidemiological studies evaluating physical inactivity as a risk factor for heart disease. It classifies them as to their general approach.

I. Retrospective and prevalence studies (data collected in the past not for epidemiologic purposes)
   A. Large general population groups, with activity level decided from job title or death certifcate, coronary artery disease diagnosed from death certificate (populations of Philadelphia, Britain, Wales, Baltimore, Chicago, and California).
   B. Population groups, with activity level gleaned from job title, leisure activity, and questionnaire; coronary artery disease diagnosed from death certificates and medical records (including a North Dakota study and The Report on the Fellowship of Cycling Old Timers).
   C. Occupational groups, with activity level arrived at from job classification of salary level; coronary artery disease diagnosed from death certificates or industrial/medical records (including studies of London busmen and postment, Israel kibbutzim, American railmen and postmen, South African railmen, Bell Telephone employees, Evans County, Georgia,

residents, Dupont Chemical Company employes, and the Chicago Peoples Gas Company employees).

D. Occupational groups, with activity level taken from job title or questionnaire; coronary artery disease diagnosed by electrocardiogram (ECG) (Finnish lumberjacks versus nonlumberjacks and British Civil Service).

E. Population groups, with physical fitness level decided through exercise test; coronary artery disease diagnosed by clinical evaluation or risk-factors assayed (Aerobic Institute in Dallas and the Masai tribe).

F. Population groups, with activity level of job and leisure time learned via questionnaire; coronary artery disease diagnosed from medical records (Health Insurance Plan of Greater New York and Harvard Graduates).

G. Hospital groups, with activity level gotten from job title or questionnaire; coronary artery disease diagnosed from medical records (Toronto Veterans Administration and Malmo, Sweden, patients).

II. Prospective studies involving apparently healthy men (in these studies the populations were chosen for study, factors were assayed, and then they were followed for heart disease endpoints).

A. Occupational groups, with activity levels assessed from job title and/or job evaluation; coronary artery disease diagnosed from medical records (Chicago Peoples Gas Company employees, London busmen, Western Electric employees, American railmen, Italian railmen, Los Angeles Civil Service employees, and San Francisco longshoremen).

B. Population studies, with activity level determined through questionnaires, coronary artery disease diagnosed by medical evaluation (seven countries, Framingham, Massachusetts; Western Collaborative; Evans County, Georgia; Gotesburg, Sweden; and Puerto Rico).

C. Occupational and other groups, with leisure time and activity level assessed from questionnaire; coronary artery disease diagnosed by medical evaluation and death certificates (British Civil Service workers, patients in the Los Angeles American Cancer Society registries, and Harvard Alumni).

D. Population and occupational groups, with physical fitness assessed by physiological data; coronary artery disease diagnosed by medical evaluation (Framingham, Massachusetts; Peoples Gas Company employees, Finland, American railmen, and the Seattle Heart Watch).

These studies have previously been reviewed and only recent investigations will be disucssed here.

Weekend activity, the electrocardiogram, and coronary heart disease Epstein and colleagues (1976) studied the relationship of vigorous exercise during leisure time to the resting ECG. From 1968 to 1970, approximately 17,000 middle-aged, male executive civil servants, on a randomly selected Monday morning, recorded their leisure-time activities of the previous weekend. Active men had significantly fewer ECG abnormalities than the men not reporting vigorous exercise. Blood pressure, serum cholesterol, and smoking habits were examined along with the relation of vigorous exercise to the ECG. The only relationship found was increased ECG abnormalities with elevated blood pressure. However, follow-up studies of these men for coronary disease end points have not revealed any protection due to leisure-time activity.

Treadmill performance was found to be inversely related to body weight, percentage of body fat, lipids, glucose, and systolic blood pressure.

Regular exercise resulting in increased aerobic capacity was associated with a reduction in risk factors.

Aerobic institute Investigations at the Aerobic Center in Dallas used treadmill performance to quantitate physical fitness (Cooper et al., 1977). In a cross-sectional study of 3000 men, treadmill performance was found to be inversely related to body weight, percentage of body fat, lipids, glucose, and systolic blood pressure. In a longitudinal study men who were treadmill tested both before and after an elective exercise program were analyzed to determine if their performance had improved. Those men who reached the upper quartile of improved aerobic fitness exhibited decreases in lipids, diastolic blood pressure, serum glucose, uric acid, and weight. In this study regular exercise resulting in increased aerobic capacity was associated with a reduction in risk factors.

High-density lipoproteins and exercise Recently, cross-sectional studies found runners to have higher levels of high-density lipoprotein cholesterol (Wood and Haskell, 1979) and prospective studies found high levels of high-density lipoprotein cholesterol to be protective against coronary heart disease (Castelli et al., 1977). Leanness, high social status, moderate alcohol consumption, and being female are also possibly related to elevated high-density lipoprotein levels.

Longshoremen study Paffenbarger et al. (1978a) analyzed a 22 year follow-up of longshoremen from 1951 to 1972, a total of 59,401 man years, for a relationship between CHD and energy expenditure on the job. Age-adjusted frequencies of other risk factors were compared between the high-energy and low-energy expenditure groups and little difference was found. Three para-

Low energy output, smoking more than one pack of cigarettes a day, and high blood pressure put longshoremen at increased risk of fatal heart attack.

meters were found to put the longshorement at increased risk for fatal heart attack: these parameters include low energy output, smoking more than one pack of cigarettes a day, and an elevated systolic blood pressure (equal to or greater than the mean).

Men with a physical activity index below 2000 kcal per week were at 64% higher risk than classmates with a higher activity index.

Harvard alumni Paffenbarger et al. (1978b) studied 36,000 Harvard University alumni who entered college between 1916 and 1950. Records of their physical activity were gathered from their student days and during their middle-aged years. In the 6-10 year follow-up, 572 men had their first myocardial infarction. Men with a physical activity index below 2000 kcal per week were at 64% higher risk than classmates with a higher activity index. Three high-risk characteristics were identified in this study: low physical activity index (less than 2000 kcal per week, cigarette smoking, and hypertension). Presence of any one characteristic was accompanied by a 50% increase in risk; the presence of two characteristics tripled the risk. Maintenance of a high physical activity index (by running only 2 miles a day, for example) could possibly have reduced the heart attack rate by 26%.

Framingham study Kannel and Sorlie (1979) found that the effect of being sedentary on overall mortality and cardiovascular mortality was rather modest compared to the other risk factors. A low correlation was noted between physical activity level and the major risk factors.

The study by Kramsch is the most important animal study supporting the value of exercise in primary prevention.

Animal studies Kramsch et al. (1979) studied two groups of eight monkeys on controlled diets who were exercised on a treadmill for 18 months. For the next 24 months, one group was fed an atherogenic diet, while both groups continued exercising. Two additional groups of sedentary monkeys were similarly fed a control and an atherogenic diet. Serum cholesterol was higher in both groups on the atherogenic diet but less elevated in those who were exercising. Ischemic ECG changes were seen only in the sedentary group on an atherogenic diet. Angiographic stenoses were marked in the sedentary group on an atherogenic diet but absent in those who were exercising and on the same diet. Postmortems showed larger left ventricles and coronary arteries in the exercised group. The atherogenic diet caused lesions in all major arteries, but less in the exercised than in the sedentary monkeys. This is the most important animal study supporting the value of exercise in the primary prevention of atherosclerosis. There have been few other animal studies of primary prevention. Most studies have dealt with the indirect effect of exercise on blood pressure and lipids and have been unconvincing as support for the exercise hypothesis.

Controversy Recent reports have disproven the hypothesis that marathon running provides absolute protection against dying from atherosclerosis. Thompson et al. (1979) investigated the circumstances of death by considering the medical and activity histories of 18 individuals who died during or immediately after jogging. They concluded that superior physical fitness does not guarantee protection against exercise-induced death.

Koplan (1979) attempted to calculate the randomly expected numbers of cardiovascular deaths in runners while running. This is an important question since a person dying of cardiovascular causes during recreational running is frequently assumed to have died because of that exercise. Using data from the National Center of Health Statistics, Koplan found that approximately 100 cardiovascular deaths per year are predicted on a purely temporal basis in runners in the United States. Reported cases do not seem to exceed this number.

Role of exercise in secondary prevention of coronary heart disease

Echocardiographic and animal studies show exercise to alter cardiac reserve, although they have failed to yield consistent, conclusive results (Froelicher, 1979). At best, the studies suggest that increases in left ventricular mass do not occur in younger subjects unless high levels of training are used and may never occur in older subjects. However, animal studies provide some of the strongest evidence for the health benefits of regular exercise.

Animal studies provide some of the strongest evidence for the health benefits of regular exercise.

Role of exercise in tertiary prevention of coronary heart disease

There is some question as to whether middle-aged patients with coronary artery disease can carry out enough physical exertion to stimulate collateral development greater than the ischemia secondary to their disease. Neill and Oxedine (1979) studied the effects of exercise training on coronary collaterals developing in response to gradual coronary occlusion in dogs. They used ameroid constrictors, which initially were nonobstructive but slowly absorbed body fluids and gradually expanded over 2-3 weeks. After placement of a constrictor on the proximal left circumflex coronary artery, 33 dogs were randomly assigned to either exercise or sedentary groups. Coronary collateral flow was evaluated within 2 months. The exercised dogs developed greater epicardial collateral connections to the occluded left circumflex, as judged by higher blood flow and a lesser pressure drop distally. However, no difference in collaterals was found angiographically. Injected

These investigators concluded that exercise can promote coronary collateral development without improving perfusion of ischemic myocardium.

microspheres demonstrated that exercised dogs were not better protected against subendocardial ischemia induced by increased heart rate in the myocardium supplied by the collaterals. These investigators concluded that exercise can promote coronary collateral development without improving perfusion of ischemic myocardium. The results raise the question that even if collateral development does occur, does it influence significantly myocardial perfusion?

Moskowitz et al. (1979) reported the effects of cage size and level of exercise on myocardial infarction size after coronary artery occlusion in rats. Isolation in small cages or treadmill exercise resulted in an approximate doubling of the infarction size when compared to rats in larger cages. Urinary catecholamines were also elevated in rats placed in small cages. Mild exercise did not increase infarct size. Thus, cage size, level of activity, and sympathoadrenal function appear to be important determinants of myocardial infarction size after coronary occlusion in the rat. This study approximates the clinical situation of progressive ambulation early after an infarction and supports the current rationale.

Lee et al. (1979) studied the hemodynamic effects of physical training on CHD patients with impaired ventricular function. Eighteen CHD patients with an ejection fraction of 0.40 or less were entered into an exercise training program. Maximal symptom-limited exercise testing and cardiac catheterization were performed initially as well as 12-14 months after exercise training. Functional capacity improved and resting and submaximal heart rates were significantly lower; however, there were no significant changes in pulmonary artery or left ventricular and diastolic pressure, cardiac index, stroke index, left ventricular and diastolic volume, or ejection fraction. An increase in work capacity was not correlated with improvement in ventricular function, and exercise training did not cause deterioration of ventricular function. These authors concluded that exercise training can be beneficial even for patients with impaired ventricular function.

These authors concluded that exercise training can be beneficial even for patients with impaired ventricular function.

DeBusk, et al. (1979) studied the cardiovascular effects of exercise training very early after a clinically uncomplicated myocardial infarction. From 3-11 weeks after infarction, 28 men underwent gymnasium training, and 12, home training, 30 were followed as controls. These patients were highly selected and showed an annual mortality of only 2%. High-risk patients, including those with ventricular gallops and other evidence of heart failure, were excluded. Patients were randomized to the training programs only after stratification. If they had S-T-segment depression or angina pectoris they were assigned only to gymnasium training or to no training. By the eleventh week functional capacity increased substantially in all three groups: gymnasium training—66%; home training—41%; controls—34%. Functional capacity increased more in the gymnasium-trained group than in the group that had no training, but this difference was significant only in patients without exercise-induced S-T segment depression or angina. All 31 groups lowered their heart rate response to submaximal work. These authors concluded that (a) symptom-limited treadmill testing is safe and provides useful guidlines for cardiac rehabilitation; (b) patients who demonstrate nonischemic responses to treadmill testing soon after infarction may safely undergo unsupervised exercise training at home; and (c) formal training may not be required to restore functional capacity to nearly normal values soon after a myocardial infarction in selected patients. This report is rather exciting since exercise training has commenced traditionally no sooner than 2-8 weeks after a myocardial infarction. However, the sample size and careful patient selection make it difficult to draw solid conclusions.

Patients who demonstrate nonischemic responses to treadmill soon after myocardial infarction can safely undergo unsupervised exercise training.

Nolewajka et al. (1979) studied 20 male patients 3-6 months postmyocardial infarction. One half of the patients were randomly assigned to an exercise program. The exercise program was maintained 5 days a week at a heart rate of 60%-70% of their maximal heart rate obtained during a bicycle ergometer test. They were considered to have a training effect if their heart rate dropped at least 10 beats at an oxygen consumption of 1.2 L per min. Both groups underwent coronary angiography, invasive resting left ventricular function studies, and intracoronary artery injection of radionuclide microspheres before and after a 7-month period. No differences were found in disease progression, resting myocardial perfusion or function, or myocardial collateralization.

Paterson et al. (1979) studied 79 patients under 54 years of age, 3-12 months postmyocardial infarction with CO_2 rebreathing during submaximal bicycle exercise both before and after 6 and 12 months of exercise training. Thirty-seven were randomized to a low-intensity activity as controls. Over the year of training only the predicted maximal oxygen consumption of the high-intensity training group increased. At 6 months their heart rates were significantly reduced at each workload, with a widened A-VO_2 difference, but there was no change in stroke volume. By the end of the year their stroke volume had increased by 10%. These observations were interpreted as showing that only peripheral changes occur in such patients after 6 months of high-intensity training, while longer periods can result in an increase in myocardial contractility.

These observations were interpreted as showing that only peripheral changes occur in such patients after 6 months of high-intensity training.

Kavanagh et al. (1979) evaluated prognostic indices in 601 patients who initiated a vigorous 3-year exercise-centered rehabili-

Participation in an exercise-centered rehabilitation program may possibly reduce the reinfarction rate.

tation program 8 months postmyocardial infarction. Over the 3-year period 23 had a fatal and 21 had a nonfatal recurrence of a myocardial infarction. The most significant prognostic factor was noncompliance with the exercise program. Patients who dropped out of the exercise program had a reinfarction rate of approximately 50%, whereas those who stayed in the exercise program had only about a 2% recurrence rate. Patients with persistent angina, aneurysm, enlarged heart, elevated serum cholesterol, and those persisting in smoking cigarettes increased their risks twofold. S-T segment depression during the exercise test carried a risk ratio of greater than three, while multiformed exercise-induced premature ventricular contractions (PVCs) had a risk ratio of less than two. There was a low yearly fatality rate of 1.2% in the 610 patients and only 0.7% in those without exercise-induced S-T segment depression. Age, hypertension, persistent resting ECG abnormalities, or the physiologic response to exercise testing had little influence on the prognosis of patients who stayed in an exercise program. However, a combination of ST-segment depression and high serum cholesterol yielded a risk ratio of greater than four. The prognosis for patients with these risk factors, however, remained at least as good as comparable patients not receiving exercise training. Patients with the high-risk prognostic features had less risk reduction, but their prognosis remained more favorable than that of subjects who did not exercise. The high risk of being a dropout in part can be attributed to bias--the sickest patients could not tolerate the program. Comparison of the trained patients to those randomized to low-energy activities showed no difference in morbidity and mortality.

CONCLUSIONS

Regular physical activity is performed by over 15 million health-conscious Americans. Yet there is no definitive evidence of its efficacy in either the primary, secondary, or tertiary prevention fo CHD. Epidemiologists have been hampered in their research by numerous problems including diagnosing reliably coronary disease, distinguishing between associations and causality, and selection and premorbid job transfers; quantifying activity levels; and accounting for the variability of risk prediction in different populations. The type of exercise that is beneficial, and its method of protection is uncertain. Some beneficial action may be mediated hormonally by the lowering of catecholamine levels. Recent studies continue to have limitations, but physical inactivity appears to involve some risk.

Animal studies have provided substantial evidence of the cardiovascular benefits of regular physical activity. Improved coronary circulation has been demonstrated in exercise-trained animals by increased capillary density, reduced myocardial infarction size, maintenance of coronary flow in response to hypoxia, and increased collateral perfusion after occlusion. Studies using various animal models have reported improvement in cardiac function secondary to exercise training. Improved intrinsic contractility, faster relaxation, enzymatic alterations, calcium availability, and enhanced autonomic and hormonal control of function have all been implicated. However, animal studies have failed to find beneficial risk factor changes observed in active humans or regression of atherosclerotic lesions.

Exercise training can be effective in achieving physiologic, psychologic, and vocational goals of cardiac rehabilitation, but beneficial effects on morbidity and mortality remain undocumented.

Exercise training can be effective in achieving the physiologic, psychologic, and vocational goals of cardiac rehabilitation, but beneficial effects on morbidity and mortality remain undocumented. Perhaps the greatest benefit of physical training is the increase in the angina threshold; however, changes in intrinsic function and coronary blood flow remain uncertain. Some data suggest that significant results occur only after longer periods of training (more than one year). Further work with noninvasive techniques is needed to characterize individuals who will benefit from training as well as to demonstrate physiologic changes.

ANNOTATED BIBLIOGRAPHY

Berglund, G.; Wilhelmsen, L.; Sannerstedt, R., et al. 1978. Coronary heart-disease after treatment of hypertension. *Lancet* 1:1-9.
A report on the incidence of coronary heart disease among patients treated for hypertension.

Blackburn, H. 1974. Progress in the epidemiology and prevention of coronary heart disease. In *Progress in Cardiology*, eds. P. N. Yu and J. F. Goodwin, Chapter 1. Philadelphia: Lea & Febiger Publishers.
A good progress report on coronary heart disease epidemiology as of 1974.

Castelli, W.; Doyle, J. T.; Gordon, T., et al. 1977. HDL cholesterol and other lipids in coronary heart disease: The cooperative lipoprotein phenotyping study. *Circulation* 55:767-772.
One of the many studies showing the effect of exercise on cholesterol.

Cobb, S., and Rose, R. M. 1973. Hypertension, peptic ulcer, and diabetes in air traffic controllers. *J. A. M. A.* 224:489-492
A carefully done study demonstrating that hypertension is more prevalent among air traffic controllers than would generally be expected.

Cooper, J. K.; Meyer, B.; Blide, R., et al. 1977. The important role of fitness determination and stress testing in predicting coronary incidence. *Ann. N. Y. Acad. Sci.* 301:642-652.
A unique contribution to preventive medicine.

Criqui, M. H.; Wallace, R.; and Heiss, G. 1979. Cigarette smoking and high density lipoprotein cholesterol: The lipid research clinic's prevalence study. *Circulation* 60:11-53.
The data suggest that cigarette smoking has an independent effect on the concentration of HDL cholesterol.

Dayton, S.; Pearce, M. L.; Hashimoto, S., et al. 1969. A controlled clinical trial of a diet high in unsaturated fats in preventing complications of arteriosclerosis. *Circulation* 39:40. Suppl. II, 2:1-11, 63.
The first report on a "closed" population demonstrating reduced incidence of atherosclerotic disease among patients treated with polyunsaturated fatty acids to reduce their serum cholesterol levels.

DeBusk, R. F.; Houston, N.; Haskell, W., et al. 1979. Exercise training soon after myocardial infarction. *Am. J. Cardiol.* 44: 1223-1229.
One of many important studies from Stanford rehabilitation program.

Epstein, L.; Miller, G. J.; Stitt, F. W., et al. 1976. Vigorous exercise in leisure time, coronary risk-factors, and resting electrocardiogram in middle-aged male civil servants. *Br. Heart J.* 38:403-409.
One of many good studies by J. N. Morris on physical inactivity.

Fisch, I. R.; Freedman, S. H., and Myatt, A. V. 1972. Oral contraceptives, pregnancy, and blood pressure. *J. A. M. A.* 222:1507-1510.
Data on the relationship between taking oral contraceptives and hypertension.

Froelicher, V. F. 1972. Animal studies of effect of chronic exercise on the heart and atherosclerosis: A review. *Am. Heart J.* 84:496-506.

————. 1977. Does exercise conditioning delay progression of myocardial ischemia in coronary atherosclerotic heart disease? In *Cardiovascular clinics*, eds. E. Corday and A. Brest, pp. 11-31. Philadelphia: F. A. Davis, Co.

These three references are state of the art at the time of their publication.

————. 1978. Exercise in the prevention of coronary atherosclerotic heart disease. In *Exercise and the heart; Cardiovascular clinics*, Vol. 9, No. 3, eds. A. Brest and N. Wenger, pp. 13-23. Philadelphia: F. A. Davis, Co.
These three references are state of the art at the time of their publication.

Froehlicher, V. F.; Battler, A.; and McKirnan, M.D. 1980. Physical activity and coronary heart disease. *Cardiology* 65:153-191. Shows the problems with echo studies.

Froelicher, V. F.; Jensen, D.; Atwood, E., et al. 1980. Cardiac rehabilitation: Evidence for improvement in myocardial perfusion and function. *Arch. Phys. Med. Rehab.* 61:517-522.
The first study using both radionuclide ejection fraction and thallium images before and after cardiac rehabilitation.

Garraway, W. M.; Whisnant, J. P.; Furlan, A. J., et al. 1979. The declining incidence of stroke. *N. Engl. J. Med.*, 300:449-452.
Incidence data on stroke in the population served by the Mayo Clinic in Rochester, Minnesota, comparing the two 5-year periods —1945-49 and 1970-74.

Harburg, E.; Gleibermann, L.; Falph, P., et al. 1978. Skin color, ethnicity, and blood pressure; I: Detroit blacks. *Am. J. Public Health*, 68:1177-1183.
A study demonstrating an inverse relationship between blood pressure and degree of skin pigmentation.

Haynes, R. B.; Sackett, D. L.; Taylor, D. W., et al. 1978. Increased absenteeism from work after detection and labeling of hypertensive patients. *J. Engl. J. Med.* 299:741-744.
A study demonstrating increased absenteeism in industry among patients who have recently been labeled as having hypertension.

Hypertension Detection and Follow-up Program Cooperative Group. 1977. Blood pressure studies in 14 communities: A two-stage screen for hypertension. *J. A. M. A.* 237:2385-2391.
Prevalence data on hypertension.

————. 1979. Five-year findings of the hypertension, detection and follow-up program. *J. A. M. A.* 242:2562-2571; 2572-2577.
Two classical reports describing the reduction in mortality and serious cardiovascular morbidity of middle-aged men and women treated carefully by stepped-care, as compared with the usual treatment of patients with mild hypertension.

Jensen, D.; Atwood, C.; Froelicher, V. F., et al. 1980. Improvement in ventricular function during exercise studied with radionuclide ventriculography after cardiac rehabilitation. *Am. J. Card.* 46:770-777.

Nineteen patients were studied with radionuclide ejection fractions before and after 6 months of exercise training. An improved ejection fraction was found during submaximal exercise.

Kannel, W. B., and Sorlie, P. 1979. Some health benefits of physical activity: The Framingham study. *Arch. Intern. Med.* 139: 857-861.
Shows physical inactivity to fall below the cardinal risk factors in importance.

Kavanagh, T.; Shephard, R. J.; Chisholm, A. W., et al. 1979. Prognostic indexes for patients with ischemic heart disease enrolled in an exercise-centered rehabilitation program. *Am. J. Cardiol.* 44: 1230-1240.
A very important study from a pioneering group.

Koplan, J. P. 1979. Cardiovascular deaths while running. *J. A. M. A.* 242:2578-2579.
Thoughtful and provocative reading.

Kramsch, D. M.; Aspen, A. J.; Abramowitz, B. M., et al. 1979. Cardiovascular effects of exercise in primate atherosclerosis. *Circulation* 59,60:652.
Only published in abstract form but will be a classic.

Lee, A. P.; Ice, R.; Blessey, R., et al. 1979. Long-term effects of physical training on coronary patients with impaired ventricular function. *Circulation* 60:1519-1526.
Even bad ventricles can benefit from exercise.

McIlhany, M. L.; Schaffer, J. W., and Hines, E. A. 1975. The heritability of blood pressure: An investigation of 200 pairs of twins using the cold pressor test. *Johns Hopkins Med. J.* 136:57-64.
A study of twins, demonstrating concordance of the cold-pressor response and therefore suggesting its heritability.

Michell, A. R. 1978. Salt appetite, salt intake, and hypertension: A deviation of perspective. *Perspect. Biol. Med.* 21.335-347.
A general review of the salt hypothesis as a cause of hypertension.

Mills, E., and Thompson, M. 1978. The economic costs of stroke in Massachusetts. *N. Engl. J. Med.* 299:415-418.
A careful analysis of the economic impact of stroke in Massachusetts. The figures, however, are estimates and in most cases are not based on actual cost.

Moskowitz, R. M.; Burns, J. J.; DiCarlo, E. F., et al. 1979. Cage size and exercise effects on infarct size in rat after coronary artery cauterization. *J. Appl. Physiol.* 47:393-396.
Support for progressive early ambulation.

National Center for Health Statistics. 1975. *Blood pressure of persons 18-74 years: United States, 1970-71.* National Health

Survey, Series 11, No. 150. Washington, D.C., U. S. Government Printing Office.
A summary of the blood pressure data collected by the 1970-71 National Health Survey.

Neill, A., and Oxedine, R. 1979. Do collaterals improve perfusion during exercise? *Circulation* 60:1501-1508.
Even if collaterals are found do they do any good?

Nolewajka, A. J.; Kostuk, W. J.; Rechnitzer, P. A., et al. 1979. Exercise and human collateralization: An angiographic and scinigraphic assessment. *Circulation* 60:114-121.
A negative study.

Paffenbarger, R. S.; Brand, R. J.; Sholtz, R. I., et al. 1978a. Energy expenditure, cigarette smoking, and blood pressure level as related to death from specific diseases. *Am. J. Epidemiol.* 108.12-18.

————; Wing, A. L.; and Hyde, R. T. 1978b. Physical activity as an index of heart attack risk in college alumni. *Am. J. Epidemiol.* 108:161-175.
Classics supporting the exercise hypothesis.

Paterson, D. H.; Shephard, R. J.; Cunningham, D., et al. 1979. Effects of physical training on cardiovascular function following myocardial infarction. *J. Appl. Physiol.* 47:482-489.
It takes one year to get central cardiac changes.

Stamler, R.; Stamler, J.; Riedlinger, W. F., et al. 1978. Weight and blood pressure: Findings in hypertension screening of 1 million Americans. *J. A. M. A.* 240:1607-1610.
A large survey of more than a million population, demonstrating once again the relationship between body weight and blood pressure.

————. 1979. Family (parental) history and prevalence of hypertension results of a nationwide screening program. *J. A. M. A.* 241:43-46.
More data on familial aggregation of hypertension based on a nationwide screening program.

Thompson, P. D.; Stern, M. P.; Williams, P., et al. 1979. Death during jogging or running. *J. A. M. A.* 242:1265-1267.
The double-edged sword of exercise.

Tsai, S. P.; Lee, E. S.; and Hardy, R. J. 1978. The effect of a reduction in leading causes of death: Potential gains in life expectancy. *Am. J. Public Health* 68:966-971.
A careful statistical analysis of potential gains in life expectancy, including a method of correcting for competing risks.

Veterans Administration. Cooperative Study Group on Antihypertensive Agents. 1967. Diastolic blood pressure 115-129 mm Hg. *J. A. M. A.* 202:1028-1034.
The original Veterans Administration study on the efficacy of intervention in serious hypertension.

———. 1970. Diastolic blood pressure 90-114 mm Hg. *J. A. M. A.* 213:1143-1152.
The subsequent Veterans Administration intervention study showing the efficacy of treating lower levels of diastolic blood pressure.

Weinstein, M. C., and Stason, W. B. 1976. *Hypertension: A policy perspective.* Cambridge, Mass.: Harvard University Press.
A policy analysis including several recommendations, among which is one suggesting that extensive independent screening for hypertension would not be cost effective.

Wood, P. D., and Haskell, W. L. 1979. The effect of exercise on plasma high density lipoproteins. *Lipids* 14:417-427.
The best summary of this subject.

Wright, I. S., and Fredrickson, D. T., eds. 1974. *Cardiovascular diseases: Guidelines for prevention and care.* Reports of the Inter-society Commission for Heart Disease Resources. Washington, D.C.: U. S. Government Printing Office.
An excellent summary of the data upon which cardiovascular disease prevention is based, including a set of policy recommendations.

An excellent summary of the data upon which cardiovascular disease prevention is based.

10 Smoking and Disease

William A. Norcross

Dr. Norcross is a graduate of Duke University School of Medicine and is on the Family Medicine faculty of the University of California, San Diego, School of Medicine. In addition to his clinical activities he is a busy teacher in the medical school and community and was given the Warner-Chilcott award for teaching in family medicine.

Brief Contents

Overview

Cigarette smoking is the single most preventable cause of death. Primary care practitioners should maintain a continuing helping attitude toward their patients' efforts to quit. As role models physicians should neither smoke nor adopt a hostile attitude toward their smoking patients. Like any addictive behavior smoking may require large amounts of time, energy, and patience to correct. Patients should be encouraged to continue their efforts even after multiple failures. Different treatment modalities may have to be explored to find the one most suitable.

Cigarette smoking is the single most preventable cause of death.

HISTORY

Tobacco, or *Nicotiana tabacum*, is an herb of the nightshade family. When cured, its leaves can be used for smoking, chewing, and sniffing. The plant is native to the Western hemisphere and probably has been used by aboriginal peoples since ancient times. It was carried to France in 1559 by Jean Nicot and to England in 1585 by Sir Francis Drake. Sir Walter Raleigh popularized pipe smoking among Elizabethan courtiers and the practice quickly spread throughout the rest of Europe and Western Asia. Opposition arose, however, and smoking was punishable by death or excommunication in parts of Germany and Turkey. In Russia the punishment for repeated smoking was castration. By comparison even the most ardent antismoking activism today is mild.

Tobacco has always played a vital role in the economy of the United States.

Tobacco has always played a vital role in the economy of this country. It was the principal crop in the Jamestown colony and cultivated not only in the fields but also in the streets and marketplace. At the conclusion of the Civil War the largest Union and Confederate armies disbanded near Durham, North Carolina, 4 miles south of the farm of Washington Duke, the first of the great tobacco barons. Soldiers from both sides brought samples home, effectively disseminating the product across the country.

With the development of efficient cigarette-rolling machines, the industry boomed and tobacco became widely available to the American public. By the beginning of the twentieth century the tobacco industry had amassed fortunes for its investors. Tobacco itself acquired a salubrious reputation: a textbook of medicine at the time prescribed tobacco smoking for the therapy of chronic bronchitis. Figure 10-1 is a 1928 advertisement that proclaims smoking as "The modern way to diet!" and is "For men who pride themselves on keeping fit."

Figure 10.1.

The popularity of smoking continues despite widespread dissemination of its harmful effects. The tobacco industry thrives; tobacco farmers receive federal subsidies for their crops; and the

DAILY NEWS, TUESDAY, OCTOBER 16, 1928 15

"I know an easy way to keep from getting fat...... Light a Lucky instead of eating sweets."

Nazimova

THE modern way to diet! Light a Lucky when rich sweets tempt you. That's what thousands of lovely women are doing—successfully. The delicately toasted flavor of Luckies makes them a delightful alternative for sweets. Toasting does it. Toasting removes the impurities and improves the flavor of the finest tobacco.

Men who pride themselves on keeping fit discovered this long ago. They know that Luckies do not affect the wind nor impair their physical condition—many prominent athletes have testified to this fact. They discovered, too, that Luckies don't irritate the throat—a fact subscribed to by 20,679 doctors.

Here's the best diet news of the year: light a Lucky and you won't miss sweets.

Nazimova
Brilliant Dramatic Star who made her first appearance last night with Civic Repertory Theatre in "The Cherry Orchard."

LUCKY STRIKE
"IT'S TOASTED"
CIGARETTES

"It's toasted"

No Throat Irritation-No Cough.

Reach for a Lucky instead of a sweet

©1928, The American Tobacco Co., Manufacturers

Figure 10-1 Advertisement in 1928 newspaper which proclaimed that cigarette smoking is not only stylish but healthful.

incidence of smoking maintains a steady increase among segments of our population, particularly among female teen-agers.

EPIDEMIOLOGY

Prevalence of smoking behavior in 15-16 year-old girls rose from 10%-20% during the period 1968-1975.

Parents who smoke influence teenagers to smoke.

A 1971 survey of junior and senior high school students revealed that more than 90% of them were aware of the correlation between smoking and lung cancer. Despite this, the prevalence of smoking behavior in 15-16 year-old girls rose from 10%-20% during the period 1968-1975; the prevalence for boys remained unchanged at 18% during the same period of time.

The family environment seems to influence smoking behavior in the young. In a household of nonsmokers, only 4% of teenagers will develop the habit; in a household in which at least one other member smokes, 25% of teenagers will become regular smokers. Peer pressure also exerts a strong influence on adolescent smoking behavior. Up to now efforts to interrupt the initiation of smoking behavior in the young have been virtually fruitless.

The cost of smoking to society is staggering. According to the latest Surgeon General's Report, smoking is responsible for 81 million lost workdays per year and 350,000 deaths. In 1975 estimated costs of smoking, including such factors as tobacco production, disease, fire, disability, was $41.5 billion. Cigarette smoking is recognized to be the single most important preventable cause of death.

BIOCHEMICAL AND PHYSIOLOGIC ASPECTS OF SMOKING

Cigarette smoke contains over 4000 compounds including tar, carbon monoxide, nicotine (the only known psychoactive component), and the carcinogens 3:4 benzopyrene, 1:12 benzpyrelene, arsenous oxide, and radioactive polonium compounds.

The major immediate physiologic effects—tachycardia, arrhythmias, increased blood pressure, bronchial constriction, and increased myocardial oxygen consumption—seem to occur via nicotine-mediated release of catecholamines. Chronic smoking increases carboxyhemoglobin with a resultant increase in red cell mass (secondary polycythemia).

Passive smoking—the involuntary breathing of exhaled mainstream smoke (which is drawn through the tobacco) and sidestream smoke (which arises from the burning core)—causes eye and nose irritation due to acrolein, ammonia, and aldehydes as well as nicotine effects such as tachycardia and hypertension.

Smoking affects the metabolism of many drugs, predominantly through the induction of microsomal enzyme systems. Thus, for example, the dose of theophylline required to achieve a therapeutic effect in a smoker will be 1½ to 2 times the dose required for a nonsmoker. Smoking also decreases the pharmacologic effects of pentazocine, imipramine, propoxyphene, diazepam, and chlorpromazine. Smokers have decreased blood levels of vitamin C and may also have impaired metabolism of vitamin B_{12} and impaired bone mineralization. Evidence suggests that smoking potentiates platelet aggregation and reduces whole blood coagulation time, which may account for its enhancing effects on estrogen-induced thromboembolic disease.

Smoking decreases the pharmacologic effects of many drugs and vitamins and enhances estrogen-induced thromboembolic disease.

The greatest effect of cigarette smoking, however, is undoubtedly on the respiratory system where it induces basal cell hyperplasia of the bronchial epithelium, loss of cilia, and nuclear changes. Even young smokers with an average age of 25 years but with a smoking history of 10-pack years almost invariably have histologic evidence of respiratory bronchiolitis. Smoking impairs ciliary movement and macrophage function, which in turn contributes to infection and alveolar occlusion—the presumed antecedents of chronic obstructive pulmonary disease.

HEALTH HAZARDS

The Fetus

A smoking mother subjects the fetus to a variety of severe health risks.

Babies born to smoking mothers average 150-250 gm less in weight than those born to nonsmoking mothers; a smoking mother is twice as likely to deliver a baby less than 2500 grams in weight than a nonsmoking mother. The ratio of placental weight to birth weight increases with smoking, possibly as a compensatory response to elevated blood carboxyhemoglobin. The available data disclose no correlation between smoking and congenital defects; however, smoking doubles the risk of spontaneous abortion and increases significantly the risk of many complications including bleeding, abruptio placentae, placenta previa, premature delivery, premature and prolonged rupture of membranes, and overall perinatal mortality. One prospective study showed the risk of stillbirths by abruptio placentae to be magnified sixfold in smoking mothers.

One prospective study showed the risk of stillbirths by abruptio placentae to be magnified sixfold in smoking mothers.

Curiously, several studies have demonstrated a lower incidence of preeclampsia among smoking mothers, a protective effect that seems "dose-related." This protective effect is limited, however, in that if the smoking mother does develop preeclampsia, her baby is more likely to die than that of a preeclamptic nonsmoking mother.

The duration of smoking-associated risks is unknown, but the United States Collaborative Perinatal Project discovered that the risk of placenta previa is correlated to past smoking history, raising the specter that such behavior creates a chronic condition that may have a long-standing effect on the outcome of future pregnancies. Studies on the effects of smoking on lactation are conflicting. Nicotine is present in breast milk and at least one suspected case of "nicotine poisoning" (restlessness, vomiting, diarrhea, and tachycardia) was reported in a breast-fed infant. Cigarette smoking also causes tobacco-treated dichlorodiphenyltrichloroethane (DDT) to be secreted in breast milk.

Nicotine is present in breast milk.

Infancy and Childhood

Children who live with smoking parents are at greater risk for several health problems. Whether these problems are the consequence of exposure to toxins in utero or later to ambient tobacco smoke in the home, or a result of other factors, is unknown.

Children who live with smoking parents are subject to health risks.

The effect of cigarette smoking on the mental and physical development of children is controversial. The United States Collaborative Perinatal Project shows little or no effect on the longterm mental and motor development of children. A smaller study also found no correlation between maternal smoking and physical and intellectual measures of offspring up to the age of 7 years.

The effect of cigarette smoking on the mental and physical development in children is controversial.

Most available data suggest a correlation between parental smoking and the incidence of respiratory illness (bronchitis and pneumonia) in infants during the first year of life and possibly later. This evidence, coupled with the observations of a reduction in mean peak expiratory flow rate in 5-year old children who had bronchitis or pneumonia during the first year of life, as compared to a control group, suggests a possibly ominous linkage between parental smoking, respiratory infection, and permanent deficit in pulmonary function.

Perhaps even more alarming is the association between maternal smoking during pregnancy and sudden infant death syndrome —the leading cause of death in the first year of childhood. Whether the increased incidence of this catastrophic syndrome is related to the effects of smoking in utero, to passive tobacco smoking in the home, or to other factors is unknown.

Maternal smoking is associated with the sudden infant death syndrome.

Adults

Overall mortality is increased strikingly by smoking. Adult smokers

Table 10-1 Mortality Ratios of Current Cigarette-Only Smokers—By Cause of Death, in Eight Prospective Epidemiologic Studies*

	STUDY									
	A	B		C	D	E	F	G		H
		Age in years						Sex		
		45-64	65-79					M	F	
All cancers		2.14	1.76	2.21	1.62		1.97			
Lung and bronchus	14.0	7.84	11.59	12.14	3.64	14.2	10.73	7.0	4.5	15.9
Larynx		6.09	8.99	9.95	13.59		13.10			
Buccal cavity	13.0	{9.90	{2.93	4.09	7.04	3.9	2.80			1.0
Pharynx				12.54	2.81					
Esophagus	4.7	4.17	1.74	6.17	2.57	3.3	6.60			0.7
Bladder and other	2.1	2.20	2.96	2.15	0.98	1.3	2.40	1.8	1.6	6.0
Pancreas	1.6	2.69	2.17	1.84	1.83	2.1		3.1	2.5	
Kidney		1.42	1.57	1.45	1.11	1.4	1.50			
Stomach		1.42	1.26	1.60	1.51	1.9	2.30	0.9	2.3	0.8
Intestines		{1.01	{1.17	1.27	1.27	1.4	0.50			0.9
Rectum	2.7			0.98	0.91	0.6	0.80			1.0
All cardiovascular		1.90	1.31	1.75			1.57			
Coronary heart disease	1.6	2.03	1.36	1.74	1.96	1.6	1.70	1.7	1.3	2.0
Cerebrovascular lesions	1.3	1.38	1.06	1.52	1.14	0.9	1.30	1.0	1.1	1.8
Aortic Aneurysm (non-syphilitic)	6.6	2.62	4.92	5.24		1.8		1.6		
Hypertension		1.40	1.42	1.67	2.51	1.6	1.20	1.3	1.4	1.0
General arteriosclerosis	1.4			1.86		3.3	2.00	2.0	2.0	
All respiratory diseases (non-neoplastic)							2.85			
Emphysema and/or bronchitis	24.7			10.08			2.30	1.6	2.2	4.3
Emphysema without bronchitis		6.55	11.41	14.17		7.7				
Bronchitis				4.49		11.3				
Respiratory tuberculosis	5.0			2.12	1.27					
Asthma				3.47						
Influenza and pneumonia	1.4	1.86	1.72	1.87		1.4	2.60			2.4
Certain other conditions										
Stomach ulcer	{2.5	4.06	4.13	4.13	{2.06					
Duodenal ulcer		2.86	1.50	2.98		6.9	2.16			0.5
Cirrhosis	3.0	2.06	1.97	3.33	1.35	2.3	1.93	2.4	0.8	4.0
Parkinsonism	0.4			0.26						
All causes	1.64	1.88	1.43	1.84	1.22	1.52	1.70	1.4	1.2	1.78

*Study A: Doll, R., and Peto, R. 1976. Mortality in relation to smoking: 20 years' observation on male British doctors. *Br. Med. J.* 2:1525-1536; Hammond, E. C. 1966. Smoking in relation to the death rates of one million men and women. In *Epidemiological Approaches to the Study of Cancer and Other Chronic Diseases,* W. Haenszel, ed. U.S. Public Health Service, National Cancer Institute Monograph 19, pp. 127-204; Study C: Kahn, H. A.: The Dorn study of smoking and mortality among U.S. veterans: Report on 8½ years of observation. In Haenszel, *Ibid,* pp. 1-125; Study D: Hirayama, T. 1972. Smoking in relation to the death rates of 265,118 men and women in Japan. A report on 5 years of follow-up. Presented at the American Cancer Society's 14th Science Writers' Seminar,24-29 Mar 1972, at Clearwater Beach, Florida, Study E: Best, E.W.R. 1966. A Canadian study of smoking and health. Ottawa: Dept. of National Health and Welfare; Study F: Hammond, E. C., and Horn, D. 1958. Smoking and death rates—Report on 44 months of follow-up on 187,783 men. I. Total mortality. II. Death rates by cause. *J.A.M.A.* 166: 1159-1172, 1294-1308; Study G: Cederlof, R.; Friberg, L.; Hrubec Z., et al. 1975. The relationship of smoking and some social covariables to mortality and cancer morbidity. A 10-year follow-up in a probability sample of 55,000 Swedish subjects age 18-69. Part ½, Sweden: Karolinska Institute; Study H: Weir, J. M., and Dunn, J. E., Jr. 1970. Smoking and mortality: A prospective study. *Cancer* 25:105-112.

Table 10-1.

of all age groups have a mortality rate that is more than 1½ times that of nonsmokers (Table 10-1).

Adult mortality rate of smokers is more than 1½ times that of nonsmokers.

The association of cigarette smoking and cancer of the lung and bronchus is well known, but cigarette smoking is also associated with cancer of the larynx, pharynx, mouth, esophagus, bladder, kidney, stomach, and pancreas.

Cigarette smoking is a well-known contributory factor in emphysema and chronic bronchitis. Impairments in pulmonary function have been demonstrated in young, relatively asymptomatic smokers. Studies also show that smoking impairs the normal function of the cilia of the respiratory epithelium, pulmonary alveolar macrophages, and the surfactant system.

Smoking seems to exert an additive effect on persons with a hereditary predisposition to chronic obstructive pulmonary disease (for example, alpha 1-antitrypsin deficiency). Smoking may also have an additive effect on environmental and occupational agents that cause pulmonary disease and lung cancer—chromate, nickel, coal gas, asbestos, uranium, arsenic, hematite, beryllium, and copper.

Smoking is associated in a dose-related fashion to peptic and gastric ulcers. Smoking diminishes pancreatic bicarbonate secretion, which may be a potentiating factor in the development of duodenal ulcer. The risk of dying from gastric ulcer disease is approximately twice as great for smokers as for nonsmokers.

Women over the age of 35 years should avoid the combination of smoking and oral contraceptives.

Finally, cigarette smoking is a strong, independent, dose-related risk factor for coronary artery disease and sudden death, and is associated with cerebrovascular disease, subarachnoid hemorrhage, peripheral vascular disease (including thromboangiitis obliterans), aortic aneurysm, and malignant hypertension. Interestingly enough, smoking does not seem to be correlated with the nonmalignant form of hypertension. For women over the age of 35 years the combination of smoking and oral contraceptive use appears to be a substantial risk factor for myocardial infarction.

Involuntary Smoking

Sidestream smoke contains a greater amount of toxic substances than mainstream smoke.

Our knowledge of the effects of involuntary, or passive smoking is limited but growing, and as it grows, so does the evidence incriminating it as a serious threat to health. Sidestream smoke contains a greater amount of toxic substances than mainstream smoke. Levels of carbon monoxide as high as 110 ppm (highest permissible 8-hour industrial exposure to carbon monoxide is 50 ppm) has been measured in ambient tobacco smoke. This level varies widely with the size of the space, ventilation, and products smoked.

Passive smoking also induces health problems.

The most obvious effect of ambient tobacco smoke on healthy young nonsmokers is eye and nose irritation (principally due to acrolein). Nonsmokers with underlying diseases such as asthma and other chronic obstructive pulmonary disease may experience acute episodes of respiratory decompensation when exposed to ambient tobacco smoke. Recent studies also show that nonsmokers exposed to long-term involuntary smoking develop disease in the small airways of the lung (White and Froeb, 1980).

Involuntary smoking significantly accelerates the development of exercise-induced angina.

Aronow (1978) found that involuntary smoking significantly accelerates the development of exercise-induced angina in both ventilated and unventilated environments. By inference one could conclude therefore that involuntary smoking predisposes to myocardial infarction and even death.

As previously described, smoking parents very likely endanger the health of their children by increasing the risk of bronchitis and pneumonia during the first year of life, by increasing the risk of sudden infant death syndrome, and quite possibly by impairing physical and mental development.

Pipes and Cigars

Overall mortality for pipe and cigar smokers is only slightly greater than that for nonsmokers.

In general the health risks of pipe and cigar smoking are intermediate between nonsmoking and cigarette smoking, probably because pipe and cigar smokers inhale less deeply. Data from major prospective epidemiological studies show that overall mortality for pipe and cigar smokers is only slightly greater than that for nonsmokers (cigar smokers have slightly higher death rates than pipe smokers).

Although the overall cancer mortality for cigar and pipe smokers is only slightly greater than for nonsmokers, the upper respiratory and upper digestive tracts seem to be vulnerable targets for malignancy. Deaths from coronary artery disease, chronic obstructive pulmonary disease, and lung, bladder, and pancreatic carcinoma are only slightly greater in pipe and cigar smokers than nonsmokers; deaths from cancer of the oral cavity, pharynx, larynx, and esophagus are equal in all smokers.

Marijuana

Little is known about the long-term effects of marijuana smoking; it may well be decades before we have prospective data as reliable as those for tobacco smoking. Nonetheless, preliminary evidence suggests that marijuana has certain deleterious effects and may well be as great a threat to health as tobacco.

Marijuana exhibits short-term bronchial dilator activity in humans; however, chronic smoking appears to cause functional impairment principally of the trachea and upper airways. Whether this leads to clinically significant obstructive pulmonary disease in not known. Whether marijuana is associated with an increased risk for lung cancer is also unknown, although studies have shown a similar effect to tobacco on the division of cultured human lung cells. The risk of heart disease in marijuana smokers is unestablished; however, the observed increased heart rate and increased left ventricular work could be detrimental to patients with established heart disease.

Marijuana smoking is probably just as hazardous as tobacco smoking.

In summary, there is no good reason to assume that the risks involved with marijuana smoking are any less than those associated with tobacco smoking.

THERAPY

There appears to be no voluntary behavior as costly, debilitating, and lethal, yet resistant to treatment, as smoking. Primary care practitioners should consistently encourage patients to stop smoking by maintaining helpful rather than hostile attitudes, even if patients repeatedly fail in their efforts to stop. Different treatment modalities may be explored over a period of time to find the one most suitable.

Cigarette safety precautions should be stressed, including use of car ashtrays and the avoidance of smoking in bed. Pregnant women especially should not smoke. Parents should be encouraged strongly to smoke out of doors and away from the house and other enclosed spaces. They should also be advised of the role modeling they provide in regard to smoking behavior.

Chronic smoking behavior is best explained by nicotine addiction.

The psychopharmacology of tobacco smoking behavior has been excellently reviewed by Schachter (1978). To summarize briefly, the data suggest that chronic smoking behavior is best explained by nicotine addition. The therapy of smoking can then be divided into three approaches: (a) prevention, (b) cessation, and (c) modification of smoking behavior. None of these approaches has met with resounding success, but even if a few people can be prevented from smoking the benefits in terms of costs, resources, health, and happiness will be immense.

The greatest benefits can probably be gained through prevention. Habituation to smoking occurs most commonly during adolescence within the social framework of a smoking peer group. Efforts to dissuade young persons from smoking by educating them to the health consequences have not been highly effective. Providing adolescent behavioral training in coping with peer pressure may be a more effective approach. One of the most promising efforts to date is the health education program, "Know Your Body," given to junior high school students. Ten sessions are devoted to role modeling, group discussion, and behavior rehearsal —all to help develop the behavioral skills necessary to resist social pressures to smoke. Initial results from this program demonstrate a 67% reduction in new smokers.

One of the most promising efforts toward primary prevention of smoking is a health education program directed at junior high school students.

Many approaches to terminate smoking have high short-term success rates; so far none have demonstrated a consistently high long-term success rate.

Whatever method is tried, the smoker should probably seek the goal of total cessation within one week or less.

Whatever method is tried, the smoker should probably seek the goal of total cessation within one week or less. Some authorities advocate stopping abruptly ("cold turkey"). Prolonged reduction of smoking is associated with a high failure rate—as the number of daily cigarettes dwindles, the reward value of each one increases immensely. For this reason expensive sequential filters designed to gradually decrease the amount of inhaled cigarette smoke are rarely successful.

The only drug effective in the treatment of smoking seems to be nicotine itself. A nicotine chewing gum enabled one group to achieve a 23% abstinence rate at one year. Benzodiazepines or other sedatives have no place in the therapy of smoking.

Behavioral modification techniques provide the best therapeutic approaches.

Efforts at behavioral modification (in the group or individual setting) have met with moderate success, and probably provide the best therapy for smoking cessation that currently is available. Several programs exist in most urban-suburban areas. Perhaps the best resource is the local American Cancer Society, which provides a number of therapies including patient education material, self-help packets for the person who prefers to attempt smoking cessation alone, and regular group meetings, which use behaviorial modification techniques along with group support. Some local branches of the American Cancer Society maintain a Smoker's Quitline, staffed by an ex-smoker who is trained to help people with the problems of smoking cessation.

Both Smoke Enders and Schick Laboratories have effective, but expensive programs. Nonetheless the costs are miniscule compared to those of continued smoking and may well be supportive for motivated patients.

The Schick Laboratories utilize aversion therapy (electric shocks, rapid smoking, etc.), which is best applied to young, motivated patients without chronic cardiac or pulmonary disease.

If physicians would like to help patients stop smoking they can employ a number of techniques themselves.

To practitioners who would like to work with patients themselves, or for whom the above resources are not available, a number of techniques can be employed in the group or individual setting. They should begin by having patients list their reasons for wanting to stop. This alone provides forceful motivation. Without attempting to cut down the number, practitioners should have the patients keep a log of each cigarette smoked, noting the time of day, the activity engaged in, a "need rating," and whether it was smoked. The log will be most successful if it can be wrapped about the cigarette package with rubber bands—necessitating its removal with each cigarette. This log will give patients insight into the behavioral forces involved in their smoking pattern. Frequently smokers will diminish their smoking behavior spontaneously after simple reflection on the environmental and emotional factors that trigger the behavior. Over a period of time (variable according to patient, but less than a week) the least important cigarettes will begin to be deleted. Next, physicians should have the patients throw away all their cigarettes, lighters, ashtrays, and other smoking paraphernalia, warning them to expect irritability within the next week (also warning family members!). Physicians should warn patients that as the lungs "heal" themselves, increased cough and sputum production may occur and persist for weeks to months. Ex-smokers should reward themselves. This is best done by using the money saved from cigarettes to buy a gift. Patients should be seen frequently and given continued positive reinforcement. If this is done in a group setting, other group members can be potent sources of support. The group members can exchange telephone numbers for communication outside the formal sessions.*

Physicians should warn patients that as the lungs "heal" themselves, increased cough and sputum production may occur.

Theoretically a low-tar, low-nicotine cigarette would be less harmful to those who cannot stop smoking, and in fact this appears to be the case. Recent evidence shows that the death rate from lung cancer is lower among smokers of low-tar and low-nicotine cigarettes than those who smoke high-tar, high-nicotine cigarettes. Furthermore, the histology of the bronchial epithelium of smokers has been observed to have improved over the past two decades coincident with the increased use of filters and cigarettes that are lower in tar and nicotine. Smokers of low-tar, low-nicotine cigarettes have reduced risk of myocardial infarction and chronic coughing. Thus smokers who cannot stop completely should be encouraged to switch to the lowest tar and nicotine cigarettes available.

For those who cannot stop smoking, a low-tar, low-nicotine cigarette offers lower risks.

Smokers who cannot stop completely should be encouraged to switch.

Health Benefits of Smoking Cessation

One encouraging point can be made to smokers: stopping the

*A number of other helpful approaches are outlined in *Calling It Quits*, a DHEW Publication No. (NIH) 79-1824.

behavior is associated with a reduction in the severity of its consequences. The risks of lung cancer and other smoking-related cancers drop dramatically after discontinuing the habit, particularly when the smoker stops prior to 20 years of involvement. The effect of cessation on chronic obstructive pulmonary disease, while not as striking as that for cancer, is noteworthy nonetheless. Although chronic smoking leads inevitably to irreversible functional pulmonary impairment in many people, both mortality and morbidity will diminish from the time smoking ceases. Studies also show similar effects on coronary artery disease and myocardial infarction. At least one study suggests that the risk of death from coronary artery disease diminishes within one year of cessation of smoking. Since the risk of developing cancer, chronic obstructive pulmonary disease, and heart disease rises to striking levels after 20 years of smoking, and since most smokers begin the habit in their late teens and early 20s, primary care practitioners should strongly urge smokers to stop before they reach the age of 40 years. As mentioned previously, it is never too early for a woman who is considering childbearing to forgo the smoking habit. And since sudden infant death syndrome, bronchitis, and pneumonia are increased in children under a year of age in households with smoking parents, eliminating the behavior may well benefit this vulnerable age group.

Most health risks decline soon after smoking ends.

All smokers should be strongly urged to stop before the age of 40 years. It is never too early for childbearing women to stop.

ANNOTATED BIBLIOGRAPHY

Aronow, W. 1978. Effect of passive smoking on angina pectoris. *N. Engl. J. Med.* 299:21-24, 1978.
Exercise-induced angina accelerates when patients with angina pectoris are exposed to passive cigarette smoking.

Auerbach, O.; Hammond, E. C.; and Garfinkel, L. 1979. Changes in bronchial epithelium in relation to cigarette smoking, 1955-1960 vs. 1970-1977. *N. Engl. J. Med.* 300:381-386.
Pathologic changes in the bronchial epithelium of smokers occur less frequently in the samples taken from 1970 to 1977. The authors postulate that this may be attributable to the increased use of filter cigarettes and low-tar, low-nicotine cigarettes.

Bell, B.A., and Symon L. 1979. Smoking and subarachnoid hemorrhage. *Br. Med. J.* 1:577-578.
This paper demonstrates an association between smoking and subarachnoid hemorrhage.

Bloxham, C. A.; Beevers, D. G.; and Walker, J. M. 1979. Malignant hypertension and cigarette smoking. *Br. Med. J.* 1:581-583.

This paper demonstrates the association between smoking and malignant hypertension.

Butler, N. R., and Goldstein, H. 1973. Smoking in pregnancy and subsequent child development. *Br. Med. J.* 4:573-575.
This study demonstrates a statistically significant decrease in height and reading ability at ages 7 and 11 years in children of mothers who smoked, as compared to those who did not.

Doll, R., and Hill, A. B. 1964. Mortality in relation to smoking: Ten years' observation of British doctors, Parts 1 and 2. *Br. Med. J.* 1:1399-1410; 1460-1467.

———., and Peto, R. 1976. Mortality in relation to smoking: 20 years' observation on male British doctors. *Br. Med. J.* 2:1525-1536.

Doyle, J. T.; Dawber, T. R.; Kannel, W. B., et al. 1964. The relationship of cigarette smoking to coronary heart disease: The second report of the combined experience of the Albany, NY and Framingham, MA studies. *J. A. M. A.* 190:886-890.
The above three references are representative samples of the large epidemiologic studies from which much of the present knowledge about smoking and chronic diseases is derived.

Durden, R. F. 1975. *The Dukes of Durham, 1865-1929.* Durham, N.C.: Duke University Press, p. 17.
A history of the Duke family and their tobacco fortune. Provides insight into the historical and economic development of the tobacco industry.

Hammond, E. C. 1966. Smoking in relation to the death rates of one million men and women. In *Epidemiological approaches to the study of cancer and other chronic diseases*, ed. W. Haensyel. U. S. Public Health Service, National Cancer Institute Monograph 19:127-204.
Another of the samples of epidemiologic studies from which we derive much of our present knowledge about smoking and chronic diseases.

———, and Garfinkel, L. 1969. Coronary heart disease, stroke, and aortic aneurysm: Factors in the etiology. *Arch. Environ. Health* 19:167-182.
Among other things this paper demonstrates an association between smoking and aortic aneurysm.

———, and Horn, D. 1958. Smoking and death rates: Report on forty-four months of follow-up on 187,783 men, I: Total mortality; II: Death rates by cause. *J. A. M. A.* 166:1159-1172, 1294-1308.

An epidemiologic study from which we derive much of our present knowledge of smoking and chronic diseases.

Harlap, S., and Davies, A. M. 1974. Infant admissions to hospitals and maternal smoking. *Lancet* 1:529-532.
The children of mothers who smoke are more likely to develop bronchitis and pneumonia during the first year of life.

The children of mothers who smoke are more likely to develop bronchitis and pneumonia.

Kahn, H. A. 1966. The Dorn study of smoking and mortality among U. S. veterans: Report on 8½ years of observation. In *Epidemiological approaches to the study of cancer and other chronic diseases*, ed. W. Haensyel, U. S. Public Health Service, National Cancer Institute Monograph 19:1-125.
An epidemiological study from which we derive much of our present knowledge of smoking and chronic diseases.

Kline, J.; Stein, Z. A.; Susser, M., et al. 1977. Smoking: A risk factor for spontaneous abortion. *N. Engl. J. Med.* 297:793-796.
This study demonstrates that maternal smoking approximately doubles the risk of miscarriage.

This study demonstrates that maternal smoking approximately doubles the risk of miscarriage.

Meyer, M. B., and Tonascia, J. A. 1977. Maternal smoking, pregnancy complications, and perinatal mortality. *Am. J. Obstet. Gynecol.* 128:494-502.
Retrospective study showing that maternal smoking is correlated with perinatal mortality and a host of other complications of pregnancy.

Naeye, R. L. 1979. Data from the U. S. Collaborative Prenatal Project presented at the Science Writers' Seminar of the American Heart Association, reported by J. Elliott. *J. A. M. A.* 241:867-868.
These data suggest little or no effect of maternal smoking on the subsequent physical and mental development of children.

————; Ladis, B.; and Drage, J. S. 1976. Sudden infant death syndrome: A prospective study. *Am. J. Dis. Child.* 130: 1207-1210.
Sudden infant death syndrome is associated with parental smoking.

National Institute of Health. 1976. *Teenage smoking: National patterns of cigarette smoking, age 12 through 18 in 1972 and 1974*. U. S. Department of Health, Education, and Welfare Publication No. (NIH) 76-931. Washington, D.C.: U. S. Government Printing Office.
Epidemiologic survey of adolescent smoking patterns demonstrating the alarming increase in smoking among adolescent females.

Niewoehner, D. E., Kleinerman, J.; and Rice, D. B. 1974. Pathologic changes in the peripheral airways of young cigarette smokers. *N. Engl. J. Med.* 291:755-758.
Respiratory bronchiolitis is demonstrated to be a very common pathologic finding in the bronchioles of asymptomatic young smokers. This may be a precursor to emphysema.

Schachter, S. 1978. Pharmacological and psychological determinants of smoking. *Ann. Intern. Med.* 88:104-114.
Review of the data that explore the etiology of chronic smoking behavior. The author demonstrates that smoking is best explained in terms of nicotine addiction.

Tashkin, D. P.; Soares, J. R.; Hepler, R. S., et al. 1978. Cannabis, 1977. *Ann. Intern. Med.* 89:539-549.
Review of the health risks of marijuana smoking.

United States Department of Health, Education, and Welfare. *Smoking and Health: 1979 Report of the Surgeon General.* Washington, D.C.: U. S. Government Printing Office.
The definitive resource on smoking. An organized, readable review and summary of the world's literature on smoking and health.

White, J. R., and Froeb, H. F. 1980. Small-airways dysfunction in nonsmokers chronically exposed to tobacco smoke. *N. Engl. J. Med.* 302:720-723.
First paper that demonstrates that healthy adult nonsmokers can suffer deficits in pulmonary function through the effects of ambient tobacco smoke.

Wynder, E. L., and Hoffmann, D. 1979. Tobacco and health. *N. Engl. J. Med.* 300:894-903.
Comprehensive review of the therapy of smoking.

Comprehensive review of the therapy of smoking.

11 Nutrition in Prevention

Vicky Newman

Ms. Newman is a Registered Dietitian who received her M.S. in foods and nutrition from San Diego State University. She is a nutritionist/research associate at the University of California Medical Center, San Diego, and is a widely traveled consultant and lecturer.

Brief Contents

Overview

Good nutrition plays a vital role in the control of chronic diseases and in delaying their age of onset. Because of the complexity and refinement of today's foods, consumers need all the help they can get in making appropriate choices. The purpose of this chapter is to give primary care providers some insight into the evidence for nutrition's role in disease prevention and to provide practical dietary suggestions.

THE ROLE OF NUTRITION IN PREVENTION

Nearly half of the average American's daily calories now come from highly refined products—isolated fats, refined sugars, and alcohol.

The American diet has changed dramatically during this century. Meat and fat consumption—particularly isolated vegetable fat—has increased while carbohydrate consumption has decreased. Also, a much higher percentage of the carbohydrates now eaten comes from sugar and refined sources. This has resulted in a decreased intake of starch and fiber as well as of several vitamins and minerals. Consumption of isolated fats, refined sugars, and alcohol has increased to the point where nearly half of the average American's daily calories come from these highly refined products.

It is difficult to separate out the effect on our health of one dietary change from the others, because they all are interrelated. The chronic diseases linked to diet—obesity, cancer of the colon, diverticular disease, diabetes, cardiovascular disease, and hypertension—probably result from a change in more than one dietary component. For example, the increase in sugar and fat consumption along with the decrease in fiber consumption plays a role in the causation of obesity. The increase in adult onset diabetes during this century could be in part the result not only of increased obesity but also the decreased intake of fiber and chromium, which are found in fibrous grains.

Epidemiologically, cancers of the breast, bowel, and rectum are as closely related to a low-fiber diet as they are to a high-fat diet.

Epidemiologically, cancers of the breast, bowel, and rectum are as closely related to a low-fiber diet as they are to a high-fat diet. Hypertension could be provoked by the increased ingestion of highly salted convenience foods or by the decrease in potassium-rich fruits, vegetables, grains, and legumes.

DIETARY CHANGES RELATED TO DISEASE

Calories

During this century the intake of total calories has remained relatively constant while expenditure has decreased. This combination is clearly implicated in the causation of obesity. If obesity is defined as being 20% or more above desirable weight, then about 40% of American women aged 40-49 years and about 32% of American men in the same age category are obese (Van Itallie, 1979). Obesity is a major risk factor in the development of diabetes, hypertension, cardiovascular disease, and certain types of cancer.

About 40% of American women aged 40-49 years and about 32% of American men in the same age category are obese.

The increase in obesity rates may be the result of more than simply excess calories relative to needs: another factor to consider is the increased caloric density of the diet due to the increase in fat and sugar and the decrease in complex carbohydrates and fiber. Highly refined diets that are high in fat and sugar appear to be more completely absorbed than those containing fiber (Van Itallie, 1979).

More Animal Protein, Less Vegetable Protein

The total protein intake of the average American has remained approximately the same for the past century. However, the source of protein has changed (Page and Friend, 1978). Early in the century half of the protein came from grains, legumes, potatoes, and other vegetable sources, while the other half came from animal products. Today only one-third of our protein comes from vegetable products, while two-thirds comes from animal products. Beef consumption has doubled during this time, while poultry consumption has tripled (Brewster and Jacobson, 1978).

The change toward more animal protein consumption has contributed to the increase in dietary fat and the decrease in carbohydrate and fiber.

This change toward more animal protein has contributed both to the increase in fat and the decrease in carbohydrate and fiber in the average diet. Compare a piece of hamburger to a pinto bean. The beef is primarily a combination of protein and fat, while the pinto bean is primarily protein, starch, and fiber. The average American also eats daily about twice the protein that his body requires for building and repair (Brewster and Jacobson, 1978). The extra protein will be either burned as energy or stored as fat. Thus cutting down on animal protein portions can help to save calories and fat (both in and on the body) as well as money.

Many epidemiologic studies suggest that a move toward less animal and more vegetable protein may be a healthy step.

A move toward less animal protein and more vegetable protein may also be a healthy step. Vegetarians have a lower incidence of several chronic diseases including cardiovascular disease, cancer, hypertension, osteoporosis, and diverticular disease than meat eaters.

Several studies have noted lower serum cholesterol and triglyceride levels in vegetarians (Sacks et al., 1975; Sanders et al., 1978). Replacement of animal by vegetable protein can lower significantly serum cholesterol levels in human subjects (Carroll et al., 1978; Sirtori et al., 1979). And recently a study of Seventh-Day Adventists showed the risk of fatal coronary heart disease among nonvegetarian Seventh-Day Adventist males, aged 35-64 years, to be three times greater than vegetarian Seventh-Day Adventist males of comparable age (Phillips et al., 1978).

Replacement of animal by vegetable protein can lower significantly serum cholesterol levels in human subjects.

It is also interesting to note that epidemiological data derived from human populations show a positive correlation between animal protein in the diet and mortality from coronary heart disease to be at least as strong as that between dietary fat and heart disease (Carroll et al.,1978). This may be due, however, to several dietary differences in addition to the difference in protein source. For example, vegetarian diets are generally higher than meat-based diets in fiber as well as several vitamins and minerals. The higher Vitamin C intake in the diet of vegetarians may confer considerable protection against elevated cholesterol levels and cardiovascular disease (Ginter, 1978).

Cancer of the breast, uterus, and colon have been found to be strongly associated with intake of total protein.

Cancer of the breast, uterus, and colon have been found to be strongly associated with intake of total protein, particularly from meat (Gori, 1979). Seventh-Day Adventists, 50% of whom follow a lacto-ovo-vegetarian diet, suffer considerably less from some forms of cancer when compared to other populations living in the same district, even when controlled for the fact they do not drink or smoke. This is particularly true of cancer of the breast and colon (Phillips, 1975).

It also appears that lacto-ovo-vegetarian women experience less osteoporosis than omnivorous women (Marsh et al., 1980). And several vegetarian populations studied recently have been found to have lower blood pressure and less hypertension than nonvegetarians living in the same areas (Anholm, 1978; Armstrong et al. 1979; Sacks et al., 1974). In addition, vegetarians also seem to have less diverticular disease than nonvegetarians (Gear et al., 1979). This is probably related more to the higher fiber content of the vegetarian diet than to the type of protein.

Diets high in protein, particularly from animal sources, may also play a role in the development of renal stone disease.

Diets high in protein, particularly from animal sources, may also play a role in the development of renal stone disease. Increased dietary protein has been reported to elevate both the intestinal absorption and urinary excretion of calcium as well as to increase the passive absorption and endogenous production of oxalate. Animal protein also contains much less magnesium than vegetable protein, which may be significant since magnesium supplementation decreases the stone recurrence rate in chronic stone formers (Johannson, 1979).

Less Carbohydrates

Consumption of total carbohydrates has declined during this century. But perhaps as important the composition of dietary carbohydrate has shifted from primarily starches (potatoes, legumes, and grains) to primarily sugars and from less refined to more refined forms.

More Sugar, Less Starch

The average American consumes about 12 tablespoons of refined sugar a day, much of it in soft drinks.

Consumption of sugars and other sweeteners is up one-third since 1909-13 (Page and Friend, 1978), to approximately 130 pounds per person per year (USDA, 1980), or about 12 tablespoons per day. The largest increase in use of refined sugar has been in beverages such as soft drinks. Soft drink consumption has more then doubled in the past 15 years (Page and Friend, 1978). In 1976 the average American drank approximately 330 12-ounce cans of soda in one year (Brewster and Jacobson, 1978).

The controversy regarding the relationship of sugar to disease continues. Recently the joint publication by the United States Department of Agriculture (USDA) and the Department of Health, Education, and Welfare (U. S. DHEW) *Nutrition and Health* (USDA, 1980, p. 15) stated:

> Contrary to widespread opinion, too much sugar in your diet does not seem to cause diabetes. The most common type of diabetes is seen in obese adults, and avoiding sugar, without correcting the overweight, will not solve the problem. There is also no convincing evidence that sugar causes heart attacks or blood vessel diseases.

On the other hand there is abundant evidence showing that dietary sucrose is one among several dietary factors associated with obesity, diabetes, and cardiovascular disease in this country.

Simply increasing the amount of carbohydrates from sugar and decreasing those from starch in the diet of test animals produces undesirable changes in glucose tolerance (Reiser et al.,

1979b; Reaven, 1979) and in blood lipid levels (Reiser et al., 1979a; Grande, 1974). It is also clear to any clinician that the greater the amount of sugar eaten, the more difficult it is to control blood glucose levels.

With all the other controversy regarding sugar and health, there does seem to be remarkable agreement among experts on the relationship between sugar consumption and tooth decay. The risk increases the more frequently the sugar is eaten, especially if it is eaten in between meals or in foods that stick to the teeth (USDA, 1980). If only for this reason alone, sugar consumption is best reduced.

More Refined Carbohydrates

Besides the decrease in total carbohydrate consumption and the increase in sugar compared to starch, there has also been a general trend toward the consumption of more refined carbohydrates during this century. Unrefined carbohydrates such as whole grains, fresh potatoes, fruits, and vegetables have been replaced increasingly by refined carbohydrates such as white flour, potato flakes, juices, and juice drinks.

Concentration (refining) of carbohydrates leads to overconsumption—and the loss of fiber, vitamins, and minerals.

Refining of carbohydrates affects the body in several ways. Concentration leads to overconsumption. Also fiber, vitamins, minerals, and other helpful food components are lost. The physical disruption of food (for example, pureeing) as well as the removal of fiber can result in faster and easier ingestion, decreased satiety, and disturbed glucose homeostasis, which is probably due to inappropriate insulin release (Haber et al., 1977; O'Dea et al., 1980). Fiber depletion also allows for more complete absorption of calories (Kelsay et al., 1978). These effects favor overnutrition and if repeated often might lead to obesity and diabetes. In fact recent studies (Anderson and Chen, 1979; Anderson and Ward, 1979) indicate that a diet high in unrefined carbohydrate and fiber may be the dietary therapy of choice for patients with maturity-onset diabetes. Not only does such a diet decrease insulin requirements, but it also appears to decrease carbohydrate-induced lipemia.

A diet high in unrefined carbohydrate and fiber may be the dietary therapy of choice for patients with maturity-onset diabetes.

Less Fiber

Removal of fiber during refining also appears to be associated with an increased tendency toward cardiovascular disease, certain forms of cancer, diverticulosis, constipation, and gallbladder disease (Burkitt et al., 1974). Between 1909 and 1975 the total crude fiber content of the American diet declined by 28%, owing to the lower intake of grains, potatoes, legumes, and fruit (Heller and Hackler, 1978).

Diets plentiful in fiber-rich foods are generally accompanied by rapid passage of food residues through the gut and by increased fecal bulk. Fiber-rich foods contain a mixture of different fibers so that it is difficult to assign a physiologic effect to a specific fiber component. The characteristics and physiologic actions of the different plant fibers have recently been reviewed by Huang et al. (1978) and Anderson and Chen (1979). For the present it is probably best to emphasize unrefined fruits, vegetables, whole grains, and legumes to obtain an adequate supply of all the different fibers that play a role in the normal functioning of the body.

It is probably best to emphasize unrefined fruits, vegetables, whole grains, and legumes to obtain an adequate supply of all the different fibers.

The influence of dietary fiber on lipid metabolism and atherosclerosis has been the subject of several recent reviews (for example, Anderson and Chen, 1979; Kritchevsky, 1979a). Fecal loss of bile salts may play a major role in the hypocholesterolemic effects of certain plant fibers. Purified cellulose is ineffective, and bran is relatively ineffective in lowering serum cholesterol. However, oats and pectin (found in fruits and vegetables) as well as gums and lignin (found in grains, legumes, and vegetables) have a hypocholesterolemic effect. Preliminary observations by Anderson and Chen (1979) suggest that long-term therapy with a diet high in plant fiber from various sources is accompanied by a distinct reduction in serum low-density lipoprotein (LDL) cholesterol content and elevation of high-density lipoprotein (HDL) cholesterol content, values above those of the control, or normal, population.

Epidemiologic studies of various populations suggest that a diet high in dietary fiber may provide protection from cancer of the colon and rectum (Burkitt et al., 1974). Fiber is thought to exert its effect on the carcinogenic process in several ways. It increases fecal bulk and decreases transit time. This then reduces the concentration of carcinogens in the intestinal tract and reduces carcinogenic exposure of the intestinal epithelium. Fiber may also alter the type and number of microorganisms in the colon and possibly inhibit their production of potential carcinogens. Certain plant fibers also appear to have a detoxifying effect when fed along with various drugs and chemicals (Gori, 1979).

Theories based on correlations of various population characteristics can, of course, be misleading. For example, the incidence of colon cancer in different countries and cultures correlates much better with the consumption of fat in the diet than it does with the consumption of fiber (Carroll, 1975). But, again, as diets increase in fat they tend at the same time to decrease in fiber as well as in certain vitamins and minerals that may have a protective effect. It is difficult to separate out the effect of one dietary change from the others.

It is difficult to separate out the effect of one dietary change from the others.

Certain foods are particularly helpful in protecting against constipation.

The removal of fiber from food results in gastrointestinal problems including constipation, hemorrhoids, diverticulosis, irritable bowel syndrome, and gallbladder disease. Fiber protects against constipation by stimulating peristalsis and increasing the volume and softness of the feces. Foods particularly helpful for constipation include cabbage, carrots, and apples as well as whole-grain breads and cereals such as oats. It has been proposed that the increased volume and softness of the stools, by reducing straining during defecation, is a factor in preventing hemorrhoids (Burkitt et al., 1974); however, experimental evidence for this claim is limited.

A high-fiber diet has also been shown to be effective in the treatment of irritable bowel syndrome

Diverticulosis and its clinical consequences were virtually nonexistent in the early twentieth century, but its incidence has grown steadily in industrialized countries. The risk of the aged developing diverticula is now estimated at nearly 50% (Almy and Howell, 1980). Until recently the standard medical treatment for this condition was a low-fiber diet. However, recent research and clinical trials have shown a diet high in vegetable fiber to be far more effective. A high-fiber diet has also been shown to be effective in the treatment of irritable bowel syndrome (Manning et al., 1977).

Recent research indicates that a diet low in fiber-rich foods may be one factor predisposing people to gallblader disease. The role of fiber in this disease is unknown but may be related to the capacity for various types of fiber to bind bile acids and bile salts (Kritchevsky, 1979a). However, there has also been some interesting work done recently showing that saponins, a sterol found particularly in legumes, are effective in decreasing bile acids and cholesterol (Potter et al., 1979).

Loss of Essential Nutrients

Trace minerals that are lost in refining may be important.

In addition to concentrating calories and removing fiber, the refining and processing of grains, fruits, and vegetables results in loss of important vitamins and minerals. A large portion of vitamins E, B_6, folic acid, and pantothenic acid as well as magnesium, selenium, chromium, and silicon are removed when grains are milled. Recent research suggests that selenium plays an important role in cancer prevention (Schrauzer, 1979). Chromium, in its organic form as part of the glucose tolerance factor, is necessary for normal glucose metabolism (Altschule, 1978). Offenbacher et al. (1980) demonstrated that chromium-rich brewer's yeast improved glucose tolerance, insulin sensitivity, and cholesterol levels in elderly normal and diabetic subjects, while chromium-poor Torula yeast did not.

Certain fibrous foods also appear to contain substances that protect against cancer.

Certain fibrous foods also appear to contain substances that protect against cancer. For example, seeds and legumes are rich in protease inhibitors, which have been shown to inhibit tumor growth. There is also experimental evidence that antioxidants such as vitamin C, vitamin E, and selenium (found in fibrous foods) and indoles (found in such vegetables as broccoli, brussel sprouts, cabbage, and cauliflower) seem to protect against chemical carcinogens (Gori, 1979).

The decrease in fruit and fresh vegetable consumption during this century has led to a decreased intake of vitamin C. This has been particularly true from 1945-1970. In surveys made in the United States, including a national nutrition survey (U.S. D.H.E.W., 1974), borderline (or below) intakes of vitamin C were commonly found (ranging up to 10%-30% of infants, children, and adults, especially in lower income groups (Briggs and Calloway, 1979). Bates et al. (1977) recently reported a strong positive correlation between vitamin C status and plasma HDL cholesterol in healthy elderly men.

More Fat, Particularly Processed Vegetable Oils

Fat consumption has increased during this century by about one-fourth. Most of the increase in fat intake has come from isolated fats and oils, particularly margarines and salad oils. In 1976 use of isolated fats and oils was almost half again as much as during 1909-13, even though consumption of butter and lard dropped sharply during this time. The use of margarine has increased about eightfold; shortening, more than twofold since 1909-13. Use of salad and cooking oils tripled between the period 1947-49 and 1976 (Page and Friend, 1978).

The use of margarine has increased about eightfold; shortening, more than twofold since 1909-13.

Though total fat intake has increased, the ratio of animal to vegetable fat has fallen from 4.88 to about 1.60, and the ratio of dietary linoleic acid to saturated fatty acids has risen from 0.21 to 0.43 (Kritchevsky, 1979b). This again is due mainly to the fact that the consumption of butter, lard, and dairy products has decreased, while consumption of margarines and vegetable oils has increased. The use of hydrogenated margarines and vegetable oils has also dramatically increased the trans fatty acids in our diet (Emken and Dutton, 1979). Cholesterol intake has changed little since 1909, although there has been a slight decrease in the last 10 years.

The two chronic diseases most often linked to these changes in fat consumption are cardiovascular disease and cancer. The link between fat and cardiovascular disease centers on the effect of different types of fats and cholesterol-containing foods on serum cholesterol levels. Saturated fats are solid at room temperature and tend to raise serum cholesterol. Such fats are found predominantly in meats and dairy products as well as in vegetable fats such as palm oil, coconut oil, and cocoa butter. These saturated vegetable oils are often present in crackers, "natural" cereals, non-dairy creamers, and other convenience foods. The monounsaturated fats are liquid at room temperature but get thick when refrigerated. They neither raise nor lower serum cholesterol. Olives, peanuts, avacadoes, and most nuts (except walnuts) are high in monounsaturated fats. It is interesting to note that though peanut oil does not affect serum cholesterol, it appears to be strongly atherogenic in rats, rabbits, and rhesus monkeys (Kritchevsky, 1979b). The polyunsaturated fats are liquid at room temperature and remain so even when refrigerated. These tend to lower serum cholesterol levels. Safflower, sunflower, and corn oils are all very high in polyunsaturated fats, while soy, sesame, and cotton are less so.

Safflower, sunflower, and corn oils are all very high in polyunsaturated fats, while soy, sesame, and cotton are less so.

Hydrogenated fats are found in margarines, shortenings, and many processed foods. These fats are made by adding hydrogen to liquid oil. The more hydrogen that is added, the more saturated they become and, therefore, the more solid or plastic at room temperature. The more saturated these margarines and shortenings are, the more they tend to raise cholesterol levels. Margarines listing liquid oil as the first ingredient have a higher proportion of liquid oil than hydrogenated oil in the product.

Margarines listing liquid oil as the first ingredient have a higher proportion of liquid oil than hydrogenated oil.

Besides becoming partially saturated during hydrogenation, trans fatty acids are also produced. Although the issue is controversial, these may play an important role in the development of atherosclerosis; they may also have an adverse effect on cell membrane function (Emken and Dutton, 1979).

Several recent studies indicate that fresh cholesterol, as found in fresh eggs, may not raise serum cholesterol levels at all or certainly much less than expected (Flynn et al., 1979; Porter et al., 1977). Whereas fresh dietary cholesterol has been shown recently to be less of a problem than once thought, new data have come to light that indicate that rancid cholesterol is very atherogenic (Taylor et al., 1979). This revelation casts doubt on the earlier cholesterol-feeding experiments—which implicated dietary cholesterol in the causation of cardiovascular disease—because many of the experiments were done with crystalline cholesterol that was rancid to varying degrees. Rancid cholesterol is more likely to be present in processed foods containing dry egg yolks as well as in old butter and aged meats and cheeses.

New data that demonstrate that rancid cholesterol is atherogenic casts doubt on earlier cholesterol-feeding experiments.

Despite many reports regarding the effects of feeding fat on plasma cholesterol and triglycerides, few studies elucidate the effect of isocaloric substitution of dietary fat on HDL levels and

It is possible to increase HDL levels through diet modification.

compositions in which quantitative methods for measuring HDL levels were used. One recent study (Hjermann et al., 1979), however, did report an increased in HDL levels in hypercholesterolemic subjects fed a low-fat (25% of total calories) diet. This low-fat diet had a P/S ratio of 1.0, indicating that it contained equal amounts of polyunsaturated and saturated fat. Such a diet is often recommended to the public.

In the past decade the incidence of coronary disease has markedly decreased; there has also been a downward trend in plasma cholesterol (Glueck and Connor, 1979). However, it is difficult to know whether or not these are causally related and how much they have to do with fat or cholesterol intake. It is true that during this same period there was an increase in the availability of fat (Kritchevsky, 1979b), but the intake of dietary cholesterol did fall somewhat, and the P/S ratio of dietary fat did increase (Glueck and Connor, 1979). It must also be noted, however, that during this same 10 years it appears that, because of the increase in consumption of fruits, vegetables, and grains, fiber consumption also improved (USDA, 1979). The increased intake of fruits and vegetables plus the renewed interest in vitamin C, largely a result of Pauling's work, have also led to an increase in vitamin C intake during this period, which would help protect from atherosclerosis, according to Ginter (1978).

Certain cancers are associated strongly with total fat intake.

Cancer of the breast, uterus, and colon has been found to be strongly associated with total fat intake (Gori, 1979). Enig et al. (1978) reported significant positive correlations in the United States between total fat and vegetable fat consumption and breast and colon mortality, and negative or no correlation for animal fat. The significant positive correlation for vegetable fat could not always be explained by the effects of total unsaturated components, of individual unsaturated components, or of the saturated component; but the correlation could be explained by the trans fatty acid component. Enig concluded that if there is a relationship between dietary fat and cancer, perhaps processed vegetable fats should be more carefully investigated.

The National Cancer Institute recently reviewed the theories relating dietary fat to carcinogenesis.

The National Cancer Institute recently reviewed the theories relating dietary fat to carcinogenesis. The most widely held view is that fat in the diet has a "promotional" effect on the development of cancer, that is, it does not cause cancer directly but somehow it influences the metabolic processes of normal cells to make them more susceptible to the development of cancer caused by other agents. It has also been proposed that fat—whether unsaturated or saturated—may act as a solvent to enhance the effect of other carcinogens. Fats are also known to change the metabolism of many tissues in the human, possibly affecting the relation of various hormones to tissue growth. The case for this is strongest for breast cancer, in which the hormonal environment has been shown to influence susceptibility to cancer.

Besides altering the hormonal environment, there are other ways in which dietary fat might lead to breast cancer—through an influence on the metabolism of chemical carcinogens, on cell membrane structure, and on the immune system.

Current research indicates that a diet high in fat increases the amount of bile and sterols excreted during digestion. These normal breakdown products may conceivably be converted into carcinogens by bacteria, which are normally present in the colon. Although no such carcinogen has yet been isolated, the biochemical mechanisms by which intestinal bacteria might produce carcinogens have been elaborately studied in the laboratory.

Increased Sodium Relative to Potassium

Sodium consumption has increased during this century relative to potassium consumption. This may play an important role in the development of hypertension (Meneely and Battarbee, 1976). The relationship of excessive sodium intake to hypertension has been known for some time, but only recently has the role of adequate potassium in hypertension prevention come to light. The reason for the change in ratio between these two minerals is that intake of sodium-rich and potassium-poor processed foods has risen during this century, while intake of potassium-rich and sodium-poor foods has fallen. Such potassium-rich foods include all fruits, fresh and frozen vegetables, grains (particularly those prepared with little or no salt), legumes, and unsalted seeds and nuts. In fact, the higher potassium intake of vegetarians may be what protects them from hypertension (Armstrong et al., 1979).

Only recently has the role of adequate potassium in hypertension prevention come to light.

Potassium-rich foods include all fruits, fresh and frozen vegetables, grains (particularly those prepared with little or no salt), legumes, and unsalted seeds and nuts.

Increased Phosphorus Relative to Calcium

Phosphorus intake has risen relative to calcium during this century (Brewster and Jacobson, 1978). This change in the calcium-to-phosphorus balance may be one important reason for the appearance of osteoporosis in increasingly younger people (particularly women) during this century. Phosphorus intake has increased because more animal protein, soda pop, and processed foods are now eaten.

This change in the calcium-to-phosphorus balance may be one important reason for the appearance of osteoporosis in increasingly younger people.

DIETARY GUIDELINES

Following are some practical suggestions that primary care physicians can give their patients to help them to improve their nutritional status. Because nutrition plays such an important role in the normal functioning of the body's metabolic systems, the guidelines below will help improve patients' general health and delay the onset of chronic disease. *Nutrition and Your Health: Dietary Guidelines for Americans* (USDA, 1980) and the *Eater's Guide* (Cumming and Newman, 1981), which are both written for the lay public, may also be helpful in patient education efforts.

Eat a Variety of Foods

The greater the variety of foods, the more healthful the diet.

No single food item supplies all the essential nutrients in the amounts needed. Therefore it is necessary to eat a variety of foods to assure an adequate diet. The greater the variety, the less likely the chances of developing either a deficiency or an excess of any single nutrient. Variety also reduces the likelihood of being exposed to excessive amounts of contaminants in any single food item.

Table 11-1

One way to assure that patients obtain variety and with it a well-balanced diet is to encourage them to select foods each day from each of several groups. In the guide in Table 11-1 foods are divided into several groups on the basis of similarity in composition and nutritional value. Computerized dietary analyses in our laboratory show that representative meals based on this guide will supply at least 80% of the recommended amount of all nutrients with Recommended Dietary Allowances (RDAs) assigned. We found that the most difficult nutrients to supply in adequate amounts were vitamins E, B_6, and folic acid, as well as magnesium and zinc. The inclusion of vegetable protein and whole grains in each representative diet was necessary to supply these in adequate amounts. Also, the servings of Protein-Rich Foods had to be increased beyond the amount needed to supply adequate protein in order to supply the recommended amount of vitamin B_6, zinc, and iron.

We found that the most difficult nutrients to supply in adequate amounts were vitamins E, B_6, and folic acid, as well as magnesium and zinc.

Maintain Ideal Weight

Obesity is a major risk factor in the development of diabetes, cardiovascular disease, hypertension, and certain cancers. Thus maintenance of ideal weight is advisable. Most persons' weight should remain about the same throughout life as it was at age 18 years (when maximal skeletal growth has been achieved).

If weight loss is necessary, a gradual and steady loss of 1-2 pounds each week is recommended. Not only is weight loss at this rate more likely to be maintained but it is also less likely to be nutritionally inadequate. Long-term success depends on acquiring new and better habits of eating and exercise over a

Table 11-1 Daily food guide for a well-balanced diet*

DAILY FOOD GUIDE

Food Group	Good Sources of These Nutrients	One Serving Equals	Recommended Servings: Child (1-10 yrs)	Teen (11-18 Yrs)	Adult (19 + yrs)	Pregnant/ Breast-feeding
LEAFY GREEN VEGETABLES Romaine, red leaf lettuce; spinach and other greens; broccoli, brussel sprouts, cabbage; asparagus; parsley, watercress, scallions, mint.	Excellent sources of folic acid, vitamin A and B_6, riboflavin, and magnesium. Also supply good amounts of iron, potassium and fiber.	1 cup raw; ¾ cup cooked.	1	1	2	2
C-RICH FRUITS & VEGETABLES Citrus; tomatoes; berries; melons (papaya, mango, cantaloupe); peppers; cabbage, cauliflower, broccoli.	Excellent sources of vitamin C and potassium. Also supply folic acid, vitamin A and fiber.	1 orange; ½ grapefruit or cantaloupe; 2 lemons; 2 tomatoes; ½ cup of sliced fruit or vegetable; ½ cup of orange/grapefruit juice; 1½ cups tomato juice.	1	2	2	2
OTHER FRUITS & VEGETABLES Green beans; peas; corn; potatoes; and all other fruits and vegetables not on the preceding two lists.	Provide carbohydrates, fiber and potassium, as well as smaller amounts of other essential vitamins and minerals. If deep orange and/or yellow, also excellent sources of vitamin A.	1 medium piece of fruit or vegetable; ½ cup of sliced raw or cooked fruit or vegetable.	2	3	3	3
PROTEN-RICH FOODS Animal: meat, poultry, seafood, eggs. Vegetable: dried beans, lentils, split peas, peanuts, nuts, tofu.	All are excellent sources of protein, iron, vitamin B_6, zinc. All animal protein supplies vitamin B_{12}. Seafood supplies iodine and selenium. Vegetable protein supplies folic acid, vitamin E and magnesium.	2 oz cooked lean meat, poultry, seafood; 2 eggs; 1 cup of cooked beans; ½ cup of nuts, 4 tbs. of peanut butter; ½ cup of tofu.	1½ Try to have 1-2 servings from vegetable protein.	3-4	2	4
BREADS AND CEREALS Whole-grain and enriched breads, rolls, tortillas; noodles; oatmeal; rice, barley.	All provide carbohydrates and some protein. (Protein quality improved when eaten together with protein foods listed above or milk products). Also provide thiamin, niacin, riboflavin and iron, if enriched. Whole grains provide additional vitamin B_6, folic acid, vitamin E, magnesium, zinc and fiber.	1 slice bread, 1 tortilla; ½ bun or English muffin; 1 dinner roll; ¾ cup of dry cereal; ½ cup of cooked cereal, rice, or noodles; 1 tbs. of wheat germ.	4 Try to have 2-3 servings from whole grain products.	5	4	5
MILK PRODUCTS Milk, yogurt, kefir, cheese.	All are excellent sources of protein and calcium, in addition to vitamin A, B_{12} and riboflavin. Fortified fluid milk also contains 100 IU of vitamin D per cup. Cheese is a good source of zinc.	1 cup of milk, yogurt, or kefir; 1½ slices, 1½ ounces or ⅓ cup of grated brick-type cheese; 5 tbs. of Parmesan; or 1¼ cups of cottage cheese; 1 cup of tofu (contains no vitamin B_{12} or D).	2	3	2	4
FATS AND OILS Butter, margarine, vegetable oils, seeds, avocadoes, olives.	Provide energy because of the fat they contain. The polyunsaturated vegetable oils and seeds are good sources of the essential fatty acids and moderate to good sources of vitamin E.	1 tsp. of butter, oil, margarine, or mayonnaise; ⅛ avocado; 5 small olives; 2 tsp. of sesame or sunflower seeds; 5-7 nuts; 2 tbs. of sour cream, 2 tbs. of coffee cream; ½ tbs. of salad dressing.	3	4	4	5

*Patients should be encouraged to select the recommended servings from each food group daily.

"Crash" diets usually fail—and can be dangerous.

period of time. This is perhaps why "crash" diets usually fail in the long run.

In general physicians should caution their patients against a severely restricted caloric intake, as well as against excessive weight loss. Diets containing fewer than 800 calories may be hazardous. Some people have developed kidney stones and adverse psychologic changes; a few people have even died suddenly and without warning. Excessive weight loss to less than 85% of ideal weight may result in menstrual irregularities, infertility, hair loss, skin changes, cold intolerance, and severe constipation (USDA, 1980).

Any brisk aerobic activity will use up from 100-200 calories in 20 minutes.

Simply encouraging patients to increase their intake of fiber-rich fruits, vegetables, whole grains, and legumes, while decreasing their intake of sugar, fat, and alcohol will help immensely in weight control. These dietary changes, particularly when coupled with regular aerobic exercise, can be very effective. Any brisk aerobic activity such as walking, dancing, swimming, jogging, biking, racquetball, basketball, or tennis will use up from 100-200 calories in 20 minutes.

Avoid Too Much Fat and Saturated Fat

Because of the link between fat and cardiovascular disease and cancer, patients should be encouraged to decrease total fat consumption. They also, should be advised to eat a variety of polyunsaturated, monounsaturated, and saturated fats.

Practical suggestions that the physician can make to patients to help them to accomplish this goal include:

1. Limit beef, pork, lamb, and whole-milk cheese consumption to a combined total of 16 ounces per week. (Each ounce contains approximately 1 teaspoon of saturated fat. A piece of meat the size of your palm weighs about 3-4 ounces. One slice of American cheese, a 1-inch cube, or ¼ cup of grated cheese each weigh about 1 ounce.)
2. When you do eat meat, select the leanest cuts and remove all visible fat before eating.
3. Use poultry, fish, and legumes (peas, beans, and lentils) to replace red meat several times a week.
4. Try to avoid luncheon meat, frankfurters, and sausage because they are so high in fat.
5. Skim off the fat from broths, soups, and gravies.
6. Bake, broil, and boil meats; try to avoid frying.

7. Switch to nonfat or low-fat milk.
   a. Whole milk contains the equivalent of 2 teaspoons of butter per cup.
   b. Low-fat milk contains only about 1 teaspoon of butter per cup.
   c. Nonfat milk contains no butter.
   d. If you prefer whole milk, you can reduce your intake of fats from other sources.

Recommended cheese include cottage, farmer, ricotta, parmesan, mozzarella, Gruyere, Jarlesburg, Swiss, sapsago, edam, gouda.

8. Try to use cheeses made with part skim milk rather than those made with whole milk. Recommended cheeses include Cottage, Farmer, Ricotta, Parmesan, Mozzarella, Gruyere, Jarlesburg, Swiss, Sapsago, Edam, Gouda.
9. Decrease rich dishes made with butter and cream and try not to use products made with palm oil, coconut oil, or cocoa butter.
10. Avoid food products bearing the terms "hardened" or "hydrogenated" vegetable oil.
11. Use only small portions of fresh butter, margarine listing liquid oil as the first ingredient), and mayonnaise as spreads.
12. Use salad dressings sparingly. (One ladleful can have as much as 200 calories of fat!).

Avoid Too Much Cholesterol

The advice most people hear about cholesterol focuses on limiting its intake. While this plays a role in maintaining normal cholesterol levels, it is only one fourth of the dietary solution to a very complicated problem. It is important that patients understand that other food factors affect blood cholesterol: (a) excessive fat, particularly saturated fat; (b) inadequate fiber, and (c) excessive calories.

Large amounts of saturated fat in the diet tend to increase blood cholesterol levels. Fiber-rich foods, on the other hand, help to decrease blood cholesterol levels by decreasing the absorption of cholesterol and saturated fat from the digestive system and increasing their excretion from the body. Caloric intake is a problem if it leads to excess weight gain, since obesity is associated with elevated blood cholesterol levels.

More specifically, physicians can help their patients to maintain normal serum cholesterol levels by suggesting the following:

1. Following suggestions made elsewhere in this section, decrease saturated fat, increase fiber-rich foods, and maintain ideal weight.

2. Reduce dietary cholesterol by—
   a. Limiting portions of meat, fish, poultry, and cheese to a combined total of 6 ounces daily. (Each ounce contains 25 milligrams of cholesterol. One chicken breast equals 3 ounces; one chicken thigh equals 2 ounces; one chicken drumstick equals 2 ounces; and one wing equals 1 ounce.)
   b. Limiting eggs to an average of 6 weekly. Restriction is unnecessary for premenopausal women, children, and vegetarians.

Eat Foods With Adequate Starch and Fiber

People think of carbohydrates as being fattening but ounce for ounce they contain only half the calories of fat. Increasing the consumption of unrefined fruits, vegetables, grains, and legumes will help to control obesity by decreasing overconsumption of calories. These foods also contain good amounts of plant fiber, which has recently been shown to be beneficial in the treatment of diabetes, cardiovascular disease, and certain types of cancer. Vitamins and minerals important to normal body functioning are also plentiful in these foods.

To help patients accomplish this goal, physicians might suggest the following:

1. Increase intake of legumes (peas, beans, and lentils), potatoes, and other vegetables.
2. Eat whole-grain breads and cereals daily.
   a. Be sure the label says whole, sprouted, or malted grain as the first ingredient.
   b. Do not be fooled by the words "wheat flour"; it means white flour.
   c. Whole wheat bread can be substituted by old-fashioned oatmeal or shredded wheat in the morning.
   d. Consume whole fresh fruits instead of fruit juices or fruit drinks.
   e. Try to have a fresh fruit or vegetable with each meal, preferably from the Dark Green Leafy or C-Rich Groups (Table 11-1).

Avoid Too Much Sugar

Excessive sugar intake is definitely related to tooth decay and may also play a role in obesity, diabetes, and cardiovascular disease. Therefore it is advisable for patients to decrease use of sugar and all sweeteners. To help them accomplish this goal, physicians might suggest that they try the following:

1. Use less of all sweeteners including white sugar, brown sugar, raw sugar, honey, and syrups.
   a. Avoid adding sugar to coffee and tea.
   b. Try decreasing the amount of sweetener in your favorite recipes by one-third to one-half.
2. Eat less of foods containing sweeteners such as candy, soft drinks, ice cream, cakes, cookies, and pies.
   a. At snack time munch on fruit and raw vegetables, whole grains, and low-fat dairy products.
   b. After meals substitute fruit and milk desserts.
   c. If canned fruits are used, be sure to choose those that are canned in their own juice or in light syrup rather than in heavy syrup.
   d. Drink water instead of sweetened beverages during and between meals.
   e. Try replacing soda pop with a mixture of half club soda and half fruit juice.
3. Read food labels for clues on sugar content: if the names sucrose, glucose, maltose, dextrose, lactose, fructose, or syrup appear first, then there is a large amount of sugar in the product.

Avoid Too Much Sodium and Obtain More Potassium

Because of the link between a high-sodium, low-potassium diet and hypertension, it is advisable that patients decrease their sodium consumption and increase their potassium consumption. To accomplish this goal physicians might suggest the following:

1. To decrease sodium intake:
   a. Limit intake of salty foods such as prepared soups (1 teaspoon salt/can), potato chips, pretzels, salted nuts and popcorn, condiments (soy sauce, steak sauce, garlic salt), cheese, pickled foods, and cured meats.
   b. Use herbs and spices instead of salt for flavor.
   c. Use garlic or onion powder rather than garlic or onion salt.
   d. Decrease salt in favorite recipes to one-half or, better, one-fourth of the amount suggested.
   e. Try to add less than ¼ teaspoon of salt to food daily.
   f. Do not salt cooking water; use a bay leaf for flavor instead.
2. To increase potassium intake, use more potassium-rich foods:
   a. All fruits (not just bananas and oranges).

b. Fresh and frozen vegetables.
c. Grains, particularly those prepared with little or no salt (for example, oatmeal, rice, and noodles).
d. Legumes (peas, beans, and lentils).
e. Unsalted nuts and seeds.

If Alcohol and Coffee Are Desired Drink Them in Moderation

Alcoholic beverages tend to be high in calories and low in other nutrients. Even moderate drinkers may need to drink less if they wish to achieve ideal weight. On the other hand, heavy drinkers may lose their appetite for foods containing essential nutrients. Vitamin and mineral deficiencies occur commonly in heavy drinkers—in part, because of poor intake but also because alcohol alters the absorption and use of some essential nutrients.

Pregnant women are best advised to limit alcohol intake to 2 ounces or less on any single day.

Sustained or excessive alcohol consumption by pregnant women is associated with an increased risk of birth defects. Pregnant women therefore are best advised to limit alcohol intake to 2 ounces or less on any single day. Heavy drinking may ultimately lead to cirrhosis of the liver, neurologic disorders, and possibly predisposition toward cancer of the throat (USDA, 1980).

One or two drinks daily appear to cause no harm in adults. In fact recent work has even shown that moderate alcohol consumers appear to have a lower rate of heart disease and a lower mortality than nondrinkers or heavy drinkers.

Moderation in caffeine use is advised not only because of the well-documented relationship between excessive intake and anxiety, gastritis, and heartburn but also because of the recent suggestion that caffeine and other xanthines may aggravate fibrocystic breast disease (Minton et al., 1979).

To help patients to moderate their alcohol and caffeine consumption physicians might suggest the following:

1. Limit alcoholic beverage consumption to a daily total of 1 ounce of absolute alcohol. This would be found in approximately:
   a. Two ounces (or shots) of hard liquor.
   b. Two 5-ounce glasses of wine.
   c. Two 12 ounce cans of beer.

Limit caffeine intake to 200 milligrams daily, which is the pharmacologically active dose.

2. Limit caffeine intake to 200 milligrams daily, which is the pharmacologically active dose. This amount would be found in approximately:
   a. Two 5-ounce cups of coffee.
   b. Five 5-ounce cups of tea.
   c. Four 12-ounce cans of cola beverage (for example, Coke, Dr. Pepper, Tab, Mountain Dew, and Pepsi).

SPECIAL CONSIDERATIONS

Pregnancy and Infancy

Studies have shown a direct relationship between the diet of the mother and the health of the infant at birth. Pregnant women are therefore best advised to follow the Daily Food Guide (Table 11-1) in order to obtain an adequate supply of nutrients. Slow and steady weight gain to a term total of 25-30 pounds is advisable, preferably at the rate of 2-4 pounds during the first trimester and a pound a week thereafter.

Supplemental iron and folic acid are recommended for all pregnant women regardless of diet.

Supplemental iron and folic acid are recommended for all pregnant women regardless of diet. Dietary sources of iron and limited maternal iron stores cannot supply the recommended amounts needed for pregnancy. Thus a daily supplement of 30-60 mg of elemental iron is recommended. Daily supplementation with 400-800 mcg of folic acid is also recommended since the requirement for folic acid is markedly increased during pregnancy and because inadequate dietary intake is common.

Breast-feeding is recommended for the first 4-6 months not only because breast milk is nutritionally superior to formula but also because of its immunologic advantages. The immune benefits derived from breast milk give protection against gastroenteritis and various forms of diarrhea as well as against allergy.

Introduction of solid or semisolid food is best delayed until the infant is 4-6 months old. There are several reasons for this. Nutritionally the infant obtains all the key nutrients needed for optimal growth and development during this period from breast milk or humanized formula. It is not until 4-6 months that an infant seems to require additional iron from solid foods. Recent studies have also implicated earlier introduction of solids in the development of childhood obesity. Patients should be encouraged to use baby foods without added salt and sugar.

Use of regular cow's milk is contraindicated in the first year.

Breast milk or formula should be continued along with solid foods throughout the first year. Use of regular cow's milk, particularly the nonfat or low-fat varieties, is contraindicated because of its high mineral and protein content.

Nutritional Supplements

Substantial numbers of Americans have been found to be below recommended intake levels of certain vitamins and minerals in the absence of specific clinical deficiency signs (U.S. DHEW, 1974). A marginal deficiency of vitamins and minerals influences markedly the metabolism of drugs and environmental chemicals (Brin,

1978) as well as immunocompetence (Axelrod 1980) and behavior (Brin, 1977). Therefore certain people, particularly those eating a diet high in refined foods, may benefit from a well-balanced, low-potency multiple vitamin-mineral supplement.

Such a supplement may be particularly helpful to the following people:

1. Those whose caloric intake is below 70% of the RDA. Such a limited food intake, unless chosen very carefully, is likely to be low in essential vitamins and minerals.
   a. Below 900 calories for ages 2 through 3 years of age.
   b. Below 1000 calories for ages 2 through 10 years of age.
   c. Below 1500 calories for ages 11 and over.
2. Those whose nutrient needs are increased due to
   a. Illness or trauma.
   b. Anemia.
   c. Chronic drug therapy, because so many drugs (including oral contraceptives) decrease absorption or increase the need for certain nutrients.

It seems reasonable to assume that if food intake or quality are compromised to the point of being low in a few nutrients, they are probably low in several, particularly those that are not replaced in processed food on a regular basis. Thus nutrients that are particularly important to include in a comprehensive supplement are vitamin E, vitamin B_6, folic acid, pantothenic acid,
Table 11-2 magnesium, zinc, copper, chromium, and selenium. Table 11-2 presents recommended formulas.

Anemia

The most common form of anemia seen in this country is caused by iron deficiency. Therefore encouraging anemic patients to eat plenty of iron-rich foods is helpful. Such foods are found in the Protein Rich Foods and the Leafy Green Vegetables listed in Table 11-1. Blackstrap molasses is also rich in iron: one tablespoon contains as much iron as a 3-ounce hamburger patty. Cooking with an iron skillet also adds iron to the diet.

Iron absorption from the diet and/or from supplements is enhanced if meat, fish, poultry, and/or vitamin C is ingested at the same time. Vitamin C also helps protect folic acid from oxidative destruction. Therefore obtaining adequate vitamin C helps indirectly to protect against anemia caused by iron deficiency or folic acid deficiency. Many vitamin C-rich foods are also good sources of folic acid.

Table 11-2 Recommended vitamin-mineral supplementation for different age groups

Nutrients	Average RDA (1-12 mo)	Recommended Formula (0-12 mo)	Average RDA 1-10 yrs)	Recommended Formula (1-10 yrs)	Average RDA (11 + yrs)	Recommended Formula (11 + yrs)
Vitamin A	1370 IU*	1370 IU*	1780 IU*	1780 IU*	3000 IU*	3000 IU*
Vitamin D	400 IU†	200 IU†	400 IU†	200 IU†	300 IU†	150 IU†
Vitamin E	5 IU‡	5 IU‡	9 IU‡	9 IU‡	15 IU‡	15 IU‡
Thiamine	0.4 mg	0.4 mg	0.9 mg	0.9 mg	1.2 mg	1.2 mg
Riboflavin	0.5 mg	0.5 mg	1.1 mg	1.1 mg	1.4 mg	1.4 mg
Niacin	7.0 mg	7.0 mg	12.0 mg	12.0 mg	16.0 mg	16.0 mg
Vitamin B_6	0.45 mg	0.45 mg	1.3 mg	1.3 mg	2.0 mg	2.0 mg
Vitamin B_{12}	1.0 mcg	1.0 mcg	2.5 mcg	2.5 mcg	3.0 mcg	3.0 mcg
Folic acid	37.5 mcg	37.5 mcg	200 mcg	200 mcg	400 mcg	400 mcg
Biotin	42.5 mcg	42.5 mcg	90 mcg	90 mcg	100-200 mcg	100-200 mcg
Pantothenic acid	2.5 mg	2.5 mg	3-4 mg	3-4 mg	4-7 mg	4-7 mg
Vitamin C	35 mg	70 mg	45 mg	90 mg	58 mg	116 mg
Calcium	450 mg	150 mg	800 mg	240 mg	960 mg	320 mg
Magnesium	60 mg	45 mg	200 mg	150 mg	330 mg	248 mg
Iron	12.5 mg	12.5 mg	12 mg	12 mg	15 mg	15 mg
Zinc	4.0 mg	4.0 mg	10 mg	10 mg	15 mg	15 mg
Iodine	45.0 mcg	45.0 mcg	93 mcg	93 mcg	150 mcg	150 mcg
Copper	0.6-0.9 mg	0.6-0.9 mg	1.5-2.0 mg	1.5-2.0 mg	2.0-3.0 mg	2.0-3.0 mg
Chromium	15-50 mcg	33 mcg	33-133 mcg	83 mcg	50-200 mcg	125 mcg
Selenium	15-50 mcg	33 mcg	33-133 mcg	83 mcg	50-200 mcg	125 mcg

*1 IU vitamin A is equivalent to 0.3 mcg retinol; 3.33 IU vitamin A is equivalent to 1 mcg retinol (as preformed vitamin; does not include carotene).

†400 IU vitamin D is equivalent to 10 mcg cholecalciferol.

‡1.49 IU vitamin E is equivalent to 1 mg α-alpha-tocopherol.

Citrus Allergy and Lactose Intolerance

Both citrus allergy and lactose intolerance are commonly encountered in clinical practice.

Both citrus allergy and lactose intolerance are commonly encountered in clinical practice. Patients with citrus allergy can obtain adequate vitamin C by eating foods from the cabbage family (broccoli, brussel sprouts, cabbage, and cauliflower) on a daily basis. Melons such as cantaloupe, mango, and papaya are also rich in vitamin C. These rarely cause allergic reactions, as opposed to tomatoes and strawberries, which often do cause allergic reactions.

Many patients with mild lactose intolerance can tolerate milk if it is ingested in small amounts.

Many patients with mild lactose intolerance can tolerate milk if it is ingested in small amounts (for example, one-half cup at a time). Natural cheeses such as Cheddar, Jack, and Swiss, are also usually well tolerated. However, processed cheeses and cheese spreads often cause gastrointestinal discomfort. This is caused by their higher lactose content, which results from the addition of nonfat dry milk solids after ripening. Patients who can tolerate no milk products at all may obtain calcium and protein from canned fish containing edible bones (salmon, mackerel, and sardines) and also from tofu (soybean curd).

ANNOTATED BIBLIOGRAPHY

Almy, T. P., and Howell, D. A. 1980. Diverticular disease of the colon. *N. Engl. J. Med.* 302:324-331.
Well-documented review of diverticular disease incidence, diagnosis, and treatment (including diet).

Altschule, M. D. 1978. Chromium and the glucose tolerance factor (GTF). In *Nutritional factors in general medicine*, ed. M. D. Altschule, pp. 77-80. Springfield: Charles C. Thomas Publisher.
Brief documented review of the role of chromium in glucose metabolism.

Anderson, J. W., and Chen, W. J. L. 1979. Plant fiber: Carbohydrate and lipid metabolism. *Am. J. Clin. Nutr.* 32:346-363.
Comprehensive review of evidence that plant fibers greatly influence the absorption and subsequent metabolism of carbohydrates and fats.

————, and Ward, K. 1979. High-carbohydrate, high-fiber diets for insulin-treated men with diabetes mellitus. *Am. J. Clin. Nutr.* 32:2312-2321.
Study suggesting that diets high in plant fiber may be the dietary therapy of choice for certain patients with maturity-onset type of diabetes.

Anholm, A. C. 1978. The relationship of a vegetarian diet to blood pressure. *Prev. Med.* 7:35.

Abstract of a population study showing significantly lower blood pressure in vegetarians compared to nonvegetarians.

Armstrong, B.; Clarke, H.; Martin, C., et al. 1979. Urinary sodium and blood pressure in vegetarians. *Am. J. Clin. Nutr.* 32:2472-2476.
This study demonstrates a higher dietary potassium intake among vegetarians, which may play a role in their relatively lower incidence of hypertension.

Axelrod, A. E. 1980. Nutrition in relation to immunity. In *Modern nutrition in health and disease*, eds. R. S. Goodhart and M. E. Shils, pp. 578-596. Philadelphia: Lea & Febiger Publishers.
Comprehensive review of the relationship between nutrition and immunity.

Bates, C. J.; Mandal, A. R.; and Cole, T. J. 1977. HDL cholesterol and vitamin C status. *Lancet.* 2:611.
Documented correspondence showing strong positive correlation between vitamin C status and plasma HDL cholesterol in men but not in women.

Brewster, L., and Jacobson, M. F. 1978. *The changing American diet*. Washington, D.C.: Center for Science in the Public Interest.
Short but comprehensive book that compares USDA food consumption patterns between 1909 and 1976.

Briggs, G. M., and Calloway, D. H. 1979. Vitamin C (ascorbic acid). In *Bogert's nutrition and physical fitness*, p. 227. Philadelphia: W. B. Saunders Company.
Chapter on vitamin C, which includes information on the vitamin C status of various samples of the American population.

Brin, M. 1977. Examples of behavioral changes in marginal vitamin deficiency in the rat and man. In *Behavioral effects of energy and protein deficits*, ed. J. Brozek. Department of Health, Education, and Welfare Publ. No. (NIH) 79-1906. Washington, D.C.: U. S. Government Printing Office.
Short review of several studies demonstrating adverse behavioral changes in the rat and man, resulting from subclinical deficiencies of thiamin, riboflavin, and vitamin C.

——————. 1978. Drugs and environmental chemicals in relation to vitamin needs. In *Nutrition and drug interrelationships*, eds. J. N. Hathcock and J. Coon, pp. 131-150. New York: Academic Press, Inc.
Short review of the effects of drug intake or of environmental chemical exposure on nutrient metabolism and needs. Includes a definition of marginal deficiency and the extent of this condition in the United States.

Burkitt, D. P.; Walker, A. R. P.; and Painter, N. S. 1974. Dietary fiber and disease. *J. A. M. A.* 229:1068-1074.
Classical review of epidemiological data correlating a low-fiber intake to disease.

Carroll, K. K. 1975. Experimental evidence of dietary factors and hormone-dependent cancers. *Cancer Res.* 35:3374-3383.
Review of recent research on animal models to determine effect of diet on tumorigenesis, with discussion of the relevance of this work to human cancer.

——————; Giovannetti, P. M.; Huff, M. W., et al. 1978. Hypocholesterolemic effect of substituting soybean protein for animal protein in the diet of health young women. *Am. J. Clin, Nutr.* 31:1312-1321.
The effect of dietary protein on plasma cholesterol.

Cumming, C. A., and Newman, V. A. 1981. *Eater's guide: Nutrition basics for busy people.* New York: Prentice-Hall, Inc.
Brief, practical, and humorous book. Includes special help for dieters and for those who must eat in restaurants often.

Emken, E. A., and Dutton, H. J., eds. 1979. *Geometrical and positional fatty acid isomers.* Champaign, Ill.: American Oil Chemists Society.
Review of current research on the effect of "trans" fatty acids and hydrogenated fats on animal and human models.

Enig, M. G.; Munn, R. J.; and Keeney, M. 1978. Dietary fat and cancer trends: A critique. *Fed. Proceed.* 37:2215-2220.
Cancer mortality over a 60-year period shows significant positive correlations with dietary total fat and vegetable fat, and negative or no correlation with animal fat.

Flynn, M. A.; Nolph, G. B.; Flynn T. C., et al. 1979. Effect of dietary egg on human serum cholesterol and triglycerides. *Am. J. Clin. Nutr.* 32:1051-1057.

Two whole fresh eggs daily produced no significant increase in mean serum cholesterol.

Two whole fresh eggs daily produced no significant increase in mean serum cholesterol.

Gear, J. S. S.; Fursdon, P.; Nolan, D. J., et al. 1979. Symptomless diverticular disease and intake of dietary fibre. *Lancet* 2:511-514.
Controlled clinical trial showing that vegetarians had a significantly higher mean fiber intake and less diverticular disease than nonvegetarians.

Ginter, E. 1978. Marginal vitamin C deficiency, lipid metabolism, and atherogenesis. *Adv. Lipid. Res.* 16: 167-220.
Excellent review of animal and human literature on the role of vitamin C in lipid metabolism and atherogenesis.

Glueck, C. J., and Connor, W. E. 1979. Diet and atherosclerosis: past, present and future. *West. J. Med.* 130:117-122.
Well-documented review of clinical and epidemiologic research on the relationship between diet and atherosclerosis.

Gori, G. B. 1979. Dietary and nutritional implications in the multifactorial etiology of certain prevalent human cancers. *Cancer* (May supplement). 43:2151-2161.
The major hypotheses of the role of dietary and nutritional factors in cancer etiology are examined.

Grande, F. 1974. Sugars in cardiovascular disease. In *Sugars in nutrition*, ed. H. L. Sipple and K. W. McNutt, pp. 401-437. New York: Academic Press.
Extensive summary of human and animal studies in which sucrose was replaced isocalorically by some type of starch (for example, legumes, bread, or potatoes).

Haber, G. B.; Heaton, K. W.; and Murphy, D. 1977. Depletion and disruption of dietary fibre: Effects on satiety, plasma-glucose, and serum-insulin. *Lancet* 2:679-682.
Report of a clinical trial demonstrating that removal of fiber from food, and also its physical disruption, can result in faster ingestion, decreased satiety, and disturbed glucose homeostasis.

Heller, S. N., and Hackler, L. R. 1978. Changes in the crude fiber content of the American diet. *Am. J. Clin. Nutr.* 31:1510-1514.
Report of assessment of crude fiber in the American diet between 1909 and 1975, demonstrating a drop of 28% during that period.

Hjermann, I.; Enger, S. C.; Helgeland, A., et al. 1979. The effect of dietary changes on high density lipoprotein cholesterol: The Oslo study. *Am. J. Med.* 66:105-109.
Controlled study demonstrating that a low-fat diet with equal amounts of saturated and polyunsaturated fat resulted in higher HDL cholesterol levels.

Huang, C. T. L.; Gopalakrishna, G. S.; Nicholas, B. L. 1978. Fiber, intestinal sterols, and colon cancer. *Am. J. Clin. Nutr.* 31:516-526.
Excellent review of the relationship between fiber, intestinal sterols, and colon cancer.

Johansson, G. 1979. Magnesium metabolism studies in health, primary hyperparathyroidism, and renal stone disease. *Scan. J. Urol. Neph. Suppl.* 51:1-45.
Thorough review of the literature on the possible role of magnesium in renal stone disease.

Kelsay, J. L.; Behall, K. M.; and Prather, E. S. 1978. Effect of fiber from fruits and vegetables on metabolic responses of human subjects. 1: Bowel transit times, number of defecations, fecal

weight, urinary excretions of energy and nitrogen and apparent digestibilities of energy, nitrogen and fat. *Am. J. Clin. Nutr.* 31:1149-1153.
Cross-over clinical trial comparing the effect of a diet high in fruit and vegetable fiber to a diet low in such fiber.

Kritchevsky, D. 1979a. Metabolic effects of dietary fiber. *West. J. Med.* 130:123-127.

————. 1979b. Nutrition and heart disease. *Food Tech.* 33:39-42.
Well-documented and comprehensive reviews of human and animal research on the relationship between diet and disease.

Manning, A. P.; Heaton, K. W.; Harvey, R. F., et al. 1977. Wheat fibre and irritable bowel syndrome. *Lancet* 2:417-418.
Controlled clinical trial of patients with irritable bowel syndrome, demonstrating benefits of a diet high in wheat fiber.

Marsh, A. G.; Sanchez, T. V.; Mickelson, O., et al. 1980. Cortical bone density of adult lacto-ovo-vegetarian and omnivorous women. *J. Am. Diet Assoc.* 76:148-151.
Report of a clinical trial demonstrating that postmenopausal lacto-ovo-vegetarian women lost significantly less bone mineral mass than omnivorous women controls.

Meneely, G. R., and Battarbee, H. D. 1976. High sodium-low potassium environment and hypertension. *Am. J. Cardiol.* 38:768-785.
Review of the potentiating effect of sodium and the ameliorating effect of potassium ingestion on the incidence of hypertension.

Minton, J. P.; Foecking, M. K.; Webster, D. J. T., et al. 1979. Caffeine, cyclic nucleotides, and breast disease. *Surgery.* 86:105-109.
Forty-seven women with clinical fibrocystic breast disease were instructed to stop all methylxanthine consumption (coffee, tea, chocolate, and cola). Of those who abstained, 65% experienced complete disappearance of all palpable breast nodules and other symptoms within 1-6 months.

Stopping all methylxanthines may help fibrocystic disease.

O'Dea, K. O.; Nestel, P. J.; and Antonoff, L. 1980. Physical factors influencing postprandial glucose and insulin responses to starch. *Am. J. Clin. Nutr.* 33:760-65.
Clinical trial on human subjects demonstrating that ground rice meals elicited much higher peak responses of glucose and insulin than either of the unground samples.

Offenbacher, E. G., and Pi-Sunyer, F. X. 1980. Improvement of glucose tolerance and blood lipids in elderly subjects given

Abstract of a clinical trial demonstrating that chromium-rich brewers yeast significantly improved glucose tolerance.

chromium-rich yeast. *Am. J. Clin. Nutr.* 33:916.
Abstract of a clinical trial demonstrating that chromium-rich brewers yeast significantly improved glucose tolerance, increased insulin sensitivity, and decreased elevated serum cholesterol levels.

Page, L., and Friend, B. 1978. The changing American diet. *Bioscience* 28:192-197.
Comprehensive review of USDA statistics showing changes in food consumption patterns in the United States between 1909 and 1976.

Phillips, R. L. 1975. Role of lifestyle and dietary habits in risk of cancer among Seventh-Day Adventists. *Cancer Res.* 35:3513-3522.
Epidemiological study of life-style factors possibly accounting for the significantly lower cancer mortality rates in this population.

————; Lemon, F. R.; Beeson, W. L., et al. 1978. Coronary heart disease mortality among Seventh-Day Adventists with differing dietary habits: A preliminary report. *Am. J. Clin. Nutr.* (October supplement) 31:191-198.
Preliminary report of a 6-year prospective study. Showed risk of fatal coronary heart disease among nonvegetarian Seventh-Day Adventist males to be three times greater than vegetarian Seventh-Day Adventist males of comparable age.

Porter, M. W.; Yamanaka, W.; Carlson, S. D., et al. 1977. Effect of dietary egg on serum cholesterol and triglyceride of human males. *Am. J. Clin. Nutr.* 30:490-495.
Three-month clinical trial showing no significant association of dietary cholesterol intake with either serum cholesterol or triglycerides.

Potter, J. D.; Topping, D. L.; and Oakenfull, D. 1979. Soya, saponins, and plasma-cholesterol. *Lancet* 1:223.
Well-referenced correspondence suggesting that the hypocholesterolemic action of soy protein is attributable to the presence of plant sterols known as saponins.

Reaven, G. M. 1979. Effects of differences in amount and kind of dietary carbohydrate on plasma glucose and insulin responses in man. *Am. J. Clin. Nutr.* 32:2568-2578.
The effect of variations in kind and amount of dietary carbohydrate on plasma glucose and insulin responses in normal subjects and in patients with chemical diabetes.

Reiser, S.; Hallfrisch, J.; Michaelis, O. E., et al. 1979a. Isocaloric exchange of dietary starch and sucrose in humans. I: Effects on levels of fasting blood lipids. *Am. J. Clin. Nutr.* 32: 1659-1669.

Consumption of sucrose can increase blood lipids; males and carbohydrate-sensitive individuals may be more susceptible than others.

——————; Handler, H. B.; Gardner, L. B., et al. 1979b. Isocaloric exchange of dietary starch and sucrose in humans. II: Effects of fasting blood insulin, glucose, and glucagon on insulin and glucose responses to a sugar load. *Am. J. Clin. Nutr.* 32:2206-2216.
Sucrose feeding produces undesirable changes in several parameters associated with glucose tolerance.

Sacks, F. M.; Rosner, B.; and Kass, E. H. 1974. Blood pressure in vegetarians. *Am J. Epidemiol.* 100:390-398.
Study of vegetarians showing highly significant associations between declared consumption of animal products and systolic and diastolic blood pressure after the age and weight effects were removed.

——————; Castelli, W. P.; Donner, A., et al. 1975. Plasma lipids and lipoproteins in vegetarians and controls. *N. Engl. J. Med.* 292:1148-1151.
Multiple regression analyses showed overall consumption of animal products to be directly related to the level of cholesterol and LDL cholesterol.

Sanders, T. A. B.; Ellis, F. R.; and Dickerson, J. W. T. 1978. Studies of vegans: the fatty acid composition of plasma choline phosphoglycerides, erythrocytes, adipose tissue, and breast milk, and some indicators of susceptibility to ischemic heart disease in vegans and omnivore controls. *Am. J. Clin. Nutr.* 31:805-813.
Study demonstrating cholesterol and triglyceride concentrations to be lower in vegans (those eating no foods of animal origin) than in omnivorous controls.

Schrauzer, G. 1979. Trace elements in carcinogenesis. In *Advances in nutritional research*, vol. 2, ed. H. H. Draper, pp. 219-244. New York: Plenum Press, Inc.
Excellent review of the role of trace minerals in carcinogenesis.

Sirtori, C. R.; Gatti, E.; Mantero, O., et al. 1979. Clinical experience with the soybean protein diet in the treatment of hypercholesterolemia. *Am. J. Clin. Nutr.* 32:1645-1658.
Soybean diet is an effective regimen for inducing a significant cholesterol reduction in type II patients refractory to standard low-lipid regimes.

Taylor, C. B.; Peng, S-K, Wethessen, N. T., et al. 1979. Spontaneously occurring angiotoxic derivatives of cholesterol. *Am. J. Clin. Nutr.* 32:40-57.

Excellent review of research on animal models demonstrating the angiotoxicity of oxidized cholesterol and its relevance to cardiovascular disease in humans.

United States Department of Health, Education, and Welfare. 1974. *HANES: Health and Nutrition Examination Survey.* Department of Health, Education, and Welfare Publ. No. (HRA) 74-12191-1. Washington, D.C.: U. S. Government Printing Office.
Report of a national nutrition survey.

United States Department of Agriculture and United States Department of Health, Education, and Welfare. 1980. *Nutrition and your health: Dietary guidelines for Americans.* Washington, D.C.: U. S. Government Printing Office.
A 20-page pamphlet (size of business envelope) containing practical dietary suggestions.

Van Itallie, T. B. 1979. Obesity: The American disease. *Food Tech.* 33:60-64.
Short review of animal and human studies to determine the causes of obesity.

12 The Role of Associated Health Professionals and Community Resources

Leona M. McGann

Ms. McGann received her M.S.W. from St. Louis University School of Social Service and her M.P.H. at Michigan University, School of Public Health. She was on the faculties of the University of Wisconsin and the University of California, Berkeley, before joining Stanford University School of Medicine. She has published articles and teaching manuals on the use of community resources.

Barbaraterry Kurtz

Ms. Kurtz received her M.S.W. at the University of Michigan, her M.P.H. at the University of California, Berkeley, and was on the faculty of the University of Michigan Medical School. She has engaged in the private practice of psychiatric social work and program development in a variety of community settings.

Brief Contents

Overview

Through a few brief case presentations a family context of preventive health care is described. Qualifications and potential activities of an effective primary care team are outlined. The chapter concludes with a concise summary of community resources, which can serve as a reference and starting point for primary health care providers who need help in making use of these important preventive services.

THE FAMILY CONTEXT OF PREVENTIVE HEALTH CARE

Although the definition of the family varies over time and among cultures, the family, whatever its exact description, is the basic unit of society and is therefore an appropriate focus for preventive health care. Simple information on the nature of the family unit provides insights into the stresses and health problems that may be encountered. There is considerable diversity in family units in the United States today (Table 12-1).

Table 12-1

Table 12-1 Family Units in the United States—By Type and Number

Type of Family	Number of Family Units
Traditional families (two parents with father as breadwinner and children under 18 years of age at home)	18%
Modified traditional families (same as above with mother in workforce)	19%
Single parent living with one or more children	12%
Nuclear families with one or both parents remarried	11%
Clusters of unrelated adults; single adults	19%
Married couples without children under 18 years of age	11%
Three-generation families	4%
Other	6%

Source: Sussman, M. B. 1977. Family. In *Encyclopedia of Social Work*, Vol. 1, p. 359. Washington, D.C.: National Association of Social Wrokers.

Certain stresses correspond to life stages.

Certain stresses are inherent in each category. Divorce can lead to health problems not only for the parents but also for their children. Excessive eating, use of drugs, and disturbances in eating, sleeping, and general behavior in school performance often occur; so may reversions in older children to thumb sucking or bed-wetting. Single parenting predisposes to many stresses for both adults and children—nutrition, limited opportunities for recreation and exercise, insufficient peer contact, and financial distress. Some of the same problems, but usually at a less intense level, may be found in modified traditional families. Remarriage, particularly when children are involved, has significant potential for complex and troubling interrelationships since it involves a complete reidentification of a particular family or pair of families. About 15%-50% of patients in primary care populations have emotional or social problems, mostly accounted for by problems of social adjustment and occupational and financial problems.

The family support network, if functioning well, may be as important in preventive disease as a weak network is in contributing to it.

Research in the field of epidemiology and our own experience suggest that the family support network, if functioning well, may be as important in preventive disease as a weak network is in contributing to it.

Psychosocial aspects of prevention include (a) identification of persons and families at high risk; (b) review of the social supports available to persons through their family, or to the immediate family through its extended relation, or in the absence of these, and (c) establishing the necessary supports through friends, peer groups, clergy, and social and community agencies that collectively constitute a substitute "extended family."

Case examples drawn from different developmental stages of the family may help to clarify the important role of the primary care team in early prevention activities.

Premarital and Early Marital Stage

Case Study

A young couple, Mary and Tom—21 and 22 years of age, respectively, and college graduates—reported to their physician for their premarital blood test. Mary had been a long-time patient of the physician, having been delivered by him. He now took the opportunity to become acquainted with Mary's fiance, getting to know him as well as the couple's marital goals and expectations. During the discussion the physician learned that Tom, unlike Mary, was uncomfortable with any overt display of affection, rejecting Mary's hand-holding gesture. Further, they did not seem to be in agreement about plans for having children or in Tom's willingness for Mary to continue to work. The physician recognized the need for these issues to be discussed and for agreements to be reached before marriage. He therefore set up a future appointment with them. At that time, he felt that he might have sufficient rapport to suggest utilization of one of their religious premarital groups, or to seek counseling through planned parenthood or the health department resources.

Early Child Rearing

Case Study

Mrs. Jones, divorced for 3 years, was rearing her two children, then 6 and 9 years of age. A changed assignment resulting in a geographical move led Mrs. Jones to seek a new physician. During her initial interview the physician explored the impact of divorce and its effect on the patient's life-style. At that time she learned that the patient had altered her previous extracurricular activities, and was now centering her world on the children, probably as a subsitution for the loss of the husband-father. Finding Mrs. Jones and the children physically healthy, the physician supported her in seeking outside relationships and calling her attention to a number of single-parent groups sponsored by many organizations including the local family service agency.

Family With an Adolescent

Case Study

John's repeated complaints of stomach cramps appeared to have no organic foundation. It was the fall of his senior year at the university and like many of his classmates John was confused and uncertain about his future.

John's father had always loved his work as a well-known grower of prize tomatoes. The business could easily have been expanded through purchase of a nearby tract of land, and he had hoped his son would join him.

While John was not rejecting farming as a career, he was unable to clarify his options. The physician was uncertain about John's vocational aptitudes and, further, a number of

John's classmates had been to see him with similar concerns about their future. The doctor was therefore familiar with the fact that the local mental health director had authorized a young psychiatric social worker to join with the school counselor in sponsoring a group devoted to issues being faced by John and his classmates. The physician suggested to John that he join the group. John, initially resistant, joined when a classmate reported that he was being helped to "unfog" himself and to sort out alternatives.

Middle Age

The departure of children from the home because of employment, school, or marriage; frustrations at work frequently compounded by the company's addition of younger business graduates; and the added burden of ill, elderly in-laws—these situations can strain relations to the breaking point, frequently resulting in divorce, with years of loneliness ahead for the woman who is less likely than the man to remarry.

Case Study

This was the picture of the O'Briens, long-time patients of a primary care physician. The physician also took care of Mrs. O'Brien's mother, and was aware of the mother's increasing lack of concern for her appearance and unwillingness ever to leave her house located next door to the O'Briens. Mrs. O'Brien, looking forward to freedom from family responsibilities, was having difficulty accepting this added burden. Increased headaches and asthmatic attacks led to short escapes in illness. The next time the physician scheduled an appointment for the mother, he requested that the O'Briens both accompany her. Communication was opened at that time. The physician gave the mother medical orders to dress and take a short accompanied walk outside every day. He urged Mrs. O'Brien to free herself from the responsibility for her mother 1 or 2 days when one of the mother's grandchildren or her sister visited with her. Mr. and Mrs. O'Brien were also advised to seek counseling or to join group of couples facing similar problems.

Retirement—Death and Dying

Case Study

Mr. Thomas, a former company executive, had elected to retire early after two mild coronaries, and he and his wife had moved to be near their married daughter. Mr. Thomas managed all the couple's finances; he played golf once a week but felt restless, dissatisfied, and useless. Mrs. Thomas worried about her husband's health and her ability to manage should he die, yet did not want to be dependent on her son-in-law for advice. Their marital relationship was strained and fraught with bickering. On visits to the physician with minor complaints, Mr. Thomas was encouraged to offer his executive skills to the Retired Senior Volunteer Program. This organization placed him with a nonprofit nursing home where his management skills were tapped. Simultaneously, Mrs. Thomas joined one of the committees planning housing for seniors, and also enrolled in a class on Financial Matters Especially for Women—having seen the announcement in the physician's office.

The Thomases managed well until Mr. Thomas' stroke and death. Mrs. Thomas spoke gratefully to the physician that her course work enabled her to understand the many financial decisions she was having to make. The physician supported her in not making an early decision to move, helping her understand that the bereavement period was not a time for major changes. She had joined a widows' group and was finding their friendship and support helpful.

ASSOCIATED HEALTH PROFESSIONALS AS A TEAM

The primary care physician's ability to provide these services would be enhanced through the availability of a team. Services provided by a coordinated health team, including medicine, nursing, and social work, unite unique and overlapping functions and capabilities.

Appropriate use of the health team may prevent further deterioration in family relationships.

The following case illustrates how this help was available immediately, preventing further deterioration in family relationships.

Case Study

Seventeen-year old Kevin was a diabetic and the youngest of three children. His parents had been complaining that

Kevin had not been wearing his medic alert necklace, which states that he is a diabetic on insulin. In addition, Kevin often stayed out all night drinking, coming home in the morning to have his mother give him his shot. In desperation his parents consulted their physician. The physician saw the parents and Kevin at separate times.

During the talk with Kevin the physician realized that there were a number of problems for this boy and his family, so he referred Kevin to a social worker. The physician and the allied staff supported the family and reinforced Kevin's relationship with the social worker.

In the course of several talks with Kevin, the social worker recognized that Kevin was using his diabetes to reinforce his family ties to him. Eventually, with Kevin's consent, his parents joined in on the talks with the social worker.

It was decided that the office nurse would instruct Kevin about diabetes and teach him how to give himself his own shots. The family was encouraged to contact the Diabetic Association's group in order to end some of the isolation and guilt they felt about Kevin's disease. Finally, the social worker joined Kevin in a meeting with school officials to try to relieve his troubled situation there.

The physician-nurse combination is the core of any health team.

The physician-nurse combination is the core of any health team. Increasingly the role of the nurse is being expanded to that of a middle-level practitioner. A social worker is often the next most useful member of a primary care team and may be employed by the practice or engaged as a consultant. A family helath worker, outreach worker, or community health worker can be a great asset in a setting serving a cultural, ethnic, or socioeconomic population that is different from, or unfamiliar to, that of the other health workers. A nutritionist, although often required only on a part-time basis, can also be helpful. Supporting services may be provided by registered nurses, licensed vocational nurses, nurses aides, and medical assistants who serve in both front office and back office capacities. In the absence of a medical assistant, the roles of receptionist, laboratory technician, x-ray technician, and business manager can be delegated to other members of the team. Consultants to the team may include any of the medical specialists, a clinical pharmacist, a vocational counselor, a mental health specialist such as a clinical psychologist or marriage and family counselor, and a health educator. There are also numerous community resources that can provide services to patients on request, although they usually cannot supply staff members directly to the primary care team.

As in all group enterprises, communication is vitally important to the optimal function of the team.

As in all group enterprises, communication is vitally important to the optimal functioning of the team. In almost any setting a weekly meeting with the entire staff is desirable. Such meetings serve to provide a forum for the discussion of both patient management and office routine. They also affirm the group identity of the team. Team conferences should take place at the time of initial family assessment and during the course of treatment of an acute or chronic illness that causes disability or family disruption. Most of the time communication through an accurate ongoing medical record is sufficient for patients with acute self-limiting problems. The longer the team members operate together, the greater the likelihood that the members with less training can take on more sophisticated functions. Each team will need to work out its own protocols and priorities. In a well-organized team the expectation usually exists that as management of parents with acute and chronic disease becomes more routinized, increasing attention will be given to health education and disease prevention.

It is important for the family members to be able to identify the team as a team.

The team will also need to establish its own methods of ensuring accountability at each level of providing care, for example, orientation of the family to the practice, initial assessment education for self-care, treatment, referral, and follow-up. It is important for the family members to be able to identify the team as a team, to respect the unique contribution of each team member, and to understand the manner in which their care is to be provided.

Table 12-2

Table 12-2 provides a list of possible associated health professionals who can participate in a primary care team, together with the qualifications and principal duties that can be undertaken. In larger primary care settings additional members of the health care team may include health educators, specialized consultants in orthopedics and in psychiatry; a clinical pharmacist; and speech, physical, and occupational therapists.

MAKING USE OF COMMUNITY RESOURCES

For physicians to limit all patient care to resources located within their office would be to neglect the opportunities for optimal primary preventive health care.

Community resources are a complex network of human and environmental services ranging from health, housing, and financial, day care and educational centers, and a myriad of assistance programs including meals on wheels and homemaker services. Community resources are especially valuable in caring for elderly persons. For physicians to limit all patient care to resources located within their office would be to neglect the opportunities for optimal primary preventive health care.

Table 12-2 Summary of Requirements for Primary Care Team Personnel

Position	Education Required	Method of Qualification	Range of Activities
Nurse practitioner	Variable: R.N., A.A., B.A., P.H.N. or M.P.H. plus clinical training; specialization available at Master's level.	R.N., licensed by state; physician supervision required by law.	Obtain health history; assess health illness status; refer patient into health care system, and provide support for persons who are impaired, infirm or ill during programs of diagnosis and therapy; provide primary prevention counseling and counseling of the elderly and disabled.
Physician's assistant	A.A. or B.A., involving clinical practice; primary care orientation preferred, although specialties are sometimes available.	Usually licensed by state; physician supervision required by law.	Conduct medical triage, take medical histories, perform physical examinations. assess health and under physician supervision initiate appropriate diagnostic and therapeutic steps, participate in routine screening (for example, audiometry), provide therapeutic procedures such as injections and immunizations, provide health counseling including family planning, and refer patients to appropriate community resources.
Clinical social worker*	M.S.W.; D.S.W. or Ph.D. are also available through some universities.	Graduation from an accredited school of social work; membership in the National Association of Social Workers, Academy of Certified Social Workers, two years' supervised practice; Licensed in some states.	Provide short-term crisis intervention through supportive counseling, assist in orienting new patients to the practice; obtain initial family history, aid in locating appropriate community resources such as a nursing home, aid the family in budgeting or locating financial resources, and assess family dynamics in order to help with treatment plans including home care.
Family health worker	Few established programs or exact norms; some inhouse and community college programs.	None established.	Assist particularly in multiethnic communities to gain acceptance of primary care services; plan and carry out educational programs; arrange for transportation and financial assistance, follow up patients with chronic illness or special needs, and serve as advocate for the patient and liaison to the welfare department, school, probation department, vocation, rehabilitation, or Social Security office.

Medical assistant/ receptionist	Private schools and community college programs with curriculum that includes reception office management skills, billing and insurance, laboratory and X-ray examination procedures, and first aid.	None established.	Perform laboratory tests; supervise appointments and billing; provide sensitive first contact with patients, and early warning recognition of family problems, financial problems, and difficulties with community resources.
Nutritionist/dietitian	B.S. with courses in nutrition, chemistry, physiology, and public health plus one year's internship, Master of Science and Master of Public Health degree in nutrition are possible.	Registration by American Dietetic Association.	Promote health through assessment of food practices; counsel normal nutrition; recommend dietary modification for diseases such as diabetes; advise on optimal nutritional management on low income and for special situations such as pregnancy, growing children, and the elderly; organize educational programs and weight reduction classes.
Registered nurse	Diploma from hospital-based school, A.S. from community college, or B.S. from college or university.	R.N.; licensed in state.	Supervise total comprehensive nursing care; observe, interpret, and evaluate patients' symptoms and needs, carry out legal orders of physicians for medications and treatments; supervise auxiliary help, carry out nursing procedures and techniques, give health guidance and participate in health education; and reports, records, and evaluates for the medical record.
Public health nurse	R.N. and B.S. including specified courses and field work in public health; may have a M.P.H. degree	R.N.; licensed by state certified by state health department for public health nursing.	In addition to the above provide a special knowledge in the promotion of individual and family health; visit in the home to provide nursing care and treatment and teach family members how to carry out prescribed treatment; appraise individual and family health needs and hazards, emotional as well as physical, help families utilize community resources.
L.V.N.'s (licensed vocational or practical nurses)	Prescribed course of study in an accredited school of vocational nursing, or education and experience equivalents	Usually state licensing; services provided under the supervision of the physician or a licensed R.N.	Assist in patient examinations, give prescribed medication, perform laboratory tests, perform clerical functions such as record keeping and filing, and may supervise nurse's aides.

*Larger practices may utilize Bachelor-level social workers under the supervision of the clinical social worker.

Agencies that provide an extension to primary care services are usually available in larger communities and many are found in rural areas as well. Information about regularly used resources should be maintained in the office by a designated staff member. Directories are usually available free or for a small sum from the welfare, social service, and health departments; chambers of commerce; and medical societies. Some United Way or "Red Feather" city and/or county agencies publish a major, detailed index of all resources in the area. The Public Health Nurse attached to a local rural health department is an invaluable resource for general information including the quality of services offered. In most urban areas a person can look in the telephone directory under Information and Referral Service and call to obtain specific suggestions for individual problems. School nurses and hospital social service workers may also provide information and collaborate in counseling and planning.

In rural areas the Public Health Nurse is an invaluable resource for general information.

In most urban areas a person can look in the telephone directory under Information and Referral Service for information.

Timing and preparation are critical in making a good community referral. The patient and family should be prepared for the referral through answering their questions and providing them with background information about the resource. Involving the patient and family in the actual selection of alternative resources may help to ensure successful follow-through on the referral. Other factors that may influence the patient's acceptance and follow-through are the location of the resource and its fee scale, the family's feeling about using a resource, the extent to which the family is prepared to use the resource, and its motivation to seek help. Physicians who are knowledgeable about community resources and display information about them in their office do much to break down families' barriers of resistance to using them. Scheduling continued office visits or telephone contacts reassures the family of physicians' concern and minimizes its fear of desertion. In many instances physicians may wish to keep in touch with the agency as well as to enable a collaborative relationship to develop.

After referral to community resources, scheduling continued office visits or telephone contacts minimizes the fear of desertion.

Case Study

A physician displaying in his office information about a "parental stress hot line" was pointedly told by Mrs. Main that she had written down the phone number. She confessed that she was having increased headaches and was growing more intolerant of her two children's (aged 2 and 3½ years) acting out behavior, explaining that she did not know how to to handle them. Her husband was finishing his Ph.D. dissertation and had little time to devote to his wife or the children.

Her own mother, now living in another state, had throughout her married life been greatly involved in social activities and had left most of Mrs. Main's early upbringing to various care-takers. The physician, recognizing Mrs. Main's failure to have a mother model and her present lack of social support, advised her to join a parenting class sponsored by the local YWCA. Since another one of his patients was attending, he suggested that his receptionist arrange for them to go together to the first meeting. The meeting was held in the evening, when her children were asleep and her husband was writing. The physician set up an appointment 3 weeks in the future to assure her of his continued interest and to learn if she were accepting his advice—and if she were finding it helpful. At this visit she advised him that she was benefiting greatly from the parenting sessions, had made friends with several of the women, and had managed on another night to take a continuing high school education class in ballet dancing. Having the information on the parental stress hot line displayed in the office enabled Mrs. Main to be open about her own problems. The physician's knowledge of the resources led him to refer the patient to a program where she received the necessary help, and her children were spared becoming child abuse statistics.

Often friends living together may need as much support and understanding as a traditionally older husband and wife couple.

Case Study

Often friends living together may need as much support and understanding as a traditionally older husband and wife couple.

Mary, 70 years old, had heart disease compounded by cancer that had spread to her liver. Her friend Anne, 60 years of age, was employed as an executive in a local accounting firm and was free to work out her own hours but Anne was the sole support of her mother housed in a nursing home in another state. Both women had numerous friends but none of these friends was in a position to share major responsibility for Mary as she became increasingly disabled. The physician was aware of the home situation and the need to make certain that Anne had the necessary social supports to maintain herself as well as Mary. The physician made numerous suggestions including referral to the Home Care Agency for evaluation and ongoing nursing service, physical rearrangement of the home, use of the Meals on Wheels program three times a week to supplement the food being provided by neighbors and friends, and finally, in agreement with Mary and her friend, a referral to the Hospice Program. The physician continued the coordination of her patient's care, supporting and encouraging Anne as well as during Mary's terminal stages and following death, assuring Anne of her availability. This kind of support enabled Anne to provide care for Mary, while maintaining her own physical and emotional health.

Resources to Help Meet Health Care Costs

Viewed at the family level, no aspect of modern life causes more stress than financial matters.

Viewed at the family level, no aspect of modern life causes more stress than financial matters. These include coping with high rent or mortgages, food, education, medical care costs, and trying to save for the future while facing fears of unemployment.

Knowledge of the basic public assistance programs may allow for early referrals and prevent the family from divesting itself of all its resources.

Knowledge of the major sources of assistance beyond private insurance for meeting medical care costs and the basic public assistance programs may allow for early referrals, thus preventing the family from divesting itself of all its resources. For example, some states permit a person to own a home of any value while receiving Medicaid; a state service for crippled children may advance the money for care and arrange for repayment; a non-English-speaking patient injured at work may not realize his right to Workmen's Compensation, or to Social Security at retirement age.

Medicare meets only about 41% of older persons' average health care costs.

Medicare meets only about 41% of older persons' average health care costs. Persons without supplementary insurance to defray these costs may deprive themselves of necessities so that they can meet their bills, thus delaying, even preventing, recovery from an illness.

The major sources of financial assistance for health care are:

1. Free or part-pay services through the health department.
2. Benefits that are based on Medicare or Workmen's Compensation, or benefits based on need and financed through taxes (such as the crippled children's program and state vocational rehabilitation programs); and such comprehensive programs as exist, for example, for veterans, Native Americans, and Merchant Seamen.
3. Those few voluntary agencies that provide either funds or direct health services.

In addition, there are payments made through private insurance companies, or Health Maintenance Organization plans, or those taken from current income, savings, or loans.

Medicare is available for some disabled under 65 years of age and most people more than 65 years of age.

Medicare—Title XVIII of the Social Security Act Medicare is a federally administered health insurance program for most people 65 years and older and some people under 65 years of age who are disabled. It consists of two types of health insurance: Part A, Hospital Insurance, and Part B, Medical Insurance.

Part A Hospital Insurance helps pay for costs of care while in a hospital or skilled nursing facility and for home health care agency services (following hospitalization).

Part B Medical Insurance helps to meet doctors' and other providers' bills and charges for such services as a home health agency, laboratory, x-ray examinations, medical supplies, appliances, and ambulance care.

Medicaid finances care for the indigent or medically indigent.

Medicaid-Title XIX of the Social Security Act Medicaid is a federal and state tax-financed program in operation in all states and territories except Arizona. The program finances care for the indigent and medically indigent. The federal law mandates that all Medicaid programs must cover all persons on public assistance. This means that persons on Supplementary Security Income or Aid to Families with Dependent Children are eligible for Medicaid. The federal law provides coverage for other groups of medically indigent, which are optional for the states.

Workmen's Compensation When individuals are unable to work, or if their earnings are reduced because of a work-related illness or injury, or if a previously existing medical condition is worsened as a result of current employment the employee may be entitled to receive benefits (medical care plus monthly income) under the Workmen's Compensation program. Although there are a few exceptions, nearly all employees are covered.

There are 54 programs (50 states plus 4 territories), each of which is different. In 7 states only the state compensation fund provides the insurance coverage; in 12 states the employer may use private insurance carriers or the state compensation insurance fund; and in 35 jurisdictions coverage is available only through private insurance companies.

In addition, in almost all states the employer can insure himself against industrial accidents in his business.

The employer or the employer's insurance carrier must provide all necessary medical treatment and disability payments until the employee returns to work or reaches "maximum recovery" and a final settlement is made.

Income payments vary. There are different schedules of benefits for different degrees of disability (10%, 20%, and so on), for permanent disability (100%), or for death from work-related causes.

Employees are required to report promptly all work-related injuries or illnesses to their employers. The individual's physician (or the physician to whom the employer sends its injured employees) is usually required to submit a medical report promptly to the employer's insurance carrier or to the state industrial accident commission.

Tax-supported rehabilitation services attempt to restore to employment vocationally handicapped persons.

Rehabilitation Tax-supported rehabilitation services are available in all states. The program's goal is to restore vocationally handicapped persons to employment. Funding is provided to help obtain (a) a medical diagnosis to determine the nature and extent of the disability and the need for medical, surgical or psychiatric treatment; (b) vocational counseling to assist the individual in selecting a suitable vocational objective; (c) physical restoration to remove or reduce employment handicaps; and (d) vocational training to prepare the applicant for a new job that is compatible with his physical and mental ability. Most state vocational rehabilitation services do not provide job placement but use the services of the state employment service.

To be eligible, usually a person must be at least 16 years of age and have a substantial vocational handicap because of a mental or physical disability, or both. Rehabilitation services are not available unless retraining will enable the person to engage in an occupation for at least one year. Eligibility for the physical restoration, maintenance, and supplies are based on financial need (the state vocational rehabilitation program looks to Medicare or Medicaid as primary resources for medical care before it will authorize state funds for restorative care).

Application is made through the nearest state department of rehabilitation office.

Income and Maintenance Resources* Social Security benefits are a nationwide contributory insurance system that provides income

---

*See also Workman's Compensation (previous section). Social Security-Title II of the Social Security Act (now called "Retirement, Survivors, Disability Insurance" [RSDI]).

protection for retired persons (62 years of age and older, and their independent spouses); survivors including minor children; and persons (any age) who have been disabled for at least 5 months (and whose disability is expected to last 12 months or more, or to result in death). Surviving dependent parents 62 years of age or over may also qualify for Social Security benefits.

Almost every kind of employment and self-employment is now covered by the Social Security system, with special provisions for employment such as domestic work in or about the private home of an employer, for farm work, or for a job where "wages" are paid in cash tips. Individuals and their employers pay equal contributions. No employees can be described as "insured" unless they have worked at least 1½ years.

Persons who have credit for 10 years of work is "fully insured" for life.

Persons who have credit for 10 years of work is "fully insured" for life. This determines only the kind of benefit; the amount is related to the worker's average earnings in jobs that were covered by Social Security.

Applicants file for benefits at the nearest Social Security Administration's office.

Unemployment insurance Unemployment Insurance, sometimes called "Unemployment Insurance Benefits," or "UIB," is a federal-state program. The original federal legislation (Title IX of the Social Security Act) provided a federal tax and offsetting credits to induce states to participate in the program.

The Federal Unemployment Tax Act levies a "permanent" tax on employers for earnings of employees who are covered by state.

The Federal Unemployment Tax Act levies a "permanent" tax on employers for earnings of employees who are covered by a state unemployment insurance program.

Benefits vary and are related to the employers' wages during a "base period" preceding the period of unemployment. The combined regular and supplemental benefits can now provide some income protection to covered, unemployed persons for up to a potential maximum duration of 65 weeks (15 months).

Supplemental Security Income In January 1974, under the new Title XVI of the Social Security Act, three assistance programs—Old Age Assistance, Aid to the Blind, and Aid to the Disabled—were federalized. Supplemental Security Income (SSI) replaced these three programs, which had been administered by the states (or countries), using federal grants-in-aid funds matched by state (or state plus county) funds. In addition, the minimum ages for Aid to the Blind and for Aid to the Disabled were eliminated, so that needy, handicapped, or retarded children who were retarded from birth on may qualify.

Social Security Insurance is a form of guaranteed minimum income for certain citizens.

In effect, SSI is a form of guaranteed minimum income for groups of people considered by society as poor, the aged, blind, and/or the disabled.

Federal SSI payments, funded entirely from general tax revenues, are administered by the Social Security Administration and are uniform throughout the United States.

In addition to these federal payment levels, 42 states supplement SSI by what is called the State Supplemental Program (SSP).

Persons may qualify for SSI if they are aged (65 years or older), disabled (any age), or blind (any age), and have limited resources and little or no income.

Resources include real and personal property. Real property may consist of the home (of any value) in which the applicant resides. Personal property may include a car (of any value) if needed for transportation to work or for medical appointments, a life insurance policy with a face value of $1,500, and liquid assets of $1,500 for one person ($2,250 for a couple). Since eligibility for SSI is very detailed and complicated, patients should be referred to the Social Security office for further information.

Aid to families with dependent children This program (Title IV of Social Security Act) gives aid to families with dependent children (AFDC)—families with serious financial needs because of the death, absence, incapacity, or unemployment of one or both parents. The amount of aid received is based on family size and income minus other outside income, the standards being set by the state legislatures. There are eligibility restrictions on real and personal property but no durational residency requirements. The program is financed through federal grants-in-aid to the state plus state funds. Applications are made to the city or county social service (welfare) office nearest to where the family lives.

General Assistance General Assistance (GA) (sometimes called "General Relief" or "Home Relief") is a county or locally financed program providing financial assistance to needy individuals ineligible for the federally funded categorical aid such as SSI (for the aged, blind, or disabled) and AFDC and who have no means of support. To be eligible a person must usually be living in the community; considered physically or mentally unemployable; needed in the home to care for a dependent child, parent, or spouse; unable to earn enough to support a family at the GA level; or involuntarily unemployed and seeking employment. Other requirements include personal property limitations. Benefits are minimal, sometimes given in the form of food or clothing orders. The benefits are set locally by each county board of supervisors or other elected body. Unlike other benefit programs, there is the possibility that a lien may be placed on the person's property, and that the ability of relatives (such as parents, spouse, or children) to provide a certain amount of support be ascertained. Persons eligible for GA are not eligible automatically for Medicaid.

Applications for GA are made to the nearest office of the county (or state) social services department (welfare department) in the country in which the needy person lives.

Counseling Services

Family service agencies Public, voluntary, or private family service agencies offer professional counseling and/or short-term continued casework including diagnostic, consultative, and referral services. Various counseling techniques may be employed, among which are family conjoint therapy, group counseling, marital counseling, and family interaction sessions. Problems presented by families frequently involve marriage and parent-child relationships, individual personality problems, or problems of aging and retirement.

The agencies are financed through taxes, fees, gifts, membership, and United Way funds.

Referrals and applications are made at the agency of choice. Fees on a sliding scale are usually charged. A major source of help is the local tax-supported mental health services.

Some agencies have special programs for adolescents including the unmarried teen-ager, or for the aged; others have special programs for minority populations. Some family service agencies are sponsored by sectarian groups such as Catholics, Jews, and Lutherans, but they provide services to all.

There are also increasing numbers of qualified clinical social workers (or family and marriage counselors) as well as psychologists and psychiatrists who provide counseling privately on a fee-for-service basis.

The rise in the number of battered women and abused children are examples of major social problems rampant in the community.

Peer counseling The rise in the number of battered women and abused children are examples of major social problems rampant in the community. Primary care teams need to be ever alert to recognize signs of these problems. Parents who leave their children alone for long periods or lock them in cars or rooms, or who tell you that they cannot tolerate their screams or demands are asking for help. A black eye or unexplained hidden bruise, depressed appearance of the female spouse, or rise in blood pressure may be tell-tale signs of spouse abuse—an indication that urgent follow-up is needed. Primary care physicians should either offer counseling in their practice or refer patients to the necessary supportive help before it is too late and the child or spouse ends up with a major injury.

Social Support Services

The increasing patient population with chronic disease plus the growing number of elderly, particularly the frail elderly, frequently living alone or separated from their families, make it necessary to provide social support services to patients and their families. These social supports can assist patients within their own homes and offer help to alleviate family disintegration.

Homemaker Services Trained and supervised persons provide help with some personal care as well as meal preparation, shopping, and light housekeeping for a specified number of hours each day or week.

Home-Delivered Meals Hot meals delivered to a person's home may be provided by a commercial or nonprofit company; nonprofit organizations charge according to the person's financial situation.

Shopping Services Some grocery stores and nonprofit grocery programs may provide delivery of groceries at little or no cost to the elderly.

Home Maintenance Repair and Rehabilitation Service Increasingly, public and private programs are coming into existence to help older persons with such tasks as heavy yard work, cleaning, building of ramps, minor home repair, and installation of insulation material. Again, when these services are sponsored by a nonprofit organization, they are provided at a fee based on the homeowner's ability to pay.

Transportation Volunteer drivers, bus or taxi service at reduced rates, and specially equipped vans or cars may be part of a variety of services facilitating mobility for the elderly and/or handicapped person.

Escort Services to the Partially Ambulatory Some community agencies provide escort services (transportation assistance) to elderly persons who are unable to travel by themselves to their physician's office, the grocery store, or to the pharmacy.

Telephone Reassurance An organized telephone program uses volunteers to make daily or more frequent home calls to check that the homebound person is all right.

Friendly Visiting Service This visiting service provides volunteers who regularly call on those who request the service. The volunteer visitor is "matched" with the "visitee," and it is natural for a friendship to develop where interests are shared and friendly acts of help are given by the volunteer visitor. In addition to agencies that are established for this purpose, some churches and club groups provide this type of service.

Hospice Care These programs are organized to provide counseling and psychologic support during terminal illness, death, and bereavement. Some hospice programs include medical, nursing, and institutional care.

Health Care Resources

Health care resources outside of private physician's offices, clinics, and health centers, are available in three distinct settings:

1. The county (or city) public health department and, if separate, the county department of mental health services; another public employee who provides services is the school nurse.
2. Voluntary health agencies such as the American Heart Association and American Cancer Society.
3. Hospitals, skilled nursing the intermediate care facilities, and day health centers.

Services provided by the health department for health promotion and disease control may include:

1. Environmental sanitation
2. Health education
3. Medical services including mental health
4. Crippled children services
5. Maternal and child health services
6. Tuberculosis, venereal disease, and other communicable disease control
7. Nutrition
8. Public health laboratory
9. Vital statistics

The amount of direct medical services offered by the public health department varies.

The amount of direct medical services offered by the public health department varies. It is partially dependent on the health needs of the population and availability of private medical services. Inner-city populations may be served extensively by county health department direct medical programs. Wealthier counties may also finance educational programs ranging from nutrition to self-development. Most offer some family planning and financing for the care of crippled children (defined differently among the states). Public health nursing may offer education, coordination, planning, and/or direct bedside care, depending on the availability of the visiting nurse or other home care agency. The public health nurse is the major provider of consultation and health education to patients and their families. She can also make a home evaluation on medical referral.

Home health care services are sponsored in various ways. County health departments, hospitals, the visiting nurses association, and commercial companies are the major sponsors of skilled, coordinated services to patients in their own homes. These services include professional nursing care, physical and occupational therapy, home health aides, and medical social work. Some home health agencies are also able to offer nutritional consultation and homemaker services.

Eligibility is based on a medical referral; the patients' charges are met through Medicare, Medicaid, other government agencies, private insurance, or the persons themselves, sometimes on a sliding fee scale.

There are various types of voluntary health agencies. Some such as the American Cancer Society, Alcoholics Anonymous, or the Epilepsy Association are for specific diseases, while others are for disorders of organs (for example, the American Heart Association), or are oriented toward problems that affect health and welfare (for example, the Child Study Association of America). Their responsibilities can be divided primarily into three areas (a) education of the public, (b) education of the professional person, and (c) research or demonstration activities project funds. In some instances, for example, in the case of the American Cancer Society, direct services are offered to individuals, including transportation for medical treatment, loan of equipment such as wheelchairs, and provision of surgical dressing.

All of the foregoing organizations will provide the primary care team with excellent educational pamphlets, which should be prominently displayed in the office, as should announcements about the educational programs and group activities of these associations or departments.

The team may also wish to avail itself of their excellent professional educational programs, and some may wish to apply for research or demonstration support through their project funds.

Depending on a person's need, different levels of institutional nursing care are offered.

Institutional and day health care Depending on a person's need, different levels of institutional nursing care are offered, ranging from care of those who are ambulatory to acute care or long-term care. Facilities may offer only one level or provide for all levels of care. The names of the facilities may be misleading in that they may be called by various titles such as "convalescent hospitals," "nursing homes," or "rehabilitation centers."

Skilled nursing facilities are for individuals who may be bed patients or partially ambulatory but who need a high level of daily nursing care and a regular monthly checkup by a physician.

Skilled nursing facility Skilled nursing facilities are for individuals who may be bed patients or partially ambulatory but who need a high level of daily nursing care and a regular monthly checkup by a physician. They also provide meals including special diets, administration of medications, 24-hour supervision, and skilled nursing including respiratory therapy. Eligibility for admission is by medical recommendation but the patient must not require acute hospital care.

Medicare certifies such facilities so that they may be entitled to seek reimbursement for patients entitled to Medicare benefits. Both patients needing long-term and those needing a custodial level of care may be housed in these facilities but custodial care is not reimbursable under Medicare.

The criteria for admission to an intermediate care facility are described.

Intermediate Care Facility To be admitted to an intermediate care facility patients must be recommended by their physicians. They must be ambulatory, continent, and able to dress and feed themselves with only limited assistance. The facility provides meals including special diets, administration of medications, 24-hour supervision, and intermittent nursing care plus an activity program. Medicaid but not Medicare will reimburse the costs in this type of facility.

Senior Day Health Centers These health centers cater to the frail or at-risk elderly. For these seniors transportation is often arranged by the center, while some seniors may be expected to arrive and leave on their own. To facilitate referrals that require public transportation, the office clerk must be well informed about it. Early referral may not only prevent the person's having further mental or physical deterioration but aid in the person's return to a substantially higher level of functioning.

This program may encompass health assessment and certain treatment services such as physical therapy or personal care (for example, bathing as well as counseling).

ANNOTATED BIBLIOGRAPHY

Cassel, J. 1976. The contribution of the social environment to host resistance. *Am. J. Epidemiol.* 104:107-123.
John Cassel has contributed greatly to the field of epidemiology and primary care through his studies of the need for social supports for families as they face major life changes. This article summarizes the research; it places emphasis on the need to improve the social supports rather than attempting to reduce the exposure to stressors.

Parker, A. W. *The team approach to primary health care.* 1972. Berkeley: University of California Extension. This monograph sets forth a conceptual model for the primary health care team. While written essentially for the neighborhood setting, it has wide application to the office setting.

Sussman, M. B. 1977. What every principal should know about families: An immodest proposal. *National Elementary Principal.* 55:35. Reprinted in M.B. Sussman. 1977. Family. In *Encyclopedia of Social Work.* Vol. 1, pp. 329-340 Washington, D.C.: National Association of Social Workers.
The *Encyclopedia of Social Work* is the seventeenth edition of a two-volume series containing information about the professional practice of social work as well as the social problems and welfare institutions of our day, plus information of the wider social, political, economic health, and environmental issues. Every office could profit by having current volumes.

13 Health Promotion in Primary Care for Children

Martin T. Stein

Dr. Stein is a graduate of the University of California, Irvine, School of Medicine, and is on the faculty of the University of California, San Diego, School of Medicine, where he is Director of the Division of Ambulatory Care at University Hospital. His background includes experience with innovative health care development in low-income community settings. An active clinical teacher, he has published various studies in the area of preventive pediatric health care.

Brief Contents

Overview

The major attainable goal for preventive pediatric practice is to promote the optimal state of physical, developmental, and psychosocial well-being during infancy, childhood, and adolescence. Through a knowledge of normal developmental changes in children and a rational schedule of pediatric visits, providers of primary care to children can both monitor and encourage the early progression of lifelong health.

THE CHANGING ROLE OF PRIMARY PEDIATRIC CARE

Immunization against bacterial and viral illnesses; improvements in housing, education, and hygiene; the widespread use of antibacterial drugs—these advances in developed countries have reduced the incidence of serious and often catastrophic infectious diseases that once consumed pediatricians' time. Although pediatricians have always been concerned with issues of growth and development, up to the beginning of the twentieth century their practices were filled by patients with fulminant pneumonia, diarrhea and dehydration, paralytic polio, pertussis, and complications of common viral exanthem illnesses.

Modern technologic and socioeconomic advances have brought about a shift in pediatric care from primary disease management to early detection and prevention. Today the emphasis is on the physiologic and developmental factors that maximize a child's health, function, and sense of well-being.

Preventive pediatrics is practiced primarily in the office setting. However, optimal health promotion extends beyond the traditional well-child visit to a recognition of the important interplay between the child's family and community. Primary health care practitioners should evaluate children and their families, not only according to their vulnerabilities and illnesses (the traditional model) but also according to their strengths and resources. This expanded model yields a potentially more comprehensive perspective on preventive health services.

Primary care practitioners should evaluate children and families both by their vulnerabilities and by their strengths.

OFFICE-BASED PREVENTION

Office-based preventive pediatric care encompasses four major areas: biologic, developmental, psychosocial, and environmental.

Biologic Preventive Care

Table 13-1

Table 13-1 summarizes the important steps in biologic preventive care including immunizations, screening procedures, physical examinations, and health counseling.

Immunization Immunization against polio, diphtheria, pertussis, tetanus, measles (rubeola), rubella, and mumps at regular intervals is the most effective and most elegant form of primary disease prevention currently available to physicians. Standard immunization schedules have been developed to ensure maximum protective antibody levels. Primary care practitioners should try to help parents understand the importance of beginning immunizations in early infancy as well as completing the schedule of vaccinations. Providing parents with a wallet-sized immunization record and making sure that all children who have missed immunization visits are recalled will prevent the overlooked "immunization orphan." Surveys show that most communities average no better than a 70% level of optimal immunization among children entering school. The afebrile children with mild respiratory symptoms will develop adequate antibodies to the immunizing agents; hence mild symptoms of respiratory illness (the common cold without fever) is not a contraindication for immunization.

Mild symptoms of respiratory illness is not a contraindication for immunization.

Nutrition Beginning with the prenatal visit primary care practitioners should discuss nutritional needs at each well-child visit. At the prenatal talk they should also actively encourage breast feeding by emphasizing the immunologic and nutritional advantages of human milk compared to the modified cow's milk in infant formulas. Human milk contains all the water-soluble and fat-soluble vitamins in appropriate amounts; its protein content is more optimal both quantitatively and qualitatively; it assures a more efficient absorption of iron; it contains protective antibodies; and it is associated with a lower incidence of acute gastrointestinal disease. Preliminary evidence also suggests that breast feeding exclusively during the first 6 months of life prevents the full development of the IgE immune system and decreases the incidence and severity of asthma, allergic rhinitis, and eczema in infants with a significant atopic family history. Although more difficult to assess quantitatively, psychologic benefits may also occur through enhancement of maternal-infant bonding and attachment behavior in breast-fed babies.

Physicians should actively encourage breast feeding by emphasizing the immunologic and nutritional advantage of human milk; there may also be psychologic benefits.

The three major nutritional problems among children in the United States are obesity, iron deficiency anemia, and dental caries. Breast feeding without solid foods during the first 4-6 months of life may help to prevent obesity. Iron supplementation is not necessary with breast feeding during this time. After 6 months physicians should advise the mother to include iron-rich food such as iron-fortified baby cereal, green vegetables, meats, and eggs. A screening hematocrit or hemoglobin measurement at 9-10 months will monitor iron status; at this age anemia is defined

The three major nutritional problems among children in the United States are obesity, iron deficiency anemia, and dental caries.

Table 13-1 Pediatric Health Promotion Visits

Time	Emphasis	Procedures	Physical Examination (Age Specific Highlights)	Preventable Problems (Or Complications)
Prenatal	Family health Pregnancy Social and economical environment Development of physician-parents relationship Parents expectations for their new roles	Discussions: Breast feeding, bonding, rooming in, prepared childbirth, circumcision, care for newborn, car seat		
Newborn	Feeding Elimination Crying Infant temperament Normal reflexes Newborn care Breast feeding	Complete P.E. P.K.U. Thyroxine Silver nitrate eye drops (prevention of gonorrhea ophthalmia) Vitamin K (prevention of hemorrhagic disease of newborn)	Head (including head circumfer ence; fontanelle size and tension)	Microcephaly Craniosynostosis Hydrocephalus
			Length	Congenital dwarf Placental insufficiency
			Weight	Small or large for gestational age
			Dysmorphic facial features	Recognizable pattern of malformations (e.g., fetal alcohol syndrome or Down syndrome)
			Eyes	Cataract, coloboma strabismus, glaucoma
			Palate	Cleft palate
			Neck mass: mid-line	Goiter Thyroglossal duct cyst
			lateral	Embryonic cleft cyst
			Cardiac murmur (femoral pulses)	Congenital cardiac defect
			Cardial rate	Cardiac failure
			Abdominal mass	Hydronephrosis Wilm tumor Neuroblastoma Inguinal hernia Epigastric hernia
			Anus	Imperforate anus Anterior displacement of anus
			Back—spinal mass, dimple, hair tuft	Spine bifida Meningomyelocele Pilonidal sinus
			Hips	Congenital dislocated hip (Ortoloni maneuver—examine for hip click during flexion and abduction of hip
			Feet	Club foot

Newborn Continued			External genitalia	Ambiguous genitalia Cryptorchidism Hypospadia
			Skin	Jaundice Purulent pustules Vessicles Birth marks
			Neurological	Hypotonia Hypertonia Asymmetrical reflexes Hearing deficit Vision deficit
			Temperament	Difficult family adjustment Inappropriate caretaking and stimulation
7-10 Days	Lactation visit—for lactating mothers and infants. Provide emotional support and mechanical techniques to ensure continuous breast feeding			
2 or 3 Weeks	Same as newborn Bonding Soliciting parent concerns Colic (late day fussiness)	Complete P.E. (especially weight and head circumference) Fluoride		
2 Months	Emerging motor, visual, social and vocal skills Assess adaptation of family to infant Crying patterns Sleep patterns	Complete P.E. DPT (diphtheria-pertussis-tetanus) OPV (oral polio vaccine)		
4 Months	Nutrition (discuss pureed foods) Development Accident prevention Behaviors: tolerating delay, discriminatory smile	Complete P.E. DPT and OPV		
6 Months	As above Stranger awareness Emerging motor skills Sleep patterns	Complete P.E. DPT Syrup of ipecac		
9-10 Months	As above Language development Exploratory behavior Feeding changes: Wean, Cup, Finger foods, Decrease appetite Accident prevention Autonomy vs dependency	Complete P.E. Hematocrit (or hemoglobin) T.B. skin test		

Table 13-1 Continued

Time	Emphasis	Procedures	Physical Examination (Age Specific Highlights)	Preventable Problems (Or Complications)
15 Months	As above (especially autonomy vs dependency..."NO")	Complete P.E. (emphasis on observation of child's behavior) Measles-mumps-rubella vaccine	Head circumference	Microcephaly Hydrocephalus Craniosynostosis
			Length and weight	Failure to thrive Overnutrition
			Eyes	Strabismus Vision deficit Conjunctivitis
			Ears	Hearing deficit
			Caridac murmur	Developing left to right shunts (VSD, ASD, PDA)
			Cardiac rate	Pulmonary or cardiac disease
			Abdominal mass	(as in newborn)
			Hips	Congenital dislocation (may be missed as newborn)
			Feet	Metatarsus adductus Club foot
			Neurodevelopmental	See text
18 Months	Discussion and P.E. optional	DPT and OPV		
2 Years	Nutritional needs Growth Language Hearing Peer play Toilet training Dental care Nursery school			
3 Years	This visit is dependent on provider's interest and knowledge in assessing growth and development and providing parental counseling. Routine P.E. has a low yield and procedures are not required.	Explore with parents: ability to follow instructions, imaginary playmates, fantasy life, sexual curiosity, nightmares		

4-5 Years	Nutrition and growth Peer play Relations with parents School readiness Separation reactions Cognitive development Draw-a-person	Complete P.E. (include B.P.) Visual Acuity Audiogram Hematocrit (or hemoglobin) T.B. skin test (if high risk community) DPT and OPV	Height and weight Blood pressure Visual acuity Audiometry Teeth Eyes, nose and lungs Abdomen Neurodevelopmental	Failure to thrive Obesity Short stature Hypertension Refractive errors Hearing deficit Dental caries Allergies Inguinal hernia Cognitive deficit Visual-motor deficit Mild cerebral palsey Auditory perceptual deficit
7-8 Years	School achievements Peer and family relations Nutrition Psychosomatic problems Health attitudes Hobbies and teams Explore reality thinking (for example Santa Claus—fiction vs fact)	Complete P.E.	Height and weight Blood pressure Visual acuity Audiometry Teeth Backs Neurodevelopmental	As in pre-school As in pre-school As in pre-school As in pre-school As in pre-school Scoliosis (examine in upright plus hip flexion positions) (See text)
12 Years	Puberty—physical and emotional changes Health attitudes (exercise, diet, smoking, drugs, alcohol) Growth variability Parent and peer relations Questions about sex	Complete P.E. Visual acuity Hematocrit (or hemoglobin) Td (tetanus-diphtheria)	Height and weight Blood pressure Skin Teeth Back (girls especially) Genitalia Sexual maturity scale (Tanner Scale)	Obesity Hypertenstion Acne Dental caries Scoliosis Venereal disease Delayed puberty
Adolescence (two routine visits)	As above	Complete P.E.		

Table 13-2

as having a hematocrit less than 33% or hemoglobin less than 11 gm/100 ml (Table 13-2 indicates normal values in children). The incidence of iron deficiency anemia at 9 months of age is about 5% in middle-class infants as compared to 30%-50% in some lower socioeconomic communities. In formula-fed infants iron deficiency anemia can be prevented by using a standard infant formula that has been supplemented with 12-15 mg of elemental iron for each quart of formula.

Table 13-2 Anemia in Children*

Age	HgB < (gm/100 ml)	Hct < (%)
Birth	14	42
1-2 months	9	27
2-6 months	10	30
6 months to 4 years	11	33
More than 5 years	12	36

*Definition of Anemia: Two standard deviations below the mean hemoglobin or hematocrit for age.

Fluoride added to water or as a supplement to the child's diet has proved beneficial in preventing dental caries. Familiarity with the fluoride content of the community water supply (the local department of public health will supply this information) will dictate the need for supplementation (see Chapter 8, "Prevention in Dentistry").

It is important to monitor nutritional intake with a detailed dietary history (taken at intervals of 2-3 months in the first year of life) and to record weight and height of the child on standard growth grids. Evaluating obesity (weight exceeds height percentile) is as important as monitoring for growth failure. Height, weight, and head circumference measurements should be determined and plotted during each well-child visit.

Evaluating obesity is as important as monitoring for growth failure.

Specific guidelines for parents will encourage optimal nutritional intake for children as well as the early formation of sound nutritional habits. These guidelines include the following:

1. Omitting foods with a high sugar content; this helps to prevent obesity and dental caries.
2. Limiting excess salt in cooking and at the table; this helps prevent hypertension.

3. Offering nutritious snacks such as fruit, carrots, celery, and peanut butter; this limits excess cariogenic sugar and calories.
4. Offering nonprocessed foods such as whole-grain cereals and bread; this provides vitamins and minerals that might otherwise be lost through refinement.

The cornerstone of genetic screening is a careful family history.

Genetic Diseases Screening for genetic diseases is another biologic component of prevention in pediatric practice. The cornerstone of genetic screening is a careful family history. A family pedigree in the child's chart may prove useful as well. Significant advances have occurred in the detection of genetic diseases through biochemical screening of heterozygote carriers and amniocentesis for detection of metabolic and chromosomal diseases (see Chapter 3, "Genetic Counseling").

The most established biochemical screening procedure for genetic disease in infancy is a blood test for phenylketonuria (PKU) on all newborns. In the future an assay for galactosemia and maple syrup urine disease may be performed on the same blood sample sent for PKU. Although in most cases congenital hypothyroidism is not a genetic disease but rather an embryonic error in morphogenesis of the thyroid gland, many communities now screen all newborns for this disorder with a thyroxine determination (see Chapter 1, "Screening, Case Finding, and Prevention").

Physical Examination In pediatric practice the physical examination is the major means by which structural problems are detected. The goal of prevention-oriented primary care practitioners should be to detect physical abnormalities at the earliest possible moment to ensure effective intervention. For example, the diagnosis by physical examination of a congenitally dislocated hip at birth has a much better prognosis than if the diagnosis were made at 18 months when the toddler presented with a limp.

By 6 weeks about 80% of all congenital defects are detectable.

Although it is traditional to perform a complete examination during every well-child visit, the yield of positive findings in early childhood is low after the newborn examination. By 6 weeks about 80% of all congenital defects are detectable. Thus, although a brief periodic physical examination has some practical value, particularly in providing reassurance to parents and older children, a larger fraction of office time is better spent in the evaluation of developmental skills, the provision of anticipatory guidance, and counseling in areas of nutrition and accident prevention.

The location of the examination may vary with the child's age. Prior to 6 months, infants will tolerate examinations on the table.

Between 6 months and 3 years of age the young patients will cooperate best while sitting on their parent's lap.

Between 6 months and 3 years of age the young patients will cooperate best while sitting on their parent's lap. After 3 years (when stranger anxiety has been resolved), the examination table will no longer signify separation from parents. Physicians should allow adolescent patients privacy by examining them without a parent's being present. Table 13-1 lists important highlights of the physical examination by age. Emphasis has been placed on physical signs that are diagnostic of problems in which early intervention may prevent subsequent disability.

While performing physical examinations physicians should take the opportunity to educate and reassure parents and older children by informing them of their findings. This will tend to promote a dialogue between physician and patient (or parent), which promotes further questions and encourages improved communication about health matters in general.

Primary care practitioners should educate parents to recognize early those symptoms that may progress to serious illness.

Anticipatory Guidance As part of the biologic approach to preventive pediatrics primary care practitioners should educate parents to recognize early those symptoms that may progress to serious illness. Anticipatory guidance—teaching parents about various aspects of normal development and disease prevention—is especially necessary in the absence of support systems in the community and an extended family. It is wise for physicians to use the opportunity of episodic visits to educate parents about timely health issues and to teach them to recognize and manage early symptoms of gastrointestinal illness, upper respiratory infetions, elevated temperatures, constipation, and infant colic. For adolescent patients physicians might want to emphasize the medical consequences of smoking, alcohol, and drugs. Providing educational material in these areas will assist, but will not be a complete substitute for, personal involvement. More work needs to be done in patient education; in my experience audiovisual presentations in the waiting room have been successful.

Allergic disease is the most common chronic illness in childhood.

Preventive Allergy An often neglected area of biologic prevention is allergic disease—the most common chronic illness in childhood. The recognition of allergic diathasis in a wheezing child or a child with recurrent sneezing and runny, itchy eyes, or the child with eczema is relatively simple. However, atopic illness often takes two less obvious forms:

1. There is the child with a chronic nocturnal cough, a child who is experiencing bronchial spasms secondary to allergens in the bedroom; although the cough and bronchial spasm are usually absent during the daytime, a forced expiratory effort may induce the diagnostic wheeze during auscultation of the chest.

2. There is the child with frequent colds; a careful family history. the discovery of edematous pale nasal turbinates, and allergic "shiners" below both eyes may suggest the correct diagnosis—allergic rhinitis.

In both cases the physician may improve significantly the functioning capacity of these children with appropriate environmental elimination and pharmacologic agents (a bronchodilator or antihistamine).

Approximately 4% of all children experience a febrile convulsion.

Prevention of Simple Febrile Seizures Another relatively common, recurrent childhood problem with preventive implications is the simple febrile convulsion. Approximately 4% of all preschool children in a general practice will experience at least one generalized tonic clonic seizure accompanying a high temperature, usually in association with acute respiratory or gastrointestinal illness. Most initial seizures, which usually occur by the age of 2 years, are nonfocal, brief (less than 10 minutes), and show neither postictal paralysis nor seizure focus on the electroencephalogram. Without continuous phenobarbital therapy, one third of children with a single seizure will develop a recurrence. With daily phenobarbitol the recurrence risk is reduced from 33% to 3%. When phenobarbitol is used only in the presence of fever the recurrence rate remains 33%.

Whether one or more brief simple febrile seizure produces brain damage remains controversial. It is not known if daily phenobarbitol prophylaxis until the child reaches the age of 5 years (when simple febrile seizures no longer occur) is associated with adverse cognitive or behavioral effects on the developing brain.

Because of the limited knowledge about possible adverse effects of febrile convulsions and drug therapy, only tentative recommendations can be made for the child with one seizure.

With our limited knowledge about the potential adverse effects of simple febrile convulsions and drug therapy, one can only make tentative recommendations for a child with one simple febrile convulsion. Continuous daily therapy with phenobarbitol (5 mg/kg 24 hr) is indicated in the following situations: (a) a complex febrile seizure—that is, a focal seizure—a seizure whose duration is greater than 15 minutes (or seizures in series, with combined duration greater than 30 minutes), Todd's paralysis, or a seizure focus on the electroencephalogram; (b) a family history of epilepsy in parents or siblings; (c) abnormal neurologic examination or developmental delay at the time of the first seizure; (d) a history of perinatal asphyxia; and (e) occurrence of the initial seizure before 12 months of age.

In the child who has experienced two or more simple febrile seizures, continuous phenobarbitol therapy is also indicated. If recurrences should occur while the child is taking medication, a phenobarbitol level should be obtained to evaluate the possible need for altering the medication.

Developmental Preventive Care

The assessment of a child's development—the unfolding of skills according to a time-honored sequence that reflects a biologic maturation of the central nervous system and its response to environmental influences—is essential to preventive pediatric practice. The assumption behind periodic developmental assessment is that early detection of a developmental delay or deviation will allow for prompt remediation or at least partial amelioration of the disability. A developmental examination assesses the strengths as well as the weaknesses of the child—information that can be beneficial to parents and teachers. Although, strictly speaking, primary care providers assess the development of all organ systems, neurodevelopmental monitoring carries with it the highest yield in terms of either the discovery of a correctable problem or the reassurance arising from a normal examination.

The DDST provides an accurate and rapid screening method for certain skills.

An age-appropriate standard neurodevelopmental examination is an initial step in developmental assessment. The Denver Developmental Screening Test (DDST) has been devised as a rapid, accurate method of screening children from birth to 5 years of age in the four standard areas of skills: (a) fine motor, (b) gross motor, (c) social adaptive, and (d) language functions. The scoring sheet makes clear the wide age range at which different children reach specific milestones of development. The DDST has been standardized among various socioeconomic groups and some American ethnic minorities. It is not an intelligence test but rather a screening system for development. Scoring sheets and test equipment are readily available.

Simple tests of cognitive function are possible in the office.

Cognitive skills may be assessed in several ways. One is by asking preschool or school-age children to draw a person. This can be done in the waiting room or while the physician is taking the history. Starting with a baseline of 3 years, 3 months of "developmental age" is scored for each body part drawn. The developmental age can then be compared to the children's chronologic age. This test can also be expanded into a projective screening test of children's emotional life with respect to their family by asking them to draw a picture of the family. The results are often astounding, insightful, and at times embarrassing.

An alternative screening test for cognitive function makes use of children's emerging visual motor skills after the age of 3 years.

An alternative screening test for cognitive function makes use of children's emerging visual motor skills after the age of 3 years. At 3 years children should be able to copy a circle; at 4 years, a cross; at 5 years, a square; at 6 years, a triangle; and at 7 years, a diamond.

This simple office screening procedure is roughly correlated with intelligence. All these tests are designed to alert physicians to the children who may require further complete assessment. They can also be used to establish children's readiness for school around the age of 5 years.

In addition, physicians should try to determine children's ability to separate effectively from their parents and to play independently and cooperatively. Five-year-old children can be asked to carry out a series of tasks (for example, "Please walk to the door and open it; then return to your mother"). This will allow physicians to examine serial reception language function, an important component of successful learning.

Difficulty on any of these tests suggests the need for communication with school personnel as well as the possible need for further testing or special instruction.

Psychosocial Preventive Care

Primary care providers also should monitor psychologic maturation as a child moves from one stage of growth to another. The prevention of psychologic disabilities—for both the child and the family—requires the understanding of normal, age-appropriate psychologic stages and deviations from normal as well as preparing the parents to cope with stage-specific changes. Table 13-3 outlines the major psychologic issues at each age and the more common clinical manifestations of stress seen in children who are experiencing conflict at a particular stage. Consultation—both by phone and referral—with a child psychiatrist or psychologist can assist primary care practitioners in developing the clinical skills needed for recognition of developmental psychiatric disturbances and intervention for the less serious problems.

Table 13-3

The systematic and routine practice of "anticipatory guidance" will help parents to become familiar with normal developmental changes and prepare families for major shifts in children's behavior. The developmental tasks and setbacks, which are indicated in Table 13-3 and denoted by an asterisk, are suggested topics for discussion with parents prior to their predicted onsets. Many books written for parents are available to assist in understanding and coping with developmental conflicts. Physicians should become familiar with a few of them so that they can make appropriate recommendations for their patients. These books are included in the Annotated Bibliography; they are designated by asterisks.

Table 13-3 Psychologic Model of Child Development

	Infant (Birth to 12 months)	Toddler (1-3 years)	Preschool (4-5 years)	School Age (6-11 years)	Adolescent (> 12 years)
Goal (Erickson) (versus failure to achieve goal)	Basic trust (versus mistrust)	Autonomy (versus shame and doubt)	Initiative (versus guilt)	Industry (versus inferiority)	Identity (versus role confusion)
Psychologic dynamic	Symbiosis (attachment between parents and infant)	Separation-individuation (gradual movement away from psychologic bond with parents to sense of own self)	Ego Development (advanced stage of independence through self-initiated play and fantasy)	Superego development (moral development through peer relations and loosening of parental bond)	Separation from family and development of self identity
Developmental tasks	*Feeding (nutritional and psychologic components) Parent-infant bonding Visual and auditory attentiveness *Feeling of safety *Stranger Awareness (~ 8 mos)	*Locomotion (motor skills) *Language *Play (parallel) *Bowel and bladder control	*Play (interactive) *Fantasy (imaginary friends) *Body exploration Language and cognitive development *Identification with parents	*Peer attachments *Lossening of ties to to parents *Learning rules Cognitive development	Pubertal changes (physical and emotional) Sexual identification *Sexuality *Separation from family *Experimentation (group pressure versus family)
Developmental setbacks	Feeding problems -Regurgitation -Vomiting -Failure to thrive *Infant colic Psychosocial deprivation syndrome *Sleep-awake cycles	*Temper tantrums *Poisoning *Bowel dysfunction *Feeding disturbances Language delay Overprotectiveness versus permissiveness *Birth of new sibling *Parental illness	*Discipline Sleep disturbances Constipation Enuresis Parent conflicts	Learning disorders -Attention disorder -School failure Psychosomatic complaints -Abdominal pain -Headache -Enuresis -Encopresis -Constipation	School failure Peer rejection Acting-out behavior

*Topics especially suitable for discussion with parents prior to expected onset.

Environmental Preventive Care

Accidents are the major cause of childhood mortality and morbidity after the neonatal period.

Between birth and 15 years of age, more children die from accidents than from the next six leading causes of death.

Health is closely related to environment (see also Chapter 6, "Environmental and Occupational Health"). From a pediatric perspective, environmental health means preventing accidents, decreasing home health hazards, and in general maximizing parents' ability to provide a safe surrounding for children's growth. Accidents are the major cause of childhood mortality and morbidity after the neonatal period. Auto accidents, poisoning, trauma, drownings, and burns account for most accidents in childhood. Their occurrence is a result of the interaction among susceptible children, dangerous environments, and often a temporary instability in family environments. Between birth and 15 years of age, more children die from accidents than from the next six leading causes of death for this age group.

Physicians should make parents aware of the potential for accidental poisonings when dispensing prescriptions.

Poison Prevention Although significant decreases in certain childhood poisoning have occurred as a result of legislative intervention (for example, safety caps on potentially poisonous drugs), educating parents remains an important means of decreasing specific environmental risk factors. Physicians should make parents aware of the potential for accidental poisonings when dispensing prescriptions. Physicians should encourage the safe storage of medicines and household cleaning products. When infants begin to explore their environment with increasing curiosity (and increasing motor skills and hand-to-mouth activity) by the end of the first year, they are extremely vulnerable to accidental poisoning. A 30 ml bottle of syrup of ipecac should be provided for parents to keep at home in order to induce vomiting in case of accidental poisoning.*

Some parents might be more likely to use car seats if they were persuaded that car restraints discourage troublesome behavior.

Auto Accidents Almost half of the accidental deaths between birth and 15 years of age are due to auto accidents. Serious morbidity and mortality can be reduced by the proper use of car seats for children under 4 years; older children should use properly installed seat and lap belts. During the prenatal discussion with parents physicians should suggest that they buy an infant car seat so that newborn infants will ride home safely from the hospital. Some parents might be more likely to use car seats if they were persuaded that car restraints discourage troublesome behavior.

---

*Dose: 15 ml (1 tablespoon) with water and ambulation. Repeat in 20 minutes if vomiting does not occur. Contraindicated in caustic and hydrocarbon ingestions, coma, and seizures; therefore, physicians should advise parents to call their office, an emergency room, or a poison information center for instruction in the appropriate use of syrup of ipecac.

Drowning Childhood drownings (and the more common near-drownings) are a result of temporary neglect in supervision coupled with a high-risk environment. Home and apartment pools should be fenced in completely. Small children should never be left unsupervised in the bathtub. Parents should know how to perform cardiopulmonary resuscitation. Primary care providers can play an important role in all these matters as a routine part of health care supervision through discussions and the provision of appropriate literature.

Television Television has assumed a major role in the education of children around the world. The commercial airways broadcast violence, encourage the consumption of nutritionally limited foods—and occasionally provide worthwhile educational material. Physicians should encourage parents to place limitations on television watching at home and also to discuss the various dramatic themes and commercial messages with their children in thoughtful and challenging ways.

Advise parents to reduce the hot water temperature in their homes to 120 F.

Burns Serious scald burns in children occur more often when very high water temperatures are maintained at home. Reducing water temperatures in hot water heaters to 120 F will prevent full-thickness burns and at the same time permit comfortable bathing.

Other Hazards Each environment has its own particular hazards. For example, children in urban ghettos should be screened for evidence of lead poisoning, and in the children of agricultural workers insecticide exposure should be considered.

Practice Strategies for Prevention

Prevention requires the education of parents as well as the involvement of primary health care providers. Physicians should seek to understand the parents' goals and expectations for their children. Some problems (such as illnesses preventable by immunization or laboratory screening) require planned office visits and active intervention by the practitioner. The American Academy of Pediatrics has revised its recommended schedule for health supervision many times; a single model is not applicable to all practice settings.

At a minimum, health supervision visits should be scheduled at the time of each recommended immunization.

At a minimum, health supervision visits should be scheduled at the time of each recommended immunization. When other objectives are to be achieved additional visits can be scheduled. Table 13-1 lists a schedule that is effective in achieving the goals set forth in this chapter.

An excellent way to help primary care practitioners follow the ongoing health promotion of children is the checklist developed

Figure 13-1

Practitioners should be alert to signs of stresses that may indicate abuse or neglect.

by Dorothy Johnson, M.D., and Barbara Jones, R.N., P.N.P., which has been successfully used in several pediatric clinics (Figure 13-1). Not only should primary care practitioners provide routine preventive monitoring and intervention, but it is of critical importance that they identify children and families who are at high risk for both biologic illnesses and psychosocial stresses. Achieving optimal growth and development in children requires effective parenting as well as a supportive physical and social environment. Practitioners should be alert to signs of stresses that may indicate abuse or neglect. Such vulnerable children and families may provide clinical clues such as the following:

Child:
- Apathy or hyperactivity
- Poor hygiene (especially in infants)
- Language delay
- Delay in psychomotor development
- Physical signs of abuse
- Failure to thrive
- Absence of stranger anxiety (end of first year)
- Poor nursery and early school adaptation

Parent:
- Delivery room observation of maternal-infant interactions—lack of visual, tactile, or auditory contact when newborn is given to mother may be predictive of subsequent abuse or neglect
- Family stress—illness, employment, economic, and marital conflicts
- Unusual approach to child (tactile, visual, and auditory): for example, parent withdraws from examination table during child's examination; parent feeds baby by bottle without skin-to-skin contact; parent does not talk to infant or child
- Frequently missed appointments
- Poor compliance with therapy

These vulnerable children and families may require more frequent office visits for supportive care as well as referrals to appropriate counselors.

Numerous special techniques have been promoted for enhancing practitioners' preventive role in primary pediatric care. Many practitioners rely routinely on written material given to parents at designated time periods in children's lives. This practice could be counterproductive if too much information were given at one

Source	Request Date	Patient Identification

Age	DEVELOPMENTAL TASKS S = Social Fm = Fine Motor L = Language M = Gross Motor	White Bars = Age during which 75-100% of children accomplish task per Denver Devel.* Check Age in which task accomplished 0 4w 8w 4m 6m 8m 10m 12m	ANTICIPATORY GUIDANCE Sa = Safety Fd = Feeding Sx = Symptomatic R_x Fl = Feeling Check if Discussed	PROCE-DURES Circle If Done
2 to 4 wks	S Cuddles* Fm Follows to midline Equal movements L Responds to sound M Moro* Primitive step* Neck/elbow flexor tone* Palmar grasp*		Sa Car restraints Bathing Bedding Fd Breast feeding Preparation of formula Propping, burping Volume expectations Sx Nasal hygiene Skin care Fl Parents & siblings	Hgt Wgt HC PKU Fluoride (see text)
6 to 8 wks	S Smiles Fm Palmar grasp fades* L Listens to bell M Lifts head (prone)		Sa Falls (rolls over) Car restraints Bathing Fire retardent clothing Small objects out of reach Fd Formula or breast Future solids Sx Thermometer use Fl Sleep	Hgt Wgt Hc DPT-1 OPV-1
3 to 4 mos	S Smiles spontaneously Fm Hands together Follows 180° L Squeals, laughs, babbles M Rolls over Head steady, sitting		Sa Crawling: objects out of reach stairway "gate" Risks of walkers, jumpers Fd Review solids Spoon Formula or breast Sx Diarrhea Fl Behavior expectations	Hgt Wgt HC DPT-2 OPV-2
5 to 6 mos	S Smiles at mirror* Fm Grasps rattle Reaches for object L Coos* M Prone holds chest up		Sa Review crawling: objects, electric outlets, floor heaters Food aspiration (beans) Fd Milk Food selection Feeding techniques Sx URI Review Fl Stimulation-consistency	Hgt Wgt HC DPT-3
7 to 8 mos	S Feeds self crackers Fm Raking grasp Cube hand to hand L Turns to voice M Sits Bears some weight		Sa Review Fd Review Sx Ear Infection Fl Separation anxiety	Hgt Wgt HC Optional Visit
9 to 10 mos	S Bye-bye* Peek-a-boo Fm Thumb-finger grasp Looks for hidden object* L Mama-Dada, non-specific Imitates speech sounds M Stands holding on		Sa Review poisons (Ipecac) Fd Finger feeding Weaning Feeding techniques Sx Dental hygiene Fl Experimentation, separation Exploration	Hgt Wgt HC Hct or Hgb TB skin test Ipecac
15 mos	S Kiss* Interactive games* Pat-a-cake Fm Bangs 2 cubes L Mama-Dada, specific M Walk with help Stand alone momentarily		Sa Streets Climbing (poisons, falls, windows) Fd Decreased appetite Eating habits Sx Vomiting Review Fl Independence testing Consistent limits	Hgt Wgt HC MMR (≥ 15 mo.)

*denotes items which are not included in Denver Devel. data

Figure 13-1 Well-Child Care Checklist. Johnson, D., and Jones, B. L. 1980. The well-child care check sheet: An aid in office implementation of preventive pediatric care. *Clin. Pediat.* 19:290-92.

Age	DEVELOPMENTAL TASKS S = Social Fm = Fine Motor L = Language M = Gross Motor	White Bars = Age during which 75-100% of Children accomplish task per Denver Devel. (*) Check Age in which task accomplished 12m	18m	2y	2½y	3y	4y	5y	6y	ANTICIPATORY GUIDANCE Sa = Safety Fd = Feeding Sx = Symptomatic R_x Fl = Feeling Check if Discussed	PROCE-DURES Circle If Done
18 mos	S Drinks from cup Plays ball Uses spoon Fm Scribbles spontaneously Tower 2 cubes L 3 words (other than Mama) Jargon* M Walks well Crawls up steps* Stoops and recovers*									Sa Car restraint Window screens Running into danger Scalds Fd Complete weaning Appetite slump Sx Mouth-to-mouth resuscitation Fl Imitation of adults Tantrums Strong preferences	Hgt Wgt HC DPT-4 OPV-3
2 yrs	S Imitates* Helps with simple tasks Removes clothing Fm Tower 4 cubes Dumps raisin from bottle spontaneously L Follows directions Combines 2 words Names body parts M Kicks ball Walks up steps Throws overhand									Sa Water safety Matches Sharp or electric objects Fd Proper snacks Sx Toilet training Fl "No" Bedtime rituals Night terrors	Hgt Wgt HC TB skin test**
2½ yrs	S Wash/dry hands Fm Tower 8 cubes Vertical line (within 30°) Bowel/bladder control L Name 1 picture M Jumps Runs*									Sa Sibling torment Car restraint Play, supervision Fd Good eating habits Sx Constipation Fl Discipline: Explanation & consistency Need for play with peers	Hgt Wgt HC Optional visit
3 yrs	S Puts on clothing Plays tag Imaginery friend* Fm Copies O L Plurals First Name* M Balance 1 foot 1 second Broad jump Pedals tricycle									Sa Teach child play safety: throwing sharp objects following ball into street Fd Small portions of food Sx URI-Viral Infections Fl Decision making within limits Explaining "rules" Curiosity	Hgt Wgt BP TB skin test** Vision Hearing
4 yrs	S Separates easily from mother Dresses with help Fm Buttons up Picks longer line Draw + L Comprehends cold, tired, hungry (2 or 3) Comprehends prepositions Recognizes colors (3 of 4) Knows full name M Hops on 1 foot									Sa Supervised use of scissors, pencils Street crossing Water safety Fd Table manners Sx Nightmares Fl Genital exploration Imaginative play and fears	Hgt Wgt BP TB skin test**
5 yrs	S Dramatic play* Dresses alone Fm Draw man, 3-6 parts Copies a square (demonstr.) L Opposites (2 or 3) Hot__ Woman__ Big__ M Catches bounced ball Balances well Heel to toe walk									Sa Teaching "outdoors alone" safety: Travel to school Neighborhood play Fd Teaching food selection Sx Check regarding: eneuresls school phobia tummy aches Fl Teaching respect for feelings and property of others Home responsibility	Hgt Wgt BP Hct UA DPT-5 OPV-4 TB skin test** Vision Hearing
6 yrs	S Shares with peers* Knows street address* Knows parents' names* Fm Draw man, 6 parts Copies triangle* L Defines (6 out of 9) Ball__ Beach__ Desk__ House__ Banana__ Window__ Ceiling__ Fence__ Sidewalk__ Composition 3 of 3: Spoon__ Shoe__ Door__ M Backward heal-toe walk Skips Passes all 5 year items*									Review 5 year items	School form Hgt Wgt BP TB skin test** Immunization Update

*denotes items which are not included in Denver Devel. data
**TB Skin Test Recommended Annually in Communities with a High Rate of New Cases.

time. As an alternative physicians can offer brief, well-written statements about age-appropriate subjects at specific time periods. Also they may direct the clinic nursing staff and other health care workers to complement written material by engaging the family in discussion.

Group sessions for specific diseases have been successful; they may also serve for well-child care.

Group discussions for parents (and older children) with specific diseases have been successful in many practices. Recently the group model has been suggested as a basis for a well-child care system. It has been traditional to carry out the activities of well-child care (interviewing, examination, counseling, and procedures) in a small room with child, parent, and physician; the well-child care group model allows for all these activities to take place in a small group setting over a 1½-hour period. Five to six parent-infant pairs can be in large room at the time of the designated well-child visits. The first period of time can be devoted to a group discussion about developmental and preventive issues. During the second part physicians can perform examinations that are appropriate in the group setting. It is desirable to keep the same members of the group constant for at least the first year of the child's life.

The group well-child care setting is based on the premise that parents with infants have shared experiences with common problems, stresses, and joys. Learning about parenting in a group setting allows many parents to ask more questions, encourages openness of feelings, and sets the stage for information exchange about preventive issues that may otherwise not surface in the traditional setting. Primary health practitioners act both as knowledgeable professionals and as facilitators for the group. This model can be adapted to many different forms of practice.

Other practitioners have made use of audiovisual aids to convey information to parents and older children. Areas of preventive well-child care for which variations of this technique have been used include nutrition, home safety, first aid, poison prevention, car seats, developmental milestones, instructions to parents of newborns, and many others. That information conveyed by the office-based audiovisual method is understood and retained by parents has been documented in a program designed to educate parents in infant nutrition during the waiting period in a primary care clinic.

ANNOTATED BIBLIOGRAPHY

Anderson, F. P. 1979. Evaluation of routine physical examination of infants in the first year of life. *Pediatrics* 45:950-960.

This is a practical clinical study that demonstrates that most congenital physical abnormalities are detectable by routine physical examination during early infancy.

Bailey, E. N.; Kiehl, S.; Akram, D. S., et al. Screening in pediatric practice. *Pediatr. Clin. North. Am.* 21:123-165.
This article represents the most comprehensive review of pediatric screening practices available to the primary care physician. It is well documented with practical, cost-effective suggestions for clinic and office practice.

This article represents the most comprehensive review of pediatric screening practices.

*Boston Woman's Health Collective. 1978. *Ourselves and our children: A book by and for parents.* New York: Random House, Inc.
A provocative series of essays for parents who strive for the optimal development of their children while maintaining their own sense of self.

*Brazelton, T. B.. 1969. *Infant and mothers.* New York: Delacorte Press.
A journey for parents (and clinicians) through the stages of early child development written by an experienced pediatrician and teacher.

Erickson, E. H. 1963. *Childhood and society.* 2nd ed. New York: W. W. Norton & Company, Inc.
This is Erickson's now classic monograph that provides a model for child and adult human psychological development.

Fishman, M. A. 1979. Febrile seizures: The treatment controversy. *J. Pediatr.* 94:177-184.
This is an excellent review of available data that can assist the primary care physician in the development of a preventive approach to the child with simple febrile seizures.

*Frailberg, S. 1959. *The magic years.* New York: Charles Scribner's Sons.
Well written and stimulating. Child psychiatrist Fraiberg discusses early psychological development as if the reader were experiencing the child's inner world.

Fulginiti, V. A. 1976. Immunization practice: Some important guidelines. *Postgrad. Med.* 60:62-69.
Dr. Fulginiti provides a practical approach to some of the problems encountered in routine immunization in office practice.

*Gordon, T. 1970. *P.E.T.: Parent effectiveness training*, New York: American Library.

*Books written for parents to assist in understanding and coping with development conflicts.

A manual for parents who want to improve their communication skills with the verbal child; Gordon teaches communication of feelings as well as content of feelings.

Green, M., and Haggerty, F. J. 1977. *Ambulatory pediatrics II*, Philadelphia: W. B. Saunders Company.
This is a well-organized, reference book on both the theory and practice of pediatrics in an ambulatory setting. Included are chapters on setting up an office practice, working with schools and community agencies, a model for comprehensive child health, specific clinical problems in outpatient pediatric practice.

Illingsworth, R. S. 1972. *The normal child.* 5th ed. London: Churchill.

————. 1974. *The development of the infant and young child: Normal and abnormal.* London: Churchill Livingstone.
Both of these books provide the general practitioner of child care with clinical wisdom and practical points in managing medical and developmental problems of children.

This article provides an excellent review on modern nutritional concepts in early infant feeding.

Jelliffe, D. B., and Jelliffe, E. F. P. 1977. Current concepts in nutrition: "Breast is best." *N. Engl. J. Med.* 297:912-915.
This article provides an excellent review on modern nutritional concepts in early infant feeding.

*Levine, J. A. 1976. *Who will raise the children: New options for fathers (and mothers).* Philadelphia: J. B. Lippincott Company.
A father discusses new role definitions for fathers and mothers in raising children.

Metz, J. R.; Allen, C. M.; Barr, G., et al. 1976. A pediatric screening examination for psychosocial problems. *Pediatrics* 58:595-606.

A list of questions is described that allows easy evaluation of psychosocial stress.

These authors provide a list of questions that can be used routinely in an outpatient practice in order to evaluate areas of psychosocial stress in children.

Newkirk, G.; Stein, M.; and Bass, R. 1979. The use of the ambulatory setting for patient self-education. *J. Med. Educ.* 54:592-593.
This study demonstrates the effectiveness of an audiovisual presentation on infant nutrition provided to mothers during the waiting period in a pediatric practice. Evaluation of this method is outlined in the article.

*Pantell, R.; Fries, J. F.; and Vickery, D. M. 1977. *Taking care of your child: A parent's guide to medical care.* Reading, Mass.: Addison-Wesley Publishing Company Inc.
Pediatrician Pantell and his colleagues outline many aspects of health promotion and illness diagnosis-management for parents; the format is lucid and practical.

*Spock, B. 1976. *Baby and child care.* New York: Simon and Schuster.
Dr. Spock's now classic encyclopedia for parents on the early recognition and appropriate management of common and uncommon physical and emotional problems. Based on principles of normal development, it remains the best reference for parents.

Stein, M. 1977. The providing of well-baby care within parent-infant groups. *Clin. Pediatr.* 16:825-828.
The provision of well-baby care by means of parent-infant groups is a unique way to practice comprehensive preventative pediatrics. The article provides specific methods in the development and implementation of the group well-child care model.

14 Preventive Health Care in the Adult

Lawrence J. Schneiderman

Dr. Schneiderman is a graduate of Harvard Medical School and served on the faculty of Stanford Medical School prior to moving to the University of California, San Diego, School of Medicine, where he began the Family Medicine program. He is board certified in Internal Medicine and Family Practice and has almost 20 years' experience in patient care, teaching, and research in the area of primary care.

Brief Contents

Overview

Despite dramatic advances over the last several decades, the overall impact of medical technology on the health and longevity of American adults has been small. In contrast, the most simple—and inexpensive—acts such as eliminating the deleterious effects of smoking, alcohol, poor nutrition, and other habits appear to be profoundly effective. Health maintenance, combining biologic (examinations, tests, procedures, and medication) and behavioral (counseling, psychologic support, and education) approaches, enables primary care providers to form an effective partnership with their patients. Periodic contacts according to age and risk are recommended.

THE PREVENTION MOVEMENT IN ADULT HEALTH CARE

Prevention in adult health care gained great impetus in the 1950s when the association between smoking and lung cancer was established. Modifying behavior (avoidance or cessation of smoking) was shown to convey striking health benefits. About the same time, epidemiologic studies conducted in Framingham, Massachusetts, established the increased risk of heart disease in persons with hypercholesterolemia and hypertension. Although a causal relationship was not proved, these discoveries aroused public interest and led to active campaigns to alter diet. Many states well before this time had mandated screening for syphilis, with its obvious behavioral implications; yet campaigns for prevention have never reached as much of the public as the current campaigns to prevent heart disease have. (More recently in the Republic of China they did.)

OFFICE-BASED PREVENTION

In this chapter the goals and practice of office-based prevention will be reviewed along a pathway analogous to that presented in the previous chapter. Some of the material repeats that which has been presented in greater depth in earlier chapters. The intent is to provide the reader with a general approach to the application of this information.

Physicians can seek to achieve biologic health maintenance through such techniques as careful medical history, hypertension evaluation, mammography, immunization, hormone replacement, and nutrition; and bring about behavioral health maintenance through sensitive counseling regarding such factors as sex, contraception, alcohol, drugs, smoking, retirement, aging, and terminal illness.

Medical schools put great effort into persuading physicians about the value of a good history (personal, family, and social) and a physical examination. These can be useful guides toward screening tests and therapeutic and preventive interventions that provide biologic health maintenance. Physicians can do much more than is generally appreciated, however, in "life counseling" (that is, reaching areas outside the traditional areas taught in the medical school curriculum). Physicians should tread carefully, of course, and maintain respect for the patients' own values. However, it is reasonable to proceed on the assumption that people generally prefer knowledge to ignorance and will welcome health care providers as educators. Patients are usually very responsive to and respectful of the physicians' expression of interest in them as persons rather than as receptacles of interesting diseases. When exploring value-laden territory physicians should try to employ an approach that invites discussion rather than issues directives.

Those persons 65 years and older comprise 10% of the United States population; they occupy 30% of acute hospital beds and 90% of long-term care beds.

Elderly persons have an inescapably intimate relationship with the health care system. As people age they pay more visits to physicians, are more frequently hospitalized, and have more lengthy stays. Those over the age of 65 years comprise about 10% of the population. They occupy 30% of acute hospital beds and 90% of long-term care beds. About one fourth of the federal budget is now devoted to the various needs of the elderly, including health care services. It is estimated that these expenditures will double and even triple over the next several decades if we do no more than continue present (and generally inadequate) health policies. Thus any benefits that preventive health care can achieve in older adults will have enormous impact as this group continues to increase.

Biologic Preventive Care

Influenza daths and pneumoccal disease occur predominantly in older persons, particularly in those aged 65 years and older.

Immunization As noted in Chapter 4, influenza deaths and pneumoccal disease occur predominantly in older persons, particularly in those aged 65 years and older. Thus pneumococcal immunization and annual influenza immunization are recommended in all such persons or those with chronic pulmonary disease, chronic renal disease, diabetes, and heart disease; or patients with altered immune states such as those with lymphoproliferative disorders; or patients on immunosuppressive therapy. Tetanus toxoid (Td) is recommended every 10 years. In the presence of a possibly contaminated wound, a booster dose should be given if the interval following the last injection was greater than 5 years.

In early and middle adulthood the most serious nutritional problem is obesity.

Nutrition As persons grow older their activities tend to decline out of proportion to their dietary intake, so that in early and middle adulthood the most serious nutritional problem is obesity. In the more advanced ages, patients begin to suffer from additional dietary deficiencies, particularly in protein, the B vitamins, vitamins C and D, calcium, and iron. As teeth deteriorate, alimentary tract blood flow declines, and gastric acid and intestinal enzyme activity (for example, lactase) diminish, elderly people have more difficulty digesting meat, milk, and fibrous vegetables. These are important sources of protein, iron, calcium, and vitamin D. Physicians should encourage whole-grain bread and cereals, fruits, and reduced amounts of concentrated sweets and fats. If patients cannot chew raw fruits and vegetables, fresh juices can be made from them. Elderly patients may also find digestion enhanced when smaller amounts of food are taken at more frequent intervals and may also be helped by supplementary HCL and digestive enzymes (See Chapter 11, "Prevention and Nutrition").

Elderly patients may also find digestion enhanced when smaller amounts of food are taken at more frequent intervals.

Medication

Hormone replacement The use of estrogens in postmenopausal women, because it appears to have both benefits and risks, must be highly individualized. Estrogens are effective in decreasing the frequency and severity of postmenopausal vasomotor symptoms (hot flashes and sweating) and in overcoming symptoms associated with atrophy of the vaginal epithelium. Evidence also suggests that estrogens protect against postmenopausal osteoporosis and associated bone fractures. Studies have failed to show any difference in the risk of breast cancer, heart disease, or emotional disease between estrogen users and nonusers. Estrogen therapy appears to have adverse consequences, however. Although still a matter of dispute, most studies have demonstrated an association between conjugated estrogen use and endometrial carcinoma. At the present time, therefore, conjugated estrogens cannot be advocated for their preventive value but only for their short-term therapeutic value. When indicated they should be given at the lowest effective dose for the shortest possible time in cyclic rather than continuous doses.

At the present time conjugated estrogens cannot be recommended for their preventive value.

Aspirin Four standard aspirin tablets (total daily dose of 1300 mg) seem to have benefits that extend beyond temporary pain relief. At least two large-scale trials have been carried out in this country and Canada that show that daily aspirin may slightly reduce the frequency of strokes or death in men having transient

Daily aspirin may slightly reduce the frequency of strokes or death in men having transient ischemic attacks.

ischemic attacks. An inexplicable finding is that there is no benefit to women. Similar studies exploring the possible value of aspirin in reduction of atherosclerotic heart disease mortality reveal slight but statistically insignificant benefits. Again the reduction was greater for men than for women.

Daily aspirin is recommended only for patients with symptomatic transient ischemic attacks.

Acetylsalicylic acid is known to inhibit platelet aggregation—which provides a possible mechanism of action. These studies raise the fascinating possibility that physicians someday may have sufficient evidence to prescribe this common (yet remarkable) drug not only as an analgesic but also as a preventive. At present it is suggested only for patients with symptomatic transient ischemic attacks (for whom surgery is not an alternative). Someday it (or a similar drug) may be recommended for all middle-aged and elderly patients. Hazards that must be taken into account include gastrointestinal toxicity and bleeding.

Drugs for Treatment of Hyperlipidemia Clinical trials of cholestyramine, clofibrate, and other lipid-lowering agents have been carried out to investigate their possible benefits in reducing morbidity and mortality from atherosclerotic cardiovascular disease. Although advocates exist (see Chapter 9), these studies have revealed substantial side effects and hazards (for example, gallstones with clofibrate), and have failed to show any benefits.

Physical Examination Chapter 1, "Screening, Case Finding, and Prevention," reviews the relative merits of diagnostic procedures used and advocated in screening. Up to about the age of 60 years, in the absence of any specific disease or condition that requires ongoing attention, patients can be advised to have medical checkups approximately every 5 years. After this age, depending of course on the state of health, the frequency of examinations should probably be increased to once a year. Each medical examination should include interval history and determination of weight, blood pressure, stool for occult blood, urinalysis, mammography, breast examination, and Pap smear. Additional tests including tuberculosis skin test (where disease prevalence is high), hematocrit and hemoglobin measurement (particularly in lower socioeconomic women), sigmoidoscopy, and serum thyroxin (T_4) measurement (in the older person) should also be done.

Up till age 60 years well patients can be advised to have medical checkups approximately every 5 years.

In special populations such as sexually "migratory" persons, screening for syphilis and gonorrhea may have some limited usefulness. Sickle cell screening in the black population and Tay-Sachs disease screening in the Ashkenazi Jewish population are examples of procedures confined to certain ethnic groups. For the pregnant woman detection of Rhesus (Rh)-type and rubella antibodies are indicated; amniocentesis, for women above the age of

35 years. In the overweight patient or the patient with a strong family history of heart disease, a serum cholesterol and blood glucose measurement might provide additional incentives—if they are needed—to help the patient pursue weight reduction. In the elderly patient, attention should be paid to vision, hearing, and dentition.

Behavioral Preventive Care

Major improvements in longevity can be achieved by changing certain health habits.

Despite remarkable advances in the technology of health care, the life span for a 45-year-old man between 1900 and the present has increased only 4 years. In contrast, improvement in longevity that is two to three times that can be demonstrated in those who follow such simple health habits as avoiding smoking, taking alcohol in moderation, eating breakfast and other meals regularly, controlling one's weight, participating in regular exercise, and sleeping between 6 and 8 hours a day.

Over the past several decades a massive research effort has gone into advancing our knowledge of the basic biologic processes and mechanisms of pathogenesis. This has led to the development of what has been called "crises care technology." Unfortunately, much less is known in the area of health behavior. It is ironic of course that so much less investment of effort and resources has been made toward discovering how to stop people from smoking (a high-yield, low-cost measure) than how lung cancer can be cured (a low-yield, high-cost measure).

Although some early approaches to behavioral modification are underway (see Chapter 10, "Smoking and Disease"), this area is very much in need of new insights and discoveries.

The risk of auto accident varies directly with the number of miles driven; the risk and severity of injury can be reduced with the simple expedient of using seat belts correctly.

Pregnancy is a greater health risk than any form of contraception. Yet delaying pregnancy not only subjects a woman to the hazards of whatever form of contraception is in use (for example, thromboembolic disease with birth control pills and endometrial infection with intrauterine devices) but it also increases the risk of breast cancer.

Breast cancer mortality probably could be reduced 20% if all women practiced regular self-examination; less than 20% do.

The consequences of breast cancer, on the other hand, are reduced by regular self-examination. Most women who practice regular breast self-examination discover their own cancer. The more frequently such self-examination is done, the more favorable the clinical stage is at surgery. It is estimated that overall breast cancer mortality could be reduced nearly 20% if all women undertook regular self-examination. Unfortunately, despite more than

20 years of promotion by the American Cancer Society, less than 20% of women do regular breast self-examinations.

Important benefits might be achieved if physicians would encourage their patients to prepare for the inevitable accompaniments to growing older (for example, life after retirement or after the loss of a spouse) and make an effort to help patients maintain interests and activities in the face of declining physical strength and vigor. Physicians should be mindful of the environmental setting of elderly patients. Discussions with elderly patients and persons involved in their care can direct attention to floor coverings, stair rails, night lights, canes, and walkers and thus do much to prevent one of the most common problems of the elderly—falls and other accidents at home.

In the following section are age-specific guidelines for prevention. Several such guidelines have been developed—the most noteworthy being the "Life-Time Health-Monitoring Program" of Breslow and Somers (1977). For those using the problem-oriented approach, screening procedures can be listed under health maintenance. To facilitate care primary health practitioners would be wise to develop or adopt the Adult Health Maintenance Checksheet in Figure 14-1. This can be inserted in the chart and referred to at the time of each medical check-up to assure that preventive services are being updated.

Figure 14-1

AGE-SPECIFIC RECOMMENDATIONS

Young Adults (17-35)

For patients with no specific problems one health care visit by the age of 25 years and every 5 years thereafter would suffice.

From a strictly medical point of view, this is one of the healthiest times in a person's life. The most common causes of death result not from disease but from acts of violence such as accidents and homicide. One health care visit by the age of 25 years would suffice to provide the basis for prevention. After that visits should be scheduled every 5 years.

A single urinalysis is a simple way to screen for diabetes and proteinuria; a skin test for tuberculosis should be considered if the patient is susceptible either by race or exposure; and a rubella titer should be obtained in the female (if it has not already been done).

In the sexually migratory person, physicians should consider screening for syphilis and gonorrhea and look for evidence of genital herpesvirus infection. A pelvic examination with the patient holding a mirror offers an ideal opportunity to teach the woman patient some basic anatomy (about which a surprising

Adult Health Maintenance Checksheet

			Source			Request Date				Patient Identification						
Age Groups	25-29	30-34	35-39	40-44	45-49	50-54	55-59	60-61	62-63	64-65	66-67	68-69	70-71	72-73	74-	75**
Complete History																
Physical Exam/Rectal																
Pelvic/Pap/Breast																
Complete Urinalysis																
CBC or HCT or Hb																
T_4																
Cholesterol																
RPR or VDRL or FTA																
PPD																
dT Booster q5-10yr																
Hematest																
Health Hazard Appraisal/BP																
q5yr until 50 then q year																
Sigmoidoscopy q2-3yr after*	50															
Mammography																
Counselling:																
Self Breast																
PMP Bleeding																
Smoking																
Alcohol																
Drugs																
Auto Accident/Seat Belts																
Depression/Suicide																
Cancer Signs																
Dental Hygeine																
Other																

*Recommended

**Yearly after 75-History, Physical, Lab Counselling, Suggested

Figure 14-1 Adult health maintenance flow sheet, which can be used to maintain ongoing record on preventive care.

A pelvic examination with the patient observing in a mirror offers an excellent teaching opportunity and encourages self-care.

number are ignorant) and may go a long way toward encouraging self-care. A Pap smear should be obtained; if it is negative and confirmed by at least one additional smear, then follow-up can be carried out during the regular 5-year check-ups (more frequently in the presence of herpesvirus, since this increases the risk of cervical cancer). The National Institutes of Health, in an effort to reconcile different organizational positions, currently recommends that 3 years be the longest interval between routine Pap screenings.

Although the risk of breast cancer is low in this age group, the first visit is a good time to teach the woman self-examination techniques and suggest that she perform it once a month between her periods. Arguments have been raised that teaching this procedure may do "psychic harm," but an underlying assumption of prevention is that knowledge is better than ignorance. Breast cancer is the commonest malignancy in women: it is responsible for one in eight deaths—an established fact that stands up against any speculative psychologic risk.

For the male in the 17-35 year age group, the risk of carcinoma of the testis peaks; male patients should be taught self-examination.

On the first visit the physician can begin perhaps the most important part of preventive health care education and counseling.

The first visit is also a good time to establish the patient's "ideal weight" (assuming that obesity has not already established itself). A blood pressure should be obtained and tetanus immunization status checked. In this age group physicians can begin perhaps the most important part of preventive health care—education and counseling. The following issues should be raised:

1. Are patients smoking? If so, are they aware of the consequences?
2. Are patients practicing birth control? If not, are they aware of the consequences? (The rise in teenage venereal disease and pregnancy indicates that a great deal of misinformation afflicts the "sexually sophisticated.")
3. Are patients knowledgeable about venereal disease?
4. Have patients thought out attitudes toward abortion?
5. Are patients in danger of abusing alcohol or drugs?
6. Do patients use seat belts when driving?
7. Are patients informed about nutrition?

To treat obesity physicians should consider referral to a weight reduction group and warn patients against fads and exploiters.

Weight reduction efforts are notoriously unsuccessful when practiced in physicians' offices; physicians should therefore consider a referral to a weight reduction group. At the same time they should warn patients about the innumerable diet fads and profitable ways that obesity is exploited. Physicians can point out that weight reduction is relatively easy for the short term, but to maintain normal weight requires a life-long commitment to a certain pattern of eating, exercise, and other habits. This is also the time to point out the relationship of diet and exercise to weight. Vigorously active persons (for example, young football players) should be advised that they can continue to consume the same number of calories only as long as they continue the same exercise schedule. Counseling patients to direct their energies to new and pleasurable physical activities along with a reasonable diet and regular weight observation can be of help.

If patients have a normal blood pressure and a family history that is not prominent for heart disease, hypertension, or stroke, there is no need to measure blood pressure any more frequently than every 5 years. Physicians can direct a question or two about salt intake, and if it seems excessively high, they can suggest that the patient use herbs and spices or try to appreciate the "natural" flavor of food. Salt reduction, although not clearly demonstrated to be of preventive value has been shown to be an effective way of reducing blood pressure.

Salt reduction, although not clearly demonstrated to be of preventive value has been shown to be an effective way of reducing blood pressure.

Any woman contemplating pregnancy should be cautioned on the potential risks to her offspring of smoking, unnecessary drugs, and excessive intake of alcohol and caffeine. Other areas that physicians can explore and for which they can offer counsel are study, work, career, sexual activity, marriage, and child rearing. In all these areas, if patients sense that physicians have a genuine interest in their future well-being, there is often a gratifying discussion with untold potential benefits.

Middle-aged Adults (36-65)

As men and women approach their "middle age," they confront a variety of psychologic, social, and hormonal changes that affect their state of health. Men begin to define themselves in terms of success or failure and accept with varying degrees of grace their declining physical vigor. Women enter menopause just about the time that their children are leaving home. In the over-50-year age group, 5% have hearing problems. Certain diseases such as atherosclerotic heart disease, breast cancer, diabetes, and colorectal cancer begin to make significant inroads. In addition to their physical debilitation, these diseases and their treatments have a profound emotional impact.

In the over-50-year age group, 5% have hearing problems.

For patients who have no obvious medical problems and who have maintained good health habits, a visit to the physician every 5 years is still sufficient.

For the middle-aged person with no specific problems, a health care examination every 5 years is still sufficient.

Medical examinations should emphasize detection of hypertension, overweight, and occult blood in the stool. A urinalysis is done to screen for diabetes and proteinuria. There is no value to obtaining chest x-ray examinations in patients whose history and physical examinations are negative.

Tonometry has been traditionally recommended in this age group. A positive family history should alert physicians to recommend that this examination be done by an optometrist or ophthalmologist. (If the patient wears glasses, more than likely intraocular pressure will already have been assessed.) It is still not clear of course that treatment prevents the development of glaucoma.

Physicians should advise patients to see their dentists at least annually for examination and prophylaxis (see Chapter 8, "Prevention in Dentistry"). Tetanus booster immunization should be done every 10 years.

Women should have a pelvic examination with Pap smear, and mammography. If they have had consistently normal Pap smears, a pelvic examination need not be done more often than every 5 years. Although ovarian cancer reaches its highest incidence by the early 60s, pelvic examinations unfortunately are of little value in preventing its consequences. The starting age and frequency of mammography are issues still under study. At this time the procedure is clearly indicated for women past their menopause or for those with masses or fibrocystic disease, a previous history of breast cancer, or a positive family history of cancer and fibrocystic disease.

Though mammography is still under study it is clearly indicated for women past menopause and for certain other indications.

Although testing for occult blood in the stool is plagued by a high false-positive and false-negative rate, it is easily incorporated in the general physical examination. If, on rectal exam, a positive test is obtained physicians can give their patients a few test slides to take home and return by mail.

The major aspects of counseling in this age group involve educating patients to recognize clues to serious illness, such as weight loss, fever, change in bowel habits, change in appetite, shortness of breath, and chronic cough. Physicians should continue to reinforce good health habits including nutrition, exercise, use of seat belts, avoidance of smoking, moderation in alcohol, and recognition of and coping with psychologic stresses. A positive family history or past history of depression or alcoholism should alert physicians to be on the lookout for these conditions. An effort should be made to ensure that good communication continues within families; and patients should be reminded of importance of vacations and periods of relaxation. Physicians will benefit their patients if they can provide time for discussion about retirement, attitudes about

A positive family history or past history of depression or alcoholism should alert physicians to be on the lookout for these conditions.

menopause, and feelings about work, spouse, sexual matters, and finances.

Although, as they age people tend to decrease their exercise, the current wave of jogging and other activities raises the opposite problem. Those who have led a sedentary existence for many years should be counseled to initiate a new activity program gradually. Regular stretching and exercise should be encouraged to enhance flexibility and a general sense of well-being. A general caution is to advise patients to take 1 month to reach peak exercise conditioning for every year of inactivity (see Chapter 5, "Prevention in Sports Injuries"). For men who are beginning to experience early signs of prostatic enlargement, it may be of benefit—although no studies have addressed this question—for physicians to remind them to urinate several times a day to allow for optimal bladder function and prevent the consequences of distention and urinary retention.

A general caution is to advise patients to take 1 month to reach peak exercise conditioning for every year of inactivity.

Older Adults (65 years and Older)

When patients show no prognostically ominous tests up to this time of life and maintain good health habits, periodic medical examination for prevention can be conducted every 1 or 2 years. A complete physical examination should include a blood pressure check, test of the stool for occult blood, urinalysis to check for diabetes and proteinuria, and, in women, a breast examination and mammogram. When previous Pap smears have been negative consistently up to this point in their life, women are unlikely to develop invasive cervical cancer. Hence the pelvic exam does not have to be continued as a routine screening procedure. In this age group the physician should look for problems with hearing (after the age of 70 years approximately 25% of patients have significant hearing problems), vision, joints, feet, and nutrition. A T_4 serum measurement is worthwhile in this age group, since thyroid disease is often clinically silent and may be one of the treatable causes of mental deterioration. Physicians should advise continuing annual dental care.

For patients 65 years and older who have no particular problems the frequency of health exams should be increased only to every 1-2 years.

In this age group the physician should look for problems with hearing, vision, joints, feet, and nutrition.

Immunization should be directed against influenza on an annual basis, against tetanus every 10 years, and once against pneumococcal disease.

Nutritional counseling and referral to a podiatrist should be considered if necessary. Again physicians should counsel patients to recognize early signs and symptoms of serious illness. A particular hazard of the elderly is hypothermia; electric blankets are a relatively cheap and effective preventive measure.

Discussions can continue to cover such topics as retirement, absence of children, loss of spouse, loss of companions, loss of function and mobility, loss and reduction in income, reduction in prestige and status, and preparation for death.

At this age early recognition of cancer does not offer the same advantage that it does to younger patients. On the other hand, if cancer is detected—and particularly if it is beyond cure—prevention takes the form of palliation and preparatory discussions with famlies, which can often reduce discomfort and emotional distress. If the subject is terminal care, usually it is wise to conduct these discussions with patients privately. At some point physicians can suggest that other members of the family be included, particularly if they will be involved in the care of the patient.

Some elderly patients will carry on a vigorous, intellectually exciting life to their last day. Such people should be encouraged and observed for whatever secrets they can offer, which in turn can be transmitted to other patients.

Patients who thrive beyond 75 years have already proved they know how to live; the burden now is on those who urge aggressive intervention.

If physicians have any strong views about intervening in the health care of elderly patients, they should reflect that patients who thrive beyond 75 years have already proved they know how to live. By this time the burden of proof is on physicians who advocate aggressive medical intervention. As sensitive observers and friendly counselors, however, physicians can continue to provide assistance in minimizing the discomfort of chronic illness, the distress of physical and mental deterioration, and the inevitability of death. In doing so, physicians should make use of other members of the health team as well as community resources when possible (see Chapter 12, "The Role of Associated Health Professionals and Community Resources"). Home care, Meals-on-Wheels, supervised boarding care, senior citizen activity programs —these all exist in many communities to help maintain the highest possible quality of life.

ANNOTATED BIBLIOGRAPHY

Aspirin Myocardial Infarction Study Research Group. 1980. A randomized controlled trial of aspirin in persons recovered from myocardial infarction. *J. A. M. A.* 243:661-669.
A multicenter, randomized double-blind and placebo-controlled trial that led to the conclusion that the benefits of aspirin versus the risk are not sufficient to recommend it for routine use in patients who have survived a myocardial infarction.

Belloc, N. B. 1973. Relationship of health practices and mortality. *Prev. Med.* 2:67-81.

Breslow, L., and Enstrom, J. D. 1980. Persistence of health habits and their relationship to mortality. *Prev. Med. 9:469-483.*

————————, and Breslow, L. 1972. Relationship of physical health status and health practices. *Prev. Med.* 1:409-421.
These three articles report the results of a large epidemiologic survey in California that shows the relationship of disability and mortality to health practices.

Breslow, L., and Somers, A. R. 1977. The lifetime health-monitoring program. *N. Engl. J. Med.* 296:601-698
An authoritative practical approach to periodic health maintenance based on age-associated risk factors.

An authoritative practical approach to periodic health maintenance based on age-associated risk factors.

Canadian Cooperative Study Group. 1978. A randomized trial of aspirin and sulfinpyrazone in threatened stroke. *N. Engl. J. Med.* 299:53-59.
A detailed report by the Canadian task force on the periodic health examination. This contains good discussion and extensive bibliography.

Elwood, P. C., and Sweetam, P. M. 1979. Aspirin and secondary mortality after myocardial infarction. *Lancet* 22-29:1313-1315.
A randomized prospective double-blind clinical trial that showed no statistically significant benefit of aspirin on mortality rate of men following a myocardial infarction.

Fields, W. S.; Lemack, N. A.; Frankowski, R. F., et al. 1977. Controlled trial of aspirin in cerebral ischemia. *Stroke.* 8:301-316.
A prospective double-blind controlled trial that demonstrates the protective effect of long-term aspirin in men with transient ischemic attacks.

Foster, R. S.; Lang, S. P.; Constanza, M. C., et al. 1978. Breast self-examination practices and breast-cancer stage. *N. Engl. J. Med.* 299:265-270.
A study of over 300 women with breast cancer that demonstrates a correlation between frequency of self-examination with favorable outcome.

Horsman, Al; Gallagher, J. C.; Simpson, M., et al. 1977. Prospective trial of oestrogen and calcium in postmenopausal women. *Br. Med. J.* 2:789-792.
A prospective trial comparing the effects of estrogen, calcium, and no treatment on bone loss—estrogen has a beneficial effect.

Hutchinson, T. A.; Polansky, S. M.; and Feinstein, A. R. 1979. Postmenopausal estrogens protect against fractures of hip and distal radius. *Lancet* 2:705-709.
A retrospective study that suggests that estrogen use may have a protective effect against postmenopausal osteoporosis and bone fractures.

A conceptual article that provides a framework for health and psychological counseling.

Medalie, J. H. 1979. The family life cycle and its implications for family practice. *J. Fam. Pract.* 9:47-56.
A conceptual article that provides a framework for health and psychological counseling.

Recker, R. R.; Saville, P. D.; and Heaney, R. P. 1977. Effect of estrogens and calcium carbonate on bone loss in postmenopausal women. *Ann. Intern. Med.* 87:649-655.
A prospective study of postmenopausal women treated with estrogens, calcium, or no treatment, that suggests that hormone replacement decreases age-related bone loss.

Smith, D. C.; Prentice, R.; Thompson, D. J., et al. 1975. Association of exogenous estrogen and endometrial carcinoma. *N. Engl. J. Med.* 293:1164-1167.

Ziel, H. K., and Finkle, W. 1975. Increased risk of endometrial carcinoma among users of conjugated estrogens. *N. Engl. J. Med.* 293:1167-1170.
These two epidemiological studies demonstrate the association between endometrial carcinoma and conjugated estrogens.

Williams, R. B., and Gentry, W. D. eds. 1977. *Behavioral approaches to medical treatment.* Cambridge, Mass.: Ballinger Publishing Company.
A good resource for the current state of the art in behavioral modification treatment of various health problems.

Index

Note: Italicized page numbers indicate figure; * following page number indicates table.